Oracle Essentials
Oracle Database 10g

Other Oracle resources from O'Reilly

Related titles

Oracle in a Nutshell

Oracle PL/SQL Programming

Oracle PL/SQL Language
  Pocket Reference

Mastering Oracle SQL

Oracle SQL*Plus Pocket
  Reference

Learning Oracle PL/SQL

TOAD Pocket Reference for
  Oracle

**Oracle Books
Resource Center**

oracle.oreilly.com is a complete catalog of O'Reilly's books on Oracle and related technologies, including sample chapters and code examples.

oreillynet.com is the essential portal for developers interested in open and emerging technologies, including new platforms, programming languages, and operating systems.

Conferences

O'Reilly & Associates brings diverse innovators together to nurture the ideas that spark revolutionary industries. We specialize in documenting the latest tools and systems, translating the innovator's knowledge into useful skills for those in the trenches. Visit *conferences.oreilly.com* for our upcoming events.

Safari Bookshelf (*safari.oreilly.com*) is the premier online reference library for programmers and IT professionals. Conduct searches across more than 1,000 books. Subscribers can zero in on answers to time-critical questions in a matter of seconds. Read the books on your Bookshelf from cover to cover or simply flip to the page you need. Try it today with a free trial.

THIRD EDITION

Oracle Essentials

Oracle Database 10g

Rick Greenwald, Robert Stackowiak,
and Jonathan Stern

O'REILLY®

Beijing · Cambridge · Farnham · Köln · Paris · Sebastopol · Taipei · Tokyo

Oracle Essentials: Oracle Database 10g, Third Edition
by Rick Greenwald, Robert Stackowiak, and Jonathan Stern

Published by O'Reilly Media, Inc., 1005 Gravenstein Highway North, Sebastopol, CA 95472.

O'Reilly & Associates books may be purchased for educational, business, or sales promotional use. Online editions are also available for most titles (*safari.oreilly.com*). For more information, contact our corporate/institutional sales department: (800) 998-9938 or *corporate@oreilly.com*.

Editor:	Deborah Russell
Production Editor:	Reg Aubry
Cover Designer:	Ellie Volckhausen
Interior Designer:	David Futato

Printing History:

October 1999:	First Edition. Originally published under the title *Oracle Essentials: Oracle8 and Oracle8i*.
June 2001:	Second Edition. Originally published under the title *Oracle Essentials: Oracle9i, Oracle8i and Oracle8*.
February 2004:	Third Edition.

ISBN: 0-596-00585-7

[M]

To the four most important people in my life: my wife, LuAnn, and my daughters, Elinor Vera YuXiu Greenwald, Josephine Shang Qiong Greenwald, and Robin Yang Ru Greenwald— you give me everything.

—Rick Greenwald

For my wife, Jodie, and sons, Nick and Mike— thanks for providing the time, support, and understanding needed for projects such as this one. My love to each of you.

—Robert Stackowiak

To my wife, Heather, and my children, Zachary and Sarah—my life and joy grows as we all do together.

—Jonathan Stern

Table of Contents

Preface

The Oracle database is a product that is both rich and deep. To address the complexities and variations in this product, Oracle books and documentation tend to be long and somewhat intimidating. Most of them either cover a broad scope of functionality in a fairly cursory way or delve deeply into complex and rather narrow topics, sometimes missing the forest for the trees by concentrating on the multitude of details of a particular subject. This book aims to be different. We want to give you an in-depth explanation of the forest itself—the concepts and features of the Oracle database. With this information, you should be better prepared to tackle any particular tree in that forest, with any number of other books.

As Oracle professionals (all of whom have worked for Oracle Corporation), we've found that a lot of Oracle users need brief explanations of similar topics. For some time, we'd wanted a book that describes all the underlying principles that shape the Oracle database, written concisely for an intelligent audience. We found that the explanations were scattered among many manuals and books and were often too complex or too simplistic. After a good deal of complaining, we finally decided to write the book ourselves. As this is now the Third Edition of *Oracle Essentials*, we've concluded that a number of you were looking for the same thing!

Goals of This Book

Our main goal is to give you a foundation for using the Oracle database effectively and efficiently. Therefore, we wrote with these principles in mind:

Focus

> We've tried to concentrate on the most important Oracle issues. Every topic provides a comprehensive but concise discussion of how Oracle handles an issue, and the repercussions of that action.

Brevity

One of the first decisions we made was to concentrate on principles rather than syntax. There simply isn't room for myriad syntax diagrams and examples in this book.

Uniqueness

We've tried to make this an ideal first Oracle book for a wide spectrum of Oracle users—but not the last! You will very likely have to refer to Oracle documentation or other, more specific books for more details about using Oracle. However, we hope this book will act as an accelerator for you. Using the foundation you get from this book, you can take detailed information from other sources and put it to the best use. A companion book, *Oracle in a Nutshell*, by Rick Greenwald and David C. Kreines (O'Reilly), contains extensive syntax for a wide range of Oracle products.

This book is the result of over 40 years of experience with Oracle and other databases. We've tried to apply that experience as best we can here.

Audience for This Book

We wrote this book for people at all levels of Oracle expertise: database administrators (DBAs) who spend most of their workday interacting with Oracle; application developers who build their systems on the data available in an Oracle database; and system administrators who are concerned with how Oracle will affect their computing environments. Of course, some users interact more peripherally with the actual Oracle product, from IT managers to business users. On the one hand, anticipating the appropriate technical level of all our potential readers presented difficulties; on the other hand, we've tried to build a solid foundation from the ground up and believe that some introductory material benefits everyone. We've also tried to ensure that every reader receives all the fundamental information necessary to truly understand the topics presented.

If you're an experienced Oracle user, you may be tempted to skip over material in this book with which you are already familiar. But experience has shown that some of the most basic Oracle principles can be overlooked, even by experts. We've also seen how the same small "gotchas" trip up even the most experienced Oracle practitioners and cause immense damage if they go unnoticed. After all, an ounce of prevention provided by understanding is worth a pound of cure (especially when you're trying to get a system up and running). So we hope that even experienced Oracle users will find valuable information in every chapter of this book—information that will save them hours in their busy professional lives.

Our guiding principle has been to present this information compactly without making it overly tutorial. We figure that the most important ratio in a book like this is the amount of useful information you get balanced against the time it takes you to get it. We sincerely hope this volume provides a terrific bang for the buck.

About the Third Edition (Oracle Database 10*g*)

We were pleased that the first two editions of this book, covering the Oracle database up to the Oracle9*i* version, were well received and that O'Reilly & Associates agreed to publish this third edition. In this update to the book, we have added information about the latest release of Oracle, Oracle Database 10*g*.

For the most part our task was fairly clear-cut, because the 10*g* release is primarily incremental—the new features in the release extend existing features of the database. We've added the information about these extensions to each of the chapters, wherever this information was most relevant and appropriate.

Note that this third edition cannot possibly cover everything that is new in Oracle Database 10*g*. In general, we followed the same guidelines for this edition that we did for the first two editions. If a new feature did not seem to be broadly important, we did not necessarily delve into it; similarly, in the first two editions we did not try to produce a laundry list of every characteristic of the Oracle database. In addition, if a feature fell into an area outside the scope of the earlier editions, we did not attempt to cover it in this edition. An example is the set of detailed changes to the SQL language used in Oracle Database 10*g*; we expect that those features will be amply covered in Oracle documentation and in SQL-specific books.

Appendix A includes a chapter-by-chapter summary of the new features of Oracle Database 10*g* that are described in this book.

Structure of This Book

This book is divided into fourteen chapters and two appendixes, as follows:

Chapter 1, *Introducing Oracle*, briefly describes the range of Oracle products and provides some history of Oracle and relational databases.

Chapter 2, *Oracle Architecture*, describes the core concepts and structures (e.g., files, processes, and so on) that are the architectural basis of Oracle8.

Chapter 3, *Installing and Running Oracle*, briefly describes how to install Oracle and how to configure, start up, and shut down the database. It also covers a variety of networking issues.

Chapter 4, *Data Structures*, summarizes the various datatypes supported by Oracle and introduces the Oracle objects (e.g., tables, views, indexes). It also provides information about query optimization.

Chapter 5, *Managing Oracle*, provides an overview of issues involved in managing an Oracle system, including security, using the Oracle Enterprise Manager (EM) product, and dealing with database fragmentation and reorganization issues.

Chapter 6, *Oracle Performance*, describes the main issues relevant to Oracle performance—especially the major performance characteristics of disk, memory, and CPU tuning—and pays special attention to parallelism in Oracle.

Chapter 7, *Multiuser Concurrency*, describes the basic principles of multiuser concurrency (e.g., transactions, locks, integrity problems) and explains how Oracle handles concurrency.

Chapter 8, *Oracle and Transaction Processing*, describes online transaction processing (OLTP) in Oracle.

Chapter 9, *Oracle and Data Warehousing*, describes the basic principles of data warehouses and business intelligence configurations and how you can use Oracle to build such systems.

Chapter 10, *Oracle and High Availability*, discusses Oracle's backup and recovery facilities, including the latest failover and data-redundancy solutions.

Chapter 11, *Oracle and Hardware Architecture*, describes how the choice of various types of architectures (e.g., uniprocessor, SMP, MPP, NUMA, grid computing) affects Oracle processing.

Chapter 12, *Distributed Databases and Distributed Data*, briefly summarizes the Oracle facilities used in distributed processing—for example, two-phase commits and Oracle Streams (Advanced Queuing).

Chapter 13, *Extending Oracle Datatypes*, discusses how Oracle provides object-orientation and support of various media type extensions to the Oracle datatypes and to the overall processing framework.

Chapter 14, *Network Deployment Models*, describes how Oracle is now being used as an Internet computing platform and for grid computing, and introduces various web-related components, such as Oracle Application Server, Oracle Portal, and Java.

Appendix A, *What's New in This Book for Oracle Database10g*, lists the Oracle Database 10g changes described in this book.

Appendix B, *Additional Resources*, lists a variety of additional resources—both online and offline—so you can do more detailed reading.

Conventions Used in This Book

The following typographical conventions are used in this book:

Italic
    Used for file and directory names, emphasis, and the first occurrence of terms

Constant width
> Used for code examples and literals

Constant width italic
> In code examples, indicates an element (for example, a parameter) that you supply

UPPERCASE
> Generally indicates Oracle keywords

lowercase
> In code examples, generally indicates user-defined items such as variables

 These icons signify a tip, suggestion, or general note.

 These icons indicate a warning or caution.

How to Contact Us

Please address comments and questions concerning this book to the publisher:

O'Reilly & Associates, Inc.
1005 Gravenstein Highway North
Sebastopol, CA 95472
(800) 998-9938 (in the United States or Canada)
(707) 829-0515 (international/local)
(707) 829-0104 (fax)

There is a web page for this book, which lists errata, the text of several helpful technical papers, and any additional information. You can access this page at:

http://www.oreilly.com/catalog/oressentials3/

To comment or ask technical questions about this book, send email to:

bookquestions@oreilly.com

For more information about books, conferences, software, Resource Centers, and the O'Reilly Network, see the O'Reilly web site at:

http://www.oreilly.com

Acknowledgments

Each of the authors has arrived at this collaboration through a different path, but we would all like to thank the team at O'Reilly for making this book both possible and a joy to write. At the top of the list is Debby Russell, who was able to leverage her robust scalability throughout the deployment of this work (go edit *that* one!). Debby not only helped to create this book, but believed in the concept enough to take it on as a project—three times over. We are lucky to have her as an editor and a friend. The rest of the O'Reilly crew also deserve a lot of credit, especially Reg Aubry, the production editor; Rob Romano, who developed the figures; and John Bickelhaupt, who wrote the index. It's incredible how they were able to strike the perfect balance—always there when we needed something, but leaving us alone when we didn't.

We're all grateful to each other. Giving birth to a book is a difficult process, but it can be harrowing when split three ways. Everyone hung in there and did their best throughout this process. We'd also like to give our sincere thanks to the technical reviewers for various editions of this book. These include Craig Shallahamer of Ora-Pub, Domenick Ficarella, Jonathan Gennick, Jenny Gelhausen, and Dave Klein. This somewhat thankless but crucially important work really enhanced the value of the book you're reading.

Rick thanks the incredibly bright and gifted people who have shared their wealth of knowledge with him over the years, including Bruce Scott, Earl Stahl, Jerry Chang, and Jim Milbery. In particular, he thanks the two individuals who have been his technical mentors over the course of his entire career: Ed Hickland and Dave Klein, who have repeatedly spent time explaining to and discussing with him some of the broader and finer points of database technology.

For the later editions of this book Rick would also like to thank all those colleagues at Oracle who helped him in his time of need, checking on those last- minute clarifications, including John Lang, Bruce Lowenthal. Alice Watson, Dave Leroy, Sushil Kumar, Mughees Minhas, Daniela Hansell, Penny Avril, Mark Townsend, and Mark Drake. And a special thank you to Jenny Tsai-Smith, who always seemed to have the time and knowledge to clear up any Oracle database problem. And last, but certainly not least, my primary coauthor, Bob Stackowiak, who has become a good friend over our years of collaboration.

Robert acknowledges all his friends over the years around the world at Oracle Corporation, IBM, Harris Computer Systems, and the U.S. Army Corps of Engineers. Through personal relationships and email, they have shared a lot and provided him with incredible opportunities for learning. At Oracle, he would especially like to thank members of Andy Mendelsohn's team who have always been helpful in providing material ahead of releases, including Mark Townsend, Raymond Roccaforte, George Lumpkin, Hermann Baer, the Dutch guys in California developing Oracle

Warehouse Builder, and many others. Special thanks are also extended to Louis Nagode for the Discoverer image he captured on his laptop for this edition and to Lilian Hobbs for early access to Oracle Enterprise Manager 10g on a development server. Also, he'd like to thank his management for recognizing the value of such projects. including Greg Barker, Susan Cook, and Mark Salser. He'd also like to thank his customers, who have always had the most practical experience using the products and tools he has worked with and from whom he will continue to learn.

Jonathan thanks Murray Golding, an excellent friend and Oracle practitioner, for his insights and analogies; Sam Mele, a true friend, for plucking him from the "frozen North" and opening doors; and the Oracle Server Technologies members and their teams, including Juan Tellez, Ron Weiss, Juan Loaiza, and Carol Colrain for their help during his years at Oracle.

CHAPTER 1

Introducing Oracle

Where do we start? One of the problems in comprehending a massive product such as the Oracle database is the difficulty of getting a good sense of how the product works without getting lost in the details of implementing specific solutions. This book aims to solve this problem by giving you a thorough grounding in the concepts and technologies that form the foundation of the Oracle Database Server. Oracle also provides an Application Server and business applications, including the E-Business Suite and the Oracle Collaboration Suite,* which are outside the scope of the main body of this book.

We've tried to write a book for a wide range of Oracle users, from the novice to the experienced user. To address this range of users, we've focused on the concepts and technology behind the Oracle database. Once you fully understand these facets of the product, you'll be able to handle the particulars of virtually any type of Oracle database. Without this understanding, you may feel overburdened as you try to connect the dots of Oracle's voluminous feature set and documentation.

This first chapter lays the groundwork for the rest of the discussions in this book. Of all the chapters, it covers the broadest range of topics; most of these are discussed further later in the book, but some of the basics—for example, the brief history of Oracle and the contents of the different "flavors" of the Oracle database products—are unique to this chapter.

Oracle has grown from its humble beginnings as one of a number of databases available in the 1970s to the market leader of today. In its early days, Oracle Corporation was known more as an aggressive sales and promotion organization than a technology supplier. Over the years, the Oracle database has grown in depth and quality,

---

* Previous versions of this book did cover *i*FS. In Oracle Database 10*g*, however, this product is now known as Oracle Files and is now a part of the Oracle Collaboration Suite. For this reason, *i*FS is not covered in this edition.

and its technical capabilities now are generally recognized as the most advanced. With each release, Oracle has added more power and features to its already solid base while improving the manageability.

Several recent Oracle database releases are the focus of this book:

Oracle8i

Oracle8*i*, released in 1999, added a new twist to the Oracle database—a combination of enhancements that made the Oracle8*i* database the focal point of the world of Internet (the *i* in 8*i*) computing.

Oracle9i

Oracle9*i*, released in 2001, introduced Real Application Clusters as a replacement for Oracle Parallel Server, and added many management and data warehousing features.

Oracle Database 10g

Oracle Database 10*g*, released in 2003 and the current release, enables grid (the *g* in 10*g*) computing. A *grid* is simply a pool of computers that provides needed resources for applications on an as-needed basis. The goal is to provide computing resources that transparently scale to the user community, much as an electrical utility company can deliver power to meet peak demand by accessing energy from other power providers' plants via a power grid. Oracle Database 10*g* further reduces the time, cost, and complexity of database management through the introduction of self-managing features such as the Automated Database Diagnostic Monitor, Automated Shared Memory Tuning, Automated Storage Management, and Automated Disk Based Backup and Recovery. One important key to Oracle Database 10*g*'s usefulness in grid computing is the ability to provision CPUs and data.

Before we dive into the specific foundations of these releases, we must spend a little time describing some Oracle basics—how databases evolved to arrive at the relational model, a brief history of Oracle Corporation, and an introduction to the basic features and configurations of the database.

The Evolution of the Relational Database

The relational database concept was described first by Dr. Edgar F. Codd in an IBM research publication entitled "System R4 Relational" appearing in 1970. Initially, it was unclear whether any system based on this concept could achieve commercial success. Nevertheless, Relational Software, Incorporated (RSI) began in 1977 and released Oracle V.2 as the world's first relational database within a couple of years. By 1985, Oracle could claim more than 1,000 relational database customer sites. By comparison, IBM would not embrace relational technology in a commercial product until the Query Management Facility in 1983.

Why has relational database technology grown to become the de facto database technology since that time? A look back at previous database technology may help to explain this phenomenon.

Database management systems were first defined in the 1960s to provide a common organizational framework for what had been data stored in independent files. In 1964, Charles Bachman of General Electric proposed a network model with data records linked together, forming intersecting sets of data, as shown on the left in Figure 1-1. This work formed the basis of the CODASYL Data Base Task Group. Meanwhile, the North American Aviation's Space Division and IBM developed a second approach based on a hierarchical model in 1965. In this model, data is represented as tree structures in a hierarchy of records, as shown on the right in Figure 1-1. IBM's product based on this model was brought to market in 1969 as the Information Management System (IMS). As recently as 1980, almost all database implementations used either the network or hierarchical approach. Although several competitors utilized these technologies, only IMS remains.

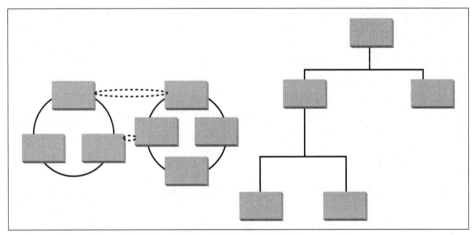

Figure 1-1. Network model (left) and hierarchical model (right)

Relational Basics

The relational database uses the concept of linked two-dimensional tables consisting of rows and columns, as shown in Figure 1-2. Unlike the hierarchical approach, no predetermined relationship exists between distinct tables. This means that the data needed to link together the different areas of the network or hierarchical model need not be defined. Because relational users don't need to understand the representation of data in storage to retrieve it (many such users created ad hoc queries against the data), ease of use helped popularize the relational model.

Relational programming is nonprocedural and operates on a set of rows at a time. In a master-detail relationship between tables, there can be one or many detail rows for

DEPTNO	DEPTNAME	LOCATION
10	Accounting	San Francisco
20	Research	San Francisco
30	Sales	Chicago
40	Operations	Dallas

EMPNO	EMPNAME	TITLE	DEPTNO
71712	Johnson	Clerk	10
83321	Smith	Mgr	20
85332	Stern	SC Mgr	30
88888	Carter	Mgr	10

Figure 1-2. Relational model with two tables

each individual master row, yet the statements used to access, insert, or modify the data would simply describe the set of results. In many early relational databases, data access required the use of procedural languages that worked one record at a time. Because of this set orientation, programs can access more than one record in a relational database more easily. Relational databases can be used more productively to extract value from large groups of data.

The contents of the rows in Figure 1-2 are sometimes referred to as *records*. A column within a row is referred to as a *field*. Tables are stored in a database *schema*, which is a logical organizational unit within the database. Other logical structures in the schema often include the following:

Views

Provide a single view of data derived from one or more tables or views. The view is an alternative interface to the data, which is stored in the underlying table(s) that make up the view.

Sequences

Provide unique numbers for column values.

Stored procedures

Contain logical modules that can be called from programs.

Synonyms

Provide alternative names for database objects.

Indexes

Provide faster access to table rows.

Database links

Provide links between distributed databases.

The relationships between columns in different tables are typically described through the use of *keys*, which are implemented through referential integrity constraints and their supporting indexes. For example, in Figure 1-2, you can establish a link between the DEPTNO column in the second table, which is called a *foreign key*, to the DEPTNO column in the first table, which is referred to as the *primary key* of that table.

Finally, even if you define many different indexes for a table, you don't have to understand them or manage the data they contain. Oracle includes a *query optimizer* (described in Chapter 4) that chooses the best way to use your indexes to access the data for any particular query.

The relational approach lent itself to the Structured Query Language (SQL). SQL was initially defined over a period of years by IBM Research, but it was Oracle Corporation that first introduced it to the market in 1979. SQL was noteworthy at the time for being the only language needed to use relational databases, because you could use SQL:

- For queries (using a SELECT statement)
- As a Data Manipulation Language or DML (using INSERT, UPDATE, and DELETE statements)
- As a Data Definition Language or DDL (using CREATE or DROP statements when adding or deleting tables)
- To set privileges for users or groups (using GRANT or REVOKE statements)

Today, SQL contains many extensions with ANSI/ISO standards that define its basic syntax.

How Oracle Grew

In 1983, RSI was renamed Oracle Corporation to avoid confusion with a competitor named RTI. At this time, the developers made a critical decision to create a portable version of Oracle (Version 3) that ran not only on Digital VAX/VMS systems, but also on Unix and other platforms. By 1985, Oracle claimed the ability to run on more than 30 platforms. Some of these platforms are historical curiosities today, but others remain in use. (In addition to VMS, early operating systems supported by Oracle included IBM MVS, DEC Ultrix, HP/UX, IBM AIX, and Sun's Solaris version of Unix.) Oracle was able to leverage and accelerate the growth of minicomputers and Unix servers in the 1980s. Today, Oracle is portable to both Microsoft Windows and Linux, which are the leading operating systems on popular commodity servers.

In addition to multiple platform support, other core Oracle messages from the mid-1980s still ring true today, including complementary software development and decision support tools, ANSI standard SQL across platforms, and connectivity over standard networks. Since the mid-1980s, the database deployment model has evolved from dedicated database application servers to client/server to Internet computing implemented with PCs and thin clients accessing database applications via browsers—and, to the grid with Oracle Database 10g.

Oracle introduced many innovative technical features to the database as computing and deployment models changed (from offering the first distributed database to the first Java Virtual Machine in the core database engine). Oracle also continues to support emerging standards such as XML and .NET. Table 1-1 presents a short list of Oracle's major feature introductions.

Table 1-1. History of Oracle technology introductions

Year	Feature
1979	Oracle Release 2—the first commercially available relational database to use SQL
1983	Single code base for Oracle across multiple platforms
1984	Portable toolset
1986	Client/server Oracle relational database
1987	CASE and 4GL toolset
1988	Oracle Financial Applications built on relational database
1989	Oracle6
1991	Oracle Parallel Server on massively parallel platforms
1993	Oracle7 with cost-based optimizer
1994	Oracle Version 7.1 generally available: parallel operations including query, load, and create index
1996	Universal database with extended SQL via cartridges, thin client, and application server
1997	Oracle8 generally available: including object-relational and Very Large Database (VLDB) features
1999	Oracle8*i* generally available: Java Virtual Machine (JVM) in the database
2000	Oracle9*i* Application Server generally available: Oracle tools integrated in middle tier
2001	Oracle9*i* Database Server generally available: Real Application Clusters; OLAP and data mining API in the database
2003	Oracle Database 10*g* enables grid computing and simplifies and automates key management tasks

The Oracle Family

Oracle Database 10g Database Server describes the most recent major version of the Oracle Relational Database Management System (RDBMS) family of products that share common source code. This family includes:

- Personal Oracle, a database for single users that's often used to develop code for implementation on other Oracle multiuser databases
- Oracle Standard Edition, which was named Workgroup Server in its first iteration as part of the Oracle7 family and is sometimes simply referred to as Oracle Server

- Oracle Enterprise Edition, which includes all Standard Edition functionality and additional functionality
- Oracle Lite, used primarily for mobile applications

Oracle8 was introduced in 1997 with larger size limitations and management features, such as partitioning, aimed at very large database implementations. In 1998, Oracle announced Oracle8*i*, which is sometimes referred to as Version 8.1 of the Oracle8 database. The *i* was added to denote added functionality supporting Internet deployment in the new version. Oracle9*i* followed, with Application Server available in 2000 and Database Server in 2001. Oracle Database 10*g* was introduced in 2003; the *g* denotes Oracle's focus on emerging grid deployment models. The terms Oracle, Oracle8, Oracle8*i*, Oracle9*i* and Oracle Database 10*g* (or Oracle10*g*) might appear to be used somewhat interchangeably in this book, because Oracle Database 10g includes all the features of previous versions. When we describe a new feature that was first made available specifically in certain releases, we've tried to note that fact to avoid confusion, recognizing that many of you may have old releases of Oracle. We typically use the simple term Oracle when describing features that are common to all these releases.

Oracle has focused development around a single source code model since 1983. While each database implementation includes some operating system–specific source code at very low levels in order to better leverage specific platforms, the interfaces that users, developers, and administrators deal with for each version are consistent. Because features are consistent across platforms for implementations of Oracle Standard Edition and Oracle Enterprise Edition, companies can migrate Oracle applications easily to various hardware vendors and operating systems while leveraging their investments in Oracle technology. This development strategy also enables Oracle to focus on implementing new features only once in its product set, instead of having to add functionality at different times to different implementations.

Oracle Standard Edition

Oracle Standard Edition refers to a specific database offering, once known as Workgroup Server. From a functionality and pricing standpoint, this product intends to compete in the entry-level multiuser and small database category, supporting smaller numbers of users. These releases are available today on Windows and Unix platforms such as HP Compaq, HP/UX, IBM AIX, Linux, and Sun Solaris.

Oracle Enterprise Edition

Oracle Enterprise Edition is aimed at larger-scale implementations that require additional features. Enterprise Edition is available on far more platforms than the Oracle release for workgroups and includes advanced management, networking, programming, and data warehousing features, as well as a variety of special-purpose options, such as clustering, which are available at extra cost.

Oracle Personal Edition

Oracle Personal Edition is the single-user version of Oracle Enterprise Edition. Personal Edition is most frequently used for development on a single machine. Because the features match those of Enterprise Edition, a developer can write applications using the Personal Edition and deploy them to multi-user servers. Some companies deploy single-user applications using this product. However, Oracle Lite offers a much more lightweight means of deploying the same applications.

Oracle Lite

Oracle Lite, once known as Oracle Mobile, is intended for single users who are using wireless/mobile devices. It differs from other members of the Oracle database family in that it doesn't use the same database engine. Instead, Oracle developed a lightweight engine compatible with the limited memory and storage capacity of handheld devices. Oracle Lite is described in more detail at the end of this chapter.

Because the SQL supported by Oracle Lite is largely the same as the SQL for other Oracle databases, you can run applications developed for those database engines using Oracle Lite. Replication of data between Oracle Lite and other Oracle versions is a key part of most implementations.

Table 1-2 summarizes the situations in which you would typically use each database product. We've used the Oracle product names to refer to the different members of the Oracle database family.

Table 1-2. Oracle family of database products

Database name	When appropriate
Oracle Standard Edition	Version of Oracle server for a small number of users and a smaller database
Oracle Enterprise Edition	Version of Oracle for a large number of users or a large database with advanced features for extensibility, performance, and management
Oracle Personal Edition	Single-user version of Oracle typically used for development of applications for deployment on other Oracle versions
Oracle Lite	Lightweight database engine for mobile computing on notebooks and handheld devices

Summary of Oracle Features

The Oracle database is a broad and powerful product. The remainder of this book examines different aspects of Oracle such as data structures, performance, and parallel processing. But before you can understand each of the different areas of Oracle in depth, you must familiarize yourself with the range of features in the Oracle database.

The rest of this chapter gives you a high-level overview of the basic areas of functionality in the Oracle product family. By the end of this chapter, you will at least have some orientation points to guide you in exploring the topics in the rest of this book.

To give some structure to the broad spectrum of the Oracle database, we've organized the features into the following sections:

- Database application development features
- Database connection features
- Distributed database features
- Data movement features
- Performance features
- Database management features

At the end of each of the following sections describing database features we've included a subsection called "Availability," which indicates the availability of each feature in specific Oracle products. You should be aware that as this feature list grows and Oracle implements packaging changes in new versions, the availability of these features in the version you implement may vary slightly.

 In this chapter, we've included a lot of terminology and rather abbreviated descriptions of features. Oracle is a huge system. Our goal here is to quickly familiarize you with the full range of features in the system. Subsequent chapters will provide additional details. Obviously, though, whole books can be (and have been!) written about each of the feature areas summarized here.

Database Application Development Features

The main use of the Oracle database system is to store and retrieve data for applications. The features of the Oracle database and related products described in this section are used to create applications. We've divided the discussion in this section into two categories: database programming and database extensibility options. Later in this chapter, we describe the Oracle Developer Suite, a set of optional tools used in Oracle Database Server and Oracle Application Server development.

Database Programming

All flavors of the Oracle database include different languages and interfaces that allow programmers to access and manipulate the data in the database. Database programming features usually interest two groups: developers building Oracle-based applications that will be sold commercially, and IT organizations within companies that custom-develop applications unique to their businesses. The following sections describe the languages and interfaces supported by Oracle.

SQL

The ANSI standard Structured Query Language (SQL) provides basic functions for data manipulation, transaction control, and record retrieval from the database. However, most end users interact with Oracle through applications that provide an interface that hides the underlying SQL and its complexity.

PL/SQL

Oracle's PL/SQL, a procedural language extension to SQL, is commonly used to implement program logic modules for applications. PL/SQL can be used to build stored procedures and triggers, looping controls, conditional statements, and error handling. You can compile and store PL/SQL procedures in the database. You can also execute PL/SQL blocks via SQL*Plus, an interactive tool provided with all versions of Oracle. Oracle Database 10g includes a more optimized version of the core PL/SQL engine, as Oracle9i allowed creation and storage of precompiled PL/SQL program units.

Java features and options

Oracle8i introduced the use of Java as a procedural language with a Java Virtual Machine (JVM) in the database (originally called JServer). JVM includes support for Java stored procedures, methods, triggers, Enterprise JavaBeans™ (EJBs), CORBA, and HTTP. The Accelerator is used for project generation, translation, and compilation, and can also be used to deploy/install shared libraries.

The inclusion of Java within the Oracle database allows Java developers to leverage their skills as Oracle application developers. Java applications can be deployed in the client, Application Server, or database, depending on what is most appropriate. We discuss Java development in Chapters 13 and 14.

Oracle data warehousing options for OLAP and data mining provide a Java API. These applications are typically custom built using Oracle's JDeveloper.

Large objects

Interest in the use of large objects (LOBs) continues to grow, particularly for storing nontraditional datatypes such as images. The Oracle database has been able to store large objects for some time. Oracle8 added the capability to store multiple LOB columns in each table. Oracle Database 10g essentially removes the space limitation on large objects.

Object-oriented programming

Support of object structures has been included since Oracle8i to allow an object-oriented approach to programming. For example, programmers can create user-defined datatypes, complete with their own methods and attributes. Oracle's object support includes a feature called Object Views through which object-oriented programs can make use of relational data already stored in the database. You can also store objects in the database as varying arrays (VARRAYs), nested tables, or index organized tables (IOTs). We discuss the object-oriented features of Oracle further in Chapter 13.

Third-generation languages (3GLs)

Programmers can interact with the Oracle database from C, C++, Java, COBOL, or FORTRAN applications by embedding SQL in those applications. Prior to compiling the applications using a platform's native compilers, you must run the embedded SQL code through a precompiler. The precompiler replaces SQL statements with library calls the native compiler can accept. Oracle provides support for this capability through optional "programmer" precompilers for languages such as C and C++ (Pro*C) and COBOL (Pro*COBOL). More recently, Oracle added SQLJ, a precompiler for Java that replaces SQL statements embedded in Java with calls to a SQLJ runtime library, also written in Java.

Database drivers

All versions of Oracle include database drivers that allow applications to access Oracle via ODBC (the Open DataBase Connectivity standard) or JDBC (the Java DataBase Connectivity open standard). Also available are data providers for OLE DB and for .NET.

The Oracle Call Interface

If you're an experienced programmer seeking optimum performance, you may choose to define SQL statements within host-language character strings and then explicitly parse the statements, bind variables for them, and execute them using the Oracle Call Interface (OCI).

OCI is a much more detailed interface that requires more programmer time and effort to create and debug. Developing an application that uses OCI can be time-consuming, but the added functionality and incremental performance gains often make spending the extra time worthwhile.

Why Use OCI?

Why would someone want to use OCI instead of the higher-level interfaces? In certain programming scenarios, OCI improves application performance or adds functionality. For instance, in high-availability implementations in which multiple systems share disks and implement Real Application Clusters/Oracle Parallel Server, you may want users to reattach to a second server transparently if the first fails. You can write programs that do this using OCI.

National Language Support

National Language Support (NLS) provides character sets and associated functionality, such as date and numeric formats, for a variety of languages. Oracle9*i* featured full Unicode 3.0 support. All data may be stored as Unicode, or select columns may be incrementally stored as Unicode. UTF-8 encoding and UTF-16 encoding provide support for more than 57 languages and 200 character sets. Oracle Database 10*g* adds support for Unicode 3.2. Extensive localization is provided (for example, for data formats) and customized localization can be added through the Oracle Locale Builder. Oracle Database 10*g* includes a Globalization Toolkit for creating applications that will be used in multiple languages.

Availability

All of these database programming features are included in both Oracle Standard Edition and Oracle Enterprise Edition.

Database Extensibility

The Internet and corporate intranets have created a growing demand for storage and manipulation of nontraditional datatypes within the database. There is a need for extensions to the standard functionality of a database for storing and manipulating image, audio, video, spatial, and time series information. These capabilities are enabled through extensions to standard SQL.

For more details regarding these features of Oracle, see Chapter 13.

Oracle Text and interMedia

Oracle Text includes what was previously referred to as the "ConText cartridge" with Ultrasearch capabilities. It can identify the gist of a document by searching for themes and key phrases in the document.

Oracle *inter*Media bundles additional image, audio, video, and locator functions and is included in the database license. Oracle *inter*Media offers the following capabilities:

- The image portion of *inter*Media can store and retrieve images.
- The audio and video portions of *inter*Media can store and retrieve audio and video clips, respectively.
- The locator portion of *inter*Media can retrieve data that includes spatial coordinate information.

Oracle Spatial Option

The Spatial option is available for Oracle Enterprise Edition. It can optimize the display and retrieval of data linked to coordinates and is used in the development of spatial information systems. Several vendors of Geographic Information Systems (GIS) products now bundle this option and leverage it as their search and retrieval engine.

XML

Oracle added native XML datatype support to the Oracle9*i* database and XML and SQL interchangeability for searching. The structured XML object is held natively in object relational storage meeting the W3C DOM specification. The XPath syntax for searching in SQL is based on the SQLX group specifications.

Database Connection Features

The connection between the client and the database server is a key component of the overall architecture of a computing system. The database connection is responsible for supporting all communications between an application and the data it uses. Oracle includes a number of features that establish and tune your database connections.

The following features relate to the way the Oracle database handles the connection between the client and server machines in a database interaction. We've divided the discussion in this section into two categories: database networking and Oracle Application Server.

Database Networking

Database users connect to the database by establishing a network connection. You can also link database servers via network connections. Oracle provides a number of features to establish connections between users and the database and/or between database servers, as described in the following sections.

Oracle Net

Oracle's network interface, Oracle Net, was formerly known as Net8 when used in Oracle8, and SQL*Net when used with Oracle7 and previous versions of Oracle. You can use Oracle Net over a wide variety of network protocols, although TCP/IP is by far the most common protocol today.

Features associated with Oracle Net, such as shared servers, are referred to as Oracle Net Services.

Oracle Names

Oracle Names allows clients to connect to an Oracle server without requiring a configuration file on each client. Using Oracle Names can reduce maintenance efforts, because a change in the topology of your network will not require a corresponding change in configuration files on every client machine.

Oracle Internet Directory

The Oracle Internet Directory (OID) was introduced with Oracle8i. OID serves the same function as Oracle Names in that it gives users a way to connect to an Oracle Server without having a client-side configuration file. However, OID differs from Oracle Names in that it is an LDAP (Lightweight Directory Access Protocol) directory; it does not merely support the Oracle-only Oracle Net protocol.

Oracle Connection Manager

Each connection to the database takes up valuable network resources, which can impact the overall performance of a database application. Oracle's Connection Manager, illustrated in Figure 1-3, reduces the number of Oracle Net client network connections to the database through the use of *concentrators*, which provide connection multiplexing to implement multiple connections over a single network connection. Connection multiplexing provides the greatest benefit when there are a large number of active users.

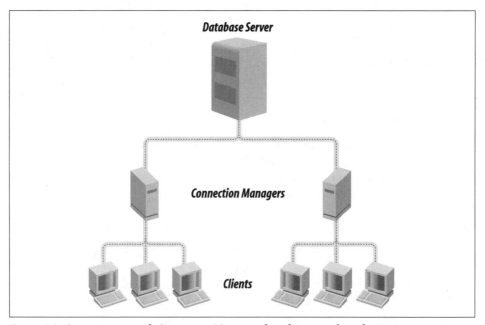

Figure 1-3. Concentrators with Connection Managers for a large number of users

You can also use the Connection Manager to provide multiprotocol connectivity when clients and servers run different network protocols. This capability replaces the multiprotocol interchange formerly offered by Oracle, but it is less important today because most companies use TCP/IP as their standard protocol.

Oracle Database 10g introduces dynamic Connection Manager configuration, enabling changing of CMAN parameters without shutting down the CMAN process.

Advanced Security Option

The Advanced Security Option was once known as the Advanced Networking Option (ANO). Key features include network encryption services using RSA Data Security's RC4 or DES algorithm, network data integrity checking, enhanced authentication integration, single sign-on, and DCE (Distributed Computing Environment) integration.

Label Security Option

Oracle Label Security controls access to data by comparing labels assigned to data with label authorizations granted to users. Multiple authorization levels are possible within a single database. Label security authorizations are managed through the Policy Manager. Policies are enforced in the database instead of through views, thus greatly simplifying management of data accessibility and providing a more secure implementation.

Availability

Advanced networking features such as the Oracle Connection Manager, Advanced Security Option, and Label Security Option have typically been available for the Enterprise Edition of the database, but not for the Standard Edition.

Oracle Application Server

The popularity of Internet and intranet applications has led to a change in deployment from client/server (with fat clients running a significant piece of the application) to a three-tier architecture (with a browser supplying everything needed on a thin client). The Oracle Application Server provides a means of implementing the middle tier of a three-tier solution for web-based applications, component-based applications, and enterprise application integration. Oracle9*i*AS and Oracle Application Server 10*g* (referenced here together as Application Server) replaced a previous Oracle Application Server (OAS) and Oracle Web Application Server. Oracle's Application Server can be scaled across multiple middle-tier servers.

This product includes a web listener based on the popular Apache listener, servlets and JavaServer Pages (JSPs), business logic, and/or data access components. Business logic might include JavaBeans, Business Components for Java (BC4J), and Enterprise JavaBeans (EJBs). Data access components can include JDBC, SQLJ, BC4J, and EJBs. TopLink provides a mapping tool that links Java objects to the database via JDBC such that the Java developer need not build SQL calls and or face broken Java applications due to database schema changes.

Oracle's Application Server offers additional solutions in the cache, portal, intelligence, and wireless areas:

Cache

Oracle Application Server Web Cache introduced a middle tier for the caching of web pages or portions of pages. An earlier cache, Oracle Application Server Database Cache, was used for caching PL/SQL procedures and anonymous PL/SQL blocks but is no longer supported with Oracle Application Server 10*g*.

Portal

The Oracle Application Server Portal is also a part of the Oracle Developer Suite (discussed later in this chapter) and is used for building easy-to-use browser interfaces to applications through servlets and HTTP links. The developed portal is deployed to the Application Server.

Business Intelligence

Application Server Business Intelligence components include the Portal, but also:

- Oracle Reports, which provides a scalable middle tier for the reporting of prebuilt query results

- Oracle Discoverer, for ad hoc query and relational online analytical processing (ROLAP)

- A deployment platform for OLAP and data mining applications custom-built with JDeveloper

These capabilities are discussed in Chapter 9.

Wireless

Oracle Wireless Edition (formerly known as Oracle Portal-to-Go) includes:

- Content adapters for transforming content to XML

- Device transformers for transforming XML to device-specific markup languages

- Personalization portals for service personalization of alerts, alert addresses, location marks, and profiles; the wireless personalization portal is also used for the creation, servicing, testing, and publishing of URL service and for user management

Availability

Because Oracle Application Server is a separate product, it can be used with various versions of the Oracle database and with either edition.

The Application Server packaging includes a Standard Edition, an Enterprise Edition, and a Java Edition (including key components for Java developers). Portal and TopLink are included in the Standard Edition. The Enterprise Edition adds the following capabilities: Forms Services, Reports Services, Discoverer Viewer, Oracle Internet Directory, Oracle Workflow, and Oracle Application Interconnect. The Java Edition bundle includes a HTTP Server, OC4J, TopLink, BC4J, and JDeveloper. For more details about Application Server, see Chapter 14.

Distributed Database Features

One of the strongest features of the Oracle database is its ability to scale up to handle extremely large volumes of data and users. Oracle scales not only by running on more and more powerful platforms, but also by running in a distributed configuration. Oracle databases on separate platforms can be combined to act as a single logical distributed database.

This section describes some of the basic ways that Oracle handles database interactions in a distributed database system.

Distributed Queries and Transactions

Data within an organization is often spread among multiple databases for reasons of both capacity and organizational responsibility. Users may want to query this distributed data or update it as if it existed within a single database.

Oracle first introduced distributed databases in response to the requirements for accessing data on multiple platforms in the early 1980s. *Distributed queries* can retrieve data from multiple databases. *Distributed transactions* can insert, update, or delete data on distributed databases. Oracle's two-phase commit mechanism, which is described in detail in Chapter 12, guarantees that all the database servers that are part of a transaction will either commit or roll back the transaction. Background recovery processes can ensure database consistency in the event of system interruption during distributed transactions. Once the failed system comes back online, the same process will complete the distributed transactions.

Distributed transactions can also be implemented using popular transaction monitors (TPs) that interact with Oracle via XA, an industry standard (X/Open) interface. Oracle8i added native transaction coordination with the Microsoft Transaction Server (MTS), so you can implement a distributed transaction initiated under the control of MTS through an Oracle database.

Heterogeneous Services

Heterogeneous Services allow non-Oracle data and services to be accessed from an Oracle database through generic connectivity via ODBC and OLE-DB included with the database.

Optional Transparent Gateways use agents specifically tailored for a variety of target systems. Transparent Gateways allow users to submit Oracle SQL statements to a non-Oracle distributed database source and have them automatically translated into the SQL dialect of the non-Oracle source system, which remains transparent to the user. In addition to providing underlying SQL services, Heterogeneous Services provide transaction services utilizing Oracle's two-phase commit with non-Oracle databases and procedural services that call third-generation language routines on non-Oracle systems. Users interact with the Oracle database as if all objects are stored in the Oracle database, and Heterogeneous Services handle the transparent interaction with the foreign database on the user's behalf.

Availability

All the technologies discussed in this section are included in both editions of the database, although Transparent Gateways are an add-on available at additional cost.

Data Movement Features

Moving data from one Oracle database to another is often a requirement when using distributed databases, or when a user wants to implement multiple copies of the same database in multiple locations to reduce network traffic or increase data availability. You can export data and data dictionaries (metadata) from one database and import them into another. Oracle Database 10g introduces a new high speed data pump for the import and export of data. Oracle also offers many other advanced features in this category, including replication, transportable tablespaces, and Advanced Queuing.

This section describes the technology used to move data from one Oracle database to another automatically.

Basic Replication

You can use basic replication to move recently added and updated data from an Oracle "master" database to databases on which duplicate sets of data reside. In basic replication, only the single master is updated. You can manage replication through the Oracle Enterprise Manager (OEM or EM). While replication has been a part of all recent Oracle releases, replication based on logs is a more recent addition, first appearing in Oracle9i Release 2.

Advanced Replication

You can use advanced replication in multimaster systems in which any of the databases involved can be updated and conflict-resolution features are needed to resolve inconsistencies in the data. Because there is more than one master database, the same data may be updated on multiple systems at the same time. Conflict resolution is necessary to determine the "true" version of the data. Oracle's advanced replication includes a number of conflict-resolution scenarios and also allows programmers to write their own. We cover replication in more detail in Chapter 12.

Transportable Tablespaces

Transportable tablespaces were introduced in Oracle8*i*. Instead of using the export/import process, which dumps data and the structures that contain it into an intermediate file for loading, you simply put the tablespaces in read-only mode, move or copy them from one database to another, and mount them. You must export the data dictionary (metadata) for the tablespace from the source and import it at the target. This feature can save a lot of time during maintenance, because it simplifies the process. Oracle Database 10*g* allows you to move data with transportable tablespaces between different platforms or operating systems.

Advanced Queuing and Streams

Advanced Queuing (AQ), first introduced in Oracle8, provides the means to asynchronously send messages from one Oracle database to another. Because messages are stored in a queue in the database and sent asynchronously when a connection is made, the amount of overhead and network traffic is much lower than it would be using traditional guaranteed delivery through the two-phase commit protocol between source and target. By storing the messages in the database, AQ provides a solution with greater recoverability than other queuing solutions that store messages in filesystems.

Oracle messaging adds the capability to develop and deploy a *content-based publish and subscribe solution* using a rules engine to determine relevant subscribing applications. As new content is published to a subscriber list, the rules on the list determine which subscribers should receive the content. This approach means that a single list can efficiently serve the needs of different subscriber communities.

In the first release of Oracle9*i*, AQ added XML support and Oracle Internet Directory (OID) integration. This technology is leveraged in Oracle Application Interconnect (OAI), which includes adapters to non-Oracle applications, messaging products, and databases.

The second release of Oracle9*i* introduced *Streams*. Streams have three major components: log-based replication for data capture, queuing for data staging, and user-defined rules for data consumption. Oracle Database 10*g* includes support for change data capture and file transfer solutions via Streams.

Extraction, Transformation, Loading

Oracle Warehouse Builder is a tool for the design of target data stores including data warehouses and a metadata repository, but it also provides a frontend to building source-to-target maps and for generating extraction, transformation, and loading (ETL) scripts. OWB leverages key embedded ETL features first made available in the Oracle9*i* database.

Availability

Although basic replication has been included with both Oracle Standard Edition and Enterprise Edition, advanced features such as advanced replication, transportable tablespaces, and Advanced Queuing have typically required Enterprise Edition.

Performance Features

Oracle includes several features specifically designed to boost performance in certain situations. We've divided the discussion in this section into two categories: database parallelization and data warehousing.

Database Parallelization

Database tasks implemented in parallel speed up querying, tuning, and maintenance of the database. By breaking up a single task into smaller tasks and assigning each subtask to an independent process, you can dramatically improve the performance of certain types of database operations.

Parallel query features became a standard part of Enterprise Edition beginning with Oracle 7.3. Parallel query became supported in Virtual Private Databases (VPD) with Oracle Database 10g. Examples of query features implemented in parallel include:

- Table scans
- Nested loops
- Sort merge joins
- GROUP BYs
- NOT IN subqueries (anti-joins)
- User-defined functions
- Index scans
- Select distinct UNION and UNION ALL
- Hash joins
- ORDER BY and aggregation
- Bitmap star joins
- Partition-wise joins
- Stored procedures (PL/SQL, Java, external routines)

When you're using Oracle, by default the degree of parallelism for any operation is set to twice the number of CPUs. You can adjust this degree automatically for each subsequent query based on the system load. You can also generate statistics for the cost-based optimizer in parallel. Parallel operations are described in more detail in Chapter 6.

Availability

You can perform maintenance functions such as loading (via SQL*Loader), backups, and index builds in parallel in Oracle Enterprise Edition. Oracle Partitioning for the Enterprise Edition enables additional parallel Data Manipulation Language (DML) inserts, updates, and deletes as well as index scans.

Data Warehousing and Business Intelligence

The parallel features discussed in the previous section improve the overall performance of the Oracle database. Oracle has also added some performance enhancements that specifically apply to data warehousing applications. For detailed explanations of these and complementary products and features related to data warehousing and business intelligence, see Chapter 9.

Bitmap indexes

Oracle added support for stored bitmap indexes to Oracle 7.3 to provide a fast way of selecting and retrieving certain types of data. Bitmap indexes typically work best for columns that have few different values relative to the overall number of rows in a table.

Rather than storing the actual value, a bitmap index uses an individual bit for each potential value with the bit either "on" (set to 1) to indicate that the row contains the value or "off" (set to 0) to indicate that the row does not contain the value. This storage mechanism can also provide performance improvements for the types of joins typically used in data warehousing. Bitmap indexes are described in more detail in Chapter 4.

Star query optimization

Typical data warehousing queries occur against a large *fact table* with foreign keys to much smaller *dimension tables*. Oracle added an optimization for this type of *star query* to Oracle 7.3. (See Figure 9-2 for an illustration of a typical star schema.) Performance gains are realized through the use of Cartesian product joins of dimension tables with a single join back to the large fact table. Oracle8 introduced a further mechanism called a *parallel bitmap star join*, which uses bitmap indexes on the foreign keys to the dimension tables to speed star joins involving a large number of dimension tables.

Materialized views

Since Oracle8*i*, materialized views have provided another means of achieving a significant speed-up of query performance. Summary-level information derived from a fact table and grouped along dimension values is stored as a materialized view. Queries that can use this view are directed to the view, transparently to the user and the SQL they submit.

Analytic functions

A growing trend in Oracle and other systems is the movement of some functions from decision-support user tools into the database. Oracle8*i* and Oracle9*i* releases featured the addition of ANSI standard OLAP SQL analytic functions for windowing, statistics, CUBE and ROLLUP, and much more. Oracle Database 10*g* further adds to this SQL library of analytic functions and statistics in the database.

OLAP Option

Introduced in Oracle9*i*, OLAP services in the OLAP Option provide a Java OLAP API and are typically leveraged to build custom OLAP applications through the use of Oracle's JDeveloper product. The OLAP Option may also be accessed via SQL.

Data Mining Option

Since Oracle9*i*, popular data-mining algorithms have been embedded in the database through the Data Mining Option and are exposed through a Java data-mining API. Data mining applications are typically custom built using Oracle's JDeveloper with DM4J.

Availability

Oracle Standard Edition lacks important data warehousing features available in the Enterprise Edition, such as bitmap indexes and many parallelization features. Enterprise Edition is recommended for data warehousing projects.

Database Management Features

Oracle includes many features that make the database easier to manage. We've divided the discussion in this section into four categories: Oracle Enterprise Manager, add-on packs, backup and recovery, and database availability.

Oracle Enterprise Manager

As part of every Database Server, Oracle provides the Oracle Enterprise Manager (EM), a database management tool framework with a graphical interface used to manage database users, instances, and features (such as replication) that can provide additional information about the Oracle environment. EM can also manage Oracle's Application Server, Collaboration Suite, and E-Business Suite.

Prior to the Oracle8*i* database, the EM software was installed on Windows-based systems, each repository accessible by only a single database manager at a time. EM evolved to a Java release providing access from a browser or Windows-based system. Multiple database administrators could then access the EM repository at the same time.

More recently, an EM HTML console was released with Oracle9iAS with important new application performance management and configuration management features. The HTML version supplemented the Java-based Enterprise Manager earlier available. Enterprise Manager 10g, released with Oracle Database 10g, also comes in Java and HTML versions. EM can be deployed in several ways: as a central console for monitoring multiple databases leveraging agents, as a "product console" (easily installed with each individual database), or through remote access, also known as "studio mode." The HTML-based console includes advanced management capabilities for rapid installation, deployment across grids of computers, provisioning, upgrades, and automated patching.

Oracle Enterprise Manager 10g has several additional options (sometimes called *packs*) for managing the Oracle Enterprise Edition database. These options, which are available for the HTML-based console, the Java-based console, or both, include:

- Database Diagnostics option
- Application Server Diagnostics option
- Database Tuning option
- Database Change Management option
- Database Configuration Management option
- Application Server Configuration Management option

Standard management pack functionality for managing the Standard Edition is now also available for the HTML-based console.

EM2Go

EM2Go is a mobile version of Enterprise Manager that provides a subset of the functionality in EM. EM2Go is accessed through a Pocket PC browser on a PDA device. Database management capabilities include alert notification and viewing, job creation and scheduling, database performance monitoring and status (including Top Sessions, locks, and SQL assessment), basic storage administration, tablespace operations management, and system configuration status. EM2Go also monitors availability and performance of Oracle Application Servers.

Availability

While both the Java- and HTML-based consoles of Enterprise Manager 10g can be used for managing Oracle, functionality is different in the two consoles. We discuss this further in Chapter 5. Oracle Application Server, Oracle E-Business Suite, and Oracle Collaboration Suite are managed through the HTML-based console.

Backup and Recovery

As every database administrator knows, backing up a database is a rather mundane but necessary task. An improper backup makes recovery difficult, if not impossible. Unfortunately, people often realize the extreme importance of this everyday task only when it is too late—usually after losing business-critical data due to a failure of a related system.

The following sections describe some products and techniques for performing database backup operations. We discuss backup and recovery strategies and options in much greater detail in Chapter 10.

Recovery Manager

Typical backups include complete database backups (the most common type), tablespace backups, datafile backups, control file backups, and archived redo log backups. Oracle8 introduced the Recovery Manager (RMAN) for the server-managed backup and recovery of the database. Previously, Oracle's Enterprise Backup Utility (EBU) provided a similar solution on some platforms. However, RMAN, with its Recovery Catalog stored in an Oracle database, provides a much more complete solution. RMAN can automatically locate, back up, restore, and recover datafiles, control files, and archived redo logs. RMAN, since Oracle9i, can restart backups and restores and implement recovery window policies when backups expire. The Oracle Enterprise Manager Backup Manager provides a GUI-based interface to RMAN. Oracle Enterprise Manager 10g introduces a new improved job scheduler that can be used with RMAN and other scripts, and that can manage automatic backups to disk.

Incremental backup and recovery

RMAN can perform incremental backups of Enterprise Edition databases. Incremental backups back up only the blocks modified since the last backup of a datafile, tablespace, or database; thus, they're smaller and faster than complete backups. RMAN can also perform point-in-time recovery, which allows the recovery of data until just prior to an undesirable event (such as the mistaken dropping of a table).

Oracle Storage Manager and Automated Disk Based Backup and Recovery

Various media-management software vendors support RMAN. Since Oracle8i, a Storage Manager has come bundled with Oracle to provide media-management services, including the tracking of tape volumes, for up to four devices. RMAN interfaces automatically with the media-management software to request the mounting of tapes as needed for backup and recovery operations.

Oracle Database 10g introduces Automated Disk Based Backup and Recovery. The disk acts as a cache, and archives and backups can then be copied to tape. The disk "cache" can also serve as a staging area for recovery.

Availability

Backup and recovery facilities are available for both Oracle Standard Edition and Enterprise Edition.

Database Availability

Database availability depends upon the reliability and management of the database, the underlying operating system, and the specific hardware components of the system. Oracle has improved availability by reducing backup and recovery times. It has done this through:

- Providing online and parallel backup and recovery
- Improving the management of online data through range partitioning
- Leveraging hardware capabilities for improved monitoring and failover

The relevant features are described in the following sections.

Partitioning option

Oracle introduced partitioning as an option with Oracle8 to provide a higher degree of manageability and availability. You can take individual partitions offline for maintenance while other partitions remain available for user access. In data warehousing implementations, partitioning is frequently used to implement rolling windows based on date ranges. Hash partitioning, in which the data partitions are divided up as a result of a hashing function, was added to Oracle8*i* to enable an even distribution of data. You can also use composite partitioning to enable hash subpartitioning within specific range partitions. Oracle9*i* added list partitioning, which enables the partitioning of data based on discrete values such as geography, and composite range-list.

Data Guard

Oracle first introduced a standby database feature in Oracle 7.3. The standby database provides a copy of the production database to be used if the primary database is lost—for example, in the event of primary site failure, or during routine maintenance. Primary and standby databases may be geographically separated. The standby database is created from a copy of the production database and updated through the application of archived redo logs generated by the production database. Data Guard, first introduced in Oracle9*i*, fully automates this process; previously, you had to manually copy and apply the logs. Agents are deployed on both the production and standby database, and a Data Guard Broker coordinates commands. A single Data Guard command is used to run the eight steps required for failover.

In addition to providing physical standby database support, Data Guard can create a logical standby database. In this scenario, Oracle archive redo logs are transformed into SQL transactions and applied to an open standby database.

Oracle Database 10g introduces several new features, including support for real-time application of redo data, integration with the Flashback database feature, and archive log compression. From Oracle Database 10g forward, rolling upgrades are supported.

Fail Safe

The Fail Safe feature provides a higher level of reliability for an Oracle database. Failover is implemented through a second system or node that provides access to data residing on a shared disk when the first system or node fails. Oracle Fail Safe for Windows, in combination with Microsoft Cluster Services, provides a failover solution in the event of a system failure.

Fail Safe is primarily a disaster recovery tool, so some downtime does occur as part of a failover operation. The recommended solution for server availability has been Real Application Clusters since Oracle9i.

Oracle Real Application Clusters

The Oracle Parallel Server (OPS) option was replaced by Real Application Clusters (RAC) beginning with Oracle9i. RAC can provide failover support as well as increased scalability on Unix, Linux, and Windows clusters. Oracle8i OPS greatly improved scalability for read/write applications through the introduction of Cache Fusion. Oracle9i RAC provided Cache Fusion for write/write applications by greatly minimizing much of the disk write activity used to control data locking. Oracle Database 10g introduces a new level of RAC portability and Oracle support by providing integrated "clusterware" for the supported RAC platforms.

With Real Application Clusters, you can run multiple Oracle instances on systems in a shared disk cluster configuration or on multiple nodes of a Massively Parallel Processor (MPP) configuration. RAC is also a key enabler for grid computing. RAC coordinates traffic among the systems or nodes, allowing the instances to function as a single database. As a result, the database can scale across dozens of nodes. Because the cluster provides a means by which multiple instances can access the same data, the failure of a single instance will not cause extensive delays while the system recovers; you can simply redirect users to another instance that's still operating.

Data Guard and RAC

Data Guard and RAC in combination replaced Parallel Fail Safe beginning with Oracle9i. Data Guard provides automated failover with bounded recovery time in conjunction with Oracle Real Application Clusters. In addition, it provides client rerouting from the failed instance to the instance that is available with fast reconnect, and automatically captures diagnostic data. With Oracle Database 10g and Enterprise Manager Version 4, it is possible to manage Data Guard configurations containing RAC primary and secondary databases implemented with Oracle Database 10g's integrated clusterware.

Automated Storage Management

Oracle Database 10g introduces Automated Storage Management (ASM), which provides optimum striping and mirroring of data for performance and availability. Because disks can now be optimally tuned via the database, ASM in Oracle Database 10g greatly simplifies this critical management task.

Availability

Advanced high-availability features such as the Partitioning Option and Real Application Clusters have typically been available for Oracle Enterprise Edition but not for Standard Edition. Oracle Data Guard is bundled with the Enterprise Edition.

Oracle Developer Suite

Many Oracle tools are available to developers to help them present data and build more sophisticated Oracle database applications. Although this book focuses on the Oracle database, this section briefly describes the main Oracle tools for application development: Oracle Forms Developer, Oracle Reports Developer, Oracle Designer, Oracle JDeveloper, Oracle Discoverer Administrative Edition and Oracle Portal. Oracle Developer Suite was known as Oracle Internet Developer Suite with Oracle9i.

Oracle Forms Developer

Oracle Forms Developer provides a powerful tool for building forms-based applications and charts for deployment as traditional client/server applications or as three-tier browser-based applications via Oracle Application Server. Developer is a fourth-generation language (4GL). With a 4GL, you define applications by defining values for properties, rather than by writing procedural code. Developer supports a wide variety of clients, including traditional client/server PCs and Java-based clients. The Forms Builder includes a built-in JVM for previewing web applications.

Oracle Reports Developer

Oracle Reports Developer provides a development and deployment environment for rapidly building and publishing web-based reports via Reports for Oracle's Application Server. Data can be formatted in tables, matrices, group reports, graphs, and combinations. High-quality presentation is possible using the HTML extension Cascading Style Sheets (CSS).

Oracle JDeveloper

Oracle JDeveloper was introduced by Oracle in 1998 to develop basic Java applications without writing code. JDeveloper includes a Data Form wizard, a Beans Express wizard for creating JavaBeans and BeanInfo classes, and a Deployment wizard. JDeveloper includes database development features such as various Oracle drivers, a Connection Editor to hide the JDBC API complexity, database components to bind visual controls, and a SQLJ precompiler for embedding SQL in Java code, which you can then use with Oracle. You can also deploy applications developed with JDeveloper using the Oracle Application Server. Although JDeveloper uses wizards to allow programmers to create Java objects without writing code, the end result is generated Java code. This Java implementation makes the code highly flexible, but it is typically a less productive development environment than a true 4GL.

Oracle Designer

Oracle Designer provides a graphical interface for Rapid Application Development (RAD) for the entire database development process—from building the business model to schema design, generation, and deployment. Designs and changes are stored in a multiuser repository. The tool can reverse-engineer existing tables and database schemas for reuse and redesign from Oracle and non-Oracle relational databases.

Designer also includes generators for creating applications for Oracle Developer, HTML clients using Oracle's Application Server, and C++. Designer can generate applications and reverse-engineer existing applications or applications that have been modified by developers. This capability enables a process called *round-trip engineering*, in which a developer uses Designer to generate an application, modifies the generated application, and reverse-engineers the changes back into the Designer repository.

Oracle Discoverer Administration Edition

Oracle Discoverer Administration Edition enables administrators to set up and maintain the Discoverer End User Layer (EUL). The purpose of this layer is to shield business analysts using Discoverer as an ad hoc query or ROLAP tool from SQL complexity. Wizards guide the administrator through the process of building the EUL. In addition, administrators can put limits on resources available to analysts monitored by the Discoverer query governor.

Oracle Portal

Oracle Portal, introduced as WebDB in 1999, provides an HTML-based tool for developing web-enabled applications and content-driven web sites. Portal application systems are developed and deployed in a simple browser environment. Portal includes wizards for developing application components incorporating "servlets" and access to other HTTP web sites. For example, Oracle Reports and Discoverer may be accessed as servlets. Portals can be designed to be user-customizable. They are deployed to the middle-tier Oracle Application Server.

Oracle Portal brought a key enhancement to WebDB, the ability to create and use *portlets*, which allow a single web page to be divided up into different areas that can independently display information and interact with the user.

Availability

All of these pieces are bundled in the Oracle Developer Suite. The Oracle Developer Suite is an additional cost option.

Oracle Lite

Oracle Lite is Oracle's suite of products for enabling mobile use of database-centric applications. Key components of Oracle Lite include the Oracle Lite Database, Mobile Development Kit, and Mobile Server (an extension of the Oracle Application Server).

Although the Oracle Lite Database engine runs on a much smaller platform than other Oracle implementations (it requires a 50K to 1 MB footprint depending on the platform), Mobile SQL, C++, and Java-based applications can run against the database. ODBC is supported. Java support includes Java stored procedures and JDBC. The database is self-tuning and self-administering. In addition to Windows-based laptops, Oracle Lite is also supported for handheld devices running WindowsCE, Palm's Computing Platform, and Symbian EPOC.

In typical usage of Oracle Lite, the user will link her handheld or mobile device running the Oracle Lite Database to a large footprint Oracle Database Server. Data will be synchronized between the two systems. The user will then remove the link and work in disconnected mode. After she has performed her tasks, she'll relink and resynchronize the data with the Oracle Database Server.

The variety of synchronization capabilities include the following:

- Bidirectional synchronization between the mobile device and Oracle's larger footprint databases
- Publish-and-subscribe-based models
- Support for protocols such as TCP/IP, HTTP, CDPD, 802.1, and HotSync

You can define priority-based replication of subsets of data. Because data distributed to multiple locations can lead to conflicts—such as which location now has the "true" version of the data—automated conflict and resolution is provided. You can also customize the conflict resolution.

The Mobile Server provides a single platform for publishing, deploying, synchronizing, and managing mobile applications. The web-based control center can be used for controlling access to mobile applications. Oracle's former "Web-to-Go" product is also part of the Mobile Server and provides centralized wizard-based application development and deployment.

CHAPTER 2

Oracle Architecture

This chapter focuses on the concepts and structures at the core of the Oracle database. When you understand the architecture of the Oracle server, you'll have a context for understanding the rest of the features of Oracle.

Instances and Databases

Many Oracle practitioners use the terms "instance" and "database" interchangeably. In fact, an instance and a database are different (but related) entities. This distinction is important because it provides insight into Oracle's architecture.

In Oracle, the term *database* refers to the physical storage of information, and the term *instance* refers to the software executing on the server that provides access to the information in the database. The instance runs on the computer or server; the database is stored on the disks attached to the server. Figure 2-1 illustrates this relationship.

The database is *physical*: it consists of files stored on disks. The instance is *logical*: it consists of in-memory structures and processes on the server. For example, Oracle uses an area of shared memory called the System Global Area (SGA) and a private memory area for each process called the Program Global Area (PGA). (The SGA is discussed further later in this chapter and both the SGA and PGA are further discussed in Chapter 6.) An instance can connect to one and only one database, although multiple instances can connect to the same database. Instances are temporal, but databases, with proper maintenance, last forever.

Users do not directly access the information in an Oracle database. Instead, they pass requests for information to an Oracle instance.

The real world provides a useful analogy for instances and databases. An instance can be thought of as a bridge to the database, which can be thought of as an island. Traffic flows on and off the island via the bridge. If the bridge is closed, the island exists but no traffic flow is possible. In Oracle terms, if the instance is up, data can

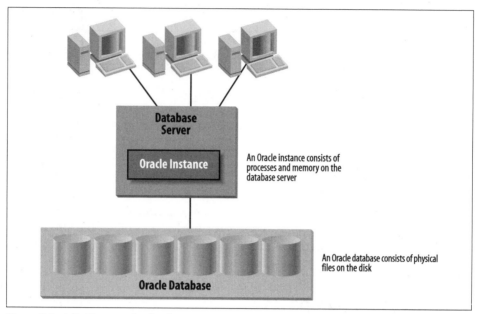

An Oracle instance consists of processes and memory on the database server

An Oracle database consists of physical files on the disk

Figure 2-1. An instance and a database

flow in and out of the database. The physical state of the database is changing. If the instance is down, users cannot access the database even though it still exists physically. The database is static: no changes can occur to it. When the instance comes back into service, the data will be there waiting for it.

The Components of a Database

When you create a database, you assign a specific name to it. You cannot change the database name once you have created it, although you can change the name of the instance that accesses the database.

This section covers the different types of files and other components that make up a complete database.

Tablespaces

Before you examine the physical files of the actual database, you need to understand a key logical structure within a database, the tablespace. All the data stored in a database must reside in a tablespace.

A *tablespace* is a logical structure; you cannot look at the operating system and see a tablespace. Each tablespace is composed of physical structures called *datafiles*; each tablespace must consist of one or more datafiles, and each datafile can belong to only one tablespace. When you create a table, you can specify the tablespace in which to create it. Oracle will then find space for it in one of the datafiles that make up the tablespace.

Figure 2-2 shows the relationship of tablespaces to datafiles for a database.

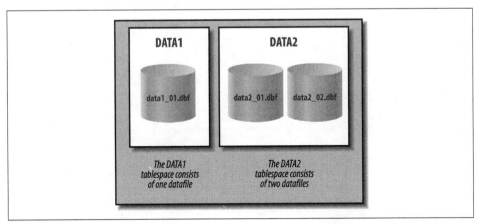

Figure 2-2. Tablespaces and datafiles

This figure shows two tablespaces within an Oracle database. When you create a new table in this Oracle database, you may place it in the DATA1 tablespace or the DATA2 tablespace. It will physically reside in one of the datafiles that make up the specified tablespace.

Oracle recommends the use of *locally managed tablespaces* (introduced in Oracle9*i*), which avoid some of the overhead of managing the tablespace. Locally managed tablespaces also enable creation of *bigfile tablespaces* (introduced in Oracle Database 10*g*), tablespaces that can be up to 8 exabytes in size (an exabyte is equivalent to a million terabytes).* Note that by default, whenever the type of extent management is not specified in Oracle Database 10*g*, permanent tablespaces that are non-SYSTEM are locally managed.

Physical Files in an Oracle Database

A tablespace is a logical view of the physical storage of information in an Oracle database. There are actually three fundamental types of physical files that make up an Oracle database:

- Control files
- Datafiles
- Redo log files

---

* The ultimate size of a bigfile depends on the limitations of the underlying operating system.

Other files are used within a database environment, such as password files and instance initialization files, but the three fundamental types just listed represent the physical database itself. Figure 2-3 illustrates the three types of files and their interrelationships.

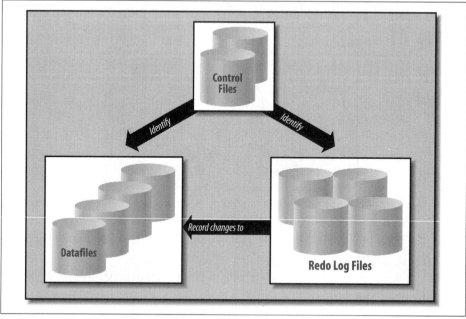

Figure 2-3. The files that make up a database

Oracle9*i* introduced the concept of Oracle Managed Files (OMFs). You can indicate the use of OMFs through an initialization parameter, and your database will automatically create, name, and delete, where appropriate, all the files that make up your database. OMFs are designed to reduce the maintenance overhead of naming and tracking the filenames for your database, as well as avoiding the problems that can result from human errors in performing these tasks. With Oracle Database 10g OMFs, bigfile tablespaces make datafiles appear completely transparent to users.

The next sections describe the roles of these three types of files and their interactions.

Control Files

The control file contains a list of files that make up the database including datafiles and redo log files. It also contains key information about the contents and state of the database, such as:

- The name of the database
- When the database was created

- Tablespace information
- Datafile offline ranges
- The log history and current log sequence information
- Archived log information
- Backup set, pieces, datafile, and redo log information
- Datafile copy information
- Checkpoint information

 Oracle Database 10g introduces a new DROP DATABASE command that can be used to delete a database and all of the files listed in the database control file.

Control file parameters

The size of a control file is influenced by the following initialization parameters, which are part of the initialization file and are set at the time you create a database (see "The Components of an Instance" later in this chapter for a discussion of the initialization file):

MAXLOGFILES
> The maximum number of redo log file groups for the database. Redo log files are described later in this chapter in the "Redo Log Files" section.

MAXLOGMEMBERS
> The maximum number of members for each redo log file group.

MAXLOGHISTORY
> The number of redo log history files the control file can contain. This history is used to simplify automatic recovery, which uses the redo logs by identifying the range of transactions held in an archived redo log.

MAXDATAFILES
> The number of datafiles the control file can track. In Oracle7, if you tried to exceed this limit you had to rebuild the control file to increase the number of datafiles that Oracle could track. In more recent Oracle database versions, this parameter determines the amount of space set aside in the control file for datafiles at the time you create the database. If you add more datafiles than specified in the MAXDATAFILES parameter, the control file will expand automatically.

MAXINSTANCES
> The amount and number of instances the control file can track. This is relevant for Real Application Clusters (or Oracle Parallel Server prior to Oracle9i), which is discussed in Chapter 6.

For more details about these parameters, please see your Oracle documentation.

In general, it's far simpler to set these MAX values to high levels to avoid encountering any problems later on. It's much easier to set the parameters for a control file a little high initially than to go through the time-consuming process of rebuilding control files when your database grows.

Of more significance, do not limit MAXLOGHISTORY in the interest of saving space. If the control file does not have enough room for redo log history, recovery will be more complex and time-consuming. When you are recovering a database, you generally want to finish the task as quickly as possible. Trying to save a little disk space by minimizing log history entries could result in more time recovering from a disaster.

Redo logs are discussed in more detail later in this chapter.

Multiple control files

A database should have at least two control files on different physical disks. Without a current copy of the control file, you run the risk of losing track of portions of your database. Losing control files is not necessarily fatal—there are ways to rebuild them. However, rebuilding control files can be difficult and introduces risk, and can be easily avoided by keeping multiple copies of the control file. You can enable multiple copies of control files by specifying multiple locations for the control files in the CONTROL_FILES parameter in the initialization file for the instance, as shown here:

```
CONTROL_FILES = (/u00/oradata/prod/prodctl1.ctl,
        /u01/oradata/prod/prodctl2.ctl,
        /u02/oradata/prod/prodctl3.ctl)
```

This parameter tells the instance where to find the control files. Oracle will ensure that all copies of the control file are kept in sync so all updates to the control files will occur at the same time.

Many Oracle systems use some type of redundant disk solution such as RAID-1 or RAID-5 to avoid data loss when a disk fails. (RAID, which stands for "redundant array of inexpensive disks," is covered in more detail in Chapter 6.) You might conclude that storing the control file on protected disk storage eliminates the need for maintaining multiple copies of control files and that losing a disk won't mean loss of the control file. But there are two reasons why this is not an appropriate conclusion:

- If you lose more than one disk in a given *striped array* or *mirror-pair* (these are discussed in more detail in Chapter 6), you will lose the data on those disks. Statistically speaking, losing two disks in a short period of time is unlikely to happen. But this type of disastrous event can occur, and it's possible that at some point you will suffer a failure or series of failures resulting in a damaged or lost control file. Because you will no doubt have your hands full recovering from the multiple disk failures, you should avoid the overhead of rebuilding control files during the recovery process. Multiplexing your control files, even when each copy is on redundant disk storage, provides an additional level of physical security for your Oracle database.

- Redundant disk storage does nothing to protect you from the unfortunately perpetual threat of human error. Someone may inadvertently delete or rename a control file, copy another file over it, or move it. A mirrored disk will faithfully mirror these actions, and multiplexed control files will leave you with one or more surviving copies of the control file when one of the copies is damaged or lost.

You do not need to be concerned with the potential performance impact of writing to multiple control files versus one control file. Updates to the control files are insignificant compared to other disk I/O that occurs in an Oracle environment.

Datafiles

Datafiles contain the actual data stored in the database. This data includes the tables and indexes that store data; the data dictionary, which maintains information about these data structures; and the rollback segments, which are used to implement the concurrency scheme you will learn about in Chapter 7.

A datafile is composed of Oracle database blocks that, in turn, are composed of operating system blocks on a disk. Oracle block sizes range from 2 KB to 32 KB.

Prior to Oracle9*i*, only a single block size could be present in the entire database. In versions of the database since the introduction of Oracle9*i*, you still set a default block size for the database, but you can also have up to five other block sizes in the database. You can only have a single block size for each tablespace, but you can mix block sizes within a database. Figure 2-4 illustrates the relationship of Oracle blocks to operating system blocks.

Datafiles belong to only one database and to only one tablespace within that database. Data is read in units of Oracle blocks from the datafiles into memory as needed, based on the work users are doing. Blocks of data are written from memory to the datafiles stored on disk as needed to ensure that the database reliably records changes made by users.

Datafiles are the lowest level of granularity between an Oracle database and the operating system. When you lay a database out on the I/O subsystem, the smallest piece you place in any location is a datafile. Tuning the I/O subsystem to improve Oracle performance typically involves moving datafiles from one set of disks to another. Oracle Database 10*g*'s Automated Storage Management (ASM) with automatic striping eliminates manual effort in this tuning task.

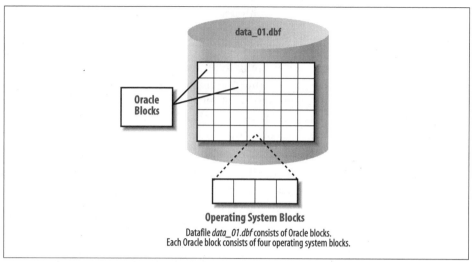

Figure 2-4. Oracle blocks and operating system blocks

Datafile structure

The first block of each datafile is called the *datafile header*. It contains critical information used to maintain the overall integrity of the database. One of the most critical pieces of information in this header is the *checkpoint structure*. This is a logical timestamp that indicates the last point at which changes were written to the datafile. This timestamp is critical for recovery situations. The Oracle recovery process uses the timestamp in the header of a datafile to determine which redo logs to apply to bring the datafile up to the current point in time.

Extents and segments

From a physical point of view, a datafile is stored as operating system blocks. From a logical point of view, datafiles have three intermediate organizational levels: data blocks, extents, and segments. An *extent* is a set of data blocks that are contiguous within an Oracle datafile. A *segment* is an object that takes up space in an Oracle database, such as a table or an index that is comprised of one or more extents.

When Oracle updates data, it attempts to update the data in the same data block. If there is not enough room in the data block for the new information, Oracle will write the data to a new data block, which may be in a different extent.

For more information on segments and extents and how they affect performance, refer to the section on "Fragmentation and Reorganization" in Chapter 5. This will be especially important if you are running an older release of Oracle. Oracle Database 10g provides a Segment Advisor that greatly simplifies segment management.

Redo Log Files

Redo log files store a "recording" of the changes made to the database as a result of transactions and internal Oracle activities. In its normal operations, Oracle caches changed blocks in memory; in the event of an instance failure, some of the changed blocks may not have been written out to the datafiles. The recording of the changes in the redo logs can be used to play back the changes that were lost when the failure occurred, thus protecting transactional consistency.

 These files are sometimes confused with rollback buffers supporting concurrency and described in Chapter 7. They are not the same!

In addition, redo log files are used for "undo" operations when a ROLLBACK statement is issued and uncommitted changes to the database are rolled back to the database image at the last commit. Automatic Undo Management automatically allocates undo (rollback) space among active sessions and first appeared in Oracle9i. Oracle Database 10g automatically determines optimal undo retention time based on system activity maximizing usage of the UNDO tablespace, where undo information is stored to roll away uncommitted transactions. Oracle Database 10g also introduces "flashback" commands that leverage undo information to flash back to a previous state of the database or tables, before tables were dropped, or for specific transaction or row history.

Multiplexing redo log files

Oracle uses specific terminology to manage redo logs. Each Oracle instance uses a *thread* of redo to record the changes it makes to the database. A thread of redo is composed of redo log groups, which are composed of one or more redo log members.

Logically, you can think of a redo log group as a single redo log file. However, Oracle allows you to specify multiple copies of a redo log to protect the all-important integrity of the redo log. By creating multiple copies of each redo log file, you protect the redo log file from disk failure and other types of disasters.

Figure 2-5 illustrates a thread of redo with groups and members. The figure shows two members per group, with each redo log mirrored.

When multiple members are in a redo log group, Oracle maintains multiple copies of the redo log files. The same arguments for multiplexing control files apply here. Redo logs are critical to the health and safety of your Oracle database and you should protect them. Simple redundant disk protection is not sufficient for cases in which human error results in the corruption or deletion of a redo log file.

Suppressing Redo Logging

By default, Oracle logs all changes made to the database. The generation of redo logs adds a certain amount of overhead. You can suppress redo log generation to speed up specific operations, but doing so means the operation in question won't be logged in the redo logs and you will not be able to recover that operation in the event of a failure.

If you do decide to suppress redo logging for certain operations, you would include the NOLOGGING keyword in the SQL statement for the operation. (Note that prior to Oracle8, the keyword was UNRECOVERABLE.) If a failure occurred during the operation, you would need to repeat the operation. For example, you might build an index on a table without generating redo information. In the event that a database failure occurs and the database is recovered, the index will not be recreated because it wasn't logged. You'd simply execute the script originally intended to create the index again.

To simplify operations in the event of a failure, we recommend that you always take a backup after an unlogged operation if you cannot afford to lose the object created by the operation or you cannot repeat the operation for some reason. In addition to using the NOLOGGING keyword in certain commands, you can also mark a table or an entire tablespace with the NOLOGGING attribute. This will suppress redo information for all applicable operations on the table or for all tables in the tablespace.

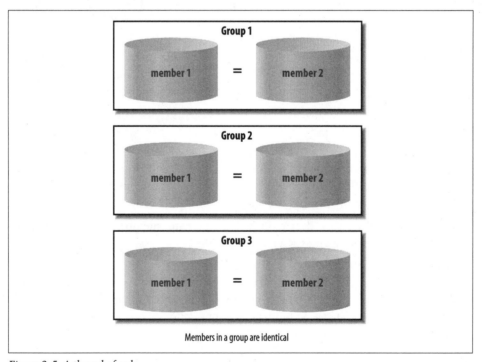

Figure 2-5. A thread of redo

There are ways you can rebuild the static part of the control file if you lose it, but there is no way to reproduce a lost redo log file; be sure to have multiple copies of the redo file.

Oracle writes *synchronously* to all redo log members. Oracle will wait for confirmation that all copies of the redo log have been successfully updated on disk before the redo write is considered done. If you put one copy on a fast or lightly loaded disk, and one copy on a slower or busier disk, your performance will be constrained by the slower disk. Oracle has to guarantee that all copies of the redo log file have been successfully updated to avoid losing data.

Consider what could happen if Oracle were to write multiple redo logs asynchronously, writing to a primary log and then updating the copies later in the background. A failure occurs that brings the system down and damages the primary log, before Oracle has completed updating all the logs. At this point you have committed transactions that are lost—the primary log that recorded the changes made by the transactions is gone, and the copies of the log are not yet up to date with those changes. To prevent this from occurring, Oracle always waits until all copies of the redo log have been updated.

How Oracle uses the redo logs

Once Oracle fills one redo log file, it automatically begins to use the next log file. Once the server cycles through all the available redo log files, it returns to the first one and reuses it. Oracle keeps track of the different redo logs by using a redo log sequence number. This sequence number is recorded inside the redo log files as they are used.

To understand the concepts of redo log filenames and redo log sequence numbers, consider three redo log files called *redolog1.log*, *redolog2.log*, and *redolog3.log*. The first time Oracle uses them the redo log sequence numbers for each will be 1, 2, and 3, respectively. When Oracle returns to the first redo log—*redolog1.log*—it will reuse it and assign it a sequence number of 4. When it moves to *redolog2.log*, it will initialize that file with a sequence number of 5.

Be careful not to confuse these two concepts. The operating system uses the redo log file to identify the physical file, while Oracle uses the redo log file sequence number to determine the order in which the logs were filled and cycled. Because Oracle automatically reuses redo log files, the name of the redo log file is not necessarily indicative of its place in the redo log file sequence.

Figure 2-6 illustrates the filling and cycling of redo logs.

Naming conventions for redo logs

The operating system names for the various files that make up a database are very important—at least to humans, who sometimes have to identify these files by their

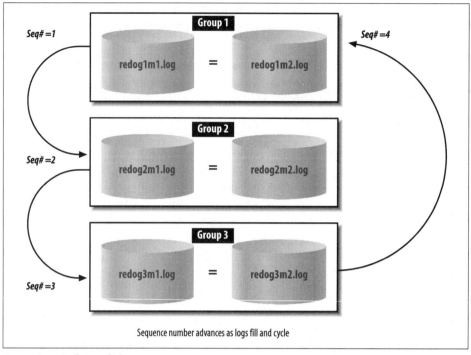

Figure 2-6. Cycling redo logs

names (if you are not using Oracle Managed Files). To add meaning and avoid errors, you should use naming conventions that capture the purpose and some critical details about the nature of the file. Here's one possible convention for the names of the actual redo log files shown in Figure 2-6:

```
redog1m1.log, redog1m2.log, ...
```

The redo prefix and .log suffixes indicate that this is redo log information. The g1m1 and g1m2 character strings capture the group and member numbers. This convention is only an example; it's best to set conventions that you find meaningful and stick to them.

Archived redo logs

You may be wondering how to avoid losing the critical information in the redo log when Oracle cycles over a previously used redo log.

There are actually two ways to address this issue. The first is quite simple: you don't avoid losing the information and you suffer the consequences in the event of a failure. You will lose the history stored in the redo file when it's overwritten. If a failure occurs that damages the datafiles, you must restore the entire database to the point in time when the last backup occurred. No redo log history exists to reproduce the changes made since the last backup occurred, so you will simply lose the effects of those changes. Very few Oracle shops make this choice, because the inability to recover to the point of failure is unacceptable—it results in lost work.

The second and more practical way to address the issue is to archive the redo logs as they fill. To understand archiving redo logs, you must first understand that there are actually two types of redo logs for Oracle:

Online redo logs
>The operating system files that Oracle cycles through to log the changes made to the database

Archived redo logs
>Copies of the filled online redo logs made to avoid losing redo data as the online redo logs are overwritten

An Oracle database can run in one of two modes with respect to archiving redo logs:

NOARCHIVELOG
>As the name implies, no redo logs are archived. As Oracle cycles through the logs, the filled logs are reinitialized and overwritten, which erases the history of the changes made to the database. This mode essentially has the disadvantage mentioned above, where a failure could lead to unrecoverable data.
>
>Choosing not to archive redo logs significantly reduces your options for database backups, as we'll discuss in Chapter 10, and is not advised by Oracle.

ARCHIVELOG
>When Oracle rolls over to a new redo log, it archives the previous redo log. To prevent gaps in the history, a given redo log cannot be reused until it is successfully archived. The archived redo logs, plus the online redo logs, provide a complete history of all changes made to the database. Together, they allow Oracle to recover all committed transactions up to the exact time a failure occurred. Operating in this mode enables tablespace and datafile backups.

The internal sequence numbers discussed earlier act as the guide for Oracle while it is using redo logs and archived redo logs to restore a database.

ARCHIVELOG mode and automatic archiving

In Oracle Database 10g, automatic archiving for an Oracle database is enabled with the following SQL statement:

```
ALTER DATABASE ARCHIVELOG
```

If the database is in ARCHIVELOG mode, Oracle marks the redo logs for archiving as it fills them. The full log files must be archived before they can be reused.

Prior to Oracle Database 10g, log files marked as ready for archiving did not mean they would be automatically archived. You also needed to set a parameter in the initialization file with the syntax:

```
LOG_ARCHIVE_START = TRUE
```

Setting this parameter started a process that is called by Oracle to copy a full redo log to the archive log destination. Oracle Database 10*g* now automatically does this. This archive log destination and the format for the archived redo log names are specified using two additional parameters, LOG_ARCHIVE_DEST and LOG_ARCHIVE_FORMAT. A setting such as the following:

```
LOG_ARCHIVE_DEST = C:\ORANT\DATABASE\ARCHIVE
```

specifies the directory to which Oracle writes the archived redo log files, and:

```
LOG_ARCHIVE_FORMAT = "ORCL%S.ARC"
```

specifies the format Oracle will use for the archived redo log filenames. In this case, the filenames must begin with ORCL and will end with .ARC. Oracle expands the %S automatically to the sequence number of the redo log padded with zeros on the left. The other options for the format wildcards are:

%s

Replaced by the sequence number without zero-padding on the left

%T

Replaced by the redo thread number with zero-padding

%t

Replaced by the redo thread number without zero-padding

If you want the archived redo log filenames to include the thread and the sequence numbers with both numbers zero-padded, set:

```
LOG_ARCHIVE_FORMAT = "ORCL%T%S.ARC"
```

The initialization file is read every time an Oracle instance is started, so changes to these parameters do not take effect until an instance is stopped and restarted. Remember, though, that turning on automatic archiving does not put the database in ARCHIVELOG mode. Similarly, placing the database in ARCHIVELOG mode does not enable the automatic archiving process.

Prior to Oracle Database 10*g*, the LOG_ARCHIVE_START parameter defaulted to FALSE. You could see an Oracle instance endlessly waiting because of dissonance between the ARCHIVELOG mode setting and the LOG_ARCHIVE_START setting. If you had turned archive logging on but had not started the automatic process, the Oracle instance would stop because it could not write over an unarchived log file marked as ready for archiving. In other words, the automatic process of archiving the file had not been done. To avoid such problems prior to Oracle Database 10*g*, you would first modify the initialization parameter and then issue the ALTER DATABASE ARCHIVELOG statement.

In Oracle Database 10*g*, the ALTER DATABASE ARCHIVELOG statement will, by default, turn on automatic archiving and the archivers are started.

You should also make sure that the archive log destination has enough room for the logs Oracle will automatically write to it. If the archive log file destination is full, Oracle will hang because it can't archive additional redo log files.

Figure 2-7 illustrates redo log use with archiving enabled.

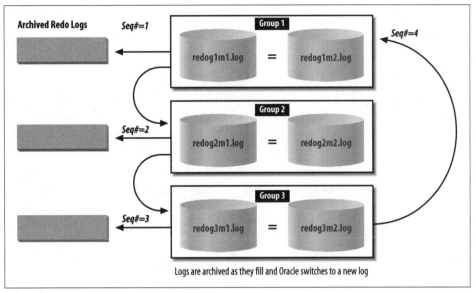

Figure 2-7. Cycling redo logs with archiving

The archived redo logs are critical for database recovery. Just as you can duplex the online redo logs, you can also specify multiple archive log destinations. Oracle will copy filled redo logs to specified destinations. You can also specify whether all copies must succeed or not. The initialization parameters for this functionality are as follows:

LOG_ARCHIVE_DUPLEX_DEST
Specifies an additional location for redundant redo logs

LOG_ARCHIVE_MIN_SUCCEED_DEST
Indicates whether the redo log must be successfully written to one or all of the locations

Starting with Oracle8*i*, you could specify up to five mandatory or optional archive log destinations, including remote systems for use in disaster recovery situations (covered in Chapter 10). Oracle8*i* also introduced automated support for multiple archiving processes to support the additional load of archiving to multiple destinations. See your Oracle documentation for the additional parameters and views that enable and control this functionality.

The Components of an Instance

An Oracle instance can be defined as an area of shared memory and a collection of background processes. The area of shared memory for an instance is called the *System Global Area,* or SGA. The SGA is not really one large undifferentiated section of memory—it's made up of various components that we'll examine in the next section, "Memory Structures for an Instance." All the processes of an instance—system processes and user processes—share the SGA.

Prior to Oracle9*i*, the size of the SGA was set when the Oracle instance was started. The only way to change the size of the SGA or any of its components was to change the initialization parameter and then stop and restart the instance. Since Oracle9*i*, you can change the size of the SGA or its components while the Oracle instance is still running. Oracle9*i* introduced the concept of the *granule*, which is the smallest amount of memory that you can add to or subtract from the SGA.

The background processes interact with the operating system and each other to manage the memory structures for the instance. These processes also manage the actual database on disk and perform general housekeeping for the instance.

There are other physical files that you can consider as part of the instance as well:

The instance initialization file
> The initialization file contains a variety of parameters that configure how the instance will operate: how much memory it will use, how many users it will allow to connect, to which database the instance actually provides access, and so on. You can alter many of these parameters dynamically at either the system-wide or session-specific level. Prior to Oracle9*i*, the only initialization file was called *INIT.ORA*. Oracle9*i* introduced a file named *SPFILE* that performs the same function as the *INIT.ORA* file but can also persistently store changes to initialization parameters that have been made while Oracle is running.
>
> *SPFILE* is a binary file that is kept on the server machine, which eliminates the need for *INIT.ORA* files on client machines. When an instance of Oracle starts up, it first looks for *SPFILE* and then for an *INIT.ORA* file.
>
> Oracle Database 10*g*'s automated features reduce the number of parameters requiring initial manual definition. Now, fewer than 40 parameters require manual definition.

The instance configuration file
> *CONFIG.ORA* is an optional parameter file. You can include it if you want to segregate a set of initialization parameters (for example, those used for Real Application Clusters).

The password file
> Oracle can use an optional password file stored as an operating system file to provide additional flexibility for managing Oracle databases. This file is

encrypted and contains userids and passwords that can be used to perform administrative tasks, such as starting and stopping the instance. Password files are typically used to implement remote access security in addition to access security by operating system, which is usually used locally (i.e., on the database server). For example, on a Unix system, any user in the DBA group can start up or shut down Oracle—the operating system group gives them the authority. However, the database server operating-system authentication always has priority over a password-file authentication and cannot be used to force the entry of a password if operating system authentication is enabled. Validating a password against the value stored in the database for a user is not possible when the database is not open. The password file forces a user to authenticate herself with a password in order to start up the database.

Figure 2-8 illustrates the memory structures and background processes, which are discussed in the following sections.

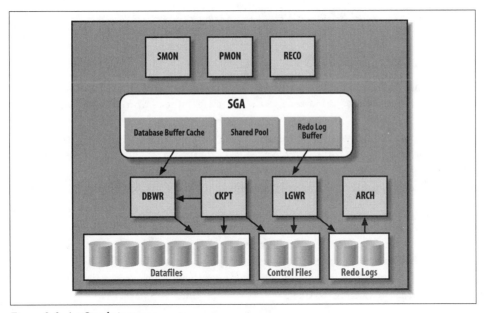

Figure 2-8. An Oracle instance

Additional background processes may exist when you use certain other features of the database: for example, shared servers (formerly the Multi-Threaded Server or MTS prior to Oracle9i), or job queues and replication. For now, we'll just describe the basic pieces of an Oracle instance and leave the optional pieces for later in the book. We'll discuss the shared server processes in Chapter 3, and replication processes in Chapter 10.

Memory Structures for an Instance

As shown in Figure 2-8, the System Global Area is actually composed of three main areas: the database buffer cache, the shared pool, and the redo log buffer.

Another type of memory pool, the large pool (not shown in Figure 2-8), was introduced in Oracle8. This optional area of the SGA is used for buffering I/O for various server processes, including those used for backup and recovery. The area is also used to store session memory for the shared server and when using the XA protocol for distributed transactions, as discussed in Chapter 12.

This alternate pool exists to reduce the demand on the shared pool for certain large memory allocations. The initialization parameter used to configure the large pool is LARGE_POOL_SIZE.

The following sections describe these areas of the SGA. For a more detailed discussion of performance issues for these areas, see "How Oracle Uses the System Global Area" in Chapter 6. Note that in Oracle Database 10g, the initialization parameters that affect the size of the SGA are now dynamic.

Database buffer cache

The database buffer cache caches blocks of data retrieved from the database. This buffer between the users' requests and the actual datafiles improves the performance of the Oracle database. If a piece of data can be found in the buffer cache, you can retrieve it from memory without the overhead of having to go to disk. Oracle manages the cache using a *least recently used* (LRU) algorithm. If a user requests data that has been recently used, the data is more likely to be in the database buffer cache; data in the cache can be delivered immediately without a disk read operation being executed.

When a user wants to read a block that is not in the cache, the block must be read and loaded into the cache. When a user makes changes to a block, those changes are made to the block in the cache. At some later time, those changes will be written to the datafile in which the block resides. This avoids making users wait while Oracle writes their changed blocks to disk.

This notion of waiting to perform I/O until absolutely necessary is common throughout Oracle. Disks are the slowest component of a computer system, so the less I/O performed, the faster the system runs. By deferring noncritical I/O operations instead of performing them immediately, an Oracle database can deliver better performance.

Oracle7 had one pool of buffers for database blocks. Oracle8 introduced multiple buffer pools. There are three pools available in Oracle8 and beyond:

DEFAULT
> The standard Oracle database buffer cache. All objects use this cache unless otherwise indicated.

KEEP
>   For frequently used objects you wish to cache.

RECYCLE
>   For objects you're less likely to access again.

Both the KEEP and RECYCLE buffer pools remove their objects from consideration by the LRU algorithm.

You can mark a table or index for caching in a specific buffer pool. This helps to keep more desirable objects in the cache and avoids the "churn" of all objects fighting for space in one central cache. Of course, to use these features properly you must be aware of the access patterns for the various objects used by your application.

Oracle Database 10g simplifes management of buffer cache size by introducing a new dynamic parameter, DB_CACHE_SIZE. This parameter replaces the DB_BLOCK_BUFFERS parameter present in previous Oracle releases.

Shared pool

The shared pool caches various constructs that can be shared among users. For example, SQL statements issued by users are cached so they can be reused if the same statement is submitted again. Another example is stored procedures, or pieces of code stored and executed within the database. These are loaded into the shared pool for execution and then cached, again using an LRU algorithm. The shared pool is also used for caching information from the Oracle data dictionary, which is the metadata that describes the structure and content of the database itself. Note that prior to Oracle Database 10g, "out of memory" errors were possible if the shared pool was undersized. Oracle Database 10g provides automatic shared memory tuning.

Redo log buffer

The redo log buffer caches redo information until it is written to the physical redo log files stored on a disk. This buffer also improves performance. Oracle caches the redo until it can be written to a disk at a more optimal time, which avoids the overhead of constantly writing the redo logs to disk.

Background Processes for an Instance

The background processes shown in Figure 2-8 are:

Database Writer (DBWR)
>   The Database Writer process writes database blocks from the database buffer cache in the SGA to the datafiles on disk. An Oracle instance can have up to 10 DBWR processes, from DBW0 to DBW9, to handle the I/O load to multiple

datafiles. Most instances run one DBWR. DBWR writes blocks out of the cache for two main reasons:

- If Oracle needs to perform a checkpoint (i.e., to update the blocks of the datafiles so that they "catch up" to the redo logs). Oracle writes the redo for a transaction when it's committed, and later writes the actual blocks. Periodically, Oracle performs a checkpoint to bring the datafile contents in line with the redo that was written out for the committed transactions.

- If Oracle needs to read blocks requested by users into the cache and there is no free space in the buffer cache. The blocks written out are the least recently used blocks. Writing blocks in this order minimizes the performance impact of losing them from the buffer cache.

Log Writer (LGWR)

The Log Writer process writes the redo information from the log buffer in the SGA to all copies of the current redo log file on disk. As transactions proceed, the associated redo information is stored in the redo log buffer in the SGA. When a transaction is committed, Oracle makes the redo information permanent by invoking the Log Writer to write it to disk.

System Monitor (SMON)

The System Monitor process maintains overall health and safety for an Oracle instance. SMON performs crash recovery when the instance is started after a failure and coordinates and performs recovery for a failed instance when you have more than one instance accessing the same database, as with Oracle Parallel Server/Real Application Clusters. SMON also cleans up adjacent pieces of free space in the datafiles by merging them into one piece and gets rid of space used for sorting rows when that space is no longer needed.

Process Monitor (PMON)

The Process Monitor process watches over the user processes that access the database. If a user process terminates abnormally, PMON is responsible for cleaning up any of the resources left behind (such as memory) and for releasing any locks held by the failed process.

Archiver (ARC)

The Archiver process reads the redo log files once Oracle has filled them and writes a copy of the used redo log files to the specified archive log destination(s).

Since Oracle8i, an Oracle instance can have up to 10 processes, numbered as described for DBWR above. LGWR will start additional Archivers as needed, based on the load, up to the limit specified by the initialization parameter LOG_ARCHIVE_MAX_PROCESSES.

Checkpoint (CKPT)

The Checkpoint process works with DBWR to perform checkpoints. CKPT updates the control file and database file headers to update the checkpoint data when the checkpoint is complete.

Recover (RECO)
   The Recover process automatically cleans up failed or suspended distributed transactions (discussed in Chapter 10).

Processes or Threads?

With all this talk about processes, you may be wondering whether Oracle actually uses threads or processes in the underlying operating system to implement these services.

For simplicity, throughout this book we use the term *process* generically to indicate a function that Oracle performs, such as DBWR or LGWR. Oracle on Windows uses one operating system process per instance; thus each "Oracle process" is actually a *thread* within the one Oracle process. Oracle on Unix uses a process-based architecture. All of the "processes" are actual operating system processes, not threads. Thus, on Unix DBWR, LGWR, and so on are specific operating system processes, while on Windows they are threads within a single process.

There are some exceptions, however. For instance, the shared server uses real threads on Windows and simulated threads on Unix.

The Data Dictionary

Each Oracle database includes a set of what is called *metadata*, or data that describes the structure of the data contained by the database including table definitions and integrity constraints. The tables and views that hold this metadata are referred to as the *Oracle data dictionary*. All the components discussed in this chapter have corresponding system tables and views in the data dictionary that fully describe the characteristics of the component. You can query these tables and views using standard SQL statements. Table 2-1 shows where you can find some of the information available about each of the components in the data dictionary.

Table 2-1. Partial list of database components and their related data dictionary views

Component	Data dictionary tables and views
Database	V$DATABASE, V$VERSION, V$INSTANCE
Shared server	V$QUEUE, V$DISPATCHER, V$SHARED SERVER
Tablespaces	DBA_TABLESPACES, DBA_DATA_FILES, DBA_FREE_SPACE
Control files	V$CONTROLFILE, V$PARAMETER, V$CONTROLFILE_RECORD_SECTION
Datafiles	V$DATAFILE, V$DATAFILE_HEADER, V$FILESTAT, DBA_DATA_FILES
Segments	DBA_SEGMENTS
Extents	DBA_EXTENTS
Redo threads, groups, and numbers	V$THREAD, V$LOG, V$LOGFILE

Table 2-1. Partial list of database components and their related data dictionary views (continued)

Component	Data dictionary tables and views
Archiving status	V$DATABASE, V$LOG, V$ARCHIVED_LOG, V$ARCHIVE_DEST
Database instance	V$INSTANCE, V$PARAMETER, V$SYSTEM_PARAMETER
Memory structure	VSGA, VSGASTAT, V$SGAINFO, V$SGA_DYNAMIC_COMPONENTS, V$SGA_DYNAMIC_FREE_MEMORY, VSGA_RESIZE_OPS, VSGA_RESIZE_CURRENT_OPS, VDB_OBJECT_CACHE, VSQL, V$SQLTEXT, V$SQLAREA
Work area memory	V$PGASTAT, V$SYSSTAT, V$SESSTAT
Processes	V$PROCESS, V$BGPROCESS, V$SESSION, V$LOCK
RMAN recovery	V$RECOVER_FILE
User passwords	V$PWFILE_USERS

The SYSTEM tablespace always contains the data dictionary tables. Data dictionary tables that are preceded by the V$ or GV$ prefixes are dynamic tables, which are continually updated to reflect the current state of the Oracle database. Static data dictionary tables can have a prefix such as DBA_, ALL_, or USER_ to indicate the scope of the objects listed in the view.

CHAPTER 3

Installing and Running Oracle

If you've been reading this book sequentially, you should understand the basics of the Oracle database architecture by now. This chapter begins with a description of how to install a database and get it up and running. (If you've already installed your Oracle database software, you can skim through this first section.) We'll describe how to create an actual database and how to configure the network software needed to run Oracle. Finally, we'll examine how to manage databases and discuss how users access databases.

Installing Oracle

Prior to Oracle8i, the Oracle installer came in both character and GUI versions for Unix. The Unix GUI ran in Motif using the X Windows system. Windows NT came with a GUI version only. Since Oracle8i, the installer is Java-based. The Oracle installer is one of the first places in which you can see the benefits of the portability of Java; the installer looks and functions the same across all operating systems. Installing Oracle is now quite simple, requiring only a few mouse clicks and answers to some questions about options and features.

Oracle has further simplified installation of Oracle Database 10g. This version of the database comes on a single CD-ROM, and can be installed in less than 30 minutes. Figure 3-1 shows a version of the launch screen of the installer for Oracle Database 10g.

Although the installation process is now the same for all platforms, there are still particulars about the installation of Oracle that relate to specific platforms. Each release of the Oracle Database server software is shipped with several pieces of documentation. Included in each release are an installation guide, release notes (which include installation information added after the installation guide was published), and a "getting started" book. You should read all of these documents prior to starting the installation process, because each of them contains invaluable information about the specifics of the installation. You will need to consider details such as

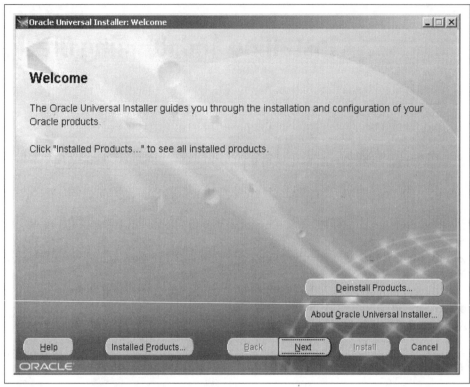

Figure 3-1. Oracle Universal Installer

where to establish the Oracle Home directory and where database files will reside. These issues are covered in detail in the documentation. In addition to the hardcopy documentation, online documentation is shipped on the database server CD-ROM, which provides additional information regarding the database and related products.

You'll typically find the installation guide in the server software CD case. The installation guide includes system requirements (memory and disk), pre-installation tasks, directions for running the installation, and notes regarding migration of earlier Oracle databases to the current release. You should remember that complete installation of the software includes not only loading the software, but also configuring and starting key services.

One of the more important decisions you need to make before actually installing Oracle concerns the directory structure and naming conventions you will follow for the files that make up a database. Clear, consistent, and well-planned conventions are crucial for minimizing human errors in system and database administration. Some of the more important conventions to consider include the following:

- Disk or mount point names
- Directory structures for Oracle software and database files
- Database filenames: control files, database files, and redo log files

The Optimal Flexible Architecture, described in the next section, provides suggestions for naming conventions for all of these files.

Optimal Flexible Architecture (OFA)

There is one more piece of documentation that you may not know about, but may find extremely valuable in creating and managing your Oracle environment. Oracle consultants working at large Oracle sites created (out of necessity) a comprehensive set of standards for Unix directory structures and filenames. This set of standards is called *An Optimal Flexible Architecture for a Growing Oracle Database* or, as it is lovingly known in the Oracle community, the OFA. The OFA provides a clear set of standards for handling multiple databases and multiple versions of Oracle on the same machine. It includes recommendations for mount points, directory structures, filenames, and scripting techniques. Anyone who knows the OFA can navigate an Oracle environment to quickly find the software and files used for the database and the instance. This standardization increases productivity and avoids errors.

While the OFA was created for Unix, the core standards can be and have been applied to Windows and other operating systems. Through the later Oracle7 releases, the OFA standards were also embedded in the Oracle installer. All system administrators and database administrators working with Oracle will find the OFA worthwhile, even if your Oracle system is already installed. The OFA exists as part of the Oracle installation guide.

Oracle Managed Files, which were new in Oracle9*i* and were discussed in Chapter 2, use the OFA for their own internal naming conventions.

Supporting Multiple Oracle Versions on a Machine

You can install and run multiple versions of Oracle on a single-server machine. All Oracle products use a directory referred to by the environment or system variable ORACLE_HOME to find the base directory for the software they will use. Because of this, you can run multiple versions of Oracle software on the same server, each with a different ORACLE_HOME variable defined. Whenever a piece of software accesses a particular version of Oracle, the software simply uses the proper setting for the ORACLE_HOME environment variable.

Oracle supports multiple ORACLE_HOME variables on Unix and Windows systems by using different directories. The OFA provides clear and excellent standards for this type of implementation.

Upgrading an Oracle Database

Oracle Database 10g includes two additional features that will help you upgrade an existing Oracle database: the Database Upgrade Assistant and rolling upgrades.

If you want to upgrade a single instance, you can use the Database Upgrade Assistant, which can be started from the Oracle Universal Installer.

One of the longstanding problems with upgrades has been the requirement to bring down the database, upgrade the database software, and then restart the database. This necessary downtime can impinge on your operational requirements. If you are using a Real Application Clusters (RAC) implementation of Oracle Database 10g, you can perform a *rolling upgrade*. A rolling upgrade allows you to bring down some of the nodes of the cluster, upgrade their software, and then bring them back online as part of the cluster. You can then repeat this procedure with the other nodes. The end result is that you can achieve a complete upgrade of your Oracle database software without having to bring down the database.

Creating a Database

As we discussed in Chapter 2, an Oracle installation can have many different databases. You should take a two-step approach for any new databases you create. First, understand the purpose of the database, and then create the database with the appropriate parameters.

Planning the Database

As with installing the Oracle software, you should spend some time learning the purpose of an Oracle database before you create the database itself. Consider what the database will be used for and how much data it will contain. You should understand the underlying hardware that you'll use—the number and type of CPUs, the amount of memory, the number of disks, the controllers for the disks, and so on. Because the database is stored on the disks, many tuning problems can be avoided with proper capacity and I/O subsystem planning.

Planning your database and the supporting hardware requires insights into the scale or size of the workload and the type of work the system will perform. Some of the considerations that will affect your database design and hardware configuration include the following:

How many users will the database have?
> How many users will connect simultaneously and how many will concurrently perform transactions or execute queries?

Is the database supporting OLTP applications or data warehousing?
> This distinction leads to different types and volumes of activity on the database server. For example, online transaction processing (OLTP) systems usually have

a larger number of users performing smaller transactions, while data warehouses usually have a smaller number of users performing larger queries.

What are the expected size and number of database objects?

How large will these objects be initially and what growth rates do you expect?

What are the access patterns for the various database objects?

Some objects will be more popular than others. Understanding the volume and type of activity in the database is critical to planning and tuning your database. Some people employ a so-called *CRUD matrix* that contains Create, Read, Update, and Delete estimates for each key object used by a business transaction. These estimates may be per minute, per hour, per day, or for whatever time period makes sense in the context of your system. For example, the CRUD matrix for a simple employee update transaction might be as shown in Table 3-1, with the checkmarks indicating that each transaction performs the operation against the object shown.

Table 3-1. Access patterns for database objects

Object	Create	Read	Update	Delete
EMP	✓	✓		
DEPT		✓		
SALARY		✓	✓	

How much hardware do I have now, and how much will I add as the database grows?

Disk drives tend to get cheaper and cheaper. Suppose you're planning a database of 100 GB that you expect to grow to 300 GB over the next two years. You may have all the disk space available to plan for the 300 GB target, but it's more likely that you'll buy a smaller amount to get started and add disks as the database grows. It's important that you plan the initial layout with the expected growth in mind.

Prior to Oracle9*i*, running out of tablespace in the middle of a batch operation meant that the entire operation had to be rolled back. Oracle9*i* introduced the concept of *resumable space allocation*. When an operation encounters an out-of-space condition, if the resumable statement option has been enabled for the session, the operation is suspended for a specific length of time, which allows the operator to correct the out-of-space condition. You even have the option to create an AFTER SUSPEND trigger to fire when an operation has been suspended.

With Automatic Storage Management (ASM), new in Oracle Database 10*g*, you can add additional disk space or take away disks without interrupting database service. Although you should still carefully estimate storage requirements, the penalty for an incorrect judgment, in terms of database downtime, is significantly reduced with ASM.

What are the availability requirements?

>What elements of redundancy, such as additional disk drives, do you need to provide the required availability? ASM also provides automatic mirroring for data, which can help to provide data resiliency.

What are my performance requirements?

>What response times do your users expect, and how much of that time can you give them? Will you measure performance in terms of average response time, maximum response time, response time at peak load, total throughput, or average load?

What are my security requirements?

>Will the application, the operating system, or the Oracle database (or some combination of these) enforce security?

The Value of Estimating

Even if you are unsure of things such as sizing and usage details, take your best guess as to initial values and growth rates, and document these estimates. As the database evolves, you can compare your initial estimates with emerging information to react and plan more effectively. For example, suppose you estimate that a certain table will be 5 GB in size initially and will grow at 3 GB per year, but when you are up and running you discover that the table is actually 3 GB, and six months into production you discover that it has grown to 8 GB. You can now revise your plans to reflect the higher growth rate and thereby avoid space problems. Comparing production measures of database size, growth, and usage patterns with your initial estimates will provide valuable insights to help you avoid problems as you move forward. In this way, documented guesses at an early stage are useful later on.

The same is true for key requirements such as availability and performance. If the exact requirements are not clear, make some assumptions and document them. These core requirements will heavily influence the decisions you make regarding redundancy and capacity. As the system evolves and these requirements become clearer, the history of these key decision criteria will be crucial in understanding the choices that you made and will make in the future.

The Automatic Workload Repository (AWR), new in Oracle Database 10g, maintains a history of workload and performance measurements, which are used by the Automatic Database Diagnostic Monitor (ADDM) to spot performance anomalies. You can also use AWR to track ongoing changes in workload.

Tools for Creating Databases

There are two basic ways to create an Oracle database:

- Use the GUI Oracle Database Configuration Assistant.
- Run character-mode scripts.

Oracle ships with a GUI utility called the Oracle Database Configuration Assistant. It is written in Java and therefore provides the same look and feel across platforms. The Assistant is a quick and easy way to create, modify, or delete a database. It allows you to create a typical preconfigured database (with minimal input required) or a custom database (which involves making some choices and answering additional questions). The Database Configuration Assistant is typically initially accessed as part of a standard installer session. The Assistant is shown in Figure 3-2.

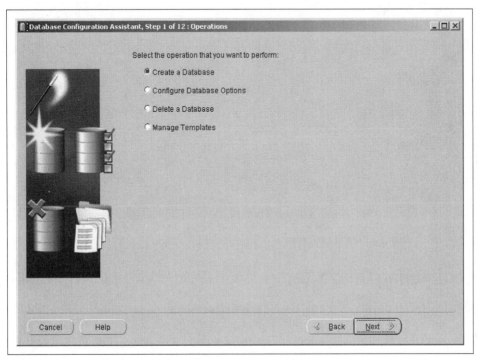

Figure 3-2. Oracle Database Configuration Assistant

If you choose to create a database, you can then select the type of database you want to create, as shown in Figure 3-3 for Oracle Database 10g. The different types of databases will be created with different default configuration values.

The alternative method for creating a database is to create or edit an existing SQL script that executes the various required commands. Most Oracle DBAs have a preferred script that they edit as needed. In Oracle7 and Oracle8, you executed the script using a character-mode utility called Server Manager; since Oracle8i, you could use SQL*Plus. The Oracle software CD-ROM also includes a sample script called *BUILD_DB.SQL*, described in the Oracle documentation. Today, most users choose to create the database with the standard installer interface.

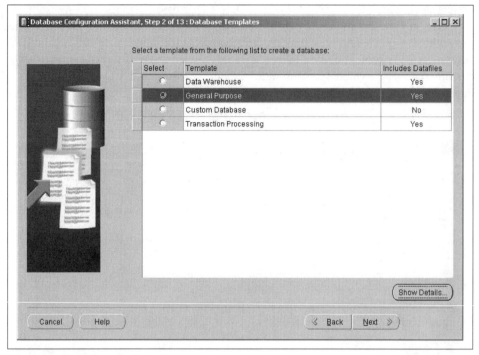

Select a template from the following list to create a database:

Select	Template	Includes Datafiles
○	Data Warehouse	Yes
○	General Purpose	Yes
○	Custom Database	No
○	Transaction Processing	Yes

Show Details...

Cancel   Help   Back   Next

Figure 3-3. Selecting a database to create

Configuring Oracle Net

Oracle Net (known as Net8 for Oracle8 and Oracle8*i*, and SQL*Net prior to Oracle8) is a layer of software that allows different physical machines to communicate for the purpose of accessing an Oracle database.

 The name Net8 was changed to Oracle Net in Oracle9*i*, and we will generally use "Oracle Net" in this chapter as a neutral term to apply to all versions of Oracle networking. The term "Oracle Net Services" in Oracle refers to all the components of Oracle Net, including dispatchers, listeners, and shared servers; these are explained later in this chapter.

A version of Oracle Net runs on the client machine and on the database server, and allows clients and servers to communicate over a network using virtually any popular network protocol. Oracle Net can also perform network protocol interchanges. For example, it allows clients that are speaking LU 6.2 to interact with database servers that are speaking TCP/IP.

Oracle Net also provides *location transparency*—that is, the client application does not need to know the server's physical location. The Oracle Net layer handles the communications, which means that you can move the database to another machine and simply update the Oracle Net configuration details accordingly. The client applications will still be able to reach the database, and no application changes will be required.

Oracle Net introduces the notion of *service names*, or *aliases*. Clients provide a service name or Oracle Net alias to specify which database they want to reach without having to identify the actual machine or instance for the database. Oracle Net looks up the actual machine and the Oracle instance, using the provided service name, and transparently routes the client to the appropriate database.

Resolving Oracle Net Service Names

The following Oracle Net configuration options resolve the service name the client specifies into the host and instance names needed to reach an Oracle database:

Local name resolution
> For local name resolution, you install a file called *TNSNAMES.ORA* on each client machine that contains entries that provide the host and Oracle instance for each Oracle Net alias. You must maintain this file on the client machines if any changes are made to the underlying database locations. Your network topology is almost certain to change over time, so use of this option can lead to an increased maintenance load.

Oracle Names service
> Using the Oracle Names software that ships with Oracle eliminates the need for a *TNSNAMES.ORA* file on each client. When a client specifies a service name, Oracle Net automatically contacts the Oracle Names server, typically located on another machine. Oracle Names replies with the host and instance information needed by the client. You can configure multiple Oracle Names servers to provide redundancy and increased performance. Oracle Names minimizes the overhead of updating the local *TNSNAMES.ORA* files when there are frequent changes to the Oracle network topology. Oracle Names can also be very useful for complex networks that are widely distributed.

Oracle Internet Directory
> The good part about the Oracle Names service is that it eliminates the need for client configuration files. The bad part is that it is proprietary—it applies only to Oracle databases. The need for a centralized naming service extends far beyond the Oracle environment. In fact, there is a well-defined standard for accessing this type of information, the Lightweight Directory Access Protocol, or LDAP. Since Oracle8*i* was released, the Oracle database has shipped with the Oracle Internet Directory (OID). OID is an LDAP-enabled directory that can fulfill the same role as the Oracle Names service. The OID is also used for a variety of other purposes, such as enabling single sign-on for the Oracle Application Server Portal product, which is described in Chapter 14. Although the use of Oracle

Names was still supported in Oracle9*i*, the future direction of this functionality clearly lies with OID. In Oracle Database 10*g*, you can export directory entries to create a local *TNSNAMES.ORA* file; this file may be used for clients not using the directory or if the directory should not be available.

Host naming

Clients can simply use the name of the host on which the instance runs. This is valid for TCP/IP networks with a mechanism in place for resolving the hostname into an IP address. For example, the Domain Name Service (DNS) translates a hostname into an IP address, much as Oracle Names translates service names. With Oracle Database 10*g*, you can use this method with either a host name, domain-qualified if appropriate, or a TCP/IP address, but the connection will not support advanced services such as connection pooling.

Third-party naming services

Oracle Net can interface with external or third-party naming and authentication services such as Kerberos or Radius. Use of such services may require Oracle Advanced Security (known as the Advanced Networking Option prior to Oracle8*i*).

These name resolution options are not mutually exclusive. For example, you can use Oracle Names and local name resolution (*TNSNAMES.ORA* files) together. In this case, you specify the order Oracle should use in resolving names in the *SQLNET. ORA* file (for example, check Oracle Names first, and if the service name isn't resolved, check the local *TNSNAMES.ORA* file). This is useful for cases in which there are corporate database services specific to certain clients. You would use Oracle Names for the standard corporate database services, such as email, and then use *TNSNAMES.ORA* entries for the client-specific database services, such as a particular development database.

Oracle Net Manager

In Oracle8, Oracle provided a GUI utility called the Net8 Assistant used to create the various configuration files required for Net8; this utility was renamed the Oracle Net Manager with the Oracle9*i* release.

Like the Database Configuration Assistant, the Oracle Net Manager is written in Java, provides the same look and feel across platforms, and is typically first accessed from the installer. The Oracle Net configuration files have a very specific syntax with multiple levels of nested brackets. Using the Oracle Net Manager allows you to avoid the errors that are common to hand-coded files. This utility, which automates the configuration of various Oracle Net components, is shown in Figure 3-4 as it appears in Oracle Database 10*g*.

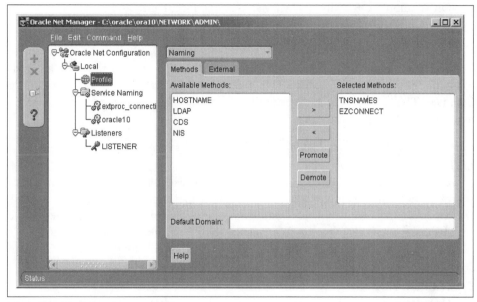

Figure 3-4. Net Manager

Auto-Discovery and Agents

Beginning with Oracle 7.3, Oracle provided auto-discovery features that allowed it to find new databases automatically. Support for auto-discovery has increased and improved with each Oracle release since then. With Oracle8*i*, the Universal Installer and Oracle Net Manager work together smoothly to automatically configure your Oracle Net network. All that is required is the *INIT.ORA* (or *SPFILE* in Oracle9*i* or more current releases) entry that maps the instance to the service or application, as described in the sidebar "Generic Service Names" later in this chapter. Auto-discovery and dynamic registration take care of the rest.

A key piece of the Oracle network that enables auto-discovery is the Oracle Intelligent Agent. The Agent is a piece of software that runs on the machine with your Oracle database(s). It acts as an agent for other functions that need to find and work with the database on the machine. For example, the Agent knows about the various Oracle instances on the machine and handles critical management functions, such as monitoring the database for certain events and executing jobs. The Agent provides a central point for auto-discovery: Oracle Net discovers instances and databases by interrogating the Agent. We'll examine the Agent again in Chapter 5.

Oracle Net Configuration Files

Oracle Net requires several configuration files. The default location for the files used to configure an Oracle Net network are as follows:

- On Windows, *ORACLE_HOME\net80\admin* for Oracle8 and *ORACLE_HOME\network\ admin* for Oracle8i and more current releases
- On Unix, *ORACLE_HOME/network/admin*

You can place these files in another location, in which case you must set an environment or system variable called TNS_ADMIN to the non-default location. Oracle then uses TNS_ADMIN to locate the files. The vast majority of systems are configured using the default location.

The files that form a simple Oracle Net configuration are as follows:

LISTENER.ORA
> Contains details for configuring the Oracle Net Listener, such as which instances or services the Listener is servicing. As the name implies, the Listener "listens" for incoming connection requests from clients that want to access the Oracle database over the network. For details about the mechanics of the Listener's function, see the later section "Oracle Net and Establishing Network Connections."

TNSNAMES.ORA
> Decodes a service name into a specific machine address and Oracle instance for the connection request. (If you're using Oracle Names or OID, as described earlier, you don't need to use the *TNSNAMES.ORA* file as part of your configuration.) This file is key to Oracle Net's location transparency. If you move a database from one machine to another, you can simply update the *TNSNAMES.ORA* files on the various clients to reflect the new machine address for the existing service name. For example, suppose that clients reach the database using a service name of "SALES". The *TNSNAMES.ORA* file has an entry for the service name SALES that decodes to a machine named HOST1 and an Oracle instance called PROD. If the Oracle database used for the SALES application is moved to a machine called HOST2, the *TNSNAMES.ORA* entry is updated to use the machine name HOST2. Once the *TNSNAMES.ORA* files are updated, client connection requests will be routed transparently to the new machine with no application changes required.

SQLNET.ORA

Provides important defaults and miscellaneous configuration details. For example, *SQLNET.ORA* contains the default domain name for your network. If you're using Oracle Names, *SQLNET.ORA* can contain the address the client uses to find the Oracle Names server and the order in which Oracle Net should resolve service names.

LDAP.ORA

For Oracle8*i* and beyond, the *LDAP.ORA* file contains the configuration information needed to use an LDAP directory, such as the Oracle Internet Directory. This information includes the location of the LDAP directory server and the default administrative context for the server. This is no longer required for an LDAP server that is registered with the Domain Name Server in Oracle Database 10*g*.

For more details on the inner workings of Oracle Net and the various configuration options and files, see your Oracle networking documentation or *Oracle Net Configuration and Troubleshooting*, by Hugo Toledo and Jonathan Gennick (see Appendix B for details).

As mentioned in Chapter 2, Oracle9*i* added a feature called a *persistent parameter file*. This file, which is named *SPFILE*, provides storage for system parameters you have changed while your Oracle9*i* instance is running, using the ALTER SYSTEM command. With the *SPFILE*, these new parameter values are preserved and used the next time you restart your Oracle instance. You can indicate whether a particular change to a system parameter is intended to be persistent (in which case it will be stored in the *SPFILE*) or temporary.

The *SPFILE* is a binary file that is kept on the server machine. By default, an Oracle9*i* or more current instance will look first for the *SPFILE* at startup and then for an instance of the *INIT.ORA* file.

The *SPFILE* can also be kept on a shared disk, so that it can be used to initialize multiple instances in an Oracle Real Application Cluster.

Starting Up the Database

Starting a database is quite simple—on Windows you simply start the Oracle services, and on Unix you issue the STARTUP command from Server Manager or SQL*Plus (since Oracle8*i*) or through Enterprise Manager. While starting a database appears to be a single action, it involves an instance and a database and occurs in several distinct phases. When you start a database, the following actions are automatically executed:

Generic Service Names

Prior to Oracle8*i*, the Listener on a database server was configured to listen for specific instance names. Clients used a Net8 service name that resolved the specific host and instance names. Starting with Oracle8*i*, you can use the SERVICE_NAMES parameter in the initialization file for an instance to specify the generic service or application name(s) the instance supports. When the instance is started on the database server, it registers the applications/services it supports with the Listener. The Oracle Net name resolution files use service names that resolve to a host and an application, not a host and an instance. The Listener on the host then directs the client to the appropriate instance based on the applications each instance is registered to support.

For example, suppose you had SALES and HR applications running on the PROD instance on the HOST1 database. Prior to Oracle8*i*, you would configure a Listener to listen for the instance called PROD. Clients for both the SALES and HR applications would use a service name that resolved to the HOST1 machine and the PROD instance. If you moved the SALES application to another instance on the same host, you would have to update the Oracle Net name resolution files to reflect the new instance name for that application. With Oracle8*i*, the PROD instance could have an *INIT.ORA/SPFILE* entry for the SERVICE_NAMES parameter, specifying that it supports the SALES and HR applications. When started, the PROD instance would register dynamically with the Listener and would be associated with SALES and HR. The entries in the Oracle Net name resolution files would decode to HOST1 and an application name of SALES or HR instead of to HOST1 and the PROD instance. The Listener would automatically direct clients that specify a service name of SALES or HR to the PROD instance.

This level of indirection avoids the need to embed instance names in the Oracle Net name resolution files, reducing administration time and increasing the flexibility of the system. Suppose that you migrate the data for the SALES application to another database. The instance name for SALES users would now be different. Prior to Oracle8*i*, you would have to update the Oracle Net naming files to reflect the change to the instance name for SALES. Since Oracle8*i*, you don't have to embed the instance name for SALES in the name resolution files. When the instance for the new database containing the SALES data is started, it will register with the Listener and will be associated with the SALES application. Clients requesting a connection to HOST1 for the application SALES will automatically be directed to the new instance by the Listener, with no changes to the Oracle Net name resolution files.

1. *Starting the instance.* Oracle reads the instance initialization parameters from the *SPFILE* or *INIT.ORA* file on the server. Oracle then allocates memory for the System Global Area and starts the background processes of the instance. At this point, none of the physical files in the database have been opened, and the instance is in the NOMOUNT state. (Note that the number of parameters that must be defined in the *SPFILE* in Oracle Database 10*g* as part of the initial installation setup is greatly reduced.)

There are problems that can prevent an instance from starting. For example, there may be errors in the initialization file, or the operating system may not be able to allocate the requested amount of shared memory for the SGA. You also need the special privilege SYSOPER or SYSDBA, granted through either the operating system or a password file, to start an instance.

2. *Mounting the database.* The instance opens the database's control files. The initialization parameter CONTROL_FILES tells the instance where to find these control files. At this point only the control files are open. This is called the MOUNT state, and at this time, the database is accessible only to the database administrator. In this state, the DBA can perform only certain types of database administration. For example, the DBA may have moved or renamed one of the database files. The datafiles are listed in the control file but aren't open in the MOUNT state. The DBA can issue a command (ALTER DATABASE) to rename a datafile. This command will update the control file with the new datafile name.

3. *Opening the database.* The instance opens the redo log files and datafiles using the information in the control file. At this point, the database is fully open and available for user access.

Shutting Down the Database

Logically enough, the process of shutting down a database or making it inaccessible involves steps that reverse those discussed in the previous section:

1. *Closing the database.* Oracle flushes any modified database blocks that haven't yet been written to the disk from the SGA cache to the datafiles. Oracle also writes out any relevant redo information remaining in the redo log buffer. Oracle then checkpoints the datafiles, marking the datafile headers as "current" as of the time the database was closed, and closes the datafiles and redo log files. At this point, users can no longer access the database.

2. *Dismounting the database.* The Oracle instance dismounts the database. Oracle updates the relevant entries in the control files to record a clean shutdown and then closes them. At this point, the entire database is closed; only the instance remains.

3. *Shutting down the instance.* The Oracle software stops the background processes of the instance and frees, or deallocates, the shared memory used for the SGA.

In some cases (e.g., if there is a machine failure or the DBA aborts the instance), the database may not be closed cleanly. If this happens, Oracle doesn't have a chance to write the modified database blocks from the SGA to the datafiles. When Oracle is started again, the instance will detect that a crash occurred and will use the redo logs to automatically perform what is called *crash recovery*. Crash recovery guarantees that the changes for all committed transactions are done and that all uncommitted or in-flight transactions will be cleaned up. The uncommitted transactions are determined after the redo log is applied and automatically rolled back.

Accessing a Database

The previous sections described the process of starting up and shutting down a database. But the database is only part of a complete system—you also need a client process to access the database, even if that process is on the same physical machine as the database.

Server Processes and Clients

To access a database, a user connects to the instance that provides access to the desired database. A program that accesses a database is really composed of two distinct pieces—a client program and a server process—that connect to the Oracle instance. For example, running the Oracle character-mode utility SQL*Plus involves two processes:

- The SQL*Plus process itself, acting as the client
- The Oracle server process, sometimes referred to as a *shadow process*, that provides the connection to the Oracle instance

Server process

The Oracle server process always runs on the computer on which the instance is running. The server process attaches to the shared memory used for the SGA and can read from it and write to it.

As the name implies, the server process works for the client process—it reads and passes back the requested data, accepts and makes changes on behalf of the client, and so on. For example, when a client wants to read a row of data stored in a particular database block, the server process identifies the desired block and either retrieves it from the database buffer cache or reads it from the correct datafile and loads it into the database buffer cache. Then, if the user requests changes, the server process modifies the block in the cache and generates and stores the necessary redo information in the redo log buffer in the SGA. The server process, however, does not write the redo information from the log buffer to the redo log files, and it does not write the modified database block from the buffer cache to the datafile. These actions are performed by the Log Writer (LGWR) and Database Writer (DBWR) processes, respectively.

Client process

The client process can run on the same machine as the instance or on a separate computer. A network connects the two computers and provides a way for the two processes to talk to each other. In either case, the concept is essentially the same—two processes are involved in the interaction between a client and the database. When both processes are on the same machine, Oracle uses local communications via Inter Process Communication (IPC); when the client is on one machine and the database server is on another, Oracle uses Oracle Net over the network to communicate between the two machines.

Application Servers and Web Servers as Clients

Although the discussion in the previous section used the terms *client* and *server* extensively, please don't assume that Oracle is strictly a client/server database. Oracle was one of the early pioneers of client/server computing and has long been based on the notion of two tasks: a client and a server. But, when you consider multi-tier computing involving web and application servers, the notion of a client changes somewhat. The "client" process becomes the middle tier, or application server. You can logically consider any process that connects to an Oracle instance a client in the sense that it is served by the database. Don't confuse this usage of the term "client" with the actual client in a multi-tier configuration. The eventual client in a multi-tier model is some type of program providing a user interface—for example, a browser running Java.

The Oracle Application Server, which is part of the overall Oracle platform, is designed to act as this middle tier. The Oracle Application Server works seamlessly with the Oracle database and shares some of the same technology. Oracle's Application Server is described in more detail in Chapter 14.

Figure 3-5 illustrates users connecting to an Oracle instance to access a database in both two-tier and three-tier configurations, involving local and network communication. The figure is based on a simplified version of the instance figure used earlier in Chapter 2 (Figure 2-8).

Figure 3-5 highlights the server process connection models as opposed to the interaction of the background processes. There is a traditional two-tier client/server connection on the left side, a three-tier connection with an application server on the right side, and a local client connection in the middle of the figure. The two-tier and three-tier connections use a network to communicate with the database, while the local client uses local IPC.

Oracle Net and Establishing Network Connections

The server processes shown in Figure 3-5 are connected to the client processes using some kind of network. How do client processes get hooked up with Oracle server processes to begin working?

The matchmaker that arranges marriages between Oracle clients and server processes is called the Oracle Net Listener. The Listener "listens" for incoming

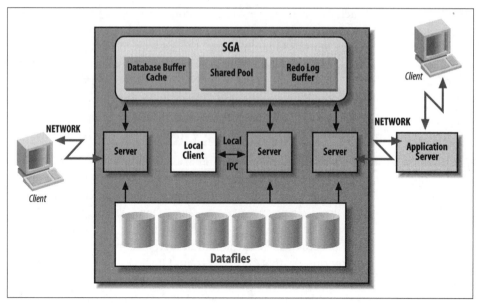

Figure 3-5. Accessing a database

connection requests for one or more instances. The Listener is not part of the Oracle instance—it directs connection requests to the instance. The Listener is started and stopped independently of the instance. If the Listener is down and the instance is up, clients accessing the database over a network cannot find the instance because there is no Listener to guide them. If the Listener is up and the instance is down, there is nowhere to send clients.

The Listener's function is relatively simple:

1. The client contacts the Listener over the network.
2. The Listener detects an incoming request and introduces the requesting client to an Oracle server process.
3. The Listener introduces the server to the client by letting each know the other's network address.
4. The Listener steps out of the way and lets the client and server communicate directly.

Once the client and the server know how to find each other, they communicate directly. The Listener is no longer required.

Figure 3-6 illustrates the previous steps for establishing a networked connection. Network traffic appears as dotted lines.

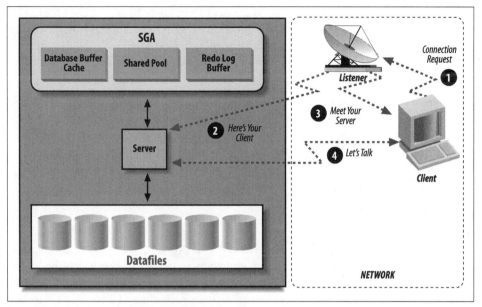

Figure 3-6. Connecting with the Oracle Net Listener

The Shared Server/Multi-Threaded Server

The server processes shown in the above diagrams are *dedicated*; they serve only one client process. So, if an application has 1,000 clients, the Oracle instance will have 1,000 corresponding server processes. Each server process uses system resources such as the memory and the CPU. Scaling to large user populations can consume a lot of system resources. To support the ever-increasing demand for scalability, Oracle introduced the Multi-Threaded Server (MTS) in Oracle7.

Since Oracle9*i*, the Multi-Threaded Server is called the *shared server*.

Shared servers allow the Oracle instance to share a set of server processes across a larger group of users. Instead of each client's connecting to and using a dedicated server, the clients use shared servers, which can significantly reduce the overall resource requirements for serving large numbers of users.

In many systems there are times when the clients aren't actively using their server process, such as when users are reading and absorbing data retrieved from the database. When a client is not using its server process in the *dedicated model*, that server process still has a hold on system resources even though it isn't doing any useful work. In the *shared server model*, the shared server can use the resources of an inactive client to do work for another client process.

You don't have to make a mutually exclusive choice between shared server processes and dedicated server processes for an Oracle instance. Oracle can mix and match dedicated and shared servers, and clients can connect to one or the other. The choice is based on your Oracle Net configuration files. In the configuration files there will be one service name that leads the client to a dedicated server, and another for connecting via shared servers. The Oracle Net manuals provide the specific syntax for this configuration.

The type of server process a client is using is transparent to the client. From a client perspective, the multithreading or sharing of server processes happens "under the covers," on the database server. The same Listener handles dedicated and multithreaded connection requests.

The steps the Listener takes in establishing a shared server connection are a little different and involve some additional background processes for the instance dispatchers and the shared servers themselves:

Dispatchers

> In the previous description of the Listener, you saw how it forms the connection between a client and server process and then steps out of the way. The client must now be able to depend on a server process that is always available to complete the connection. Because a shared server process may be servicing another client, the client connects to a dispatcher, which is always ready to receive any client request. There are separate dispatchers for each network protocol being used (e.g., dispatchers for TCP/IP, etc.). The dispatchers serve as surrogate dedicated servers for the clients. Clients directly connect to their dispatchers instead of to a server. The dispatchers accept requests from clients and place them in a request queue, which is a memory structure in the SGA. There is one request queue for each instance.

Shared servers

> The shared server processes read from the request queue, process the requests, and place the results in the response queue for the appropriate dispatcher. There is one response queue for each dispatcher. The dispatcher then reads the results from the response queue and sends the information back to the client process.

There is a pool of dispatchers and a pool of shared servers. Oracle starts a certain number of each based on the initialization parameters DISPATCHERS and SERVERS (MTS_DISPATCHERS and MTS_SERVERS prior to Oracle9*i*). You can start additional dispatchers up to the maximum number indicated by the value of the MAX_DISPATCHERS (MTS_MAX_DISPATCHERS prior to Oracle9*i*) parameter. Oracle will start additional shared servers up to the value of MAX_SHARED_SERVERS (MTS_MAX_SERVERS prior to Oracle9*i*). If Oracle starts additional processes to handle a heavier request load and the load dies down again, Oracle gradually reduces the number of processes to the floor specified by SERVERS.

The following steps show how establishing a connection and using shared server processes differ from using a dedicated server process:

1. The client contacts the Listener over the network.

2. The Listener detects an incoming request and, based on the Oracle Net configuration, determines that it is for a multithreaded server. Instead of handing the client off to a dedicated server, the Listener hands the client off to a dispatcher for the network protocol the client is using.

3. The Listener introduces the client and the dispatcher by letting each know the other's network address.

4. Once the client and the dispatcher know where to find each other, they communicate directly. The Listener is no longer required. The client sends each work request directly to the dispatcher.

5. The dispatcher places the client's request in the request queue in the SGA.

6. The next available shared server process reads the request from the request queue and does the work.

7. The shared server places the results for the client's request in the response queue for the dispatcher that originally submitted the request.

8. The dispatcher reads the results from its queue.

9. The dispatcher sends the results to the client.

Figure 3-7 illustrates the steps for using the shared servers. Network traffic appears as dotted lines.

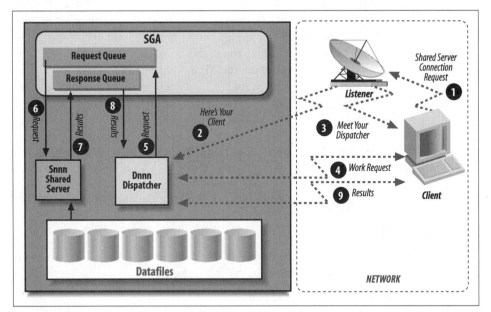

Figure 3-7. Connecting with the Oracle Net Listener (Shared Server)

Session Memory for Shared Server Processes Versus Dedicated Server Processes

There is a concept in Oracle known as *session memory* or *state*. State information is basically data that describes the current status of a session in Oracle. For example, state information contains information about the SQL statements executed by the session. When you use a dedicated server, this state is stored in the private memory used by the dedicated server. This works out well because the dedicated server works with only one client. The technical term for this private memory is the Program Global Area (PGA).

If you're using the shared servers, however, any server can work on behalf of a specific client. The session state cannot be stored in the PGA of the shared server process. All servers must be able to access the session state because the session can migrate between different shared servers. For this reason, Oracle places this state information in the SGA.

All servers can read from the SGA. Putting the state information in the SGA allows a session and its state to move from one shared server to another for processing different requests. The server that picks up the request from the request queue simply reads the session state from the SGA, updates the state as needed for processing, and puts it back in the SGA when processing has finished.

The request and response queues, as well as the session state, require additional memory in the SGA, so you should allocate more memory if you're using shared servers. By default, the memory for the shared server session state comes from the shared pool. Alternatively, in Oracle8, you could also configure something called the *large pool* as a separate area of memory for the MTS. (We introduced the large pool in Chapter 2 in the "Memory Structures for an Instance" section.) Using the large pool memory avoids the overhead of coordinating memory usage with the shared SQL, dictionary caching, and other functions of the shared pool. This allows memory management from the large pool and avoids competing with other subsystems for space in and access to the shared pool. Note that Oracle Database 10g introduces automated memory management of the SGA and PGA size.

Data Dictionary Information About the Shared Server

The data dictionary, which we introduced in Chapter 2, also contains information about the operation of the shared server in the following views:

VMTS/VSHARED_SERVER_MONITOR
    This view contains dynamic information about the shared servers, such as high-water marks for connections and how many shared servers have been started

and stopped in response to load variations. The view V$MTS was deprecated in Oracle9*i* and replaced by V$SHARED_SERVER_MONITOR.

V$DISPATCHER

This view contains details of the dispatcher processes used by the shared server. It can determine how busy the dispatchers are, to help set the floor and ceiling values appropriately.

V$SHARED_SERVER

This view contains details of the shared server processes used by the shared server. It can determine how busy the servers are, to help set the floor and ceiling values appropriately.

V$CIRCUIT

You can think of the route from a client to its dispatcher and from the dispatcher to the shared server (using the queues) as a virtual circuit. This view details these virtual circuits for user connections.

Oracle at Work

To help you truly understand how all the disparate pieces of the Oracle database work together, this section walks through an example of the steps taken by the Oracle database to respond to a user request. This example looks at a user who is adding new information to the database (in other words, executing a transaction).

Oracle and Transactions

A *transaction* is a work request from a client to insert, update, or delete data. The statements that change data are a subset of the SQL language called Data Manipulation Language (DML). Transactions must be handled in a way that guarantees their integrity. Although Chapter 7 delves into transactions more deeply, we must visit a few basic concepts relating to transactions now in order to understand the example in this section:

Transactions are logical and complete

In database terms, a transaction is a logical unit of work composed of one or more data changes. A transaction consists of one or more INSERT, UPDATE, and/or DELETE statements affecting data in multiple tables. The entire set of changes must succeed or fail as a complete unit of work. A transaction starts with the first DML statement and ends with either a commit or a rollback.

Commit or rollback

Once a user enters the data for his transaction, he can either *commit* the transaction to make the changes permanent or *roll back* the transaction to undo the changes.

System Change Number (SCN)

A key factor in preserving database integrity is an awareness of which transaction came first. For example, if Oracle is to prevent a later transaction from unwittingly overwriting an earlier transaction's changes, it must know which transaction began first. The mechanism Oracle uses is the System Change Number, a logical timestamp used to track the order in which events occurred. Oracle also uses the SCN to implement multiversion read consistency, which is described in detail in Chapter 7.

Rollback segments

Rollback segments are structures in the Oracle database used to store "undo" information for transactions, in case of rollback. This undo information restores database blocks to the state they were in before the transaction in question started. When a transaction starts changing some data in a block, it first writes the old image of the data to a rollback segment. The information stored in a rollback segment is used for two main purposes: to provide the information necessary to roll back a transaction and to support multiversion read consistency.

A rollback segment is not the same as a redo log. The redo log is used to log all transactions to the database and to recover the database in the event of a system failure, while the rollback segment provides rollback for transactions and read consistency.

Blocks of rollback segments are cached in the SGA just like blocks of tables and indexes. If rollback segment blocks are unused for a period of time, they may be aged out of the cache and written to the disk.

Oracle9*i* introduced automatic management of rollback segments. In previous versions of the Oracle database, DBAs had to explicitly create and manage rollback segments. In Oracle9*i*, you had the option of specifying automatic management of all rollback segments through the use of an UNDO tablespace. With automatic undo management, you can also specify the length of time that you want to keep undo information; this feature is very helpful if you plan on using flashback queries, discussed in the following sidebar. Oracle Database 10*g* adds an undo management retention time advisor.

Fast commits

Because redo logs are written whenever a user commits an Oracle transaction, they can be used to speed up database operations. When a user commits a transaction, Oracle can do one of two things to get the changes into the database on the disk:

- Write all the database blocks the transaction changed to their respective datafiles.

- Write only the redo information, which typically involves much less I/O than writing the database blocks. This recording of the changes can be

Flashback

In Oracle9*i*, rollback segments were also used to implement a feature called *Flashback Query*. Remember that rollback segments are used to provide a consistent image of the data in your Oracle database at a previous point in time. With Flashback Query, you can direct Oracle to return the results for a SQL query at a specific point in time. For instance, you could ask for a set of results from the database as of two hours ago.

If you use this feature, you will have to size your rollback segments to hold enough information to perform the Flashback Query. In addition, you can query only for a point in the past. Despite a few limitations of the feature, there are scenarios in which you might be able to use a Flashback Query effectively, such as going back to a point in time before a user made an error that resulted in a loss of data.

Oracle Database 10*g* has greatly expanded its flashback capabilities to include:

FLASHBACK DATABASE
> Returns (rolls back) the entire database to a particular point in time. Can be used instead of point-in-time recovery in some situations.

FLASHBACK TABLE
> Returns a specific table to a specific point in time.

FLASHBACK TRANSACTION
> Returns all the changes made by one specific transaction.

FLASHBACK DROP
> Rolls back a drop operation. When an object is dropped, it is placed in a Recycle Bin, so a user can simply un-drop the object to restore it.

SELECT Flashback clauses
> New clauses in the SELECT statement return all the versions of rows (i.e., show changes to the rows) in a particular query over a span of time.

---

replayed to reproduce all the transaction's changes later, if they are needed due to a failure.

To provide maximum performance without risking transactional integrity, Oracle writes out only the redo information. When a user commits a transaction, Oracle guarantees that the redo for those changes writes to the redo logs on disk. The actual changed database blocks will be written out to the datafiles later. If a failure occurs before the changed blocks are flushed from the cache to the datafiles, the redo logs will reproduce the changes in their entirety. Because the slowest part of a computer system is the physical disk, Oracle's fast-commit approach minimizes the cost of committing a transaction and provides maximum risk-free performance.

A Transaction, Step by Step

This simple example illustrates the complete process of a transaction. The example uses the EMP table of employee data, which is part of the traditional test schema shipped with Oracle databases. In this example, an HR clerk wants to update the name of an employee. The clerk retrieves the employee's data from the database, updates the name, and commits the transaction.

This example assumes that only one user is trying to update the information for a row in the database. Because of this assumption, it won't include the steps normally taken by Oracle to protect the transaction from changes by other users, which are detailed in Chapter 7.

Assume that the HR clerk already has the employee record on-screen and so the database block containing the row for that employee is already in the database buffer cache. The steps from this point would be the following:

1. The user modifies the employee name on-screen and the client application sends a SQL UPDATE statement over the network to the server process.

2. The server process looks for an identical statement in the shared SQL area of the shared pool. If it finds one, it reuses it. Otherwise, it checks the statement for syntax and evaluates it to determine the best way to execute it. This processing of the SQL statement is called *parsing and optimizing*. (The optimizer is described in more detail in Chapter 4.) Once the processing is done, the statement is cached in the shared SQL area.

3. The server process copies the old image of the employee data about to be changed to a rollback segment. The old version of the employee data is stored in the rollback segment in case the HR clerk cancels or rolls back the transaction. Once the server process has written the old employee data to a rollback segment, the server process modifies the database block to change the employee name. The database block is stored in the database cache at this time.

4. The server process records the changes to the rollback segment and the database block in the redo log buffer in the SGA. The rollback segment changes are part of the redo. This may seem a little odd, but remember that redo is generated for *all* changes resulting from the transaction. The contents of the rollback segment have changed because the old employee data was written to the rollback segment for undo purposes. This change to the contents of the rollback segment is part of the transaction and therefore part of the redo for that transaction.

5. The HR clerk commits the transaction.

6. The Log Writer (LGWR) process writes the redo information for the entire transaction from the redo log buffer to the current redo log file on disk. When the operating system confirms that the write to the redo log file has successfully completed, the transaction is considered committed.

7. The server process sends a message to the client confirming the commit.

The user could have canceled or rolled back the transaction instead of committing it, in which case the server process would have used the old image of the employee data in the rollback segment to undo the change to the database block.

Figure 3-8 shows the steps described here. Network traffic appears as dotted lines.

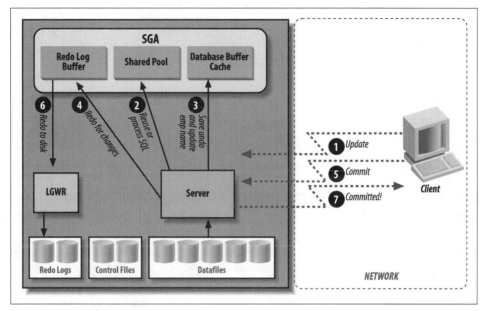

Figure 3-8. Steps for a transaction

CHAPTER 4

Data Structures

In previous chapters, we examined some distinctions between the different components that make up an Oracle database. For example, you've learned that the Oracle instance differs from the files that make up the physical storage of the data in tablespaces, that you cannot access the data in a tablespace except through an Oracle instance, and that the instance itself isn't very valuable without the data stored in those files.

In the same way, the actual tables and columns within the database are the entities stored within the database files and accessed through the database instance. The user who makes a request for data from an Oracle database probably doesn't know anything about instances and tablespaces, but does know about the structure of her data, as implemented with tables and columns. To fully leverage the power of Oracle, you must understand how the Oracle database server implements and uses these logical data structures.

Datatypes

The *datatype* is one of the attributes for a *column* or a variable in a stored procedure. A datatype describes and limits the type of information stored in a column, and limits the operations that you can perform on columns.

You can divide Oracle datatype support into three basic varieties: character datatypes, numeric datatypes, and datatypes that represent other kinds of data. You can use any of these datatypes when you create columns in a table, as with this SQL statement:

```
CREATE SAMPLE_TABLE(
    char_field CHAR(10),
    varchar_field VARCHAR2(10),
    todays_date DATE)
```

You also use these datatypes when you define variables as part of a PL/SQL procedure.

Character Datatypes

Character datatypes can store any string value, including the string representations of numeric values. Assigning a value larger than the length specified or allowed for a character datatype results in a runtime error. You can use string functions, such as UPPER, LOWER, SUBSTR, and SOUNDEX, on standard (not large) character value types.

There are several different character datatypes:

CHAR

> The CHAR datatype stores character values with a fixed length. A CHAR datatype can have between 1 and 2,000 characters. If you don't explicitly specify a length for a CHAR, it assumes the default length of 1. If you assign a value that's shorter than the length specified for the CHAR datatype, Oracle will automatically pad the value with blanks. Some examples of CHAR values are:
>
> ```
> CHAR(10) = "Rick      ", "Jon       ", "Stackowiak"
> ```

VARCHAR2

> The VARCHAR2 datatype stores variable-length character strings. Although you must assign a length to a VARCHAR2 datatype, this length is the maximum length for a value rather than the required length. Values assigned to a VARCHAR2 datatype aren't padded with blanks. The VARCHAR2 datatype can have up to 4,000 characters. Because of this, a VARCHAR2 datatype can require less storage space than a CHAR datatype, because the VARCHAR2 datatype stores only the characters assigned to the column.
>
> At this time, the VARCHAR and VARCHAR2 datatypes are synonymous in Oracle8 and later versions, but Oracle recommends the use of VARCHAR2 because future changes may cause VARCHAR and VARCHAR2 to diverge. The values shown earlier for the CHAR values, if entered as VARCHAR2 values, are:
>
> ```
> VARCHAR2(10) = "Rick", "Jon", "Stackowiak"
> ```

NCHAR and NVARCHAR2

> The NCHAR and NVARCHAR2 datatypes store fixed-length or variable-length character data using a different character set from the one used by the rest of the database. When you create a database, you specify the character set that will be used for encoding the various characters stored in the database. You can optionally specify a secondary character set as well (this is known as the *National Language Set*, or NLS). The secondary character set will be used for NCHAR and NVARCHAR2 columns. For example, you may have a description field in which you want to store Japanese characters while the rest of the database uses English encoding. You would specify a secondary character set that supports Japanese characters when you create the database, and then use the NCHAR or NVARCHAR2 datatype for the columns in question.

With Oracle9*i*, you can specify that you want to indicate the length of NCHAR and NVARCHAR2 columns in terms of characters, rather than bytes. This new feature allows you to indicate, for example, that a column with one of these datatypes is 7 characters long. The Oracle9*i* database will automatically make the conversion to 14 bytes of storage if the character set requires double byte storage.

 Oracle Database 10*g* includes the Globalization Development Kit (GDK), which is designed to aid in the creation of Internet applications that will be used with different languages. The key feature of this kit is a framework that implements best practices for globalization for Java and PL/SQL developers.

Oracle Database 10*g* also supports case- and accent-insensitive queries and sorts. You can use this feature if you want to use only base letters or only base letters and accents in a query or sort.

LONG

The LONG datatype can hold up to 2 GB of character data. It is regarded as a legacy datatype from earlier versions of Oracle. If you want to store large amounts of character data, Oracle now recommends that you use the CLOB and NCLOB datatypes. There are many restrictions on the use of LONG datatypes in a table and within SQL statements, such as the fact that you cannot use LONGs in WHERE, GROUP BY, ORDER BY, or CONNECT BY clauses or in SQL statements with the DISTINCT qualifier. You also cannot create an index on a LONG column.

CLOB and NCLOB

The CLOB and NCLOB datatypes can store up to 4 GB of character data prior to Oracle Database 10*g*. With Oracle Database 10*g*, the limit has been increased to 128 TBs, depending on the block size of the database. The NCLOB datatype stores the NLS data. Oracle Database 10*g* implicitly performs conversions between CLOBs and NCLOBs. For more information on CLOBs and NCLOBs, please refer to the discussion about large objects (LOBs) in "Other Datatypes," later in this chapter.

Numeric Datatype

Oracle uses a standard, variable-length internal format for storing numbers. This internal format can maintain a precision of up to 38 digits.

The numeric datatype for Oracle is NUMBER. Declaring a column or variable as NUMBER will automatically provide a precision of 38 digits. The NUMBER datatype can also accept two qualifiers, as in:

```
column NUMBER( precision, scale )
```

The *precision* of the datatype is the total number of significant digits in the number. You can designate a precision for a number as any number of digits up to 38. If no value is declared for *precision*, Oracle will use a precision of 38. The *scale* represents the number of digits to the right of the decimal point. If no scale is specified, Oracle will use a scale of 0.

If you assign a negative number to the *scale*, Oracle will round the number up to the designated place to the *left* of the decimal point. For example, the following code snippet:

```
column_round NUMBER(10,-2)
column_round = 1,234,567
```

will give column_round a value of 1,234,600.

The NUMBER datatype is the only datatype that stores numeric values in Oracle. The ANSI datatypes of DECIMAL, NUMBER, INTEGER, INT, SMALLINT, FLOAT, DOUBLE PRECISION, and REAL are all stored in the NUMBER datatype. The language or product you're using to access Oracle data may support these datatypes, but they're all stored in a NUMBER datatype column.

Date Datatype

As with the NUMERIC datatype, Oracle stores all dates and times in a standard internal format. The standard Oracle date format for input takes the form of DD-MON-YY HH:MI:SS, where DD represents up to two digits for the day of the month, MON is a three-character abbreviation for the month, YY is a two-digit representation of the year, and HH, MI, and SS are two-digit representations of hours, minutes, and seconds, respectively. If you don't specify any time values, their default values are all zeros in the internal storage.

You can change the format you use for inserting dates for an instance by changing the NLS_DATE_FORMAT parameter for the instance. You can do this for a session by using the ALTER SESSION SQL statement or for a specific value by using parameters with the TO_DATE expression in your SQL statement.

Oracle SQL supports date arithmetic in which integers represent days and fractions represent the fractional component represented by hours, minutes, and seconds. For example, adding .5 to a date value results in a date and time combination 12 hours later than the initial value. Some examples of date arithmetic are:

```
12-DEC-99 + 10 = 22-DEC-99
31-DEC-1999:23:59:59 + .25 = 1-JAN-2000:5:59:59
```

As of Oracle9*i*, Release 2, Oracle also supports two INTERVAL datatypes, INTERVAL YEAR TO MONTH and INTERVAL DAY TO SECOND, which are used for storing a specific amount of time. This data can be used for date arithmetic.

Other Datatypes

Aside from the basic character, number, and date datatypes, Oracle supports a number of specialized datatypes:

RAW and LONG RAW

Normally, your Oracle database not only stores data but also interprets it. When data is requested or exported from the database, the Oracle database sometimes massages the requested data. For instance, when you dump the values from a NUMBER column, the values written to the dump file are the representations of the numbers, not the internally stored numbers.

The RAW and LONG RAW datatypes circumvent any interpretation on the part of the Oracle database. When you specify one of these datatypes, Oracle will store the data as the exact series of bits presented to it. The RAW datatypes typically store objects with their own internal format, such as bitmaps. A RAW datatype can hold 2 KB, while a LONG RAW datatype can hold 2 GB.

ROWID

The ROWID is a special type of column known as a *pseudocolumn*. The ROWID pseudocolumn can be accessed just like a column in a SQL SELECT statement. There is a ROWID pseudocolumn for every row in an Oracle database. The ROWID represents the specific address of a particular row. The ROWID pseudocolumn is defined with a ROWID datatype.

The ROWID relates to a specific location on a disk drive. Because of this, the ROWID is the fastest way to retrieve an individual row. However, the ROWID for a row can change as the result of dumping and reloading the database. For this reason, we don't recommend using the value for the ROWID pseudocolumn across transaction lines. For example, there is no reason to store a reference to the ROWID of a row once you've finished using the row in your current application.

You cannot set the value of the standard ROWID pseudocolumn with any SQL statement.

The format of the ROWID pseudocolumn changed with Oracle8. Beginning with Oracle8, the ROWID includes an identifier that points to the database object number in addition to the identifiers that point to the datafile, block, and row. You can parse the value returned from the ROWID pseudocolumn to understand the physical storage of rows in your Oracle database.

You can define a column or variable with a ROWID datatype, but Oracle doesn't guarantee that any value placed in this column or variable is a valid ROWID.

ORA_ROWSCN

Oracle Database 10g supports a new pseudocolumn, ORA_ROWSCN, which holds the System Change Number (SCN) of the last transaction that modified the row. You can use this pseudocolumn to check easily for changes in the row since a transaction started. For more information on SCNs, see the discussion of concurrency in Chapter 7.

LOB

A LOB, or large object datatype, can store up to 4 GB of information. LOBs come in three varieties:

- CLOB, which can only store character data
- NCLOB, which stores National Language character set data
- BLOB, which stores data as binary information

You can designate that a LOB should store its data within the Oracle database or that it should point to an external file that contains the data.

LOBs can participate in transactions. Selecting a LOB datatype from Oracle will return a pointer to the LOB. You must use either the DBMS_LOB PL/SQL built-in package or the OCI interface to actually manipulate the data in a LOB.

To facilitate the conversion of LONG datatypes to LOBs, Oracle9*i* includes support for LOBs in most functions that support LONGs, as well as a new option to the ALTER TABLE statement that allows the automatic migration of LONG datatypes to LOBs.

BFILE

The BFILE datatype acts as a pointer to a file stored outside of the Oracle database. Because of this fact, columns or variables with BFILE datatypes don't participate in transactions, and the data stored in these columns is available only for reading. The file size limitations of the underlying operating system limit the amount of data in a BFILE.

XMLType

As part of its support for XML, Oracle9*i* includes a new datatype called XML-Type. A column defined as this type of data will store an XML document in a character LOB column. There are built-in functions that allow you to extract individual nodes from the document, and you can also build indexes on any particular node in the XMLType document.

User-defined data

Oracle8 and later versions allow users to define their own complex datatypes, which are created as combinations of the basic Oracle datatypes previously discussed. These versions of Oracle also allow users to create objects composed of both basic datatypes and user-defined datatypes. For more information about objects within Oracle, see Chapter 13.

AnyType, AnyData, AnyDataSet

Oracle9*i* and newer releases include three new datatypes that can be used to explicitly define data structures that exist outside the realm of existing datatypes.

Each of these datatypes must be defined with program units that let Oracle know how to process any specific implementation of these types.

Type Conversion

Oracle automatically converts some datatypes to other datatypes, depending on the SQL syntax in which the value occurs.

When you assign a character value to a numeric datatype, Oracle performs an implicit conversion of the ASCII value represented by the character string into a number. For instance, assigning a character value such as 10 to a NUMBER column results in an automatic data conversion.

If you attempt to assign an alphabetic value to a numeric datatype, you will end up with an unexpected (and invalid) numeric value, so you should make sure that you're assigning values appropriately.

You can also perform explicit conversions on data, using a variety of conversion functions available with Oracle. Explicit data conversions are better to use if a conversion is anticipated, because they document the conversion and avoid the possibility of going unnoticed, as implicit conversions sometimes do.

Concatenation and Comparisons

The concatenation operator for Oracle SQL on most platforms is two vertical lines (||). Concatenation is performed with two character values. Oracle's automatic type conversion allows you to seemingly concatenate two numeric values. If NUM1 is a numeric column with a value of 1, NUM2 is a numeric column with a value of 2, and NUM3 is a numeric column with a value of 3, the following expressions are TRUE:

```
NUM1 || NUM2 || NUM3 = "123"
NUM1 || NUM2 + NUM3 = "15" (12 + 3)
NUM1 + NUM2 || NUM3 = "33" (1+ 2 || 3)
```

The result for each of these expressions is a character string, but that character string can be automatically converted back to a numeric column for further calculations.

Comparisons between values of the same datatype work as you would expect. For example, a date that occurs later in time is larger than an earlier date, and 0 or any positive number is larger than any negative number. You can use relational operators to compare numeric values or date values. For character values, comparisons of single characters are based on the underlying code pages for the characters. For multicharacter strings, comparisons are made until the first character that differs between the two strings appears. The result of the comparison between these two characters is the result of the overall comparison.

If two character strings of different lengths are compared, Oracle uses two different types of comparison semantics: *blank-padded comparisons* and *non-padded*

---

comparisons. For a blank-padded comparison, the shorter string is padded with blanks and the comparison operates as previously described. For nonpadded comparisons, if both strings are identical for the length of the shorter string, the shorter string is identified as smaller. For example, in a blank-padded comparison the string "A " (a capital A followed by a blank) and the string "A" (a capital A by itself) would be seen as equal, because the second value would be padded with a blank. In a nonpadded comparison, the second string would be identified as smaller because it is shorter than the first string. Nonpadded comparisons are used for comparisons in which one or both of the values are VARCHAR2 or NVARCHAR2 datatypes, while blank-padded comparisons are used when neither of the values is one of these datatypes.

Oracle Database 10*g* includes a feature called the Expression Filter, which allows you to store a complex comparison expression as part of a row. You can use the EVALUATE function to limit queries based on the evaluation of the expression.

NULLs

The NULL value is one of the key features of the relational database. The NULL, in fact, doesn't represent any value at all—it represents the lack of a value. When you create a column for a table that must have a value, you specify it as NOT NULL, meaning that it cannot contain a NULL value. If you try to write a row to a database table that doesn't assign a value to a NOT NULL column, Oracle will return an error.

You can assign NULL as a value for any datatype. The NULL value introduces what is called *three-state logic* to your SQL operators. A normal comparison has only two states: TRUE or FALSE. If you're making a comparison that involves a NULL value, there are three logical states: TRUE, FALSE, and none of the above.

None of the following conditions are true for Column A if the column contains a NULL value:

```
A > 0
A < 0
A = 0
A != 0
```

The existence of three-state logic can be confusing for end users, but your data may frequently require you to allow for NULL values for columns or variables.

You have to test for the presence of a NULL value with the relational operator IS NULL, because a NULL value is not equal to 0 or any other value. Even the expression:

```
NULL = NULL
```

will always evaluate to FALSE, because a NULL value doesn't equal any other value.

Basic Data Structures

This section describes the three basic Oracle data structures: tables, views, and indexes.

Tables

The *table* is the basic data structure used in a relational database. A table is a collection of rows. Each *row* in a table contains one or more *columns*. If you're unfamiliar with relational databases, you can map a table to the concept of a file or database in a nonrelational database, just as you can map a row to the concept of a record in a nonrelational database.

With the Enterprise Editions of Oracle8 and beyond, you can purchase an option called Partitioning that, as the name implies, allows you to partition tables and indexes, which are described later in this chapter. Partitioning a data structure means that you can divide the information in the structure between multiple physical storage areas. A partitioned data structure is divided based on column values in the table. You can partition tables based on the range of column values in the table, the result of a hash function (which returns a value based on a calculation performed on the values in one or more columns), or a combination of the two. With Oracle9*i* you can also use a list of values to define a partition, which can be particularly useful in a data warehouse environment.

Oracle is smart enough to take advantage of partitions to improve performance in two ways:

- Oracle won't bother to access partitions that won't contain any data to satisfy the query.
- If all the data in a partition satisfies a part of the WHERE clause for the query, Oracle simply selects all the rows for the partition without bothering to evaluate the clause for each row.

Partitioning tables can also be useful in a data warehouse, in which data can be partitioned based on the time period it spans.

Equally important is the fact that partitioning substantially reduces the scope of maintenance operations and increases the availability of your data. You can perform all maintenance operations, such as backup, recovery, and loading, on a single partition. This flexibility makes it possible to handle extremely large data structures while still performing those maintenance operations in a reasonable amount of time. In addition, if you must recover one partition in a table for some reason, the other partitions in the table can remain online during the recovery operation.

If you've been working with other databases that don't offer the same type of partitioning, you may have tried to implement a similar functionality by dividing a table into several separate tables and then using a UNION SQL statement to view the data in several tables at once. Partitioned tables give you all the advantages of having several identical tables joined by a UNION statement without the complexity that implementation requires.

To maximize the benefits of partitioning, it sometimes makes sense to partition a table and an index identically so that both the table partition and the index partition map to the same set of rows. You can automatically implement this type of partitioning, which is called *equipartitioning*, by specifying an index for a partitioned table as a LOCAL index.

For more details about the structure and limitations associated with partitioned tables, refer to your Oracle documentation.

As of Oracle9*i*, you can define external tables. As its name implies, the data for an external table is stored outside the database, typically in a flat file. The external table is read-only; you cannot update the data it contains. The external table is good for loading and unloading data to files from a database, among other purposes.

Views

A *view* is an Oracle data structure constructed with a SQL statement. The SQL statement is stored in the database. When you use a view in a query, the stored query is executed and the base table data is returned to the user. Views do not contain data, but represent ways to look at the base table data in the way the query specifies.

You can use a view for several purposes:

- To simplify access to data stored in multiple tables
- To implement specific security for the data in a table (e.g., by creating a view that includes a WHERE clause that limits the data you can access through the view)

  Since Oracle9*i*, you can use *fine-grained access control* to accomplish the same purpose. Fine-grained access control gives you the ability to automatically limit data access based on the value of data in a row.

- To isolate an application from the specific structure of the underlying tables

A view is built on a collection of *base tables*, which can be either actual tables in an Oracle database or other views. If you modify any of the base tables for a view so that they no longer can be used for a view, that view itself can no longer be used.

In general, you can write to the columns of only one underlying base table of a view in a single SQL statement. There are additional restrictions for INSERT, UPDATE, and DELETE operations, and there are certain SQL clauses that prevent you from updating any of the data in a view.

You can write to a non-updateable view by using an INSTEAD OF trigger, which is described later in this chapter.

Oracle8*i* introduced *materialized views*. Materialized views can hold presummarized data, which provides significant performance improvements in a data warehouse scenario. Materialized views are described in more detail in Chapter 9.

Indexes

An *index* is a data structure that speeds up access to particular rows in a database. An index is associated with a particular table and contains the data from one or more columns in the table.

The basic SQL syntax for creating an index is shown in this example:

```
CREATE INDEX emp_idx1 ON emp (ename, job);
```

in which emp_idx1 is the name of the index, emp is the table on which the index is created, and ename and job are the column values that make up the index.

The Oracle database server automatically modifies the values in the index when the values in the corresponding columns are modified. Because the index contains less data than the complete row in the table and because indexes are stored in a special structure that makes them faster to read, it takes fewer I/O operations to retrieve the data in them. Selecting rows based on an index value can be faster than selecting rows based on values in the table rows. In addition, most indexes are stored in sorted order (either ascending or descending, depending on the declaration made when you created the index). Because of this storage scheme, selecting rows based on a range of values or returning rows in sorted order is much faster when the range or sort order is contained in the presorted indexes.

In addition to the data for an index, an index entry stores the ROWID for its associated row. The ROWID is the fastest way to retrieve any row in a database, so the subsequent retrieval of a database row is performed in the most optimal way.

An index can be either unique (which means that no two rows in the table or view can have the same index value) or nonunique. If the column or columns on which an index is based contain NULL values, the row isn't included in an index.

An index in Oracle is the physical structure used within the database. A *key* is a term for a logical entity, typically the value stored within the index. In most places in the Oracle documentation, the two terms are used interchangeably, with the notable exception of the foreign key constraint, which is discussed later in this chapter.

Four different types of index structures, which are described in the following sections, are used in Oracle: standard B*-tree indexes; reverse key indexes; bitmap indexes; and a new type of index, the function-based index, which was introduced in Oracle8*i*. Oracle also gives you the ability to cluster the data in the tables, which can improve performance. This is described later, in the section "Clusters."

B*-tree indexes

The *B*-tree index* is the default index used in Oracle. It gets its name from its resemblance to an inverted tree, as shown in Figure 4-1.

The B*-tree index is composed of one or more levels of branch blocks and a single level of leaf blocks. The branch blocks contain information about the range of values contained in the next level of branch blocks. The number of branch levels between the root and leaf blocks is called the *depth* of the index. The leaf blocks contain the actual index values and the ROWID for the associated row.

The B*-tree index structure doesn't contain many blocks at the higher levels of branch blocks, so it takes relatively few I/O operations to read quite far down the B*-tree index structure. All leaf blocks are at the same depth in the index, so all retrievals require essentially the same amount of I/O to get to the index entry, which evens out the performance of the index.

Oracle allows you to create *index organized tables* (IOTs), in which the leaf blocks store the entire row of data rather than only the ROWID that points to the associated row. Index organized tables reduce the amount of space needed to store an index and a table by eliminating the need to store the ROWID in the leaf page. But index organized tables cannot use a UNIQUE constraint or be stored in a cluster. In

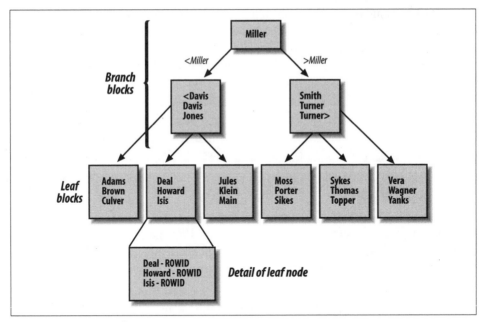

Figure 4-1. A B*-tree index

addition, index organized tables don't support distribution, replication, and partitioning (covered in greater detail in other chapters), although IOTs can be used with Oracle Streams for capturing and applying changes with Oracle Database 10*g*.

There have been a number of enhancements to index organized tables as of Oracle9*i*, including a lifting of the restriction against the use of bitmap indexes as secondary indexes for an IOT and the ability to create, rebuild, or coalesce secondary indexes on an IOT. Oracle Database 10*g* continues this trend by allowing list partitioning for index organized tables, as well as providing other enhancements.

Reverse key indexes

Reverse key indexes, as their name implies, automatically reverse the order of the bytes in the key value stored in the index. If the value in a row is "ABCD", the value for the reverse key index for that row is "DCBA".

To understand the need for a reverse key index, you have to review some basic facts about the standard B*-tree index. First and foremost, the depth of the B*-tree is determined by the number of entries in the leaf nodes. The greater the depth of the B*-tree, the more levels of branch nodes there are and the more I/O is required to locate and access the appropriate leaf node.

The index illustrated in Figure 4-1 is a nice, well-behaved, alphabetic-based index. It's balanced, with an even distribution of entries across the width of the leaf pages. But some values commonly used for an index are not so well behaved. Incremental

---

values, such as ascending sequence numbers or increasingly later date values, are always added to the right side of the index, which is the home of higher and higher values. In addition, any deletions from the index have a tendency to be skewed toward the left side as older rows are deleted. The net effect of these practices is that over time the index turns into an unbalanced B*-tree, where the left side of the index is more sparsely populated than the leaf nodes on the right side. This unbalanced growth has the overall effect of increasing the depth of the B*-tree structure due to the number of entries on the right side of the index. The effects described here also apply to the values that are automatically decremented, except that the left side of the B*-tree will end up holding more entries.

You can solve this problem by periodically dropping and recreating the index. However, you can also solve it by using the reverse value index, which reverses the order of the value of the index. This reversal causes the index entries to be more evenly distributed over the width of the leaf nodes. For example, rather than having the values 234, 235, and 236 be added to the maximum side of the index, they are translated to the values 432, 532, and 632 for storage and then translated back when the values are retrieved. These values are more evenly spread throughout the leaf nodes.

The overall result of the reverse index is to correct the imbalance caused by continually adding increasing values to a standard B*-tree index. For more information about reverse key indexes and where to use them, refer to your Oracle documentation.

Bitmap indexes

In a standard B*-tree index, the ROWIDs are stored in the leaf blocks of the index. In a *bitmap index*, each bit in the index represents a ROWID. If a particular row contains a particular value, the bit for that row is "turned on" in the bitmap for that value. A mapping function converts the bit into its corresponding ROWID. Unlike other index types, bitmap indexes include entries for NULL values.

You can store a bitmap index in much less space than a standard B*-tree index if there aren't many values in the index. Figure 4-2 shows an illustration of how a bitmap index is stored. Figure 9-3 in Chapter 9 shows how a bitmap index is used in a selection condition.

The functionality provided by bitmap indexes is especially important in data warehousing applications in which each dimension of the warehouse contains many repeating values and queries typically require the interaction of several different dimensions. For more about data warehousing, see Chapter 9.

Function-based indexes

Function-based indexes were new in Oracle8*i*. A function-based index is just like a standard B*-tree or bitmap index, except that you can base the index on the result of a SQL function, rather than just on the value of a column or columns.

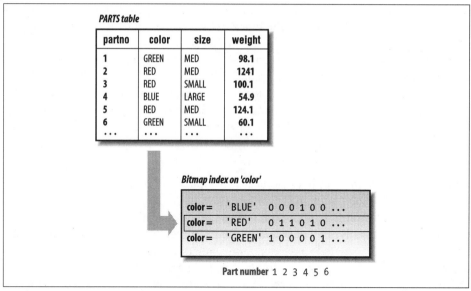

Figure 4-2. Bitmap index

Prior to Oracle8*i*, if you wanted to select on the result of a function, Oracle retrieved every row in the database, executed the function, and then accepted or rejected each row. With function-based indexes you can simply use the index for selection, without having to execute the function on every row, every time.

For example, without a function-based index, if you wanted to perform a case-insensitive selection of data you would have to use the UPPER function in the WHERE clause, which would retrieve every candidate row and execute the function. With a function-based index based on the UPPER function, you can select directly from the index.

 With Oracle Database 10*g*, you can perform case- or accent-insensitive queries; such queries provide another way to solve this problem.

This capability becomes even more valuable when you consider that you can create your own functions in an Oracle database. You can create a very sophisticated function and then create an index based on the function, which can dramatically affect the performance of queries that require the function.

Additional Data Structures

There are several other data structures available in your Oracle database that can be useful in some circumstances.

Sequences

One of the big problems that occurs in a multiuser database is the difficulty of supplying unique numbers for use as keys or identifiers. For this situation, Oracle allows you to create an object called a *sequence*. The sequence object is fairly simple. Whenever anyone requests a value from it, it returns a value and increments its internal value, avoiding contention and time-consuming interaction with the requesting application. Oracle can cache a range of numbers for the sequence so that access to the next number doesn't have to involve disk I/O; rather, it can be satisfied from the range in the SGA.

Sequence numbers are defined with a name, an incremental value, and some additional information about the sequence. Sequences exist independently of any particular table, so more than one table can use the same sequence number.

Consider what might happen if you didn't use Oracle sequences. You might store the last sequence number used in a column in a table. A user who wanted to get the next sequence number would read the last number, increment it by a fixed value, and write the new value back to the column. But if many users tried to get a sequence number at the same time, they might all read the "last" sequence number before the new "last" sequence number had been written back. You could lock the row in the table with the column containing the sequence number, but this would cause delays as other users waited on locks. What's the solution? Create a sequence.

Synonyms

All data structures within an Oracle database are stored within a specific *schema*. A schema is associated with a particular username, and all objects are referenced with the name of the schema followed by the name of the object.

For instance, if there is a table named EMP in a schema named DEMO, the table would be referenced with the complete name of DEMO.EMP. If you don't supply a specific schema name, Oracle assumes that the structure is in the schema for your current username.

Schemas are a nice feature because object names have to be unique only within their own schemas, but the qualified names for objects can get confusing, especially for end users. To make names simpler and more readable, you can create a *synonym* for any table, view, snapshot, or sequence, or for any PL/SQL procedure, function, or package.

Synonyms can be either *public*, which means that all users of a database can use them, or *private*, which means that only the user whose schema contains the synonym can use it. For example, if the user DEMO creates a public synonym called EMP for the table EMP in his schema, all other users can simply use EMP to refer to the EMP table in DEMO's schema. Suppose that DEMO didn't create a public synonym and a user called SCOTT wanted to use the name EMP to refer to the EMP table in DEMO's schema. The user SCOTT would create a private synonym in his schema. Of course, SCOTT must have access to DEMO's EMP table for this to work.

Synonyms simplify user access to a data structure. You can also use synonyms to hide the location of a particular data structure, making the data more transportable and increasing the security of the associated table by hiding the name of the schema owner.

Prior to Oracle Database 10g, if you changed the location referenced by a synonym, you would have to recompile any PL/SQL procedures that accessed the synonym.

Clusters

A *cluster* is a data structure that improves retrieval performance. A cluster, like an index, doesn't affect the logical view of the table.

A cluster is a way of storing related data values together on disk. Oracle reads data a block at a time, so storing related values together reduces the number of I/O operations needed to retrieve related values, because a single data block will contain only related rows.

A cluster is comprised of one or more tables. The cluster includes a cluster index, which stores all the values for the corresponding cluster key. Each value in the cluster index points to a data block that contains only rows with the same value for the cluster key.

If a cluster contains multiple tables, the tables should be joined together and the cluster index should contain the values that form the basis of the join.

Because the value of the cluster key controls the placement of the rows that relate to the key, changing a value in that key can cause Oracle to change the location of rows associated with that key value.

Clusters may not be appropriate for tables that regularly require full table scans, in which a query requires the Oracle database to iterate through all the rows of the table. Because you access a cluster table through the cluster index, which then points to a data block, full table scans can actually require more I/O operations, lowering overall performance.

Hash Clusters

A *hash cluster* is like a cluster with one significant difference that can make it even faster: the values for the cluster key are stored in the cluster index. Each request for data in a clustered table involves at least two I/O operations, one for the cluster index and one for the data. A hash cluster stores related data rows together, but groups the rows according to a *hash value* for the cluster key. The hash value is calculated with a hash function, which means that each retrieval operation starts with a calculation of the hash value and then goes directly to the data block that contains the relevant rows. By eliminating the need to go to a cluster index, a hash clustered table can be even faster for retrieving data than a clustered table. You can control the number of possible hash values for a hash cluster with the HASHKEYS parameter when you create the cluster.

Because the hash cluster directly points to the location of a row in the table, you must allocate all the space required for all the possible values in a hash cluster when you create the cluster.

Hash clusters work best when there is an even distribution of rows among the various values for the hash key. You may have a situation in which there is already a unique value for the hash key column, such as a unique ID. In such situations, you can assign the value for the hash key as the value for the hash function on the unique value, which eliminates the need to execute the hash function as part of the retrieval process. In addition, you can specify your own hash function as part of the definition of a hash cluster.

Oracle Database 10g introduces sorted hash clusters, where data is not only stored in a cluster based on a hash value, but is also stored in the order in which it was inserted. This data structure improves performance for applications that access data in the order in which it was added to the database.

Data Design

Tables and columns present a logical view of the data in a relational database. The flexibility of a relational database gives you many options for grouping the individual pieces of data, represented by the columns, into a set of tables. To use Oracle effectively, you must understand and follow some firmly established principles of database design.

The topic of database design is vast and deep: we won't even pretend to offer more than a cursory overview. For more information, we recommend the book *Oracle Design* by Dave Ensor and Ian Stevenson (see Appendix B for details).

When E. F. Codd created the concept of a relational database in the 1960s, he also began work on the concept of *normalized* data design. The theory behind normalized data design is pretty straightforward: a table should contain only the information that is directly related to the key value of the table. The process of assembling these logical units of information is called *normalization* of the database design.

The concept of normalized table design was tailored to the capabilities of the relational database. Because you could join data from different tables together in a query, there was no need to keep all the information associated with a particular

> ## Normalized Forms
>
> In fact, there is more than one type of normalization. Each step in the normalization process ends with a specific result called a *normalized form*. There are five standard normalized forms, which are referred to as first normal form (1NF), second normal form (2NF), and so on. The normalization process that we describe briefly in this section results in third normal form (3NF), the most common type of normalization.
>
> Explaining the complete concepts that lie behind the different normal forms is beyond the scope of this chapter and book.

object together in a single record. You could decompose the information into associated units and simply join the appropriate units together when you needed information that crossed table boundaries.

There are many different methodologies for normalizing data. The following is one example. You start by defining all the data required by your application:

1. Identify the objects your application needs to know (the *entities*). Examples of entities, as shown in Figure 4-3, include employees, locations, and jobs.

2. Identify the individual pieces of data, referred to by data modelers as *attributes*, for these entities. In Figure 4-3, employee name and salary are attributes. Typically, entities correspond to tables and attributes correspond to columns.

3. As a potential last step in the process, identify *relationships* between the entities based on your business. These relationships are implemented in the database schema through the use of structures such as foreign keys. For example, the primary key of the DEPARTMENT NUMBER table would be a foreign key column in the EMPLOYEE NAME table used to identify the DEPARTMENT NUMBER in which an employee works. A foreign key is a type of constraint; constraints are discussed later in this chapter.

Normalization provides benefits by avoiding storage of redundant data. Storing the department in every employee record not only would waste space but would also lead to a data maintenance issue. If the department name changed, you would have to update every employee record, even though no employees had actually changed departments. By normalizing the department data into a table and simply pointing to the appropriate row from the employee rows, you avoid both duplication of data and this type of problem.

However, there is an even more important reason to go through the process of designing a normalized database. You can benefit from normalization because of the planning process that normalizing a data design entails. By really thinking about the way the intended applications use data, you get a much clearer picture of the needs the system is designed to serve. This understanding leads to a much more focused database and application.

Normalization also reduces the amount of data that any one row in a table contains. The less data in a row, the less I/O is needed to retrieve it, which helps to avoid this performance bottleneck. In addition, the smaller the data in a row, the more rows are retrieved per data block, which increases the likelihood that more than one desired row will be retrieved in a single I/O operation. And the smaller the row, the more rows will be kept in Oracle's system buffers, which also increases the likelihood that a row will be available in memory when it's needed, thereby avoiding the need for any disk I/O at all.

Finally, the process of normalization includes the creation of foreign key relationships and other data constraints. These relationships build a level of data integrity directly into your database design.

Figure 4-3 shows a simple list of attributes grouped into entities and linked by a foreign key relationship.

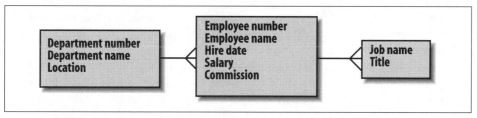

Figure 4-3. The results of the normalization process

Creating a normalized data design isn't the only data design work you will have to do. Once you've completed an optimal logical database design, you must go back and consider what indexes you should add to improve the anticipated performance of the database and whether you should designate any tables as part of a cluster or hash cluster.

Because adding these types of performance-enhancing data structures doesn't affect the logical representation of the database, you can always make these types of modifications later when you see the way an application uses the database in test mode or in production.

Constraints

A *constraint* enforces certain aspects of data integrity within a database. When you add a constraint to a particular column, Oracle automatically ensures that data violating that constraint is never accepted. If a user attempts to write data that violates a constraint, Oracle returns an error for the offending SQL statement.

Should You Normalize Your Data?

Whenever possible, we recommend that you go through the process of designing a normalized structure for your database.

Data normalization has been proven, both theoretically and in decades of practice, to provide concrete benefits. In addition, the process of creating a normalized data design is intimately intertwined with the process of understanding the data requirements for your application system. You can improve even the simplest database by the discoveries made during the process of normalization.

However, there may be times when you feel that the benefits of a fully normalized design will counteract the performance penalty that a design imposes on your production systems. For example, you may have one, two, or three contact names to be placed in their own table, with a foreign key linking back to the main row for the organization. But because you want to see all the contact names every time you request contact information, you might decide to save the overhead and added development effort of the join and simply include the three contact names in your organization table. This technique is common in decision-support/data warehousing applications.

Of course, this violation of the rules of normalization limits the flexibility of your application systems—for example, if you later decide that you need four contact names, some redesign will be necessary.

For this reason, we suggest that you always implement a fully normalized database design and then, if necessary, go back and denormalize certain tables as needed. With this approach, you will at least have to make a conscious decision to "break" the normalization, which involves an active consideration of the price of denormalization.

Constraints may be associated with columns when you create or add the table containing the column (via a number of keywords) or after the table has been created with the SQL statement ALTER TABLE. Five constraint types are supported by Oracle8 and later versions:

NOT NULL

You can designate any column as NOT NULL. If any SQL operation leaves a NULL value in a column with a NOT NULL constraint, Oracle returns an error for the statement.

Unique

When you designate a column or set of columns as unique, users cannot enter values that already exist in another row in the table for those columns.

The unique constraint is implemented by the creation of an index, which requires a unique value. If you include more than one column as part of a unique key, you will create a single index that will include all the columns in the unique key. If an index already exists for this purpose, Oracle will automatically use that index.

If a column is unique but allows NULL values, any number of rows can have a NULL value, because the NULL indicates the absence of a value. To require a unique value for a column in every row, the column should be both unique and NOT NULL.

Primary key

Each table can have, at most, a single primary key constraint. The primary key may consist of more than one column in a table.

The primary key constraint forces each primary key to have a unique value. It enforces both the unique constraint and the NOT NULL constraint. A primary key constraint will create a unique index, if one doesn't already exist for the specified column(s).

Foreign key

The foreign key constraint is defined for a table (known as the *child*) that has a relationship with another table in the database (known as the *parent*). The value entered in a foreign key must be present in a unique or primary key of another specific table. For example, the column for a department ID in an employee table might be a foreign key for the department ID primary key in the department table.

A foreign key can have one or more columns, but the referenced key must have an equal number of columns. You can have a foreign key relate to the primary key of its own table, such as when the employee ID of a manager is a foreign key referencing the ID column in the same table.

A foreign key can contain a NULL value if it's not forbidden through another constraint.

By requiring that the value for a foreign key exist in another table, the foreign key constraint enforces referential integrity in the database. Foreign keys not only provide a way to join related tables but also ensure that the relationship between the two tables will have the required data integrity.

Normally, you cannot delete a row in a parent table if it causes a row in the child table to violate a foreign key constraint. However, you can specify that a foreign key constraint causes a *cascade delete*, which means that deleting a referenced row in the parent table automatically deletes all rows in the child table that reference the primary key value in the deleted row in the parent table.

Check

A check constraint is a more general-purpose constraint. A check constraint is a Boolean expression that evaluates to either TRUE or FALSE. If the check constraint evaluates to FALSE, the SQL statement that caused the result returns an error. For example, a check constraint might require the minimum balance in a bank account to be over $100. If a user tries to update data for that account in a way that causes the balance to drop below this required amount, the constraint will return an error.

Some constraints require the creation of indexes to support them. For instance, the unique constraint creates an implicit index used to guarantee uniqueness. You can also specify a particular index that will enforce a constraint when you define that constraint.

All constraints can be either immediate or deferred. An *immediate constraint* is enforced as soon as a write operation affects a constrained column in the table. A *deferred constraint* is enforced when the SQL statement that caused the change in the constrained column completes. Because a single SQL statement can affect several rows, the choice between using a deferred constraint or an immediate constraint can significantly affect how the integrity dictated by the constraint operates. You can specify that an individual constraint is immediate or deferred, or you can set the timing for all constraints in a single transaction.

Finally, you can temporarily suspend the enforcement of constraints for a particular table. When you reenable the operation of the constraint, you can instruct Oracle to validate all the data for the constraint or simply start applying the constraint to the new data. When you add a constraint to an existing table, you can also specify whether you want to check all the existing rows in the table.

Triggers

You use constraints to automatically enforce data integrity rules whenever a user tries to write or modify a row in a table. There are times when you want the same kind of enforcement of your own database or application-specific logic. Oracle includes *triggers* to give you this capability.

 Although you can write triggers to perform the work of a constraint, Oracle has optimized the operation of constraints, so it's best to always use a constraint instead of a trigger if possible.

A trigger is a block of code that is fired whenever a particular type of database event occurs to a table. There are three types of events that can cause a trigger to fire:

- A database UPDATE
- A database INSERT
- A database DELETE

You can, for instance, define a trigger to write a customized audit record whenever a user changes a row.

Triggers are defined at the row level. You can specify that a trigger is to be fired either for each row or for the SQL statement that fires the trigger event. As with the previous discussion of constraints, a single SQL statement can affect many rows, so the specification of the trigger can have a significant effect on the operation of the trigger and the performance of the database.

There are three times when a trigger can fire:

- Before the execution of the triggering event
- After the execution of the triggering event
- Instead of the triggering event

Combining the first two timing options with the row and statement versions of a trigger gives you four possible trigger implementations: before a statement, before a row, after a statement, and after a row.

INSTEAD OF triggers were introduced with Oracle8. The INSTEAD OF trigger has a specific purpose: to implement data-manipulation operations on views that don't normally permit them, such as a view that references columns in more than one base table for updates. You should be careful when using INSTEAD OF triggers because of the many potential problems associated with modifying the data in the underlying base tables of a view. There are many restrictions on when you can use INSTEAD OF triggers. Refer to your Oracle documentation for a detailed description of the forbidden scenarios.

You can specify a *trigger restriction* for any trigger. A trigger restriction is a Boolean expression that circumvents the execution of the trigger if it evaluates to FALSE.

Triggers are defined and stored separately from the tables that use them. Because they contain logic, they must be written in a language with capabilities beyond those of SQL, which is designed to access data. Oracle8 and later versions allow you to write triggers in PL/SQL, the procedural language that has been a part of Oracle since Version 6. Oracle8*i* and beyond also support Java as a procedural language, so you can create Java triggers with those versions.

You can write a trigger directly in PL/SQL or Java, or a trigger can call an existing stored procedure written in either language.

Triggers are fired as a result of a SQL statement that modifies a row in a particular table. It's possible for the actions of the trigger to modify the data in the table or to cause changes in other tables that fire their own triggers. The end result of this may be data that ends up being changed in a way that Oracle thinks is logically illegal. These situations can cause Oracle to return runtime errors referring to *mutating tables*, which are tables modified by other triggers, or *constraining tables*, which are tables modified by other constraints. Oracle8*i* eliminated some of the errors caused by activating constraints with triggers.

Oracle8*i* also introduced a very useful set of system event triggers (sometimes called *database-level event triggers*), and user event triggers (sometimes called *schema-level event triggers*). You can now place a trigger on system events such as database startup and shutdown and on user events such as logging on and logging off.

Query Optimization

All of the data structures discussed so far in this chapter are server entities. Users request data from an Oracle server through database queries. Oracle's query optimizer must then determine the best way to access the data requested by each query.

One of the great virtues of a relational database is its ability to access data without predefining the access paths to the data. When a SQL query is submitted to an Oracle database, Oracle must decide how to access the data. The process of making this decision is called *query optimization*, because Oracle looks for the optimal way to retrieve the data. This retrieval is known as the *execution path*. The trick behind query optimization is to choose the most efficient way to get the data, because there may be many different options available.

For instance, even with a query that involves only a single table, Oracle can take either of these approaches:

- Use an index to find the ROWIDs of the requested rows and then retrieve those rows from the table.
- Scan the table to find and retrieve the rows; this is referred to as a *full table scan*.

Although it's usually much faster to retrieve data using an index, the process of getting the values from the index involves an additional I/O step in processing the query. Query optimization may be as simple as determining whether the query involves selection conditions that can be imposed on values in the index. Using the index values to select the desired rows involves less I/O and is therefore more efficient than retrieving all the data from the table and then imposing the selection conditions.

Another factor in determining the optimal query execution plan is whether there is an ORDER BY condition in the query that can be automatically implemented by the presorted index. Alternatively, if the table is small enough, the optimizer may decide to simply read all the blocks of the table and bypass the index because it estimates the cost of the index I/O plus the table I/O to be higher than just the table I/O.

The query optimizer has to make some key decisions even with a query on a single table. When a more involved query is submitted, such as one involving many tables that must be joined together efficiently or one that has a complex selection criteria and multiple levels of sorting, the query optimizer has a much more complex task.

Prior to Oracle Database 10*g*, you could choose between two different Oracle query optimizers, a rule-based optimizer and a cost-based optimizer, which are described in the following sections. With Oracle Database 10*g*, the rule-based optimizer is desupported. The references to syntax and operations for the rule-based optimizer in the following sections are provided as a convenience and are applicable only if you are running an older release of Oracle.

Rule-Based Optimization

Oracle has always had a query optimizer, but until Oracle7 the optimizer was only rule-based. The *rule-based optimizer*, as the name implies, uses a set of predefined rules as the main determinant of query optimization decisions. As noted earlier, the rule-based optimizer is desupported in Oracle Database 10g.

Rule-based optimization was sometimes a better choice than other random methods of optimization or the Oracle cost-based optimizer in early Oracle releases, despite some significant weaknesses. One weakness is the simplistic set of rules. The Oracle rule-based optimizer has about twenty rules and assigns a weight to each one of them. In a complex database, a query can easily involve several tables, each with several indexes and complex selection conditions and ordering. This complexity means that there will be a lot of options, and the simple set of rules used by the rule-based optimizer might not differentiate the choices well enough to make the best choice.

The rule-based optimizer assigns an optimization score to each potential execution path and then takes the path with the best optimization score. Another main weakness of the rule-based optimizer stems from the way it resolved optimization choices made in the event of a "tie" score. When two paths present the same optimization score, the rule-based optimizer looks to the syntax of the SQL statement to resolve the tie. The winning execution path is based on the order in which the tables occur in the SQL statement.

You can understand the potential impact of this type of tie-breaker by looking at a simple situation in which a small table with 10 rows, SMALLTAB, is joined to a large table with 10,000 rows, LARGETAB, as shown in Figure 4-4. If the optimizer chooses to read SMALLTAB first, the Oracle database will read the 10 rows and then read LARGETAB to find the matching rows for all 10 of these rows. If the optimizer chooses to read LARGETAB first, the database will read 10,000 rows from LARGETAB and then read SMALLTAB 10,000 times to find the matching rows. Of course, the rows in SMALLTAB will probably be cached, thus reducing the impact of each probe, but the two optimizer choices still offer a dramatic difference in potential performance.

Differences like this occur as a result of the ordering of the table names in the query. In the previous situation the rule-based optimizer returns the same results for the query, but it uses widely varying amounts of resources to retrieve those results.

Cost-Based Optimization

To improve the optimization of SQL statements, Oracle introduced the *cost-based optimizer* in Oracle7. As the name implies, the cost-based optimizer does more than simply look at a set of optimization rules; instead, it selects the execution path that requires the least number of logical I/O operations. This approach avoids the error discussed in the previous section. After all, the cost-based optimizer would know

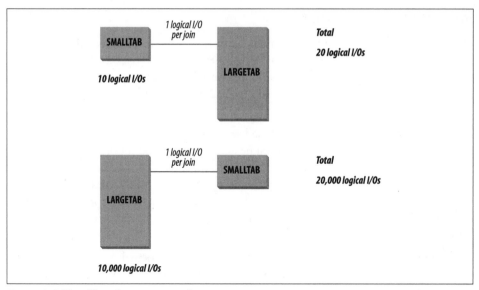

Figure 4-4. The effect of optimization choices

which table was bigger and would select the right table to begin the query, regardless of the syntax of the SQL statement.

Oracle8 and later versions, by default, attempt to use the cost-based optimizer to identify the optimal execution plan. As we've mentioned, in Oracle Database 10g, the cost-based optimizer is the only supported choice. To properly evaluate the cost of any particular execution plan, the cost-based optimizer uses statistics about the composition of the relevant data structures. These statistics are automatically gathered in Oracle Database 10g.

Statistics

Like the rule-based optimizer, the cost-based optimizer finds the optimal execution plan by assigning an optimization score for each of the potential execution plans. However, the cost-based optimizer uses its own internal rules and logic along with statistics that reflect the state of the data structures in the database. These statistics relate to the tables, columns, and indexes involved in the execution plan. The statistics for each type of data structure are listed in Table 4-1.

Oracle Database 10g also collects overall system statistics, including I/O and CPU performance and utilization.

These statistics are stored in three tables in the data dictionary, which are described in the final section of this chapter, "Data Dictionary Tables."

Table 4-1. Database statistics

Data structure	Type of statistics
Table	Number of rows
	Number of blocks
	Number of unused blocks
	Average available free space per block
	Number of chained rows
	Average row length
Column	Number of distinct values per column
	Second-lowest column value
	Second-highest column value
	Column density factor
Index	Depth of index B*-tree structure
	Number of leaf blocks
	Number of distinct values
	Average number of leaf blocks per key
	Average number of data blocks per key
	Clustering factor

You can see that these statistics can be used individually and in combination to determine the overall cost of the I/O required by an execution plan. The statistics reflect both the size of a table and the amount of unused space within the blocks; this space can, in turn, affect how many I/O operations are needed to retrieve rows. The index statistics reflect not only the depth and breadth of the index tree, but also the uniqueness of the values in the tree, which can affect the ease with which values can be selected using the index.

Oracle8 and later versions use the SQL statement ANALYZE to collect these statistics. (This is no longer needed in Oracle Database 10*g* because statistics can be gathered automatically.) You can analyze a table, an index, or a cluster in a single SQL statement. Collecting statistics can be a resource-intensive job; in some ways, it's like building an index. Because of its potential impact, the ANALYZE command has two options:

COMPUTE STATISTICS

Calculates the statistics on the entire data structure.

ESTIMATE STATISTICS

Specifies a number of rows or overall percentage of the data structure for statistical analysis. You can also let the DBMS_STATS package determine the appropriate sample size for best results.

The latter choice makes gathering the relative statistics for the data structure consume far fewer resources than computing the exact figures for the entire structure. If you have a very large table, for example, analyzing 5% or less of the table will probably produce an accurate estimate of the relative percentages of unused space and other relative data.

 The accuracy of the cost-based optimizer depends on the accuracy of the statistics it uses, so you should make updating statistics a standard part of your maintenance plan. With Oracle Database 10g, you can enable automatic statistics collection for a table, which can be based on whether a table is either stale (which means that more than 10% of the objects in the table have changed) or empty.

The use of statistics makes it possible for the cost-based optimizer to make a much more well-informed choice of the optimal execution plan. For instance, the optimizer could be trying to decide between two indexes to use in an execution plan that involves a selection based on a value in either index. The rule-based optimizer might very well rate both indexes equally and resort to the order in which they appear in the WHERE clause to choose an execution plan. The cost-based optimizer, however, knows that one index contains 1,000 entries while the other contains 10,000 entries. It even knows that the index that contains 1,000 values contains only 20 unique values, while the index that contains 10,000 values has 5,000 unique values. The selectivity offered by the larger index is much greater, so that index will be assigned a better optimization score and used for the query.

Testing the Effect of New Statistics

There may be times when you don't want to update your statistics, such as when the distribution of data in your database has reached a steady state or when your queries are already performing in an optimal way. Oracle gives you a way that you can try out a new set of statistics to see if they might make things better while still maintaining the option of returning to the old set: you can save your statistics in a separate table and then collect new ones. If, after testing your application with these new statistics, you decide you preferred the way the old statistics worked, you can simply reload the saved statistics.

In Oracle9i, you have the option of allowing the cost-based optimizer to use CPU speed as one of the factors in determining the optimal execution plan. An initialization parameter turns this feature on and off. In Oracle Database 10g, the default cost basis is calculated on the CPU cost plus the I/O cost for a plan.

Even with all the information available to it, the cost-based optimizer did have some noticeable initial flaws. Aside from the fact that it (like all software) occasionally has bugs, the cost-based optimizer used statistics that didn't provide a complete picture of the data structures. In the previous example, the only thing the statistics tell the optimizer about the indexes is the number of distinct values in each index. They don't reveal anything about the distribution of those values. For instance, the larger index can contain 5,000 unique values, but these values can each represent two rows in the associated table, or one index value can represent 5,001 rows while the rest of the index values represent a single row. The selectivity of the index can vary wildly, depending on the value used in the selection criteria of the SQL statement. Fortunately, Oracle 7.3 introduced support for collecting histogram statistics for indexes to address this exact problem. You create histograms using syntax within the ANALYZE INDEX statement when you gather statistics yourself in Oracle versions prior to Oracle Database 10g. This syntax is described in your Oracle SQL reference documentation.

Oracle8 and more recent releases come with a built-in PL/SQL package, DBMS_STATS, which contains a number of procedures that can help you to automate the process of collecting statistics. Many of the procedures in this package also collect statistics with parallel operations, which can speed up the collection process.

Influencing the cost-based optimizer

There are two ways you can influence the way the cost-based optimizer selects an execution plan. The first way is by setting the optimizer mode to favor either batch-type requests or interactive requests with the ALL_ROWS or FIRST_ROWS choice.

You can set the optimizer mode to weigh the options for the execution plan to either favor ALL_ROWS, meaning the overall time that it takes to complete the execution of the SQL statement, or FIRST_ROWS, meaning the response time for returning the first set of rows from a SQL statement. The optimizer mode tilts the evaluation of optimization scores slightly and, in some cases, may result in a different execution plan. ALL_ROWS and FIRST_ROWS are two of four choices for the optimizer mode, which is described in more detail in the next section.

Oracle also gives you a way to completely override the decisions of the optimizer with a technique called *hints*. A hint is nothing more than a comment with a specific format inside a SQL statement. You can use hints to force a variety of decisions onto the optimizer, such as:

- Use of the rule-based optimizer prior to Oracle Database 10g
- Use of a full table scan
- Use of a particular index
- Use of a specific number of parallel processes for the statement

Hints come with their own set of problems. A hint looks just like a comment, as shown in this extremely simple SQL statement. Here, the hint forces the optimizer to use the EMP_IDX index for the EMP table:

```
SELECT /*+ INDEX(EMP_IDX) */ LASTNAME, FIRSTNAME, PHONE FROM EMP
```

If a hint isn't in the right place in the SQL statement, if the hint keyword is misspelled, or if you change the name of a data structure so that the hint no longer refers to an existing structure, the hint will simply be ignored, just as a comment would be. Because hints are embedded into SQL statements, repairing them can be quite frustrating and time-consuming if they aren't working properly. In addition, if you add a hint to a SQL statement to address a problem caused by a bug in the cost-based optimizer and the cost-based optimizer is subsequently fixed, the SQL statement is still outside the scope of the optimization calculated by the optimizer.

However, hints do have a place—for example, when a developer has a user-defined datatype that suggests a particular type of access. The optimizer cannot anticipate the effect of user-defined datatypes, but a hint can properly enable the appropriate retrieval path.

 Since Oracle9*i*, you can extend the optimizer to include user-defined function and domain-based indexes as part of the optimization process.

For more details about when hints might be considered, see the sidebar "Accepting the Verdict of the Optimizer" later in this chapter.

Choosing a Mode

In the previous section we mentioned two optimizer modes: ALL_ROWS and FIRST_ROWS. The two other valid optimizer modes for all Oracle versions prior to Oracle Database 10*g* are:

RULE
> Forces the use of the rule-based optimizer

CHOOSE
> Allows Oracle to choose whether to use the cost-based optimizer or the rule-based optimizer

With an optimizer mode of CHOOSE, which is the default setting, Oracle will use the cost-based optimizer if any of the tables in the SQL statement have statistics associated with them. The cost-based optimizer will make a statistical estimate for the tables that lack statistics. It's important to understand that partially collected statistics can cause tremendous problems. If one of the tables in a SQL statement has statistics, Oracle will use the cost-based optimizer. If the optimizer is acting on incomplete information, the quality of optimization will suffer accordingly. If you're going to use the cost-based optimizer, make sure you gather complete statistics for your databases.

You can set the optimizer level at the instance level, at the session level, or within an individual SQL statement. But the big question remains, especially for those of you who have been using Oracle since before the introduction of the cost-based optimizer: which optimizer should I choose?

Why choose the cost-based optimizer?

We favor using the cost-based optimizer, even prior to Oracle Database 10*g*, for several reasons.

First, the cost-based optimizer makes decisions with a wider range of knowledge about the data structures in the database. Although the cost-based optimizer isn't flawless in its decision-making process, it does tend to make more accurate decisions based on its wider base of information, especially because it has been around since Oracle7 and has been improved with each new release.

Second, the cost-based optimizer has been enhanced to take into account improvements in the Oracle database itself, while the rule-based optimizer has not. For instance, the cost-based optimizer understands the impact that partitioned tables have on the selection of an execution plan, while the rule-based optimizer does not. As another example, the cost-based optimizer can optimize execution plans for star schema queries, which are heavily used in data warehousing, while the rule-based optimizer has not been enhanced to deal effectively with these types of queries.

The reason for this bias is simple: Oracle Corporation has been quite frank about their intention to make the cost-based optimizer *the* optimizer for the Oracle database. Oracle hasn't been adding new features to the rule-based optimizer and hasn't guaranteed support for it in future releases. As we have mentioned, with Oracle Database 10*g*, the rule-based optimizer is no longer supported

So your future (or your present, with Oracle Database 10*g*) lies in the cost-based optimizer. But there are still situations in which you might want to use the rule-based optimizer if you are running a release of Oracle prior to Oracle Database 10*g*.

Why choose the rule-based optimizer?

As the old saying goes, if it ain't broke, don't fix it. And you may be in an environment in which you've designed and tuned your SQL to operate optimally with the rule-based optimizer. Although you should still look ahead to a future in which only the cost-based optimizer is supported, there may be no reason to switch over to the cost-based optimizer now if you have an application that is already performing at its best and you are not planning to move to Oracle Database 10*g* in the near term.

The chances are pretty good that the cost-based optimizer will choose the same execution plan as a properly tuned application using the rule-based optimizer. But there is always a chance that the cost-based optimizer will make a different choice, which can create more work for you, because you might have to spend time tracking down the different optimizations.

Remember the bottom line for all optimizers: no optimizer can provide a performance increase for a SQL statement that's already running optimally. The cost-based optimizer is not a magic potion that remedies the problems brought on by a poor database and application design or an inefficient implementation platform.

The good news is that Oracle gives you a lot of flexibility in accepting, storing, or overriding the verdict of the optimizer.

Saving the Optimization

There may be times when you want to prevent the optimizer from calculating a new plan whenever a SQL statement is submitted. For example, you might do this if you've finally reached a point at which you feel the SQL is running optimally, and you don't want the plan to change regardless of future changes to the optimizer or the database.

Starting with Oracle8i, you can create a *stored outline* that will store the attributes used by the optimizer to create an execution plan. Once you have a stored outline, the optimizer simply uses the stored attributes to create an execution plan. With Oracle9i, you can also edit the hints that make up a stored outline.

Remember that storing an outline fixes the optimization of the outline at the time the outline was stored. Any subsequent improvements to the optimizer will not affect the stored outlines, so you should document your use of stored outlines and consider restoring them with new releases.

Understanding the Execution Plan

Oracle's query optimizer automatically selects an execution plan for each query submitted. By and large, although the optimizer does a good job of selecting the execution plan, there may be times when the performance of the database suggests that it's using a less-than-optimal execution plan.

The only way you can really tell what path is being selected by the optimizer is to see the layout of the execution plan. You can use two Oracle character-mode utilities to examine the execution plan chosen by the Oracle optimizer, or you can look at the execution plan in Enterprise Manager, as of Oracle Database 10g. These tools allow you to see the successive steps used by Oracle to collect, select, and return the data to the user.

The first utility is the SQL EXPLAIN PLAN statement. When you use EXPLAIN PLAN, followed by the keyword FOR and the SQL statement whose execution plan you want to view, the Oracle cost-based optimizer returns a description of the execution plan it will use for the SQL statement and inserts this description into a database table. You can subsequently run a query on that table to get the execution plan, as shown in SQL*Plus in Figure 4-5.

Accepting the Verdict of the Optimizer

Some of you may be doubting the effectiveness of Oracle query optimization, especially those of you who encountered bumpy times with the early releases of the cost-based optimizer. You may have seen cases in which the query optimizer chose an incorrect execution path that resulted in poor performance. You may feel that you have a better understanding of the structure and use of the database than does the query optimizer. For these reasons, you probably include a lot of hints to force the acceptance of the execution path you feel is correct.

We recommend using the query optimizer for all of your queries. Although the Oracle developers who wrote the query optimizer had no knowledge of your particular database, they did depend on a lot of customer feedback, experience, and knowledge of how Oracle processes queries during the creation of the query optimizer. They designed the cost-based optimizer to efficiently execute all types of queries that may be submitted to the Oracle database.

In addition, there are three advantages that the query optimizer has over your discretion in all cases:

- The optimizer sees the structure of the entire database. Many Oracle databases support a variety of applications and users and it's quite possible that your system shares data with other systems, making the overall structure and composition of the data somewhat out of your control. In addition, you have probably designed and tested your systems in a limited environment, so your idea of the optimal execution path may not match the reality of the production environment.

- The optimizer has a dynamically changing view of the database and its data. The statistics used by the cost-based optimizer can change with each new collection operation. Although the statistics typically don't change the query optimization in more or less steady-state production databases, exceptions to this rule do occur. In addition to the changing statistical conditions, the internal workings of the optimizer are occasionally changed to fix bugs or to accommodate changes in the way the Oracle database operates. In Oracle9*i*, the cost-based optimizer can even take into account the speed of the CPU, and Oracle Database 10*g* also collect statistics on I/O. If you force the selection of a particular query plan with a hint, you won't benefit from these changes in Oracle.

- A bad choice by the optimizer may be a sign that something is amiss in your database. For the most part, the query optimizer selects the optimal execution path. What may be seen as a mistake by the query optimizer can, in reality, be traced to a misconception about the database and its design or to an improper implementation. A mistake is always an opportunity to learn, and you should always take advantage of any opportunity to increase your overall understanding of how Oracle and its optimizer work.

—continued—

We recommend that you consider using hints only when you have determined them to be absolutely necessary by thoroughly investigating the causes for an optimization problem. The hint syntax was included in Oracle syntax as a way to handle exceptional situations, rather than to allow you to circumvent the query optimizer. If you've found a performance anomaly and further investigation has led to the discovery that the query optimizer is choosing an incorrect execution path, then and only then should you assign a hint to a query.

Even in this situation, we recommend that you keep an eye on the hinted query in a production environment to make sure that the forced execution path is still working optimally.

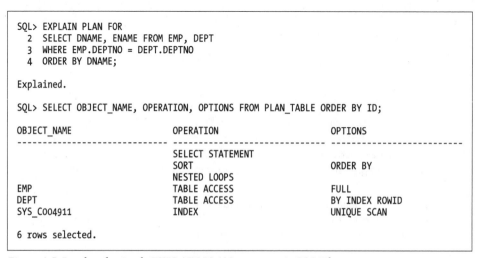

```
SQL> EXPLAIN PLAN FOR
  2   SELECT DNAME, ENAME FROM EMP, DEPT
  3   WHERE EMP.DEPTNO = DEPT.DEPTNO
  4   ORDER BY DNAME;

Explained.

SQL> SELECT OBJECT_NAME, OPERATION, OPTIONS FROM PLAN_TABLE ORDER BY ID;

OBJECT_NAME                   OPERATION                      OPTIONS
----------------------------  -----------------------------  --------------------------
                              SELECT STATEMENT
                              SORT                           ORDER BY
                              NESTED LOOPS
EMP                           TABLE ACCESS                   FULL
DEPT                          TABLE ACCESS                   BY INDEX ROWID
SYS_C004911                   INDEX                          UNIQUE SCAN

6 rows selected.
```

Figure 4-5. Results of a simple EXPLAIN PLAN statement in SQL*Plus

The execution plan is presented as a series of rows in the table, one for each step taken by Oracle in the process of executing the SQL statement. The optimizer also includes some of the information related to its decisions, such as the overall cost of each step and some of the statistics that it used to make its decisions.

The optimizer writes all of this information to a table in the database. By default, the optimizer uses a table called PLAN_TABLE; make sure the table exists before you use EXPLAIN PLAN. (The *utlxplan.sql* script included with your Oracle database creates the default PLAN_TABLE table.) You can specify that EXPLAIN PLAN uses a table other than PLAN_TABLE in the syntax of the statement. For more information about the use of EXPLAIN PLAN, please refer to your Oracle documentation.

There are times when you want to examine the execution plan for a single statement. In such cases, the EXPLAIN PLAN syntax is appropriate. There are other times when you want to look at the plans for a group of SQL statements. For these situations, you can set up a trace for the statements you want to examine and then use the second utility, TKPROF, to give you the results of the trace in a more readable format in a separate file.

You must use the EXPLAIN keyword when you start TKPROF, as this will instruct the utility to execute an EXPLAIN PLAN statement for each SQL statement in the trace file. You can also specify how the results delivered by TKPROF are sorted. For instance, you can have the SQL statements sorted on the basis of the physical I/Os they used; the elapsed time spent on parsing, executing, or fetching the rows; or the total number of rows affected.

The TKPROF utility uses a trace file as its raw material. Trace files are created for individual sessions. You can start collecting a trace file either by running the target application with a switch (if it's written with an Oracle product such as Developer) or by explicitly turning it on with an EXEC SQL call or an ALTER SESSION SQL statement in an application written with a 3GL. The trace process, as you can probably guess, can significantly affect the performance of an application, so you should turn it on only when you have some specific diagnostic work to do.

You can also view the execution plan through Enterprise Manager for the SQL statements that use the most resources.

Tuning your SQL statements isn't a trivial task, but with the EXPLAIN PLAN and TKPROF utilities you can get to the bottom of the decisions made by the cost-based optimizer. It takes a bit of work to understand exactly how to read an execution plan, but it's better to have access to this type of information than not. In large-scale system-development projects, it's quite common for developers to submit EXPLAIN PLANs for the SQL they're writing to a DBA as a formal step toward completing a form or report. While time-consuming, this is the best way to ensure that your SQL is tuned before going into production.

SQL Tuning Advisor

Oracle Database 10g includes a new tool called the SQL Tuning Advisor. This tool performs advanced optimization analysis on selected SQL statements, using workloads that have been automatically collected into the Automatic Workload Repository (AWR) or that you have specified yourself. Once the optimization is done, the SQL Tuning Advisor makes recommendations, which could include updating statistics, adding indexes, or creating an SQL Profile. This Profile is stored in the database and is used as the optimization plan for future executions of the statement, which allows you to "fix" errant SQL plans without having to touch the underlying SQL.

Data Dictionary Tables

The main purpose of the Oracle data dictionary is to store data that describes the structure of the objects in the Oracle database. Because of this purpose, there are many views in the Oracle data dictionary that provide information about the attributes and composition of the data structures within the database.

All of the views listed in this section actually have three varieties, which are identified by their prefixes:

DBA_
  Includes all the objects in the database. A user must have DBA privileges to use this view.

USER_
  Includes only the objects in the user's own database schema.

ALL_
  Includes all the objects in the database to which a particular user has access. If a user has been granted rights to objects in another user's schema, these objects will appear in this view.

This means that, for instance, there are three views that relate to tables: DBA_TABLES, ALL_TABLES, and USER_TABLES.

Some of the more common views that directly relate to the data structures are described in Table 4-2.

Table 4-2. Data dictionary views about data structures

Data dictionary view	Type of information
ALL_TABLES	Information about the object and relational tables
TABLES	Information about the relational tables
TAB_COMMENTS	Comments about the table structures
TAB_HISTOGRAMS	Statistics about the use of tables
TAB_PARTITIONS	Information about the partitions in a partitioned table
TAB_PRIVS*	Different views detailing all the privileges on a table, the privileges granted by the user, and the privileges granted to the user
TAB_COLUMNS	Information about the columns in tables and views
COL_COMMENTS	Comments about individual columns
COL_PRIVS*	Different views detailing all the privileges on a column, the privileges granted by the user, and the privileges granted to the user
LOBS	Information about large object (LOB) datatype columns
VIEWS	Information about views
INDEXES	Information about the indexes on tables
IND_COLUMNS	Information about the columns in each index

Table 4-2. Data dictionary views about data structures (continued)

Data dictionary view	Type of information
IND_PARTITIONS	Information about each partition in a partitioned index
PART_*	Different views detailing the composition and usage patterns for partitioned tables and indexes
CONS_COLUMNS	Information about the columns in each constraint
CONSTRAINTS	Information about constraints on tables
SEQUENCES	Information about sequence objects
SYNONYMS	Information about synonyms
TAB_COL_STATISTICS	The statistics used by the cost-based optimizer
TRIGGERS	Information about the triggers on tables
TRIGGER_COLS	Information about the columns in triggers

CHAPTER 5
Managing Oracle

Many Oracle users and developers are not actively aware of all the system and database management activities that go on around them. But effective management is vital to providing a reliable, available, and secure platform that delivers optimal performance. This chapter focuses on how you can manage Oracle to ensure these virtues for your environment. Much of the management responsibility usually falls upon the database administrator. However, users and developers of Oracle also need to be aware of some of the techniques described here.

The DBA is typically responsible for the following management tasks:

- Installing and upgrading the database and options
- Creating tables and indexes
- Creating and managing tablespaces
- Managing control files, online redo logs, archived redo logs, job queues, and server processes
- Creating, monitoring, and tuning data-loading procedures
- Adding users and groups and implementing security procedures
- Implementing backup and recovery plans
- Monitoring database performance and exceptions
- Reorganizing and tuning the database
- Troubleshooting database problems
- Coordinating with Oracle Worldwide Customer Support Services

Particularly in smaller companies, DBAs are also often called upon to take part in database schema design and security planning. DBAs in large enterprises may also help set up replication strategies, disaster and high-availability strategies, hierarchical storage management procedures, and the linking of database event monitoring (e.g., specific database tasks and status) into enterprise network monitors.

Oracle Database 10g is designed to enable grid computing, which can introduce additional complexities associated with managing scores of computers in a grid. Manageability of a grid must take into account disk virtualization, resource pooling, provisioning of computer resources, dynamic workload management, and dynamic control of changing grid components. Oracle's grid initiative has resulted in many significant changes in managing databases, all geared toward significantly reducing this complexity. While targeted at simplifying grid management, most of these improvements will have an even greater impact initially in simplifying management of more traditional Oracle database implementations.

 As a consequence of the grid initiative, readers of previous editions of this book will find more changes in this chapter than possibly in any other portion of this book.

All of the tasks we've just described come under the heading of managing the database. Many of the provisioning duties, including installation, initial configuration, and cloning, are discussed in Chapter 3. This chapter explores the following aspects of managing Oracle:

- Using Oracle Enterprise Manager (EM), which provides an easy-to-use interface and underlying framework for many database-management tasks, including new Oracle Database 10g capabilities
- Implementing security
- Managing database fragmentation, which can affect database performance
- Performing backup and recovery operations, which are the foundation of database integrity protection
- Working with Oracle Support

You will need an understanding of all of these areas if you're going to design and implement effective management strategies for your own Oracle database environment.

Management and Enterprise Manager

Each version of Oracle contains a new set of features that require corresponding management capabilities. This ever-increasing feature curve previously required a fairly steep learning curve on the part of the novice. Over the past few releases, Oracle has made more database features self-tuning and self-managing. Oracle Database 10g and its "Intelligent Infrastructure" is a huge step forward in this effort. Many manual steps needed to manage releases previous to Oracle Database 10g have been eliminated. Management of this infrastructure is accomplished through the self-managing capabilities of the database and through the Oracle Enterprise Manager 10g.

EM can now manage not only multiple Oracle databases, but also the Oracle Application Server, E-Business Suite, and Collaboration Suite. However, as we've mentioned, our primary focus in this book is on Oracle's database management capabilities.

Oracle Enterprise Manager Architecture

Oracle first distributed the Oracle Enterprise Manager with database packaging in Oracle7. Initial EM versions required Windows-based workstations as client machines. A browser-based EM console built using Java appeared with the Oracle8*i* database release. The HTML-based console first appeared with Oracle9 *i*AS and is now included as Enterprise Manager 10*g* with the database in Oracle Database 10*g*. Enterprise Manager 10*g* can be used for management tasks locally, remotely, and/or through firewalls. Individual consoles can manage single databases or multiple databases. Where EM is used to manage Oracle deployed on a grid of computers, or to manage multiple Oracle database instances and products, it is installed using a Grid Control Enterprise Manager CD.

EM is composed of the following components:

Oracle Management Agents
 These agents monitor databases and services on the local and remote nodes. An agent can both monitor the database and services on a remote node and communicate the results of this monitoring back to EM.

Central Console
 The console allows you to view the status of database components.

Oracle Management Service (OMS)
 This service, located in the Oracle Application Server, is deployed as an OC4J (Oracle Application Server Containers for J2EE) application and renders the HTML user interface.

Management Knowledge Center (MKC) / Management Repository
 This is the central repository of enterprise-wide management data, including hardware and software configuration data leveraged in lifecycle, cloning, and patch management.

The EM architecture is shown in Figure 5-1.

Management Agents are available for the wide variety of operating systems on which the Oracle database is available and are responsible for automatic service discovery, event monitoring, and job (predefined task) execution. Management Agents can also send Simple Network Management Protocol (SNMP) traps to database performance monitors in tools such as CA Unicenter Network and Systems Management, the HP OpenView Operations console, and IBM Tivoli. Through the agents, EM can be used to manage Oracle databases running on Unix, Linux, Windows, and many other operating systems.

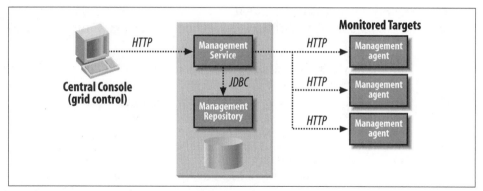

Figure 5-1. Oracle Enterprise Manager architecture

Oracle Enterprise Manager Consoles

The growth in deployment within single companies of Oracle on Windows, Linux, and Unix has resulted in growing popularity of the EM interface to manage Oracle instances residing on a mixture of operating systems. The Enterprise Manager 10*g* initially shipping with Oracle Database 10*g* provides HTML-based and Java-based consoles. (We'll describe the functionality provided by each later on.) These provide a common interface for management across multiple platforms and a framework that supports a variety of monitoring tools. The HTML console will include more and more functionality over time, including much of what is initially only in the Java console.

The Enterprise Manager 10*g* interface and framework are used for monitoring and managing events, jobs, new database self-monitoring features, reports, roles and privileges, and audit trails. An EM console and the underlying Intelligent Infrastructure (described in a subsequent section) are installed as part of the normal Oracle Database 10*g* database installation process. Much of the functionality in previous Enterprise Manager optional packs, such as diagnostics and tuning, performance, and change management, are now included in EM and are built upon the new infrastructure. EM automatically discovers target databases as soon as it is installed.

The HTML console can manage many database tasks and components, including backup and recovery, export and import, instances, Real Application Clusters (RAC), schema, security (users and roles), the OLAP option, and Data Guard. Included is *i*SQL*Plus, a new browser-based version of SQL*Plus. The Java console enables additional management of Advanced Queues, instances, replication, HTML DB, schema, security, the Spatial Option, storage, Streams, workspace, Fail Safe, LogMiner, and Text. Both also provide SQL Scratchpads, the SQL*Plus worksheet, and management of the OLAP Option and materialized views (Summary Advisor).

Most network and database connectivity management is available in the Java console, although the HTML console now provides some Oracle Net administration.

Advanced security management is also through the Java console, including the Enterprise Security Manager, Wallet Manager, Policy Manager, and Directory Manager.

Additional functionality is provided in options (sometimes called *packs*) to Enterprise Manager in the areas of diagnostics, tuning, change management, and configuration management. The following options are now fully integrated into the EM console and are built upon the new management infrastructure:

Database Diagnostics option
> This option, which monitors databases on single systems and across systems, aids in identifying performance bottlenecks and providing tools for problem resolution.

Application Server Diagnostics option
> This option enables the monitoring of an application that has been deployed using the middle-tier Application Server for availability and overall response.

Database Tuning option
> This option provides recommendations for improving transaction and query performance.

Database Change Management option
> This option is used in the evaluation and implementation of database schema changes.

Database Configuration Management option
Application Server Configuration option
> These options are used to track operating systems and associated hardware, as well as software installations and patches. They also provide automated replication and patching.

Finally, the HTML console also contains wireless-enabled features and can be used for management of the Oracle Application Server, including real-time and historical performance monitoring, events monitoring and statistics, J2EE diagnostics, unified Application Server management, application deployment, and cluster management.

A simple management interface is also deployable through the Oracle Application Server Portal. Five management portlets are prepackaged for use with the Portal, providing displays of target summaries, outstanding alerts (notifications where thresholds are reached or exceeded), metric details, availability timelines, and executive summary information.

The HTML Console Interface

Let's have a closer look at managing Oracle through the HTML console that is available as part of a normal Oracle Database 10g instance installation. Logging into Enterprise Manager brings you to the home page of your database (see Figure 5-2).

Four tabs are shown to provide quick EM navigation: a home tab (your initial location), an administration tab, a maintenance tab, and a performance tab. At the top of the console page, there are also links to setup (for setting up and managing additional administrators, notification methods, etc.), preferences (e.g., notification schedules), help, and logout. The following describe what you'll see in each of the tabbed areas:

Home Page

The Home Page is segmented into the following areas: general characteristics (e.g., status, instance name, version, host, listener names, and Oracle home), host CPU, active sessions, space usage, advise (a link to the Automatic Database Diagnostic Monitor (ADDM) findings, which are described later in this chapter), high availability (instance recovery time and archiving status), activity summary of scheduled and running jobs, and related alerts. The page also includes related links to Advisor Central, all metrics, manage metrics, iSQL*Plus, alert history, blackouts (periods during which data collection activities are suspended), metric collection errors, alert log content, jobs, and configuration monitoring.

Administration Page

The Administration Page has links to instance administration (initialization parameters, undo management, and memory parameters), storage administration (control files, tablespaces, datafiles, rollback segments, redo log groups, archive logs, and temporary tablespace groups), security administration (user, roles, and profiles), the database resource manager (resource monitors, consumer groups, and plans), the scheduler (jobs, schedules, programs, job classes, windows, and window groups), data warehouse administration (OLAP cubes, dimensions, and measures and summary management materialized views, view logs, and refresh groups), schema administration (tables, indexes, views, synonyms, sequences, database links, source types, and user types), and workload administration (workload repository and SQL Tuning Sets).

Maintenance Page

The Maintenance Page has links to utilities (export to files, import from files, load data from files, SQL Access Advisor (described later), gather statistics, reorganize objects, and make tablespace locally managed), recovery (backup, recovery, backup settings, recovery settings, backup management, and recovery catalog), and software management (patching).

Performance Page

The Performance Page graphically shows parameters such as host run queue length, paging rate, instance service time (CPU used, concurrency, scheduler, administrative, configuration, system I/O, application, network, user I/O, commit, and other workload), and instance throughput (logins and transactions, physical reads and redo size). The page also has additional monitoring links to

Top Sessions, Top SQL, Advisor Central, blocking sessions, database locks, instance activity, and top consumers.

Advisor Central provides links to many of the new tuning tools in Oracle Database 10g, including ADDM, SQL Tuning, SQL Access, the Memory Advisor, Mean Time to Recovery (MTTR) management, the Segment Advisor, and undo management tools.

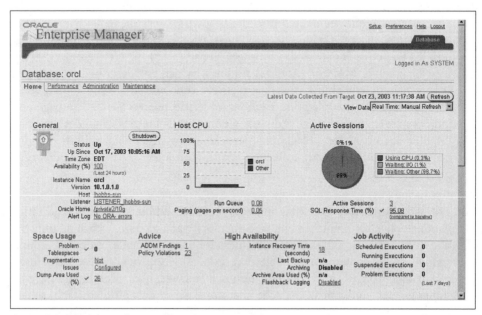

Figure 5-2. HTML console

Oracle Database 10g also includes a more sophisticated scheduler that enables control of when and where jobs take place. The scheduler programs describe the names of programs to be run, the types of programs, and the program arguments. Jobs are created through the link in the Administrator Page to specify what is to be executed (e.g., a specific PL/SQL program you name for execution) and an execution schedule. Job parameters specified include description, log level, job class, whether a job can be restarted, and the PL/SQL statement to be used. Jobs can be scheduled to run immediately or at specific times. A schedule can be shared by multiple jobs.

EM2Go

EM2Go is a mobile version of Enterprise Manager introduced with Oracle Database 10g. It can be used for remote wireless management of database instances and Oracle Application Server. Providing a subset of the functionality in Enterprise Manager, EM2Go leverages the previously described Oracle Management Service, associated Management Repository, and Oracle Agents in the EM architecture. The Enterprise

Manager Console is accessed through a Pocket PC browser on a PDA device. Communication between the Console and OMS and between OMS and the agents is via HTTP. The administrator begins by logging into Oracle Enterprise Manager from the EM2Go home page by entering the appropriate EM username and password. Upon logging in, the administrator is presented with a summary of alerts, database and Application Server availability, and links to more detailed information describing the alerts, availability, and performance of the targets being monitored.

Database administration capabilities in EM2Go include the ability to perform basic administration tasks on control files, tablespaces, datafiles, rollback segments, redo segments, redo log groups, and archive logs. The performance management interface has links into the current Top Sessions, which identify the sessions consuming the most time and resources, their associated SQL statements, and wait status, as well as information on locks, and the Top SQL assessment.

Host monitoring provides a view of the health of the underlying hardware and operating system. Application Server monitoring includes performance statistics and enables setting of thresholds to more easily determine the severity of reported statistics.

Oracle Database 10*g* Self-Tuning and Management

A major focus in Oracle Database 10*g* is the introduction of new self-tuning and management features in the database. Necessary for grid computing, these new features also make managing more familiar database environments much easier. Out of the box, the Oracle installation process builds an Intelligent Infrastructure. The infrastructure includes a workload repository (Automatic Workload Repository, or AWR) that is automatically populated with database statistical information gathered via "instrumentation" in the database code at very low overhead. Active session history is typically gathered every second, and the AWR is populated by default every 30 seconds. The Intelligent Infrastructure includes automatic setup of maintenance tasks that a DBA would normally schedule (such as ANALYZE to build statistics needed for the cost-based optimizer), server-generated alerts that occur just-in-time (not through a polling mechanism, as was present in previous EM deployment), and an advisory infrastructure.

The new self-tuning and management features that DBAs and others can leverage include:

Automatic Database Diagnostic Manager (ADDM)
> ADDM automatically tracks changes in database performance and makes recommendations on how to improve performance. Steps needed to resolve system utilization problems are typically reduced from watching events, exploring V$

tables, and identifying related SQL to simply reviewing the recommendations and accepting them. ADDM leverages data gathered in the workload repository. ADDM can be accessed through Advisor Central in EM.

Automatic SQL Tuning Optimizer

Rather than reviewing sessions with "bad SQL" by examining parameters such as system utilization and wait events, then observing Top Sessions in Enterprise Manager to identify such sessions and reviewing an explain plan, you can now simply review the ADDM recommendations, follow a link to SQL Tuning, and accept the recommendations. The SQL Tuning Optimizer performs a more extensive optimization investigation, and stores the results of this process in a Profile for automatic use by Oracle in the future. These Profiles can be used with packaged applications, as well as with your own custom code, and are used by the optimizer in subsequent resubmission of the SQL statements.

Automatic Shared Memory Advisor

The Memory Advisor is an expert system that eliminates manual adjustment of the buffer pool and shared pool sizes previously required to eliminate out-of-memory errors.

Segment Advisor

Use of the Segment Advisor eliminates the need to identify fragmented objects and then to use Enterprise Manager to reorganize the objects. The Segment Advisor advises which objects to shrink and allows you to simply accept the recommendations.

Single Command Flashback Recovery

The FLASHBACK DATABASE statement enables you to quickly revert the database to a state it was in at a past moment in time. Oracle Database 10g uses a log file containing data block images for changed blocks and other information. You can simply recover the table with a single FLASHBACK TABLE command. For more information on all of the new FLASHBACK commands, see Chapter 10.

Automated Undo Management (AUM) Tuning

AUM, the database feature that automatically allocates undo (rollback) space among active sessions, first appeared in Oracle9i. Oracle Database 10g AUM Tuning automatically determines optimal undo retention time based on system activity, and maximizes usage of the undo tablespace.

Automated Storage Management (ASM)

ASM provides a filesystem and volume manager in the database, enabling the automated striping of files and automating mirroring of database extents. DBAs simply define a pool of storage or disk group and manage the disk group through EM. Workloads can be dynamically rebalanced without taking the database down, so the DBA can add to the pool of storage while the database is available. ASM includes support of datafiles, log files, control files, archive logs, and RMAN and backup sets, and can be applied to a single system, or a RAC or grid computing environment.

Implementing Security

One of the most important aspects of managing the Oracle database effectively in a multiuser environment is the creation of a security scheme to control access to and modification of the database. In an Oracle database you grant security clearance to individual users or database roles, as described in the following sections.

Security management is typically performed at three different levels:

- Database level
- Operating system level
- Network security level

At the operating system level, DBAs should have the ability to create and delete files related to the database, whereas typical database users should not. Oracle includes operating system–specific security information as part of its standard documentation set. In many large organizations, DBAs or database security administrators work closely with computer system administrators to coordinate security specifications and practices.

Database security specifications control user database access and place limits on user capabilities through the use of username/password pairs. Such specifications may limit the allocation of resources (disk and CPU) to users and mandate the auditing of users. Database security at the database level also provides control of the access to and use of specific schema objects in the database.

Usernames, Privileges, Groups, and Roles

The DBA or database security administrator creates *usernames* to provide valid user identifiers that can be used to connect to the database. Two user accounts are automatically created as part of the installation process and are assigned the DBA role: SYS and SYSTEM. (The DBA role is described in a subsequent section.)

Each database username has a password associated with it that prevents unauthorized access. Oracle can check to ensure that passwords:

- Are at least four characters long
- Differ from the username
- Do not match any word on an internal list of simple words
- Differ from the previous password (if there is one) by at least three characters

Oracle can check for these characteristics each time a password is created or modified as part of enforced security policies.

Once a user has successfully logged into the database, that user's access is restricted based on *privileges*, which are the rights to execute certain SQL statements. Some privileges may be granted systemwide (such as the ability to delete rows anywhere in the database) or may apply only to a specific schema object in the database (such as the ability to delete rows in a specific table).

Roles are named groups of privileges and may be created, altered, or dropped. In most implementations, the DBA or security administrator creates usernames for users and assigns roles to specific users, thereby granting them a set of privileges. This is most commonly done today through the Oracle Enterprise Manager (EM) console, described previously in this chapter. For example, you might grant a role to provide access to a specific set of applications, such as "human resources," or you might define multiple roles so that users assigned a certain role can update hourly pay in the human resources applications, while users assigned other roles cannot.

Every database has a pseudo-role named PUBLIC that includes every user. All users can use privileges granted to PUBLIC. If database links are created using the keyword PUBLIC, they will be visible to all users who have privileges to the underlying objects for those links and synonyms. Note that as database vulnerability seems to be an increasing concern, you may want to consider limited privileges for the PUBLIC role.

Security Privileges

Four basic security privileges are applied to the data in an Oracle database:

SELECT
> Perform queries

INSERT
> Put rows into tables or views

UPDATE
> Update rows in tables or views

DELETE
> Remove rows from tables, table partitions, or views

In addition to these data-specific privileges, several other privileges apply to the objects within a database schema:

CREATE
> Create a table in a schema

DROP
> Remove a table in a schema

ALTER
> Alter tables or views

All of these privileges can be handled with two simple SQL statements. The GRANT statement gives a particular privilege to a user or role, while the REVOKE statement takes away a specific privilege. You can use GRANT and REVOKE to modify the privileges for an individual or a role. You can use either of these statements with the keyword PUBLIC to issue or revoke a privilege for all database users.

The DBA Role, SYSDBA, and SYSOPER

The DBA role is one of the most important default roles in Oracle. The DBA role includes most system privileges. By default, it is granted to the users SYS and SYSTEM, both created at database creation time. Base tables and data dictionary views are stored in the SYS schema. SYSTEM schema tables are used for administrative information and by various Oracle tools and options. Therefore, it is strongly recommended that you create at least one more administrative user.

The DBA role does not include basic database administrative tasks included in the SYSDBA or SYSOPER system privileges. Therefore, SYSDBA or SYSOPER should be specifically granted to administrators. They will CONNECT AS either SYSDBA or SYSOPER to the database and will have access to a database even when it is not open. SYSDBA privileges can be granted to users by SYS or by other administrators with SYSDBA privileges. When granted, the SYSDBA privileges allow a user to perform the following database actions from the command line of SQL*Plus or the browser-based *i*SQL*Plus, or through EM's point-and-click interface:

STARTUP
Start up a database instance.

SHUTDOWN
Shut down a database instance.

ALTER DATABASE OPEN
Open a mounted but closed database.

ALTER DATABASE MOUNT
Mount a database using a previously started instance.

ALTER DATABASE BACKUP CONTROLFILE
Start a backup of the control file. However, backups are more frequently done through RMAN today, as described in the "Backup and Recovery" section later in this chapter.

ALTER DATABASE ARCHIVELOG
Specify that the contents of a redo log file group must be archived before the redo log file group can be reused.

ALTER DATABASE RECOVER
Apply logs individually or start automatic application of the redo logs.

CREATE DATABASE

Create and name a database, specify datafiles and their sizes, specify logfiles and their sizes, and set parameter limits.

DROP DATABASE

Delete a database and all of the files included in the control file.

CREATE SPFILE

Create a server parameter file from a text initialization (*INIT.ORA*) file.

RESTRICTED SESSION

Allow connections to databases started in Restricted mode. Restricted mode is designed for activities such as troubleshooting and some types of maintenance, similar to what SYS can do.

Administrators connected as SYSOPER can perform a more limited set of statements: STARTUP and SHUTDOWN, CREATE SPFILE, ALTER DATABASE OPEN or MOUNT or BACKUP, ALTER DATABASE ARCHIVELOG, ALTER DATABASE RECOVER, and also the RESTRICTED SESSION privilege.

Database administrators are authenticated using either operating system authentication or a password file. The CONNECT INTERNAL syntax supported in earlier releases of Oracle is no longer available. When operating system authentication is used, administrative users must be named in the OSDBA or OSOPER defined groups. For password file authentication, the file is created with the ORAPWD utility. Users are added by SYS or by those having SYSDBA privileges.

 With each release of Oracle, fewer default users and passwords in combination are automatically created during database and options installation and creation. Regardless, we recommend that you reset all default passwords that are documented in Oracle.

Auditing Security, Policies, and Policy Violations

If you're suspicious about the actions of a particular user and are considering reducing that user's level of privileges, you may want to make use of Oracle's audit capabilities to audit that user's actions at the statement level, privilege level, or schema object level. Auditing can also gather data about database activities for planning and tuning purposes. Auditing of connections with administrative privileges to an instance and audit records recording database startup and shutdown occur by default.

You can also audit sessions at the user level, which captures some basic but extremely useful statistics such as the number of logical I/Os, the number of physical I/Os, and the total time logged on. As noted previously, gathering performance statistics is low in terms of overhead, and Oracle Database 10g automatically gathers statistics in populating the Automatic Workload Repository (AWR).

Audit records always contain the following information:

- Username
- Session identifier
- Terminal identifier
- Name of schema object accessed
- Operation performed or attempted
- Completion code of the operation
- Date and timestamp

The records may be stored in a data dictionary table (AUD$ in the SYS schema), which is also called the database audit trail, or in an operating system audit trail.

To turn on auditing, set the AUDIT_TRAIL parameter in the initialization file. To generate audit information, you must set this parameter and specify the desired auditing options with the AUDIT statement. A typical use of the AUDIT statement is the auditing of a specific schema object (e.g., a table) for a certain action (e.g., UPDATE) to see who has been modifying that table.

Oracle9*i* added fine-grained auditing, which enabled selective audits of SELECT statements with bind variables based on access of specified columns. Oracle Database 10*g* adds extended SQL support for fine-grained auditing. You can now perform granular auditing of queries, UPDATE, INSERT, and DELETE operations through SQL.

How can you quickly identify potential threats? Enterprise Manager 10*g*'s visual interface to a policy framework in the EM repository aids management of security in the Oracle Database 10*g* release. Security policies or rules are built and stored in a policy library. Violations of rules are reported as critical, warning, or informational through the EM interface. Out of the box, security violations are checked on a daily basis. Policies may be adjusted according to business demands, and violations can be overridden when they are reported.

View-Based Security

You can think of views as virtual tables defined by queries that extract or derive data from physical "base" tables. Because you can use them to create different representations of the data for different groups of users, you can use views to present only the rows or columns that a certain group of users should be able to access.

For example, in a human resources application, users from the HR department may have full access to the employee base table, which contains basic information such as employee names, work addresses, and work phone numbers, as well as more restricted information such as Social Security numbers, home addresses, and home telephone numbers. For other users in the company, you'll want to hide more personal information by providing a view that shows only the basic information.

In many situations, creating a Virtual Private Database (VPD) or leveraging the Label Security Option, described in subsequent sections of this chapter, provide a more secure means of restricting access to certain data.

Fine-Grained Access Control

Implementing security can be a very time-consuming process, especially if you want to base security on an attribute with a wide range of values. A good example of this type of situation in the human resources scenario previously described would be the need to limit the data an HR representative can see to only the rows relating to employees that he supports. Here you're faced with a situation in which you might have to define a view for every HR representative, which might mean *many* different views. And if you want to grant write access for a representative's own employees and read access for other employees, the situation gets even more complex. The smaller the scope, or *grain*, of the access control you desire, the more work is involved in creating and maintaining the security privileges.

Oracle offers a type of security that you can use to grant this type of fine-grained access control (FGAC). *Security policies* implemented as PL/SQL functions can be associated with tables or views enabling creation of a Virtual Private Database. A security policy returns a condition that's dynamically associated with a particular SQL statement, which transparently limits the data that's returned. In the HR example, suppose that each representative supports employees with a last name in a particular alphabetic range, such as A through G. The security policy would return a WHERE clause, based on a particular representative's responsibilities, that limits the rows returned. You can keep the range for each representative in a separate table that is dynamically queried as part of the security policy function. This simplifies management of allowable access if roles and responsibilities change frequently.

You can associate a security policy with a particular view or table by using the built-in PL/SQL package DBMS_RLS, which also allows you to refresh, enable, or disable a security policy.

Oracle Database 10g VPD is even more fine-grained, enabling enforced rewrites when a query references a specific column. Performance of queries in VPD implementations is also improved in Oracle Database 10g through the support of parallel query. Fine-grained security can also be based on the type of SQL statement issued. The security policy previously described could be used to limit UPDATE, INSERT, and DELETE operations to one set of data, but allow SELECT operations on a different set of data. For a good description of FGAC through PL/SQL, see *Oracle PL/SQL Programming* by Steven Feuerstein and Bill Pribyl (see Appendix B for details).

Label Security Option

The Oracle Label Security Option eliminates the need to write VPD PL/SQL programs to enforce row-level label security where sensitivity labels are desired. These collections of labels, label authorizations, and security enforcement options can be applied to entire schema or to specific tables.

Sensitivity labels are defined based on a user's need to see and/or update data. They consist of a level denoting the data sensitivity, a category or compartment that further segregates the data, and a group used to record ownership (which may be hierarchical in nature) and access.

Standard group definitions given to users provide them access to data containing those group labels. Inverse groups in the data can be used to define what labels a user must have in his profile in order to access it.

Policies are created and applied, sensitivity labels are defined, and user labels are set and authorized through a policy manager tool accessible through EM. You can also add SQL predicates and label functions and manage trusted program units, Oracle VPD fine-grained access control policies, and VPD application contexts. Label Security policy management is now possible in Oracle Database 10g when using the Oracle Internet Directory.

Security and Application Roles and Privileges

Applications can involve data and logic in many different schemas with many different privileges. To simplify the issues raised by this complexity, roles are frequently used in applications. Application roles have all the privileges necessary to run the applications, and users of the applications are granted the roles necessary to execute them.

Application roles may contain privileges that should be granted to users only while they're running the application. Application developers can place a SET ROLE statement at the beginning of an application to enable the appropriate role and disable others only while the application is running. Similarly, you can invoke a DBMS_SESSION.SET_ROLE procedure from PL/SQL.

Another way to accomplish application security is by encapsulating privileges in stored procedures. Instead of granting direct access to the various tables for an application, you can create stored procedures that provide access to the tables and grant access to the stored procedures instead of the tables. For example, instead of granting INSERT privileges for the EMPLOYEE table, you might create and grant access to a stored procedure called HIRE_EMPLOYEE that accepts as parameters all the data for a new employee.

When you run a stored procedure normally, the procedure has the access rights that were granted to the owner of the procedure; that owner is the schema in which the procedure resides. If a particular schema has access to a particular database object, all stored procedures that reside in that schema have the same rights as the schema. When any user calls one of those stored procedures, that user has the same access rights to the underlying data objects that the procedure does.

For example, suppose there is a schema called HR_REP. This schema has write access to the EMP table. Any stored procedure in the HR_REP schema also has write access to the EMP table. Consequently, if you grant a user access to a stored procedure in the HR_REP schema, that user will also have write access to the EMP table regardless of her personal level of security privilege. However, she will have access only through the stored procedures in the schema.

One small but vitally important caveat applies to access through stored procedures: the security privilege must be *directly* granted to the schema, not granted by means of a role.

If you attach the keyword AUTHID CURRENT_USER to a stored procedure when it's compiled, security restrictions will be enforced based on the username of the user invoking the procedure, rather than the schema that owns the stored procedure (the definer of the procedure). If a user has access to a particular database object with a particular privilege, that user will have the same access through stored procedures compiled with the AUTHID CURRENT_USER.

Distributed Database and Multi-Tier Security

All the security features available for undistributed Oracle databases are also available for the distributed database environment, which is covered in Chapter 12. However, the distributed database environment introduces additional security considerations. For example, user accounts needed to support server connections must exist in all of the distributed databases forming the system. As database links (which define connections between distributed database instances) are created, you will need to allow the user accounts and roles needed at each site.

For large implementations, you may want to configure global authentication across these distributed databases for users and roles. Global authentication allows you to maintain a single authentication list for multiple distributed databases. Where this type of external authentication is required, Oracle's Advanced Security Option, discussed in the next section, provides a solution.

In typical three-tier implementations, the Oracle Application Server runs some of the application logic, serves as an interface between the clients and database servers, and provides much of the Oracle Identity Management (OIM) infrastructure. The Oracle Internet Directory (OID) provides directory services running as applications on an Oracle database. The directory synchronization service, provisioning integrated service, and delegated administrative service are part of OID. The Oracle Database 10g certificate authority (an X.509 v3 certificate authority) and single sign-on reside in the Application Server. Security in middle-tier applications is controlled by applications' privileges and preserving client identities through all three tiers.

EM is commonly used to configure valid application users to Oracle's LDAP-compliant OID server. A user who accesses an application for which he is not authenticated is redirected to a login server. Once there, he is prompted for a username and password that are checked against the OID server. A cookie is returned and the user is redirected from the login server to the application.

Advanced Security Option

The Oracle Advanced Security Option (ASO), formerly known as the Advanced Networking Option (ANO), is used in distributed environments linked via Oracle Net in which there are concerns regarding secure access and transmission of data. This option specifically provides data encryption during transmission to protect data from unauthorized viewing over Oracle Net, as well as Net/SSL, and between thin JDBC clients and the database. Encryption algorithms supported include RC4_40, RC4_56, RC4_128, RC4_256, DES_40, 2-Key Triple-DES (3DES), and 3-Key 3DES. Communications packets are protected against data modification, transaction replay, and removal through use of MD5 and SHA-1 algorithms.

ASO also provides support for a variety of identity authentication methods to ensure that user identities are accurately known. Third-party authentication services supported include Kerberos, Cybersafe, RADIUS, and DCE. RADIUS enables support of third-party authentication devices including smart cards and token cards. Public Key Infrastructure (PKI) authentication, popular for securing Internet-based e-commerce applications, uses X.509 v3 digital certificates and can leverage Entrust Profiles stored in Oracle Wallets. Oracle Database 10g adds authentication capabilities for users who have Kerberos credentials, and enables Kerberos-based authentication across database links.

Oracle Wallets can store multiple certificates in a variety of formats, including X.509 certificates in PKCS #12 format. Oracle Wallets are managed through a Wallet Manager accessible through EM and support the Triple-DES (3DES) algorithm for securing the wallets. User wallets may be stored and retrieved from the Oracle Internet Directory. A user migration tool is included to migrate database users to OID.

In a typical scenario, the Oracle Enterprise Security Manager configures valid application users to the LDAP-compliant OID server. An X.509 certificate authority creates private key pairs and publishes them in Oracle wallets (through Oracle Wallet Manager) to the LDAP directory.

A user who wants to log in to a database server will need a certificate and a private key, which can be retrieved from that user's password-protected wallet, which resides in the LDAP directory. With Oracle Database 10g, users and servers can be provisioned using keys of up to 4096 bit that can be honored at runtime. When the user's key on the client device is sent to the database server, it is matched with the paired key retrieved by the server via SSL from the LDAP directory and the user is authenticated to use the database.

Fragmentation and Reorganization

Fragmentation is a problem that can negatively impact performance—and one that many DBAs have struggled to manage. Fragmentation can be an unwanted phenomenon if it results in small parts of noncontiguous "free space" that cannot be reused.

In Oracle, a collection of contiguous blocks is referred to as an *extent*. A collection of extents is referred to as a *segment*. Segments can contain anything that takes up space—for example, a table, an index, or a rollback segment. Segments typically consist of multiple extents. As one extent fills up, a segment begins to use another extent. As fragmentation occurs, by database activity that leaves "holes" in the contiguous space represented by extents, segments acquire additional extents. As fragmentation grows, performance is negatively impacted.

Resolving Fragmentation

In Oracle Database 10g, resolving fragmentation becomes fairly trivial. You can perform an online segment shrink using the Segment Advisor interface accessible through EM. ADDM recommends segments to shrink, and you simply choose to accept the recommendations.

Prior to Oracle Database 10g, the common means of reducing fragmentation in Oracle9i was through an online reorganization accomplished through a CREATE TABLE . . . AS SELECT online operation—that is, the copying of the contents of one table to another while the original table is updated. Changes to the original table were tracked and applied to the new table. Physical and logical attributes of the table could be changed during this online operation, thus allowing an online reorganization.

Compare and contrast these methods to reducing fragmentation in Oracle database versions prior to Oracle9i. The general recommendation was to avoid fragmentation through careful planning. But the usual way to solve fragmentation was to reorganize a table by exporting the table, dropping it, and importing it. The data was unavailable while the table was in the process of being reorganized. Many DBAs claimed that they saw improved performance after reorganizing segments into a single extent. Over time, a decrease in performance reoccurred as the number of extents the table occupied increased.

Oracle performance increased as a result of these reorganization operations, but this improvement was *not* due to a decrease in the number of extents. When a table is dropped and recreated, several things happened that increased performance:

1. Each block was loaded as full of rows as possible.

2. As a consequence, the high-water mark of the table (the highest block that has ever had data in it) was set to its lowest point.

3. All indexes on the table were rebuilt, which meant that the index blocks were as full as possible. The depth of the index, which determined the number of I/Os it takes to get to the leaf blocks or the index, was sometimes minimized.

By eliminating fragments and shrinking segments in a much more automated and online fashion, Oracle Database 10g greatly simplifies solving fragmentation problems; the result is that optimal conditions exist for performance.

Backup and Recovery

This section provides only a very brief overview of standard backup and recovery options. For more detailed information about backup and recovery options, refer to Chapter 10.

Even if you've taken adequate precautions, critical database records can sometimes be destroyed as a result of user error or hardware or software failure. The only way to prepare for this type of potentially disastrous situation is to perform regular backup operations.

Two basic types of potential failures can affect an Oracle database: *instance failure*, in which the Oracle instance terminates without going through the shutdown process; and *media failure*, in which the disks that store the information in an Oracle database are corrupted or damaged.

After an instance failure, Oracle will automatically perform crash recovery; you can use Real Application Clusters (Oracle Parallel Server prior to Oracle9i) to automatically perform instance recovery when one of its instances crashes. However, DBAs must initiate recovery from media failure. The ability to recover successfully from this type of failure is one of the greatest challenges a DBA faces—it's also the place where the value of the DBA becomes most apparent! The recovery process includes restoring older copies of the damaged datafile(s) and rolling forward by applying archived and online redo logs.

To ensure successful recovery, the DBA should have prepared for this eventuality by performing the following actions:

- Multiplexing online redo logs by having multiple log members per group on different disks and controllers

- Running the database in ARCHIVELOG mode so that redo log files are archived before they are reused
- Archiving redo logs to multiple locations
- Maintaining multiple copies of the control file(s)
- Backing up physical datafiles frequently—ideally, storing multiple copies in multiple locations

Running the database in ARCHIVELOG mode ensures that you can recover the database up to the time of the media failure; in this mode, the DBA can perform online datafile backups while the database is available for use. In addition, archived redo logs can be sent to a standby database (explained in Chapter 10) in which they may be applied.

RMAN, first introduced in Oracle8 and greatly enhanced since, provides an easy-to-use frontend to manage this process. RMAN is accessible today through EM interfaces.

Types of Backup and Recovery Options

There are two major categories of backup:

Full backup
> Includes backups of datafiles, datafile copies, tablespaces, control files (current or backup), or the entire database (including all datafiles and the current control file). Reads the entire file and copies all blocks into the backup set, skipping only datafile blocks that have never been used (with the exception of control files and redo logs where no blocks are skipped).

Incremental backup
> Includes backups of datafiles, tablespaces, or the whole database. Reads the entire file and backs up only those data blocks that have changed since a previous backup.

You can begin backups through the Recovery Manager (RMAN) or the Oracle Enterprise Manager interface to RMAN, which uses the database export facility, or you can initiate backups via standard operating system backup utilities.

RMAN was introduced with Oracle8 and replaced the Enterprise Backup Utility available for some previous Oracle7 releases. In general, RMAN supports the most database backup features, including open or online backups, closed database backups, incremental backups at the Oracle block level, corrupt block detection, automatic backups, backup catalogs, and backups to sequential media. RMAN added capabilities in Oracle9*i* for one-time backup configuration, recovery windows to determine and manage expiration dates of backups, and restartable backups and restores. Also added was support for testing of restores and recovery.

In Oracle Database 10*g*, RMAN can perform image copy backups of the database, tablespaces, or datafiles. RMAN can be used to apply incremental backups to datafile image backups. The speed of incremental backups is increased through a change tracking feature by reading and backing up only changed blocks.

Recovery options include the following:

- Complete database recovery to the point of failure
- Tablespace point-in-time recovery (recovery of a tablespace to a time different from the rest of the database)
- Time-based or point-in-time database recovery (recovery of the entire database to a time before the most current time)
- Recovery until the CANCEL command is issued
- Change-based or log sequence recovery (to a specified System Change Number, or SCN)

You can recover through the use of RMAN (utilizing the recovery catalog or control file) or via SQL or SQL*Plus.

RMAN in Oracle Database 10*g* improves the reliability of backups and restores through a number of added features. The current database supports the backup and restore of standby control files. RMAN now automatically retries a failed backup or restore operation. During recovery, RMAN automatically creates and recovers datafiles that have never been backed up. Where backups are missing or corrupt during the restore process, RMAN now automatically uses an older backup.

To speed backups and restoration, Oracle Database 10*g* introduces the Flash Recovery Area, organizing recovery files to a specific area on disk. These files include control files, archived log files, flashback database logs, datafile copies, and RMAN backups. You can set a RETENTION AREA parameter to retain needed recovery files for specific time windows. Backup files and archivelogs that age beyond the time window are automatically deleted. Oracle Database 10*g*'s ASM (described earlier in this chapter) can configure the Flash Recovery Area. If availability of disk space is an issue, RMAN in Oracle Database 10*g* also has the ability to compress backup sets.

Making Sure the Backup Works

The key to providing an adequate backup and recovery strategy is to simulate recovery from failure using the backups from your test system before going live in production. Many times, backup media that were thought to be reliable prove not to be, or backup frequencies that were thought to be adequate prove to be too infrequent to allow for timely recoveries. It's far better to discover that recovery is slow or impossible in test situations than after your business has been impacted by the failure of a production system.

Additional Backup Capabilities

A number of Oracle Backup Solutions Program (BSP) partners certify their products to perform backup and recovery to disk and tape storage devices using RMAN. Oracle bundles Legato's Single Server Version (LSSV) tape storage management product at no charge on popular Unix platforms (such as AIX, HP-UX, Linux, Solaris, and Tru64 Unix) and Windows platforms. The LSSV's capabilities include the following:

- Media management, including tape labeling, media tracking, and retention policy management
- Ability to use up to four locally connected tape drives and up to four concurrent data streams
- Installation integrated into the Oracle installer
- Integration with EM for administration

There are some limitations when using LSSV. The product doesn't provide networked backups; it provides support for only a limited number of tape devices; and it doesn't support robotic libraries or backups of operating system files, network attached storage (NAS), or storage area networks (SAN). Legato offers optional products providing these additional backup capabilities.

There are other Oracle BSP partners, such as Computer Associates, EMC, Hewlett-Packard, Sun, IBM Tivoli, and Veritas. Current partners are generally posted at *http://otn.oracle.com* (the Oracle Technology Network). You may want to check with your favorite backup vendor about their current certification in support of Oracle's Media Management Interface Library (MML), the interface to RMAN.

Working with Oracle Support

Regardless of the extent of your training, there are bound to be some issues that you can't resolve without help from Oracle Corporation. Part of the job of the DBA is to help resolve any issues with the Oracle database. Oracle offers several levels of support including basic product support, advanced support, and incident support. Each of these support options cost extra, but regardless of your support level, you can get the most from Oracle by understanding how to best work with them.

Resolving problems with the assistance of Oracle Worldwide Customer Support Services can initially be frustrating to novice DBAs and others who may report problems. Oracle responds to database problems reported as Service Requests (SRs), formerly known as Technical Assistance Requests (TARs), based on the priority or severity level at which those problems are reported. If the problem is impacting your ability to complete a project or do business, the problem should be reported as "priority level 2" in order to assure a timely response. If the problem is initially assigned a lower level and the response hasn't been adequate, you should escalate the problem-resolution priority.

If business is halted because of the problem, the priority level assigned should be "priority level 1." However, if a problem is reported at level 1, the caller must be available for a callback (even if after hours). Otherwise, Oracle will assume that the problem wasn't as severe as initially reported and may lower the priority level for resolution.

Reporting Problems

You can report problems via phone, email, or the web browser-based MetaLink interface. The MetaLink support, included with basic product support, has grown extremely popular as answers to similar problems can be rapidly found and may result in eliminating time required for a physical response. MetaLink provides proactive notifications, customized home pages, technical libraries and forums, product life-cycle information, a bug database, and the ability to log SRs (TARs). When contacting technical support, you will need your Customer Support Identification (CSI) number. Oracle Sales Consultants can also provide advice regarding how to report problems. Additionally, Oracle Worldwide Customer Support Services offers training for DBAs regarding effective use of Support services.

Automated Patching in Oracle Database 10g

Oracle Support issues Metalink Notes whenever software bugs or vulnerabilities are discovered and issues appropriate patches. Automated patching and notification provided with Oracle Database 10g can reduce the time delay between Oracle's discovery of such problems and your reaction to them. Alerts can now be issued to your Enterprise Manager 10g console alerting you to the newly discovered bugs or vulnerabilities. Through the Enterprise Configuration Management capabilities in Enterprise Manager 10g, you'll see a link to the patch and the target where the patch should be applied.

In RAC and grid environments, "rolling" patch updates can be applied across your nodes without taking the cluster or grid down. (We described the process of applying rolling patch updates in Chapter 3.) Further, you can roll back a patch (e.g., uninstall it) on an instance if you observe unusual behavior and want to remove the patch.

CHAPTER 6

Oracle Performance

As this book illustrates, the Oracle database has a wide range of features. As you gain experience with Oracle, you'll reap more of the benefits it has to offer. One area on which you will inevitably focus is performance tuning. This chapter gives you the basics you'll need to understand before you can address performance issues.

Oracle database performance tuning has been extensively documented in the Oracle community. There are numerous books that provide detailed and excellent information; many of these are listed in Appendix B. This book is focused more on the concepts of the Oracle database, so we won't delve too deeply into specific tuning recommendations. Instead, we'll touch on the importance of tuning and discuss some basic notions of how Oracle uses resources. Here, we're simply laying a foundation for understanding Oracle performance issues. This understanding will help you implement the tuning procedures most suited for your own particular implementation scenario. Where appropriate, we'll provide some basic tuning guidelines.

Performance Tuning Basics

Database performance is one of the trickiest components of the operation of your database. One of the curious aspects of performance is that "good performance" is defined by its absence rather than by its presence. You can recognize bad performance easily, but good performance is usually defined as simply the absence of bad performance. Performance is simultaneously a very simple topic—any novice user can implicitly understand it—and an extremely complex topic that can strain the ingenuity of the most proficient database administrator.

Before getting into a specific discussion of Oracle performance, it makes sense to define a basic methodology for investigating performance problems.

There are three basic steps to understanding how to address performance issues with your Oracle database:

- Define performance problems

- Check the performance of the Oracle server software
- Check the overall performance of the server machine

Defining Performance Problems

The first step in performance tuning is to determine if there actually *is* a performance problem. In the previous section, we mentioned the concept of poor performance, which even end users can recognize. But what exactly is poor performance?

Poor performance is inevitably the result of disappointment—a user feels that the system is not performing as expected. Consequently, you must first evaluate how real the unmet expectations are in the first place.

If performance expectations are realistic—for example, if performance has degraded from an earlier level, you then need to identify which of the system's components are causing the problems. You must refine a general statement like "the system is too slow" to identify which types of operations are too slow, what constitutes "too slow," and when these operations are slowing down. For example, the problem may occur only on specific transactions and at specific times, or all transactions and reports may be performing below the users' expectations.

Once you've defined the performance expected from your system, you can begin to try to determine where your performance problem lies. Performance problems occur when there is a greater demand for a particular resource than the resources available to service that demand, and the system slows down while applications wait to share the resource.

Oracle Server Performance

The first place to begin looking for resource bottlenecks is the Oracle database software. You can use the Oracle Enterprise Manager (described in more detail in Chapter 5) to identify less than optimal use of Oracle's internal resources. Bottlenecks within your database result in sessions waiting unnecessarily, and performance tuning is aimed at removing these bottlenecks.

Oracle's dynamic performance views are one of the most powerful tools for detecting bottlenecks within your Oracle database. All of these performance views have names that begin with "V$", and, from Oracle9*i* on, there are also global views (for all nodes in a Real Application Clusters database) that begin with "GV$". Two views, in particular, identify the sources of these waits; these are invaluable for guiding your analysis:

V$SYSTEM_EVENT
    Provides aggregated, system-wide information about the resources for which sessions are waiting

V$SESSION_WAIT

> Provides detailed, session-specific information about the resources for which individual sessions are waiting

You can use these two views to pinpoint the resources that are causing the most waits. Focusing on the resources presenting the largest source of waiting will provide the largest performance improvements.

 Oracle Database 10*g* includes an enhanced wait model that makes it easier to determine exactly who is waiting for what resource at what time.

You may find that your problem has a simple source, such as a lower-than-expected database buffer cache hit ratio, which indicates that the cache is not working at its optimal level. For a resource like the cache, which is controlled by the Oracle server software, you can simply increase the initialization parameter DB_BLOCK_BUFFERS to increase the size of the cache, which may improve the hit ratio.

Other situations may not be quite so clear-cut. For instance, you may find that it takes a relatively long time to fetch database rows from the disk. This situation may be caused by contention on the database server's disks, which could be caused by less than optimal placement of Oracle files on disk or by other applications on the server.

Later in this chapter, we'll show you how Oracle uses its own internal resources, such as disk and memory, and how understanding this will help you to manage the resources allocated to the Oracle database software.

Machine Resource Usage

You can also run into performance issues with resources for the database server itself or on the machine on which the database server is running. If your Oracle database is not properly configured, adding machine resources may help reduce performance bottlenecks, but this is a fairly expensive way to solve the problem. Further, the problem will likely resurface as these additional resources are consumed. But if your Oracle database is properly configured and you find that the host computer is experiencing resource shortages, adding machine resources is in order.

The performance of your Oracle database is based on how it uses machine resources and what resources are available. These machine resources include processing power or CPU, memory, disk I/O, and network bandwidth. You can trace the bulk of database performance problems back to a bottleneck on one or more of these resources.

Network bandwidth can be a bottleneck, but because the network enables communication between the server and the client, the use of this bandwidth is more a function of the client applications communicating with the database server than a problem with the database server software. For this reason, this chapter focuses on how Oracle uses the three key machine resources: CPU, memory, and disk I/O. The slowest device in a computer is the disk drive and, as a result, the most common source of database performance issues is disk I/O. The majority of this chapter therefore focuses on performance as it relates to physical disk I/O.

Network bandwidth does come into play when using your Oracle database to supply data over the Internet, because there is typically less network bandwidth available over the Web. Although you can't typically surmount this type of problem simply by improving the performance of your Oracle database; you can monitor network bottlenecks with Enterprise Manager, as discussed later, with Oracle Database 10g.

The database server machine may bottleneck on multiple resources, including CPU and I/O. In fact, computer environments are designed so that one resource can try to compensate for the lack of another resource, which can lead to a deficit in the compensating resource as well. If you run out of physical memory, the operating system will swap areas of memory out to the disk, which can cause I/O bottlenecks. You can identify your machine resource usage using tools provided by the machine vendor or operating system utilities. For example, on Unix systems, you can use *sar, iostat,* and *vmstat*; on Windows, you can use the Performance Monitor.

With the latest version of Enterprise Manager in Oracle Database 10g, you can get information on many types of system resource utilization.

When All Else Fails

You may still have performance problems with your application system even if you have not identified a problem in any of the areas previously described. In this case, your performance problem may not lie in the database server, but in the design of the application or the database itself. At this point, you will face the difficult problem of having to analyze the interaction of individual modules and SQL statements in your application system and the database server. You may find that you get lucky and find a handful of SQL statements that are causing your performance problem. However, it's more likely that you will have to reconsider the design of your application system—in particular, if you are running an older release of the Oracle database.

Enterprise Manager 10g and the Automatic Database Diagnostic Monitor (ADDM) for Oracle Database 10g can automatically identify SQL statements that are using the most resources or are less-than-optimal. The SQL Tuning Advisor component can even suggest solutions for the identified performance problems. (These tools are described later in this chapter.)

Needless to say, more complex application redesign is far beyond the scope of this book, so the rest of this chapter will concentrate on helping you to understand Oracle machine resources.*

A Final Note on Performance

Performance is based in the real world. Whenever you attempt to address performance problems, you must make sure to carefully monitor the areas that you are attempting to improve, both before and after your changes. You must use a systematic approach not only for discovering the source of a performance problem, but also for implementing the appropriate solution.

Oracle and Disk I/O Resources

From the perspective of machine resources, an input/output operation, or I/O, can be defined as the operating system of the computer reading or writing some bytes from or to the underlying disk subsystem of the database server. I/Os can be small, such as 4 KB of data, or large, such as 64 KB or 128 KB of data. The lower and upper limits on the size of an I/O operation vary according to the operating system. Your Oracle database also has a block size that you can define; we refer to this as the *database block size*.

An Oracle database issues I/O requests in two basic sizes:

Single database block I/Os
> For example, one 8 KB datablock at a time. This type of request reads or writes a specific block. For example, after looking up a row in an index, Oracle uses a single block I/O to retrieve the desired database block.

Multiblock I/Os
> For example, 32 database blocks, each consisting of 8 KB, for a total I/O size of 256 KB. Multiblock I/O is used for large-scale operations, such as full table scans. The number of blocks in one multiblock I/O is determined by the initialization parameter DB_FILE_MULTIBLOCK_READ_COUNT.

The Oracle database can read larger amounts of data with multiblock I/Os, so there are times when a full table scan might actually retrieve data faster than an index-based retrieval (e.g., if the selectivity of the index is low). Oracle can perform multiblock operations faster than the corresponding collection of single-block operations.

---

* For more details about the vast topic of Oracle performance, refer to the tuning books mentioned in Appendix B.

I/O Planning Principles for an Oracle Database

When you're planning the disk layout and subsequent placement of the various files that make up your database, you need to consider the different reasons Oracle performs I/O and the potential performance impacts.

The main destinations of the I/O operations Oracle performs are the following:

- Redo logs
- Data contained in tables
- Indexes on the tables
- The data dictionary, which goes in the SYSTEM tablespace
- Sort activity, which goes in the TEMP tablespace of the user performing the sort
- Rollback information, which is spread across the datafiles of the tablespace containing the database's rollback segments
- Archived redo logs, which go to the archived log destination (assuming the database is in ARCHIVELOG mode)

The following simple principles for managing these types of I/O can optimize Oracle's use of the database server's disk subsystem:

Use disk-striping technologies to spread I/O evenly across multiple spindles
These technologies are covered in detail in the next section, "Using RAID Disk Array Technology."

Use tablespaces to clearly segregate and target different types of I/O
Using tablespaces to segregate objects simplifies tuning later on. Oracle implements I/O activity at the level of the datafile, or the physical object the operating system sees as a file. Placing specific objects in specific tablespaces allows you to accurately measure and direct the I/O for those objects by tracking and moving the underlying datafiles as needed. For example, consider a database with several large, busy tables. Placing multiple large tables in a single tablespace makes it difficult to determine which table is causing the I/O to the underlying datafiles. Segregating the objects allows you to directly monitor the I/O associated with each object. Your Oracle documentation details the other factors to consider in mapping objects to tablespaces.

Place redo logs and redo log mirrors on the two least-busy devices
This placement maximizes throughput for transactional systems. Oracle writes to all copies of the redo log file, and this I/O is not completed until all copies have been successfully written to. If you have two copies of the redo log file, one on a slow device and the other on a fast device, your redo log I/O performance will be constrained by the slower device.

Distribute "system overhead" evenly over the available drives

System overhead consists of I/O to the SYSTEM tablespace for the data dictionary, the TEMP tablespace for sorting, and the tablespaces that contain rollback segments for undo information. You should consider the system profile in spreading the system overhead over multiple drives. For example, if the application generates a lot of data changes versus data reads, the I/O to the rollback segments may increase due to higher writes for changes and higher reads for consistent read functionality.

Sort activity can also affect disk I/O. If you can get the majority of sorts to occur in memory through tuning the SORT_AREA_SIZE parameter in the initialization file, you can then minimize physical I/O to the TEMP tablespace. Oracle constantly queries and updates the data dictionary stored in the SYSTEM tablespace. This information is cached in the shared pool section of the SGA, so sizing your shared pool properly is key to overall performance. With Oracle Database 10*g*, you can allow Oracle to automatically and dynamically size the different pools in the SGA.

Use a different device for archiving and redo log files

To avoid archiving performance issues due to I/O contention, make sure that the archive log destination uses different devices from those used for the redo logs and redo log mirrors.

Some other principles to consider from the perspective of database availability include the following:

If taking database backups to disk, store the backups on devices that don't contain any database components

This protects the system from the potential loss of the database and the needed backups from the failure of an I/O device.

Make sure the device used for the archive log destination doesn't contain any database components or database backups

If the failure of a single device results in the loss of both database components and archived redo logs, or backup components and archived redo logs, recovery will be endangered.

> Fault-tolerant disk arrays don't eliminate the need for a sound backup and recovery strategy. Fault-tolerant storage merely reduces the likelihood of undergoing database recovery due to the failure of a single drive. For full coverage of Oracle databases and high availability, see Chapter 10.

Using RAID Disk Array Technology

One of the most powerful ways to reduce performance bottlenecks due to disk I/O is the use of RAID disk arrays. RAID stands for Redundant Array of Inexpensive (or

Independent) Disks and is used to group disks into arrays for two reasons: redundancy and performance. The use of RAID for redundancy is detailed in Chapter 10. Our focus in this chapter is on the performance aspects of RAID technology.

RAID Basics

RAID disk arrays provide a hardware solution for both reliability and performance. There are different levels of RAID hardware; the following are most relevant to performance:

RAID-0

Where availability isn't a concern, the disks can be configured as RAID-0, which is nonredundant disk *striping*.

RAID-1

Provides the simplest form of redundancy, full duplication of data, which is referred to as *mirroring*.

RAID-0+1

Combines the one-to-one mirroring of RAID-1 with the striping of RAID-0.

RAID-3

Provides redundancy by storing parity information on a single disk in the array. This parity information can help to recover the data on other disks should they fail. RAID-3 saves on disk storage compared to RAID-1, but isn't often used because the parity disk can be a bottleneck.

RAID-5

Uses parity data for redundancy in a way that is similar to RAID-3, but stripes the parity data across all of the disks, like the way in which the actual data is striped. This alleviates the bottleneck on the parity disk.

There are additional levels of RAID, including RAID-6, which adds dual parity data, and RAID-7 and RAID-8, which add performance enhancements to the characteristics of RAID-5.

RAID groups disk drives into arrays to automatically spread I/O operations across multiple spindles, reducing contention on individual drives. For example, suppose you place a datafile containing an index on a single drive. If multiple processes use the index simultaneously, they will all issue I/O requests to the one disk drive, resulting in contention for the use of that drive.

Instead, suppose you place the same datafile on a "disk" that is actually an array of five physical disks. Each physical disk in the array can perform I/O operations independently on different data blocks of the index, automatically increasing the amount of I/O Oracle can perform without causing contention.

Simply using disk arrays won't, by itself, give you optimal I/O performance. As discussed earlier, you also have to think about how to logically place the different types of Oracle files across the available drives, even if the drives are grouped into arrays.

Disk-striping technology for RAID arrays can be implemented in various ways, as described in the following sections. All of these are transparent to your Oracle database. Oracle Database 10g striping considerations are made simpler through the introduction of Automatic Storage Management (ASM). ASM provides automatic striping and rebalancing of stripe sets. By default, ASM also provides automated mirroring.

Host-based software

With host-based striping, logical volume–management software runs on the database server. Examples of this type of software include Hewlett Packard's Logical Volume Manager (LVM) and Veritas Software's Volume Manager, which act as an interface between the operating system that requests I/O and the underlying physical disks. The volume-management software groups disks into arrays, which are then seen by the operating system as single "disks." The actual disks are usually individual devices attached to controllers or disks contained in a prepackaged array containing multiple disks and controllers. This striping is handled by the volume-management software and is completely transparent to Oracle. Figure 6-1 illustrates host-based volume management.

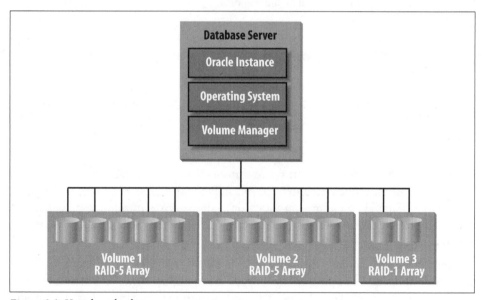

Figure 6-1. Host-based volume management

Oracle9i Release 2 introduced its own volume manager for Linux and Windows with the Real Application Clusters option. Oracle Database 10g includes a portable cluster filesystem and volume manager in the database that is leveraged by ASM.

Dedicated storage subsystems

Dedicated storage systems, often referred to as *disk farms*, contain disks, controllers, CPUs, and (usually) memory used as an I/O cache. Vendors include EMC, Hewlett-Packard (formerly Compaq) and Storagetek. These subsystems offload the task of managing the disk arrays from the database server. The I/O subsystem is attached to the server using controllers. These dedicated storage devices are sometimes grouped into *storage area networks* (SANs) to denote their logical organization as a separate set of networked devices. The disk arrays are defined and managed within the dedicated I/O subsystem, and the resulting logical "disks" are seen by the operating system as physical disks.

This type of disk-volume management is completely transparent to the database server and offers many benefits:

- The database server does not spend CPU resources managing the disk arrays.
- The I/O subsystem uses memory for an I/O cache, so the performance of Oracle I/O can improve dramatically (for example, from an average I/O time of 10–12 milliseconds to 3–5 milliseconds).
- Write I/O is completed as soon as the data has been written to the subsystem's cache.
- The I/O subsystem will de-stage the data from cache to actual disk later.
- Read I/O can be satisfied from the cache. The subsystem can employ some type of algorithm to sense I/O patterns and preload the cache in anticipation of pending read activity.

Note that you must back up the cache with some type of battery so a power failure doesn't result in the loss of data that was written to the cache, but hasn't yet been de-staged to the physical disk. Otherwise, data that Oracle assumes made it to disk may be lost, thereby potentially corrupting the database. Figure 6-2 illustrates a database server with a dedicated I/O subsystem.

Combined host-based and I/O subsystem volume management

In this configuration, disks are grouped into arrays within the I/O subsystem and grouped again into coarser arrays using operating system volume management. On EMC systems, for example, the physical disks are grouped into either RAID-1 mirrored disk pairs or into a RAID-S striped configuration using four disks per stripe set. RAID-S is the term EMC (*http://www.emc.com*) uses for their specialized striping hardware and software.

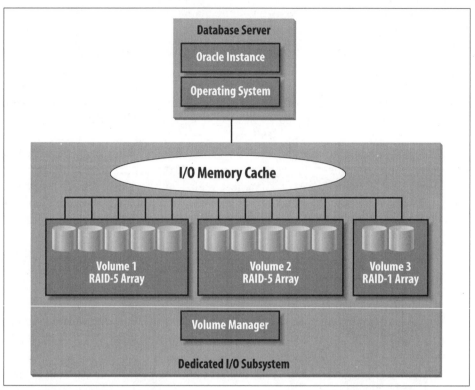

Figure 6-2. Dedicated I/O subsystems

Using EMC technology as an example, the operating system sees horizontal sections of disk space across each RAID-1 disk or RAID-S array as single "disks." You can use the operating system volume management to group these "disks" into arrays. With RAID-1 disks, this configuration delivers the benefits of using a dedicated I/O subsystem with its own cache and processing power while leveraging striping for simplicity. With RAID-S arrays you get the benefit of the dedicated I/O subsystem and further simplify disk management by a striping multiplier effect. An array of five "disks" at the operating system level could map back to five arrays of four disks each in the I/O subsystem. This configuration maps a logical disk seen by Oracle to 20 physical disks in the underlying I/O subsystem. Figure 6-3 illustrates a logical drive on the database server mapping to horizontal sections across multiple RAID-S arrays.

Flexibility, Manageability, and Disk Arrays

Many systems today use some type of RAID technology that groups multiple individual disk drives, also referred to as *spindles*, into arrays. Each disk array is then treated as a single logical disk for the purpose of planning I/O. Striping allows you to simply spread I/O across multiple disks, without incurring the planning and admin-

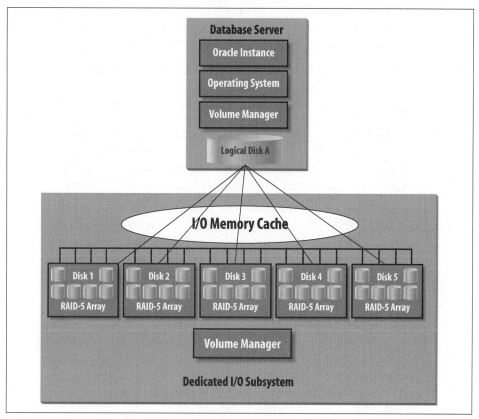

Figure 6-3. Combining host-based striping and an EMC I/O subsystem

istrative overhead of dealing with many individual disk drives. Striping is transparent to Oracle, but this doesn't mean that a DBA or system administrator can ignore it. Understanding the mapping of Oracle database files to arrays, and the arrays to the underlying disks and controllers, is crucial to planning and maintaining your Oracle database.

The decision about how many disks should be in each array is often the topic of intense debate. At one extreme, using multiple disks without grouping any of them into arrays provides the most control and flexibility because every disk is visible and can be targeted in isolation by placing certain files on each disk. However, this approach requires more planning and can result in more ongoing administration, because you will have to deal with every individual disk drive. As databases become larger and larger, this approach becomes unmanageable.

At the other extreme, you can group all disks into one single array, seen by the operating system and Oracle as a single "disk." This makes for extremely simple planning and administration; no effort is required to analyze where you should place the various files, as there is only one "disk." However, this approach sacrifices flexibility and leads to brute force solutions to I/O bottlenecks. If I/O performance across the array is unsatisfactory, the solution is to add more controllers and disks. The entire set of disks becomes a black box that either works or doesn't work as a unit.

The most useful configuration is one that balances manageability with flexibility. For example, consider a system with 1,000 disks. Neither a single array of 1,000 disks nor a set of 1,000 individual disks is likely to be appropriate. Perhaps 50 arrays of 20 disks each would provide the needed I/O performance without any undue administrative burden. If less flexibility is needed, 20 arrays of 50 disks are more suitable. On the other hand, grouping all the disks into one array may be the simplest way to manage a system with only five disks. For the 'right' answer, you must assess your needs to determine the appropriate balance.

Oracle Database 10g simplifies this debate by automating the striping and stripe set rebalancing process. ASM divides files into 1 MB extents and spreads the extents evenly across each disk group. Pointers are used to track placement of each extent (instead of using a mathematical function such as a hashing algorithm to stripe the data). So when the disk group configuration changes, individual extents can be moved. In comparison to traditional algorithm-based striping techniques, the need to rerun that algorithm and reallocate all of the data is eliminated. Extent maps are updated when rebalancing the load after a change in disk configuration, opening a new database file, or extending a database file by enlarging tablespace. By default, each 1 MB extent is also mirrored, so management of redundancy is also simplified. Mirroring can be extended to triple mirroring or can be turned off. Although you still have to consider how many disk groups to use, implementation of these groups with striping and redundancy is automated with ASM.

How Oracle I/O and Striped Arrays Interact

In almost all large databases, some type of disk striping increases disk I/O rates without adding too heavy an administrative burden for managing a large number of datafiles across many individual disks. The disks may be organized into RAID arrays using a volume manager on the database server, a dedicated I/O subsystem, or a combination of both.

If you are using an Oracle release without ASM, when you set up striped disk arrays, you can set the *chunk size* used to stripe across the disks. The chunk size is the amount of data written to one disk before moving to the next disk in the array. Understanding the interaction between different stripe chunk sizes and the two sizes of Oracle I/O is critical in maximizing your I/O performance.

Consider an Oracle database with an 8 KB data block size and the DB_FILE_ MULTIBLOCK_READ_COUNT initialization parameter set to 32. There will be two sizes of I/O by Oracle: a single 8 KB data block and a 256 KB multiblock read (32 times 8 KB). Suppose you then configure a four-disk array for use by Oracle with a chunk size of 64 KB so that the 256 KB of data will be spread across the four drives, with 64 KB on each.

Each 8-KB I/O will hit one spindle, as the 8 KB will lie within one 64-KB chunk.* Striping can increase performance for small I/Os by maximizing concurrency: each disk can service a different I/O. The multiblock I/Os of 256 KB may hit all four disks. If the chunk size was 256 KB instead of 64 KB, on average each 256-KB I/O call would hit one disk. In this case, the multiblock I/O will require fewer I/O calls with a larger chunk size on the disks. In either case, a single disk will clearly satisfy single-data-block I/O calls. Striping can increase I/O rates for large reads by driving multiple disks with a single I/O call, as illustrated with a 64-KB chunk size and a 256-KB multiblock I/O.

Figure 6-4 illustrates the interaction of different-sized Oracle I/Os with arrays striped using different chunk sizes.

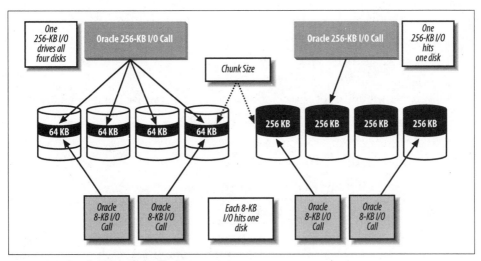

Figure 6-4. Oracle I/O and chunk size interaction

Oracle and Parallelism

The ability to parallelize operations is one of the most important features of the Very Large Database (VLDB). Database servers with multiple CPUs, which are called *symmetric multiprocessing* (SMP) machines, are the norm today for most database serv-

---

* It's difficult to say exactly what will occur due to the alignment of the stripe-chunk boundaries with Oracle data blocks, but to illustrate the single versus multiple disk point, let's assume the simple case—they line up! For a more detailed discussion of striping issues, see the document "Configuring Oracle Server for VLDB," by Cary Millsap of hotsos.com, formerly with Oracle Corporation (see Appendix B). Anyone who is tempted is welcome to perform detailed testing for all the permutations of stripe chunk size and Oracle I/O. If you happen to perform this extensive testing, please tell all the rest of us what you find!

ers. As performance demands increase and data volumes continue to grow, you will increasingly need to use multiple processors and disks to reduce the time needed to complete a given task. Oracle supports parallelism within a single SMP server as well as parallelism across multiple nodes, using Oracle Parallel Server/Real Application Clusters. Executing a SQL statement in parallel will consume more of all three machine resources—CPU, memory, and disk I/O—but complete the overall task faster.

Parallelism affects the amount of memory and CPU resources used to execute a given task in a fairly linear fashion—the more parallel processes used, the more resources consumed for the composite task. Each parallel execution process has a Program Global Area (PGA) that consumes memory and performs work. Each parallel execution process takes its own slice of CPU, but more parallel processes can reduce the total amount of time spent on disk I/O, which is the place in which bottlenecks can most readily appear.

Two types of parallelism are possible within an Oracle database:

Block-range parallelism
Driven by ranges of database blocks

Partition-based parallelism
Driven by the number of partitions or subpartitions involved in the operation

The following sections describe these types of parallelism.

Block-Range Parallelism

In 1994, Oracle 7.1 introduced the ability to dynamically parallelize table scans and a variety of scan-based functions. This parallelism was based on the notion of *block ranges*, in which the Oracle server would understand that each table contained a set of data blocks that spanned a defined range of data. Oracle7 implemented block-range parallelism by dynamically breaking a table into pieces, each of which was a range of blocks, and then used multiple processes to work on these pieces in parallel. Oracle's implementation of block-range parallelism was unique in that it didn't require physically partitioned tables to achieve parallelism.

With block-range parallelism, the client session that issued the SQL statement transparently becomes the parallel execution coordinator, dynamically determining block ranges and assigning them to a set of parallel execution (PE) processes. Once a PE process has completed an assigned block range, it returns to the coordinator for more work. Not all I/O occurs at the same rate, so some PE processes may process more blocks than others. This notion of "stealing work" allows all processes to participate fully in the task, providing maximum leverage of the machine resources.

Block-range parallelism scales linearly based on the number of PE processes, provided you have adequate hardware resources. The key to achieving scalability with parallelism lies in hardware basics. Each PE process runs on a CPU and requests I/O to a device. If you have enough CPUs reading enough disks, parallelism will scale. If the system encounters a bottleneck on one of these resources, scalability will suffer. For example, four CPUs reading two disks will not scale much beyond the two-way scalability of the disks and may even sink below this level if the additional CPUs cause contention for the disks. Similarly, 2 CPUs reading 20 disks will not scale to a 20-fold performance improvement. The system hardware must be balanced for parallelism to scale.

Most large systems have far more disks than CPUs. In these systems, parallelism results in a randomization of I/O across the I/O subsystem. This is useful for concurrent access to data as PE processes for different users read from different disks at different times, resulting in I/O that is distributed across the available disks.

A useful analogy for dynamic parallelism is eating a pie. The pie is the set of blocks to be read for the operation, and the goal is to eat the pie as quickly as possible using a certain number of people. Oracle serves the pie in helpings, and when a person finishes his first helping, he can come back for more. Not everyone eats at the same rate, so some people will consume more pie than others. While this approach in the real world is somewhat unfair, it's a good model for parallelism because if everyone is eating all the time, the pie will be consumed more quickly. The alternative is to give each person an equal serving and wait for the slower eaters to finish.

Figure 6-5 illustrates the splitting of a set of blocks into ranges.

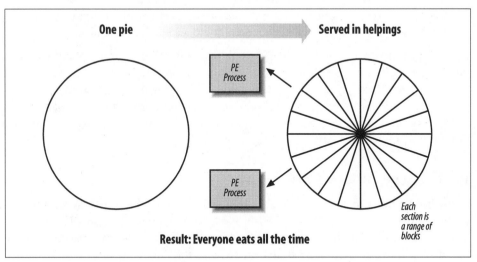

Figure 6-5. Dynamic block-range parallelism

Parallelism for Tables and Partitions of Tables

With *partitioned tables*, introduced in Oracle8, an operation may involve one, some, or all of the partitions of a partitioned table. There is essentially no difference in how block-range parallelism dynamically splits the set of blocks to be read for a regular table as opposed to a partitioned table. Once the optimizer has determined which partitions should be accessed for the operation, all the blocks of all partitions involved are treated as a pool to be broken into ranges.

This assumption by the optimizer leads to a key consideration for using parallelism and partitioned tables. The degree of parallelism (i.e., the number of parallel execution processes used for the table as a whole) is applied to the set of partitions that will be used for an operation. The optimizer will eliminate the use of partitions that do not contain data an operation will use. For instance, if one of the partitions for a table contains ID numbers below 1,000, and if a query requests ID numbers between 1,100 and 5,000, the optimizer understands that this query will not access this partition.

Since Oracle9*i*, you can also partition tables based on a list of specific values, although this type of partitioning is typically used to partition tables for maintenance operations.

The use of a subset of partitions has important implications for setting a degree of parallelism that provides good scalability for queries that scan some versus all of a table's partitions. A level of parallelism that may be good for the partitioned table as a whole may cause I/O contention for a query that accesses only one partition stored on fewer disks, as multiple parallel processes try to access the same disk.

If you expect that your queries will use partition elimination or pruning and you plan on using parallelism, you should stripe each partition over a sufficient number of drives to scale effectively. This will ensure scalability regardless of the number of partitions accessed. This striping can be achieved manually through the use of multiple datafiles on multiple disks, through the use of striped arrays, or through a combination of both approaches.

What Can Be Parallelized?

Many people think that Oracle can parallelize only simple table scans. While the parallelization of a table scan is involved in most parallelized operations, Oracle actually can parallelize far more than simple scans. The list of operations that can be parallelized using block-range parallelism includes the following:

- Tablespace creation
- Index creation and rebuilds
- Online index reorganizations and rebuilds
- Index organized table reorganizations and movements

- Table creation, such as summary creation using CREATE TABLE...AS SELECT
- Partition-maintenance operations, such as moving and splitting partitions
- Data loading
- Imposing integrity constraints
- Statistics gathering (automatically gathered in Oracle Database 10*g*)
- Backups and restores
- DML operations (INSERT, UPDATE, DELETE)
- Query processing operations

The specific features of query processing that may be parallelized include:

- Table scans
- Nested loops
- Sort merge joins
- Hash joins
- Bitmap star joins
- Index scans
- Partition-wise joins
- Anti-joins (NOT IN)
- SELECT DISTINCT
- UNION and UNION ALL
- ORDER BY
- GROUP BY
- Aggregations
- User-defined functions

Oracle Database 10*g* has added the ability to run the OLAP AGGREGATE statement and the Import utility in parallel.

Controlling Oracle's Parallel Resource Usage

An Oracle instance has a pool of parallel execution (PE) processes that are available to the database users. Controlling the maximum number of active PE processes is important; too many PE processes will overload the machine, leading to resource bottlenecks and performance degradation. The pool of PE processes is governed by the following two initialization parameters:

PARALLEL_MIN_SERVERS
> A number that acts as a floor for the pool of PE processes. When the instance is started, it will spawn this number of PE processes. A typical value is twice the number of CPUs.

PARALLEL_MAX_SERVERS

A number that acts as a ceiling for the pool of PE processes. As users request parallel operations, the instance will spawn additional PE processes up to this value. This limits the maximum parallel activity on the system and can be used to avoid overloading the machine. The effective ceiling for a given machine will vary. If the load decreases, the instance will gradually scale the pool back to PARALLEL_MIN_SERVERS.

A user session requests a number of PE processes from the pool based on the degree of parallelism for the operation the session is performing.

Setting the degree of parallelism

The degree of parallelism governs how many parallel-execution processes can be used for a given operation. The degree of parallelism is determined in three mutually exclusive ways:

1. If a table has default parallelism enabled using ALTER TABLE *tablename* PARALLEL, the optimizer will set the degree of parallelism automatically. In Oracle 7.3 and 8.0.3, default parallelism was set to the minimum of two values: the number of CPUs in the machine or the number of distinct devices used to store the table.* Based on customer feedback, in Oracle 8.0.4 (and subsequent releases) default parallelism defaults to the number of CPUs to recognize the prevalent use of striped disk arrays. Large tables in which parallelism is useful are typically stored on one or more striped disk arrays so that the resulting number of actual spindles used is greater then the number of CPUs. CPU count represents a more realistic value for default parallelism.

2. You can set the parallelism for a table to an explicit value using ALTER TABLE *tablename* PARALLEL N, where N is the desired degree of parallelism. This technique is useful where you want to override the optimizer's default value because of hardware characteristics. For example, you should set the parallelism if the machine can handle a degree of twice the number of CPUs for a particular table.

3. You can override any table-level setting and explicitly set the degree using the PARALLEL optimizer hint for queries or the PARALLEL clause, which is valid for some statements, such as CREATE INDEX or CREATE TABLE AS SELECT. This is useful if you want to use more resources for a particular task, such as an index build, but leave the degree of parallelism for other operations unchanged.

---

* If you use operating-system or disk-subsystem striping to stripe a datafile over more than one disk, this striped datafile presents itself to Oracle as a single datafile on a single device. Using a single array of five disks will not equate to five devices for default parallelism. Using five datafiles, each on a separate array, will. So, take care when using default parallelism and transparent or OS-level disk striping in these earlier Oracle versions.

Intra-operation parallelism

For any operation involving more than one step, such as a scan and sort, a degree of parallelism of *N* will actually use 2 x *N* PE processes, one set per suboperation. For example, *N* scanner processes will feed *N* sorter processes. At the end of the overall task, the coordinator combines the results from the separate PE processes. Figure 6-6 illustrates transparent parallelism within and between sets of PE processes.

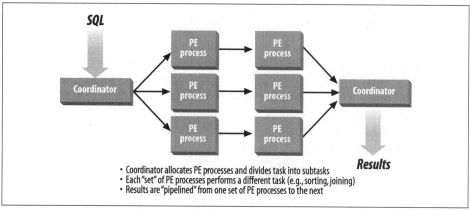

Figure 6-6. Intra-operation and inter-operation parallelism

Adaptive Parallelism

Determining the optimal degree of parallelism in the presence of multiple users and varying workloads has proven challenging. For example, a degree of 8 for a query may provide excellent performance for 1 or 2 users, but what if 20 users query the same table? This scenario would call for 160 PE processes (8 PEs for each of the 20 users), which could overload the machine. Setting the degree to a lowest common denominator value (for example, 2) provides effective parallelism for higher user counts, but does not leverage resources fully when fewer users are active.

Oracle8*i* introduced the notion of *self-tuning adaptive parallelism*. This feature automatically scales down parallelism as the system load increases and scales it back up as the load decreases. When an operation requests a degree of parallelism, Oracle will check the system load and lower the actual degree the operation uses to avoid overloading the system. As more users request parallel operations, the degree they receive will become lower and lower until operations are executing serially. If activity decreases, subsequent operations will be granted increasing degrees of parallelism. This adaptability frees the DBA from the difficult task of trying to determine the optimal degree of parallelism in the face of constant changes in workload.

Adaptive parallelism takes two factors into account in determining the degree of parallelism granted to an operation:

- System load.

- Parallelism resource limitations of the user's consumer group if the Database Resource Manager is active. (The Database Resource Manager is described later in this chapter.) This is important, because it means that adaptive parallelism respects resource plans if they're in place.

The following two initialization parameters enable adaptive parallelism:

PARALLEL_AUTOMATIC_TUNING
When set to TRUE, enables the adaptive parallelism feature.

PARALLEL_MIN_PERCENT
Determines what percentage of the requested parallelism an operation must be granted. For example, suppose this parameter were set to 50 and an operation requested a degree of 8. If Oracle grants the operation a degree of 4, the operation will continue as it received the minimum 50% of the requested degree of parallelism. If Oracle grants a degree less than 4, which would be less than 50% of the requested degree of 8, an error will be returned to the user. If you are using adaptive parallelism, set PARALLEL_MIN_PERCENT to 0 to allow Oracle to scale parallelism down as needed.

Partition-Based Parallelism

A small subset of Oracle's parallel functionality is based on the number of partitions or subpartitions accessed by the statement to be parallelized. For block-range parallelism, the piece of data each PE process works on is a range of blocks. For partition-based parallelism, the pieces of data that drive parallelism are partitions or subpartitions of a table. The operations in which parallelism is based on the number of partitions or subpartitions include the following:

- Updates and deletes
- Index scans
- Index creation and rebuilds on partitioned tables

Parallelism for partitions and subpartitions of a table

Oracle8 introduced support for parallel Data Manipulation Language (DML), or the ability to execute INSERT, UPDATE, and DELETE statements in parallel. This type of parallelism improves the performance of large bulk operations (for example, an update to all the rows of a very large table).

In Oracle8 the degree of parallelism for updates and deletes is tied to the number of partitions involved, while in Oracle8*i* and beyond the degree of parallelism for updates and deletes is tied to the number of partitions or subpartitions involved. A table with 12 partitions (for example, one partition for each month of the year) can have a maximum degree of 12 for a parallel update or delete. An update to only one month of data would have no parallelism because it involves only one partition. If the table were created using Oracle's composite partitioning (for example, with 4 hash subpartitions by PRODUCT_ID within each month), the maximum degree of parallelism for the entire table would be 48, or 12 partitions with 4 subpartitions each. An update to one month of data could have a degree of 4 because each month contains four hash subpartitions. If the table is not partitioned, Oracle cannot perform updates or deletes in parallel.

Oracle8 and more recent releases can execute index creation, index rebuilds, and index scans for partitioned indexes in parallel using the same semantics as parallel DML: one PE process per partition or subpartition of the index.

Fast full index scans for nonpartitioned tables

People often assume that the Oracle database can parallelize index scans only if the target index is partitioned. Oracle 7.3 introduced the ability to perform parallel index scans on nonpartitioned indexes for a certain case. If the index scan operation were "unbounded," meaning that the entire index was going to be accessed to satisfy the query, then Oracle 7.3 and higher would use block-range parallelism to access the entire index in parallel. While Oracle can perform index scans for nonpartitioned indexes, this feature applies to a narrow set of queries. Partition-based index scans apply to a much broader range of queries.

Parallel insert for nonpartitioned and partitioned tables

Oracle can execute an INSERT statement of the form INSERT INTO *tableX* SELECT...FROM *tableY* in parallel for nonpartitioned and partitioned tables. Oracle uses a set of PE processes executing block-range parallelism for the SELECT portion of the INSERT statement. These PE processes pass the rows to a second set of PE processes, which insert the rows into the target table. The target table can be a nonpartitioned or partitioned table. Parallelism for an insert is not exactly block-range or partition-based.

Oracle and Memory Resources

Accessing information in memory is much faster than accessing information on a disk. An Oracle instance uses the database server's memory resources to cache the information accessed to improve performance. Oracle utilizes an area of shared memory called the System Global Area (SGA) and a private memory area for each server process called the Program Global Area (PGA). Operating systems use virtual memory, which means that an Oracle instance can use more memory than is physically available on the machine.

Prior to Oracle9*i*, you could specify the size for the SGA or any of its components—database buffer cache, shared pool, or large pool—only in the initialization file, and the size of these memory allocations could not be changed without shutting down and restarting the instance. Oracle9i enabled dynamic resizing of these pools based on a minimum memory allocation called a *granule*. Oracle Database 10g automatically manages shared memory.

Exhausting a database server's supply of physical memory will cause poor performance. If you are running an older release of Oracle, you should gauge the size of the various memory areas Oracle uses or add more memory to the machine to prevent a memory deficit from occurring. What constitutes the right size for the various areas is a function of your application behavior, the data it uses, and your performance requirements.

How Oracle Uses the System Global Area

Oracle uses the SGA for the following operations:

- Caching of database blocks containing table and index data in the database buffer cache
- Caching of parsed and optimized SQL statements, stored procedures, and data dictionary information in the shared pool
- Buffering of redo log entries in the redo log buffer before they're written to disk

In versions prior to Oracle 9i, the amount of memory allocated to each of these areas within the SGA is determined at instance startup and cannot be altered without restarting the instance. The initialization parameters that allocate memory are:

DB_BLOCK_BUFFERS
    Specifies the number of database blocks the database buffer cache can contain

SHARED_POOL_SIZE
    Specifies the size of the shared pool, in bytes

LOG_BUFFER
    Specifies the size of the redo log buffer, in bytes

Of these three memory areas, the majority of tuning efforts focus on the database buffer cache and the shared pool.

The database buffer cache

Tuning the database buffer cache is relatively simple: You assess what percentage of the database blocks requested by users are read from the cache versus from the disk. This percentage is termed the *hit ratio*. If response times are too high and this ratio is lower than 90% (as a rule of thumb), increasing the value of the initialization parameter DB_BLOCK_BUFFERS may increase performance.

You can use the Oracle Enterprise Manager to get information about the cache hit ratio.

It's tempting to assume that continually increasing the size of the database buffer cache will translate into better performance. However, this is true only if the database blocks in the cache are actually being reused. Most OLTP systems have a relatively small set of core tables that are heavily used (for example, lookup tables for things such as valid codes). The rest of the I/O tends to be random, accessing a row or two in various database blocks in the course of the transaction. Because of this, having a larger buffer cache may not contribute to performance because there isn't much reuse of data blocks occurring.

In addition, not all operations read from the database buffer cache. For example, large full-table scans are limited to a small number of buffers to avoid adversely impacting other users by dominating the cache. If your application performs a lot of table scans, increasing the buffer cache may not help performance because the cache will not contain the needed data blocks. Parallel table scans completely bypass the buffer cache and pass rows directly to the requesting user process. As with most performance issues, your understanding of how your application is actually using your data is the key that will help guide your database buffer-cache tuning.

The shared pool

The shared pool is used at several points during the execution of every operation that occurs in an Oracle database. For example, the shared pool is accessed to cache the SQL sent to the database and for the data dictionary information required to execute the SQL. Because of its central role in database operations, a shared pool that is too small may have a greater impact on performance than a database buffer cache that is too small. If the requested database block isn't in the database buffer cache, Oracle will perform an I/O to retrieve it, resulting in a one-time performance hit. A shared pool that is too small will cause poor performance for a variety of reasons affecting all users. These reasons include the following:

- Not enough data dictionary information can be cached, resulting in frequent disk access to query and update the data dictionary.
- Not enough SQL can be cached, leading to memory "churn," or the flushing of useful statements to make room for incoming statements. A well-designed application issues the same statements repeatedly. If there isn't enough room to cache all the SQL the application uses, the same statements get parsed, cached, and flushed over and over, wasting valuable CPU resources and adding overhead to every transaction.

- Not enough stored procedures can be cached, leading to similar memory churn and performance issues for the program logic stored and executed in the database.

Once you've diagnosed which of these problems is occurring, the solution is fairly simple: increase the size of the shared pool. Shared pool sizes in the 150–250 MB range are not uncommon for large, active databases. For more information about examining shared pool activity to identify problems, see the appropriate *Oracle Tuning Guide*, as well as the third-party books listed in Appendix B.

The redo log buffer

While the redo log buffer consumes a very small amount of memory in the SGA relative to the database buffer cache and the shared pool, it's critical for performance. Transactions performing changes to the data in the database write their redo information to the redo log buffer in memory. The redo log buffer is flushed to the redo logs on disk when a transaction is committed or when the redo log buffer is one-third full. Oracle "fences" off the portion of the redo log buffer that's being flushed to disk to make sure that its contents aren't changed until the information is safely on disk. Transactions can continue to write redo information to the rest of the redo log buffer (the portion that isn't being written to disk and therefore isn't fenced off by Oracle). In a busy database, transactions may generate enough redo to fill the remaining unfenced portion of the redo log buffer before the I/O to the disks for the fenced area of the redo log buffer is complete. If this happens, the transactions will have to wait for the I/O to complete because there is no more space in the redo log buffer. This situation can impact performance. The ratio that detects this waiting is calculated using system statistics from the dynamic performance view V$SYSSTAT as:

```
redo log space requests / redo entries
```

As a general rule, if this ratio is greater than 1:5,000 you should increase the size of the redo log buffer. You can keep increasing the size of the redo log buffer until the ratio does not get any lower.

Alternatively, the statistic "redo buffer allocation retries" can be used. It is also available through V$SYSSTAT and is an indication of how often a session waited for space in the redo log buffer. An example of the query you may use to obtain the statistic is:

```
SELECT name, value FROM V$SYSSTAT
   WHERE name = 'redo buffer allocation retries';
```

You should monitor these statistics over a period of time to gain insight into the trend. The values at one point in time reflect the cumulative totals since the instance was started, and aren't necessarily meaningful as a single data point. Note that this is true for all statistics used for performance tuning. Ideally, the value of "redo buffer allocation retries" should be close to 0. If you observe the value rising during the monitoring period, you should increase the size of the redo log buffer.

Automatic sizing for the SGA

Oracle Database 10*g* helps to eliminate tuning SGA pools with automatic sizing for the SGA. The database automatically allocates memory for each of the SGA pools, and you only have to specify the total amount of memory required by setting the SGA_TARGET parameter. Oracle Database 10*g* proactively monitors the memory requirements for each pool and dynamically reallocates memory when appropriate. You can still specify the minimum amount of memory for any of the SGA pools while using automatic SGA sizing. A few SGA pools, including the Keep cache, Recycle cache, Streams cache and caches for nonstandard database block sizes, are still manually sized.

How Oracle Uses the Program Global Area

Each server has a Program Global Area (PGA), which is a private memory area that contains information about the work the server process is performing. There is one PGA for each server process. The total amount of memory used for all the PGAs is a function of the number of server processes active as part of the Oracle instance. The larger the number of users, the higher the number of server processes and the larger the amount of memory used for their associated PGAs. Using the Multi-Threaded Server (known as shared servers from Oracle9*i* on) reduces total memory consumption for PGAs because it reduces the number of server processes.

The PGA consists of a working memory area for things such as temporary variables used by the server process, memory for information about the SQL the server process is executing, and memory for sorting rows as part of SQL execution. The initial size of the PGA's working memory area for variables, known as *stack space*, cannot be directly controlled because it is predetermined based on the operating system you are using for your database server. The other areas within the PGA can be controlled as described in the following sections.

Memory for SQL statements

When a server process executes a SQL statement for a user, the server process tracks the session-specific details about the SQL statement and the progress by executing it in a piece of memory in the PGA called a *private SQL area*, also known as a *cursor*. This area should not be confused with the shared SQL area within the shared pool. The shared SQL area contains shareable details for the SQL statement, such as the optimization plan. Optimizers and optimization plans are discussed in Chapter 4.

The private SQL area contains the session-specific information about the execution of the SQL statement within the session, such as the number of rows retrieved so far.

Once a SQL statement has been processed, its private SQL area can be reused by another SQL statement. If the application reissues the SQL statement whose private SQL area was reused, the private SQL area will have to be reinitialized.

Each time a new SQL statement is received, its shared SQL area must be located (or, if not located, loaded) in the shared pool. Similarly, the SQL statement's private SQL area must be located in the PGA or, if it isn't located, reinitialized by the server process. This reinitialization is relatively expensive in terms of CPU resources.

A server process with a PGA that can contain a higher number of distinct private SQL areas will spend less time reinitializing private SQL areas for incoming SQL statements. If the server process doesn't have to reuse an existing private SQL area to accommodate a new statement, the private SQL area for the original statement can be kept intact. Although similar to a larger shared pool, a larger PGA avoids memory churn within the private SQL areas. Reduced private SQL area reuse, in turn, reduces the associated CPU consumption, increasing performance. There is, of course, a trade-off between allocating memory in the PGA for SQL and overall performance.

OLTP systems typically have a "working set" of SQL statements that each user submits. For example, a user who enters car rental reservations uses the same forms in the application repeatedly. Performance will be improved if the user's server process has enough memory in the PGA to cache the SQL those forms issue. Application developers should also take care to write their SQL statements so that they can be easily reused, by specifying bind variables instead of different hard-coded values in their SQL statements. This technique is discussed in more detail in Chapter 8.

The number of private SQL areas, and therefore the amount of memory in the PGA they consume, is determined by the intialization parameter OPEN_CURSORS. You should set this parameter based on the SQL your application submits, the number of active users, and the available memory on the server.

Memory for sorting within the PGA

Each server process uses memory in its PGA for sorting rows before returning them to the user. If the memory allocated for sorting is insufficient to hold all the rows that need to be sorted, the server process sorts the rows in multiple passes called *runs*. The intermediate runs are written to the temporary tablespace of the user, which reduces sort performance because it involves disk I/O.

Sizing the sort area of the PGA is a critical tuning point. A sort area that's too small for the typical amount of data requiring sorting will result in temporary tablespace disk I/O and reduced performance. A sort area that's significantly larger than necessary will waste memory. The correct value for the sort area depends on the amount of sort activity performed on behalf of your application, the size of your user population, and the available memory on the database server. The sort area is determined by the following initialization parameters, which can be modified dynamically at the system and session level without restarting the instance:

SORT_AREA_SIZE

Specifies the maximum amount of memory a server process can use for sorting before using the temporary tablespace stored on disk.

SORT_AREA_RETAINED SIZE

Specifies the lower bound on sort memory that the server process will retain after completing sorts. Setting this parameter equal to SORT_AREA_SIZE means that each server process will eventually allocate and hold memory in the PGA equal to SORT_AREA_SIZE. Setting SORT_AREA_RETAINED_SIZE to a value lower than SORT_AREA_SIZE will reduce total memory consumption, and server processes will release memory after completing sorts, freeing memory up for use by other processes. If most sorts use the maximum amount of memory as defined by SORT_AREA_SIZE, you can set SORT_AREA_RETAINED_SIZE to the same value. This avoids shrinking and growing the sort memory repeatedly.

Each parallel execution process allocates its own sort area. So, if SORT_AREA_SIZE is 4 MB and you execute a query using a degree of parallelism of 8, the PE processes can allocate up to 32 MB of memory for sorting. Keep this in mind when setting the SORT_AREA_SIZE and degrees of parallelism to avoid unexpectedly high memory consumption.

Automatic sizing for the PGA

As with the SGA, Oracle Database 10g also provides automatic sizing for the PGA. You can set a parameter (WORKAREA_SIZE_POLICY) to tell the Oracle database to automatically allocate memory for the different PGA memory pools, based on the total amount of PGA memory allocated by the PGA_AGGREGATE_TARGET parameter. The allocation is based on the needs of the individual SQL statements. Using automatic sizing for the PGA eliminates the need to size individual portions of the PGA, such as SORT_SIZE_AREA.

Oracle and CPU Resources

The Oracle database shares the CPU(s) with all other software running on the server. If there is a shortage of CPU power, reducing Oracle or non-Oracle CPU consumption will improve the performance of all processes running on the server.

If all the CPUs in a machine are busy, the processes line up and wait for a turn to use the CPU. This is called a *run queue* because processes are waiting to run on a CPU. The busier the CPUs get, the longer processes can spend in this queue. A process in the queue isn't doing any work, so as the run queue gets longer, response times degrade.

 You can use the standard monitoring tools (and Enterprise Manager with Oracle Database 10g) for your particular operating system to check the CPU utilization for that machine.

Tuning CPU usage is essentially an exercise in tuning individual tasks: it reduces the number of commands required to accomplish the tasks and/or reduces the overall number of tasks to be performed. You can do this tuning through workload balancing, SQL tuning, or improved application design. This type of tuning requires insight into what these tasks are and how they're being executed.

As mentioned earlier, an in-depth discussion of all the various tuning points for an Oracle database is beyond the scope of this book. However, there is a set of common tasks that typically result in excess CPU consumption. Some of the usual suspects to examine if you encounter a CPU resource shortage on your database server include the following:

Bad SQL

Poorly written SQL is the number one cause of performance problems. An Oracle database attempts to optimally execute the SQL it receives from clients. If the SQL contained in the client applications and sent to the database is written so that the best optimization plan Oracle can identify is still inefficient, Oracle will consume more resources than necessary to execute the SQL. Tuning SQL can be a complex and time-consuming process because it requires an in-depth understanding of how Oracle works and what the application is trying to do. Initial examinations can reveal flaws in the underlying database design, leading to changes in table structures, additional indexes, and so on. Changing the SQL requires retesting and a subsequent redeployment of the application—until Oracle Database 10g.

Oracle Database 10g comes with a SQL Tuning Advisor, which can not only recognize poorly written SQL, but also create an optimizer plan to circumvent the problem and replace the standard optimization plan with the improved plan. With this capability, you can improve the performance of poorly written SQL without changing any code in the application.

Excessive parsing

As we discussed in the section "Memory for SQL statements," Oracle must parse every SQL statement before it is processed. Parsing is very CPU-intensive, involving a lot of data dictionary lookups to check that all the tables and columns referenced are valid. Complex algorithms and calculations estimate the costs of the various optimizer plans possible for the statement to select the optimal plan. If your application isn't using bind variables (discussed in Chapter 8), the database will have to parse every statement it receives. This excessive and unnecessary parsing is one of the leading causes of performance degradation. Another common cause is a shared pool that's too small, as discussed previously in the section "The shared pool." Keep in mind that you can avoid the creation of execution plans by using stored outlines, as described in Chapter 4. And, as of Oracle9*i*, you also have the ability to edit the hints that make up a stored outline.

Database workload

If your application is well designed and your database is operating at optimal efficiency, you may experience a shortage of CPU resources for the simple reason that your server doesn't have enough CPU power to perform all the work it's being asked to do. This shortage may be due to the workload for one database (if the machine is a dedicated database server) or to the combined workload of multiple databases running on the server. Underestimating the amount of CPU resources required is a chronic problem in capacity planning. Unfortunately, accurate estimates of the CPU resources required for a certain level of activity demands detailed insight into the amount of CPU power each transaction will consume and how many transactions per minute or second the system will process, both at peak and average workloads. Most organizations don't have the time or resources for the system analysis and prototyping required to answer these questions. This is perhaps why CPU shortages are so common, and why the equally common solution is to simply add more CPUs to the machine until the problem goes away. Real Application Clusters and the grid (described mainly in Chapter 14) are attempts to at least make adding more CPU horsepower easier.

Non-database workload

Not all organizations have the luxury of dedicating an entire machine to an Oracle database to ensure that all CPU resources are available for that database. Use operating system utilities to identify the top CPU consumers on the machine. You may find that non-Oracle processes are consuming the bulk of the CPU resources and adversely impacting database performance.

Database Resource Manager

The previous section described some of the ways that you can end up with poor performance through a lack of CPU resources. The Database Resource Manager (DRM), first introduced in Oracle8*i* and enhanced in Oracle9*i*, can help you automatically avoid some of these problems.

DRM works by leveraging consumer groups you've identified and enabling you to place limits on the amount of computer resources that can be used by that group. Implementing the DRM ensures that one group or member of a group does not end up using an excessive amount of any one resource, as well as acting to deliver guaranteed service levels for different sets of users.

The following DRM features can be combined to protect against poor performance:

Predicting resource utilization
> The DRM can leverage the query optimizer cost computations to predict the amount of resources that a given query will take and the query execution time. Note that, by default, the query optimizer uses a CPU + I/O cost model in Oracle Database 10g. In Oracle9i, the query optimizer used an I/O cost model based on single block reads.

Switching consumer groups
> The DRM can switch consumer groups dynamically. You might want to give a particular consumer group a high allocation of CPU resources. But if a single query from that group looks as if it will take up too many CPU resources and affect the overall performance of the machine, the consumer group can be switched to another group that has a smaller CPU allocation—for example, a consumer group designed for batch operations.

Limiting number of connections
> The DRM can limit the number of connections for any particular consumer group. If the limit on connections for a group has been reached and another connection request comes in, the connection request is queued until an existing connection is freed. By limiting the overall number of connections for a consumer group, you can place some rough limits on the overall resources that particular group might require.

Monitoring

We began this chapter by pointing out that, on one level, poor performance is easy to define—it occurs when the expectations of your user community, in terms of response time, are not met.

Of course, this is a situation you want to actively avoid. You can accomplish this by proactively monitoring potential sources of performance degradation. Oracle has a number of tools you can use to monitor resource usage and performance.

Dynamic Performance Views

The dynamic performance views mentioned earlier in this chapter are a key source of information about the operation of the Oracle database. Although Oracle supplies an increasing number of automatic and graphical methods for tracking and examining the same information, most of these tools use the V$ tables to obtain the data they need.

Enterprise Manager

Enterprise Manager (EM) was described in detail in Chapter 5, although certain features of EM are worth highlighting here in terms of their use in performance monitoring and tuning.

Enterprise Manager provides both high-level and detailed views of resource utilization for Oracle servers, and these can give a quick indication of the cause of performance problems. EM also has a complete system of alerts and thresholds, which can be set up to proactively inform you that a particular resource is nearing a critical usage level. Enterprise Manager includes a set of advisors, which can be run to give you suggestions on how to optimize performance in different areas, such as tuning SQL statements or suggesting new materialized views (both new in Oracle Database 10g.)

Enterprise Manager 10g has the ability to immediately spot the SQL statements that have used the most database resources and SQL statements that may not be fully optimized, as well as presenting the execution plan for these statements. These tools are handy for calling out specific statements that may be impacting the operation of the Oracle database environment.

Enterprise Manager 10g also includes a new type of performance analyzer called Application Performance Management (APM). APM gives you the ability to set up *beacons*, which are client processes that periodically execute transactions and report the response time. APM goes beyond the Oracle environment to help you understand performance from an end user's point of view, which can, in turn, help you to spot other sources of performance problems, such as network transmission slowdowns.

Automatic Workload Repository and Diagnostics

The Automatic Workload Repository (AWR) is a new feature in Oracle Database 10g. The AWR captures and stores information about resource utilization by Oracle workloads. By default, statistics are captured every 30 minutes and are stored for 7 days.

AWR helps Oracle Database 10g to identify potential performance issues by comparing workloads over time, and acts as the foundation for many of the manageability features in Oracle Database 10g, such as the Automatic Database Diagnostic Monitor (ADDM). The ADDM automatically identifies and reports on resource bottlenecks, such as CPU contention, locking issues, and poor performance from specific SQL statements.

Real Application Clusters and Performance

Oracle9*i* introduced an evolution of the Oracle Parallel Server (OPS) technology called Real Application Clusters. In the past, OPS had been primarily used for availability, because there were performance penalties for using OPS with OLTP and some other types of applications.

Real Application Clusters have eliminated these problems, making it possible for most applications to scale over a cluster of machines. Oracle claims that with Real Application Clusters, each new machine can add as much as 90% of the performance of the standalone machine. Even if this new technology doesn't reach these heights, you can still deploy the same application on a Real Application Cluster that you can on a single database server, with the capability of adding more nodes to the cluster, rather than upgrading your database server to increase overall throughput.

Oracle Database 10*g* has added cluster workload management, a feature that lets you specify how different services, or workloads, use the nodes in a cluster. Cluster workload management gives you the ability to provision the nodes in a cluster to different parts of the overall application workload.

Real Application Clusters are discussed in more detail in Chapter 8.

CHAPTER 7

Multiuser Concurrency

All information systems fulfill a single purpose: to collect, store, and retrieve information. As systems grow to handle many different users with many different needs, problems can arise as a result of the conflicting demands for concurrent access to the same data.

Concurrent user access is one of the most central and vexing issues for applications accessing data from databases. Implementing concurrent user access, or *concurrency*, can affect two of the most important facets of any application: the underlying integrity of the data and the performance of the application system.

As Ken Jacobs, Vice President at Oracle, put it in his classic paper entitled "Transaction Control and Oracle7," a multiuser database must be able to handle concurrently executing transactions in a way that "ensure(s) predictable and reproducible results." This goal is the core issue of data integrity, which, in turn, is the foundation of any database system.

As multiple users access the same data, there is always the possibility that one user's changes to a specific piece of data will be unwittingly overwritten by another user's changes. If this situation occurs, the accuracy of the information in the database is compromised, which can render the data useless or, even worse, misleading. At the same time, the techniques used to prevent this type of loss can dramatically reduce the performance of an application system, as users wait for other users to complete their work before continuing. These techniques act like a traffic signal, so you can't solve this type of performance problem by increasing the resources available to the database. The problem isn't due to a lack of horsepower—it's caused by a red light.

Although concurrency issues are central to the success of applications, they are some of the most difficult problems to predict because they can stem from such complex interactive situations. The difficulties posed by concurrent access continue to increase as the number of concurrent users increases. Even a robust debugging and testing environment may fail to detect problems created by concurrent access, because these problems are created by large numbers of users who may not be available in a test environment. Concurrency problems can also pop up as user access patterns change throughout the life of an application.

If the problems raised by concurrent access aren't properly handled by the underlying database software, developers may find themselves suffering in a number of ways. They will have to create their own customized solutions to these problems in their software, which will consume valuable development time. They will frequently find themselves adding code during the late stages of development and testing to work around the underlying deficiencies in the database, which can alter the design of the application. Worst of all, they may find themselves changing the optimal design of their data structures to compensate for weaknesses in the capabilities of the underlying database.

There is only one way to deal successfully with the issues raised by concurrent data access. The database that provides the access must implement strategies to transparently overcome the potential problems posed by concurrent access. Fortunately, Oracle has excellent methods for handling concurrent access.

This chapter describes the basics of concurrent data access and gives you an overview of the way that Oracle handles the issues raised by concurrent access. If you've worked with large database systems in the past and are familiar with concurrent user access, you might want to skip the first section of this chapter.

Basics of Concurrent Access

To prepare you to deal with the problems posed by multiuser concurrent access to data, we'll review some of the basic concepts that relate to concurrency.

Transactions

The *transaction* is the bedrock of data integrity in multiuser databases and the foundation of all concurrency schemes. A transaction is defined as a single indivisible piece of work that affects some data. All of the modifications made to data within a transaction are uniformly applied to a database with a COMMIT statement, or the data affected by the changes is uniformly returned to its initial state with a ROLLBACK statement. Once a transaction is committed, the changes made by that transaction become permanent and are made visible to other transactions and other users.

Transactions always occur over time, although most transactions occur over a very short period of time. Because the changes made by a transaction aren't official until the transaction is committed, each individual transaction must be isolated from the effects of other transactions. The mechanism used to enforce transaction isolation is the lock.

Locks

A database uses a system of *locks* to prevent transactions from interfering with each other. Transactions can interfere with each other by allowing one transaction to change a piece of data that another transaction is also in the process of changing. Figure 7-1 illustrates a system without locks. Transaction A reads a piece of data; Transaction B reads the same piece of data and commits a change to the data. When Transaction A commits the data, its change unwittingly overwrites the changes made by Transaction B, resulting in a loss of data integrity.

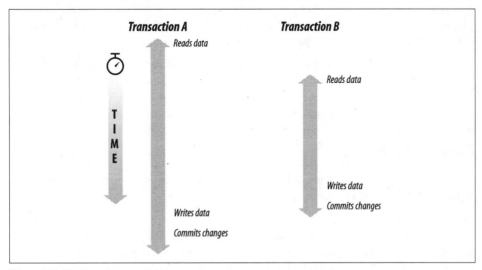

Figure 7-1. Transactions over time

Two types of locks are used to avoid this type of problem. The first is called a *write lock*, or an *exclusive lock*. An exclusive lock is applied and held while changes are made to data in the course of a transaction and released when the transaction is ended by either a COMMIT or a ROLLBACK statement. A write lock can be held by only one user at a time, so only one user at a time can change that data.

Some databases also use *read locks*, or *shared locks*. A read lock can be held by any number of users who are merely reading the data, because the same piece of data can be shared among many readers. However, a read lock prevents a write lock from being placed on the data, as the write lock is an exclusive lock. In Figure 7-1, if a read lock were placed on the data when Transaction A began, Transaction B would be able to read the same data but would be prevented from acquiring a write lock on the data until Transaction A ended.

Oracle uses read locks only when a SQL operation specifically requests them with the FOR UPDATE clause in a SELECT statement. You shouldn't use the FOR

UPDATE clause routinely because it unduly increases the probability that readers will interfere with writers—a situation that normally never occurs with Oracle, as you will see shortly.

Concurrency and Contention

The safeguards that enforce isolation between concurrent users of data can lead to their own problems if they're improperly implemented. As you can see from the example described above, a single transaction can cause significant performance problems as the locks it places on the database prevent other transactions from completing. The interference caused by conflicting locks is called *contention*. The more contention in a database, the slower the potential response times and throughput.

In most databases, increased concurrent access to data results in increased contention and decreased performance, in terms of both response time and throughput. Oracle's multiversion read concurrency scheme can greatly reduce contention, as you will see later in this chapter.

Integrity Problems

Some basic integrity problems can result if transaction isolation isn't enforced. Four of these problems are common to many databases:

Lost updates
> The most common type of integrity problem. Occur when two writers are both changing the same piece of data, and one writer's changes overwrite the other writer's changes. This is the problem that exclusive locks are designed to prevent.

Dirty reads
> Occur when a database allows a transaction to read data that has been changed by another transaction but hasn't been committed yet. The changes made by the transaction may be rolled back, so the data read may turn out to be incorrect. Many databases allow dirty reads to avoid contention caused by write locks.

Nonrepeatable reads
> Occur as a result of changes made by another transaction. One transaction makes a query based on a particular condition. After the data has been returned to the first transaction, but before the first transaction is complete, another transaction changes the data so that some of the previously retrieved data no longer satisfies the selection condition. If the query is repeated in the same transaction, it would return a different set of results, so any changes made on the basis of the original results may no longer be valid. Data that was read once can return different results if it's read again later in the same transaction.

Phantom reads

Also occur as a result of changes made by another transaction. One transaction makes a query based on a particular condition. After the data has been returned to the first transaction, but before the first transaction is complete, another transaction inserts into the database new rows that meet the selection criteria for the first transaction. If the transaction is making changes based on the assumption that the only rows that satisfied the condition were returned, a phantom read could result in improper data. Although all the data read by the first query is returned for the second query, additional data also should have been returned, so any changes made on the basis of the original results may no longer be valid.

Serialization

The goal of a complete concurrency solution is to provide the highest level of isolation between the actions of different users accessing the same data. As defined by the SQL92 standard, this highest level is called *serializable*. As the name implies, serializable transactions appear as though they have been executed in a series of distinct, ordered transactions. When one transaction begins, it is isolated from any changes that occur to its data from subsequent transactions.

To the user, a serializable transaction looks as though it has the exclusive use of the database for the duration of the transaction. Serializable transactions are predictable and reproducible, the two cardinal virtues of data integrity.

Of course, it's not trivial to have a database server support thousands of users while each one thinks he is the only one. But Oracle manages to pull off this quietly dramatic feat.

Oracle and Concurrent User Access

Oracle solves the problems created by concurrent access through a technology called *multiversion read consistency*, sometimes referred to as MVRC. Multiversion read consistency guarantees that a user sees a consistent view of the data she requests. If another user changes the underlying data during the query execution, Oracle maintains a version of the data as it existed at the time the query began. If there were transactions underway but uncommitted at the time the query began, Oracle will ensure that the query ignores the changes made by those transactions. The data returned to the query will reflect all committed transactions at the time the query started.

This feature has two dramatic effects on the way queries impact the database. First, Oracle doesn't place any locks on data for read operations. This means that a read operation will never block a write operation. Even if a database places a single lock on a single row as part of a read operation, it can still cause contention in the database, especially because most database tables tend to concentrate update operations around a few "hot spots" of active data.

Second, a user gets a complete "snapshot" view of the data, accurate at the point in time that the query began. Other databases may reduce the amount of contention in the database by locking an individual row only while it's being read, rather than over the complete duration of the row's transaction. A row that's retrieved at the end of a result set may have been changed since the time the result set retrieval began. Because rows that will be read later in the execution of the query weren't locked, they could be changed by other users, which would result in an inconsistent view of the data.

Oracle's Isolation Levels

Oracle, like many other databases, uses the concept of *isolation levels* to describe how a transaction will interact with other transactions and how it will be isolated from other transactions. An isolation level is essentially a locking scheme implemented by the database that guarantees a certain type of transaction isolation.

An application programmer can set an isolation level at the session level (ALTER SESSION) or transaction level (SET TRANSACTION). More restrictive isolation levels will cause more potential contention, as well as delivering increased protection against data integrity problems.

Two basic isolation levels are used frequently within Oracle: READ COMMITTED and SERIALIZABLE. (A third level, READ ONLY, is described later in this section.) Both of these isolation levels create serializable database operations. The difference between the two levels is in the duration for which they enforce serializable operations:

READ COMMITTED
    Enforces serialization at the statement level. This means that every statement will get a consistent view of the data as it existed at the start of that statement. However, because a transaction can contain more than one statement, it's possible that nonrepeatable reads and phantom reads can occur within the context of the complete transaction. The READ COMMITTED isolation level is the default isolation level for Oracle.

SERIALIZABLE
    Enforces serialization at the transaction level. This means that every statement within a transaction will get the same consistent view of the data as it existed at the start of the transaction.

Because of their differing spans of control, these two isolation levels also react differently when they encounter a transaction that blocks their operation with a lock on a requested row. Once the lock has been released by the blocking transaction, an operation executing with the READ COMMITTED isolation level will simply retry the operation. Because this operation is concerned only with the state of data when the statement begins, this is a perfectly logical approach.

On the other hand, if the blocking transaction commits changes to the data, an operation executing with a SERIALIZABLE isolation level will return an error indicating that it cannot serialize operations. This error makes sense, because the blocking transaction will have changed the state of the data from the beginning of the SERIALIZABLE transaction, making it impossible to perform any more write operations on the changed rows. In this situation, an application programmer will have to add logic to his program to return to the start of the SERIALIZABLE transaction and begin it again.

 There are step-by-step examples of concurrent access later this chapter (in the "Concurrent Access and Performance" section) that illustrate the different ways in which Oracle responds to this type of problem.

One other isolation level is supported by Oracle: you can declare that a session or transaction has an isolation level of READ ONLY. As the name implies, this level explicitly prohibits any write operations and provides an accurate view of all the data at the time the transaction began.

Oracle Concurrency Features

Three features are used by Oracle to implement multiversion read consistency:

Rollback segments
Rollback segments are structures in the Oracle database that store "undo" information for transactions in case of rollback. This information restores database rows to the state they were in before the transaction in question started. When a transaction starts changing some data in a block, it first writes the old image of the data to a rollback segment. The information stored in a rollback segment provides the information necessary to roll back a transaction and supports multiversion read consistency.

A rollback segment is different from a redo log. The redo log is used to log all transactions to the database and recover the database in the event of a system failure, while the rollback segment provides rollback for transactions and read consistency.

Blocks of rollback segments are cached in the System Global Area just like blocks of tables and indexes. If rollback segment blocks are unused for a period of time, they may be aged out of the cache and written to disk.

System Change Number (SCN)

To preserve the integrity of the data in the database, it's critical to keep track of the order in which actions were performed. Oracle must preserve the ordering of transactions with respect to time. The mechanism Oracle uses is the System Change Number.

The SCN is a logical timestamp that tracks the order in which events occurred. Oracle uses the SCN information in the redo log to reproduce transactions in the original and correct order when applying redo. Oracle also uses the SCN to determine when to clean up information in rollback segments that's no longer needed, as you will see in the following sections.

> In Oracle Database 10g, there is now a new pseudocolumn on each row that contains the SCN, ORA_ROWSCN. You can quickly determine if a row has been updated since it was retrieved by comparing the value read from this pseudocolumn at the start of a transaction with the value read from this pseudocolumn at the end of the transaction.

Locks in data blocks

A database must have a way of determining if a particular row is locked. Most databases keep a list of locks in memory, which are managed by a lock manager process. Oracle keeps locks with an area of the actual block in which the row is stored. A data block is the smallest amount of data that can be read from disk for an Oracle database, so whenever the row is requested, the block is read, and the lock is available within the block. Although the lock indicators are kept within a block, each lock affects only an individual row within the block.

In addition to the above features, which directly pertain to multiversion read consistency, another implementation feature in Oracle provides a greater level of concurrency in large user populations:

Nonescalating row locks

To reduce the overhead of the lock-management process, other databases will sometimes *escalate* locks to a higher level of granularity within the database. For example, if a certain percentage of rows in a table are locked, the database will escalate the lock to a table lock, which locks all the rows in a table including rows that aren't specifically used by the SQL statement in question. Although lock escalation reduces the number of locks the lock manager process has to handle, it causes unaffected rows to be locked. Because each row's lock is kept within its data block, there is never any need for Oracle to escalate a lock.

A lock manager called the Distributed Lock Manager (DLM) has historically been used with Oracle Parallel Server to track locks across multiple instances of Oracle. This is a completely different and separate locking scheme that doesn't affect the way Oracle handles row locks. The technology used in Oracle Parallel Server has been improved and renamed in Oracle9*i* as Real Application Clusters, and the technology used in the DLM has been integrated into the core of the product. Real Application Clusters are described in more detail in Chapter 8.

How Oracle Handles Locking

If you've read this chapter from the beginning, you should now know enough about the concepts of concurrency and the features of Oracle to understand how the database can handle multiuser access. However, to make it perfectly clear how these features interact, we'll walk you through three scenarios: a simple write to the database, a situation in which two users attempt to write to the same row in the same table, and a read that takes place in the midst of conflicting updates.

For the purposes of these examples, we'll use the scenario of one or two users modifying the EMP table, a part of the standard sample Oracle schema that lists data about employees via a form.

A Simple Write Operation

This example describes a simple write operation, in which one user is writing to a row in the database. In this example, an HR clerk wants to update the name for an employee. Assume that the HR clerk already has the employee record on-screen. The steps from this point are as follows:

1. The client modifies the employee name on the screen. The client process sends a SQL UPDATE statement over the network to the server process.

2. The server process obtains a System Change Number (SCN) and reads the data block containing the target row.

3. The server records row lock information in the data block.

4. The server process copies the old image of the employee data about to be changed to a rollback segment and then modifies the employee data, which includes writing the SCN to the ORA_ROWSCN pseudocolumn with Oracle Database 10*g*.

5. The server process records the changes to the rollback segment and the database block in the redo log buffer in the SGA. The rollback segment changes are part of the redo, because the redo log stores all changes resulting from the transaction.

6. The HR clerk commits the transaction.

7. Log Writer (LGWR) writes the redo information for the entire transaction, including the SCN that marks the time the transaction was committed, from the redo log buffer to the current redo log file on disk. When the operating system

confirms that the write to the redo log file has successfully completed, the transaction is considered committed.

8. The server process sends a message to the client confirming the commit.

A Conflicting Write Operation

The write operation previously described is a little different if there are two users, Client A and Client B, who are trying to modify the same row of data at the same time. The steps are as follows:

1. Client A modifies the employee name on the screen. Client A sends a SQL UPDATE statement over the network to the server process.

2. The server process obtains an SCN for the statement and reads the data block containing the target row.

3. The server records row lock information in the data block.

4. The server process then copies the old image of the employee data about to be changed to a rollback segment. Once the server process has written the old employee data to a rollback segment, the server process modifies the cached database block to change the employee name, which includes writing the SCN to the ORA_ROWSCN pseudocolumn with Oracle Database 10g.

5. The server process records the changes to the rollback segment and the database block in the redo log buffer in the SGA. The rollback segment changes are part of the redo, because the redo log stores all changes resulting from the transaction.

6. Client B modifies the employee name on the screen and sends a SQL UPDATE statement to the server.

7. The server process obtains an SCN and reads the data block containing the target row.

8. The server process sees that there is a lock on the target row from the information in the header of the data block, so it takes one of two actions. If the isolation level on Client B's transaction is READ COMMITTED, the server process waits for the blocking transaction to complete. If the isolation level for Client B's transaction is SERIALIZABLE, an error is returned to the client.

9. Client A commits the transaction, the server process takes the appropriate action, and the server sends a message to Client A confirming the commit.

10. If Client B executed the SQL statement with the READ COMMITTED isolation level, the SQL statement then proceeds through its normal operation.

The previous example illustrates the default behavior of Oracle when it detects a problem caused by a potential lost update. Because the SERIALIZABLE isolation level has a more drastic outcome when it detects a write conflict than the READ COMMITTED isolation level, many developers prefer the latter level. They can avoid some of the potential conflicts by checking for changes prior to issuing an update, by either comparing values in a row or using the Oracle Database 10g row SCN. Alternatively, they can use the SELECT FOR UPDATE syntax in their SQL to avoid the problem altogether.

A Read Operation

By looking at how a user reads data from the table, you can appreciate the beauty of Oracle's read consistency model. In this scenario, Client A is reading a series of rows from the EMP table, while Client B modifies a row before it is read by Client A, but after Client A begins her transaction:

1. Client A sends a SQL SELECT statement over the network to the server process.

2. The server process obtains an SCN for the statement and begins to read the requested data for the query. For each data block that it reads, it compares the SCN of the SELECT statement with the SCNs for any transactions that were uncommitted in the relevant rows of the data block. If the server finds an uncommitted transaction with a later SCN than the current SELECT statement, the server process uses data in the rollback segments to create a "consistent read" version of the data block, current as of the time the SELECT was issued. This is what provides the multiversion read consistency.

3. Client B sends a SQL UPDATE statement for a row in the EMP table that has not yet been read by Client A's SELECT statement. The server process gets an SCN for the statement and begins the operation.

4. Client B commits his changes. The server process completes the operation, which includes recording information in the data block that contained the modified row that allows Oracle to determine the SCN for the update transaction.

5. The server process for Client A's read operation comes to the newly modified block. It sees that the data block contains changes made by a transaction that has an SCN that is later than the SCN of the SELECT statement. The server process looks in the data block header, which has a pointer to the rollback segment that contains the data as it existed when Client A's transaction started. The rollback segment uses the old version of the data to create a version of the block as it existed when the SELECT statement started. Client A's SELECT statement reads the desired rows from this consistent version of the data block.

Figure 7-2 illustrates the process of reading with multiversion read consistency.

Concurrent Access and Performance

When you read through all the steps involved in the above processes, you may assume that Oracle would be a very slow database. This is not at all true. Oracle has

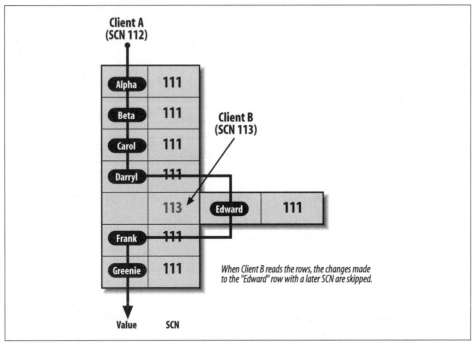

Client A
(SCN 112)

Alpha	111
Beta	111
Carol	111
Darryl	~~111~~
113	Edward	111
Frank	~~111~~
Greenie	111

Client B
(SCN 113)

When Client B reads the rows, the changes made
to the "Edward" row with a later SCN are skipped.

Value   SCN

Figure 7-2. Multiversion read consistency

consistently turned in benchmarks that make it one of the fastest databases, if not the fastest, on the market today.

Oracle provides good performance while implementing multiversion read consistency by minimizing and deferring unnecessary I/O operations. To assure the integrity of the data in a database, the database must be able to recover in the event of a system failure. This means that there must be a way to ensure that the data in the database accurately reflects the state of the committed data at the time of the crash. Oracle can do this by writing changed data to the database whenever a transaction commits. However, the redo log contains much less information than the entire data block for the changed data, so it's much "cheaper" to write to disk. Oracle writes the redo information to disk as soon as a transaction commits and defers writing the changed data blocks to the database until several sets of changed blocks can be written together. Oracle can restore the database using the redo logs, and these procedures cut down on time-consuming I/O operations.

However, when you're considering the performance of a database, you have to think about more than simple I/O operations. It doesn't really matter how fast your database runs if your transaction is waiting for another transaction to release a lock. A faster database may complete the blocking transaction faster, but your transaction is still at a dead stop until the blocking transaction completes. Because most databases perform a mixture of reading and writing, and because Oracle is the only database on the market that doesn't use read locks, Oracle will essentially always deliver the lowest amount of database contention. Less contention equals greater throughput for a mixed application load.

There is also more than one type of performance. Performance for database operations is measured in milliseconds; performance for application developers is measured in months. Because Oracle provides much less contention with its read consistency model, developers have to spend less time adding workarounds to their applications to handle the results of contention.

It's not as though Oracle is the only database to give you a concurrency solution you can use to implement applications that provide adequate data integrity. But the multiversion read consistency model makes it easy for you to get a consistent view of data without excessive contention and without having to write workarounds in your application. If it sounds as if we're big fans of Oracle's locking scheme, well—we are.

Workspaces

Oracle9i introduced a new feature that relates to concurrency, Workspace Manager.

Workspace Manager allows current, proposed, and historical versions of a row to exist together in the same table. It ensures that each user sees the appropriate version of a row along with the rest of the data in the database. For instance, a group may be working on a set of changes to an overall compensation package, but not want proposed changes to be seen until they have received final approval.

Workspace Manager uses workspaces to accomplish this. A *workspace* is a virtual environment that one or more users share to make changes to the data in the database. Users enter a workspace to make changes to data. A workspace logically groups collections of new row versions in one or more version-enabled tables, and isolates these versions until they are explicitly merged with production data or until they are discarded. A user in a workspace sees all of the data in the database, as it existed when the workspace was created or last refreshed, as well as the changes made from the workspace. Changes to data made from within a workspace are only visible to users within the workspace.

To use workspaces to version data in a table, you must first enable the table for versioning. Workspace Manager can version-enable one or more user tables in the database. The unit of versioning is a row. When a table is version-enabled, all rows in the table can support multiple versions of the data. Versioned rows are stored in the same table as the original rows. The versioning infrastructure is not visible to the users of the database, and application SQL statements to select, insert, modify, and delete data continue to work in the usual way with version-enabled tables. Workspace Manager version-enables a table by renaming the table, adding a few columns to the table to store versioning metadata, creating a view on the version-enabled table using the original table name and defining INSTEAD OF triggers on the view for SQL DML operations.

Savepoints are used to create new row versions, and allow users to roll back changes to rows in version-enabled tables and see the state of the database as it existed as of a particular milestone. Modifying a row after a savepoint is created causes a new version of that row to be created. Subsequent changes are applied to this new version in the workspace until another savepoint is created. Users can compare differences between any two savepoints.

A rollback operation deletes changes made in the workspace. A user can delete either all changes made since the workspace was created or only changes made after a savepoint. The user can limit the rollback to one or more version-enabled tables.

A table can be version-enabled with the history option. If the history option is specified, Workspace Manager adds a timestamp to the row version every time it is changed. The history option works with savepoints to provide a history of changes made to each row version created by a savepoint. This allows users in a workspace to go back to any point in time and view the entire database from the perspective of changes made in that workspace. The history option allows you to choose either to make a copy of the row version each time a change is made to it or to overwrite values in the row version with the most recent changes. If you keep all changes when version-enabling a table, you keep a persistent history of all changes made to all row versions in the table.

Workspaces can be organized into hierarchies, to implement cascading groups of changes. Child workspaces can be merged and refreshed with their parent workspace. Merging a workspace involves applying changes made in a child workspace to its parent workspace. Refreshing a workspace involves applying changes made in the parent workspace to a child workspace. With Oracle Database 10g, you can even allow a child workspace to have more than one parent workspace. This feature allows a user in the child workspace to see all of the changes made across all of the parent workspaces in one place before they are merged into production. A user can work in more than one workspace in a particular session. A user with workspace privileges can freeze access to a workspace to allow no access to the workspace, read-only access, or single-writer access.

You can choose to allow two or more workspaces to version the same row at the same time. This allows multiple proposals to be developed concurrently or to create multiple variations of a data scenario for "what-if" analysis. When a row is changed in both the child and parent workspace (usually through the merge of another child workspace into the parent), a data conflict is created. Conflicts can be checked and resolved at any time. Conflicts are automatically detected when a merge or refresh operation is requested. The list of conflicts is presented to the user in a conflict view. Conflicts are resolved manually using a Workspace Manager procedure. For each conflict, you can choose to keep the row from the child workspace, the row from the parent workspace, or the common base row's original data values. You must resolve conflicts before you can perform a merge or refresh operation.

Workspace Manager provides exclusive and shared version locks to prevent conflicts between workspaces. These locks eliminate row conflicts between a parent workspace and a child workspace. They can also be used to reserve rows you will be updating in the future. You can enable locking on a workspace, for a user session, on specified rows, or a combination of the three.

Workspace Manager is tightly integrated with the Oracle database. Oracle Database 10g Workspace Manager enhancements include the ability to export and import version-enabled tables, to use SQL*Loader to bulk load data into version-enabled tables, to trigger events based on workspace operations, and to define workspaces that are continually refreshed.

CHAPTER 8

Oracle and Transaction Processing

The insatiable corporate appetite for ever larger and more sophisticated transaction-processing systems has been one of the main forces driving the evolution of computing technology. As we discussed in the previous chapter, transactions form the foundation of business computing systems. In fact, transaction processing (TP) was the impetus for business computing as we know it today. The batch-oriented automation of core business processes like accounting and payroll drove the progress in mainframe computing through the 1970s and 1980s. Along the way, TP began the shift from batch to users interacting directly with systems, and online transaction processing (OLTP) was born. In the 1980s the computing infrastructure shifted from large centralized mainframes with dumb terminals to decentralized client/server computing with graphical user interfaces (GUIs) running on PCs and accessing databases on other machines over a network.

The client/server revolution provided a much better user interface and reduced the cost of hardware and software, but it also introduced additional complexity in systems development, management, and deployment. After a decade of use, system administrators were being slowly overwhelmed by the task of managing thousands of client machines and dozens of servers, so the latter half of the 1990s has seen a return to centralization. One of the major focuses of Oracle Database 10*g* is reduced management overhead, and the concept of grid computing (discussed in Chapter 14) is, in part, aimed at correcting some of the counterproductive effects of decentralized computing. Chapter 5 covers Oracle Database 10*g* management in much more detail. OLTP is one of the areas addressed by the consolidation of data processing represented by the grid.

Although many of the specific features covered in this chapter are touched upon in other chapters of this book, this chapter examines all of these features in light of their use in large OLTP systems—a topic of great importance to Oracle users.

OLTP Basics

Before we discuss how Oracle specifically handles OLTP, we'll start by presenting a common definition of online transaction processing.

What Is a Transaction?

The concept of a transaction and the relevant Oracle mechanics for dealing with transactions are discussed in Chapter 7. To recap that discussion, a *transaction* is a logical unit of work that must succeed or fail in its entirety. Each transaction typically involves one or more Data Manipulation Language (DML) statements such as INSERT, UPDATE, or DELETE, and ends with either a COMMIT to make the changes permanent or a ROLLBACK to undo the changes.

The industry bible for OLTP, *Transaction Processing: Concepts and Techniques,* by Jim Gray and Andreas Reuter (see Appendix B), introduced the notion of the *ACID* properties of a transaction. A transaction must be the following:

Atomic
> The entire transaction succeeds or fails as a complete unit.

Consistent
> A completed transaction leaves the affected data in a consistent or correct state.

Isolated
> Each transaction executes in isolation and doesn't affect the states of others.

Durable
> The changes resulting from committed transactions are persistent.

If transactions execute serially—one after the other—their use of ACID properties can be relatively easily guaranteed. Each transaction starts with the consistent state of the previous transaction and, in turn, leaves a consistent state for the next transaction. Concurrent usage introduces the need for sophisticated locking and other coordination mechanisms to preserve the ACID properties of concurrent transactions while delivering throughput and performance.

What Does OLTP Mean?

Online transaction processing can be defined in different ways: as a type of computing with certain characteristics, or as a type of computing in contrast to more traditional batch processing.

General characteristics

Most OLTP systems share some of the following general characteristics:

High transaction volumes and large user populations
> The benefits of large, centralized systems have driven the ever-increasing scale of today's modern OLTP systems.

Well-defined performance requirements
> OLTP systems often involve Service Level Agreements that state the expected response times.

High availability
> These systems are typically deemed mission-critical with significant costs resulting from downtime. The universal availability of the Web clearly increases availability requirements.

Scalability
> The ability to increase transaction volumes without significant degradation in performance allows OLTP systems to handle fluctuations in business activity.

With the expansion of user communities based on opening up systems on the Web, OLTP demands have increased, in terms of both overall performance and availability. Web users expect the system to be up all the time and to perform quickly—if your order-entry site is down or slow, web users will go elsewhere.

Online versus batch

Online transaction processing implies direct and conversational interaction between the transaction processing system and its users. Users enter and query data using forms that interact with the backend database. Editing and validation of data occur at the time the transactions are submitted by users.

Batch processing occurs without user interaction. Batches of transactions are fed from source files to the operational system. Errors are typically reported in exception files or logs and are reviewed by users or operators later on. Virtually all OLTP systems have a batch component: jobs that can execute in off-peak hours for reporting, payroll runs, posting of accounting entries, and so on.

Many large companies have batch-oriented mainframe systems that are so thoroughly embedded in the corporate infrastructure that they cannot be replaced or removed. A common practice is to "frontend" these legacy systems with OLTP systems. Users interact with the OLTP system to enter transactions. Batch files are extracted from the OLTP system and fed into the downstream legacy applications. Once the batch processing is done, extracts are produced from the batch systems and are used to refresh the OLTP systems. This extraction process provides the users with a more sophisticated interface with online validation and editing, but it preserves the flow of data through the entrenched batch systems. While this process seems costly, it's typically more attractive than the major surgery required to remove the older systems. To compound the difficulty, in some cases the documentation of these older systems is incomplete and the employees who understand the inner workings have retired or moved on.

The financial services industry has been a leader in information technology for transaction processing, so this notion of feeding legacy downstream applications is very common in banks and insurance companies. For example, users enter insurance claims into an online system. Once all the data has been entered, if the claim has been approved it is extracted and fed into legacy systems for further processing and payment.

Oracle features such as transportable tablespaces and Streams, discussed elsewhere in this book, are aimed in part at providing the functionality required by distributed OLTP systems in a more timely fashion than traditional batch jobs.

OLTP Versus Decision Support

Mixed workloads—OLTP and reporting—are the source of many performance challenges and the topic of intense debate. The data warehousing industry had its genesis in the realization that OLTP systems could not realistically provide the needed transaction throughput while supporting the enormous amount of historical data and ad hoc query workload that business analysts needed for things like multiyear trend analysis.

The issue isn't simply one of adequate machine horsepower; rather, it's the way data is modeled, stored, and accessed, which is typically quite different. In OLTP, the design centers on analyzing and automating business processes to provide consistent performance for a well-known set of transactions and users. While data warehousing certainly involves analysis and requires performance, the nature of the workload isn't easy to predict. Ad hoc queries that can consume significant resources occur along with scheduled reports.

Reporting and query functions are part of an OLTP system, but the scope and frequency are typically more controlled than in a data warehouse environment. For example, a banking OLTP system will include queries for customer status and account balances, but not multiyear transaction patterns.

The OLTP system typically provides forms that allow well-targeted queries that are executed efficiently and don't consume undue resources. However, hard and fast rules—for example, that OLTP systems don't include extensive query facilities—don't necessarily hold true. The I/O performed by most OLTP systems tends to be approximately 70–80% read and 20–30% write. Most transactions involve the querying of data, such as product codes, customer names, account balances, inventory levels, and so on. Users submitting tuned queries for specific business functions are a key part of OLTP. Ad hoc queries across broad data sets are not.

Decision support systems and OLTP systems could access much of the same data, but these types of systems also typically have different requirements in terms of CPU, memory, and data layout, which makes supporting a mixed workload less than optimal for both types of processing. Real Application Clusters, with dynamic service provisioning in Oracle Database 10g, makes it possible to allocate individual nodes for individual workloads. It also makes it more feasible to deploy these mixed workloads to a single database (albeit with multiple database instances).

Oracle's OLTP Heritage

Oracle has enjoyed tremendous growth as the database of choice for OLTP in the midrange computing environment. Oracle6 introduced non-escalating row-level locking and read consistency (two of the most important of Oracle's core OLTP features), but Oracle7 was really the enabler for Oracle's growth in OLTP. Oracle7 introduced many key features, including the following:

- Multi-Threaded Server (MTS)
- Shared SQL
- Stored procedures and triggers
- XA support
- Distributed transactions and two-phase commits
- Data replication
- Oracle Parallel Server (OPS)*

Oracle 8.0 enhanced existing functionality and introduced additional OLTP-related features including the following:

- Connection pooling
- Connection multiplexing
- Data partitioning
- Advanced Queuing (AQ)
- Index organized tables
- Internalization of the Distributed Lock Manager (DLM) for Oracle Parallel Server
- Internalization of the triggers for replicated tables and parallel propagation of replicated transactions

Oracle8i provided the following additional enhancements and technologies for OLTP:

- Support for Java internally in the database kernel
- Support for distributed component technologies: CORBA V2.0 and Enterprise JavaBeans (EJB) v1.0

---

* OPS was actually available for DEC VMS in 1989 and for NCR Unix with the last production release of Oracle6 (Version 6.0.36), but it became widely available, more stable, and more popular in Oracle7.

- Publish/subscribe messaging based on Advanced Queuing
- Cache Fusion for Oracle Parallel Server
- Online index rebuild and reorganization
- Database Resource Manager (DRM)
- Use of a standby database for queries
- Internalization of the replication packages used to apply transactions at the remote sites

Oracle9*i* continued this trend, with the introduction of Real Application Clusters, which extended the benefits of Oracle Parallel Server to OLTP applications. Oracle Database 10*g* improves the capabilities of Real Application Clusters for deployment to a new computing model, grid computing. But many of the capabilities that enable OLTP with Oracle have been core to the database product for many years.

The remainder of this chapter examines many of these features in more depth.

Architectures for OLTP

Although all OLTP systems are oriented toward the same goals, there are several different underlying system architectures that you can use for the deployment of OLTP, including the traditional two-tier model, a three-tier model, and a model that encompasses the use of the Web.

Traditional Two-Tier Client/Server

The late 1980s saw the rise of two-tier client/server applications. In this configuration, PCs acted as clients accessing a separate database server over a network. The client ran both the GUI and the application logic, giving rise to the term *fat clients*. The database server processed SQL statements and returned the requested results back to the clients. While database servers were relatively simple to develop using visual tools, client/server systems were difficult to deploy and maintain—they required fairly high-bandwidth networks and the installation and regular upgrading of specific client software on every user's PC.

Figure 8-1 illustrates the two-tier architecture.

Stored Procedures

Oracle7 introduced stored procedures written in PL/SQL, Oracle's proprietary language for writing application logic. These procedures are stored in the database and executed by clients issuing remote procedure calls (RPCs) as opposed to executing SQL statements. Instead of issuing multiple SQL calls, occasionally with intermediate logic to accomplish a task, the client issues one procedure call, passing in the

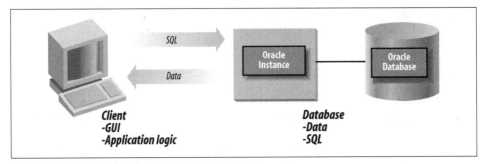

Figure 8-1. Two-tier client/server architecture

required parameters. The database executes all the required SQL and logic using the parameters it receives.

Stored procedures can also shield the client logic from internal changes to the data structures or program logic. As long as the parameters the client passed in and received back don't change, no changes are required in the client software. Stored procedures move a portion of the application logic from the client to the database server. By doing so, stored procedures can reduce the network traffic considerably. This capability increases the scalability of two-tier systems. Figure 8-2 illustrates a two-tier system with stored procedures.

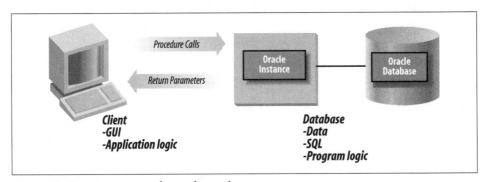

Figure 8-2. Two-tier system with stored procedures

Three-Tier Systems

The OLTP systems with the largest user populations and transaction throughput are typically deployed using a three-tier architecture. In the past, the three-tier architecture involved a transaction processing (TP) monitor, but now it more frequently uses an application server. Clients access a TP monitor or application server in the middle tier that, in turn, accesses a database server on the backend. The notion of a TP monitor dates back to the original mainframe OLTP systems. Of course, in the mainframe environment all logic ran on one machine. In an open system environment, application servers typically run on a separate machine (or machines), adding a middle tier between clients and the database server.

There are various classes of application servers:

- Older, proprietary servers such as Tuxedo from BEA Systems on Unix and Windows, or CICS from IBM on mainframes
- Industry-standard application servers based on Java 2 Enterprise Edition (J2EE)
- The Microsoft .NET application server environment as part of the Windows operating systems for servers, for example, Windows 2000 or Windows 2003

Application servers provide an environment for running services that clients call. The clients don't interact directly with the database server. Some examples of calling services provided by an application server or a TP monitor on a remote machine seem similar in many ways to the stored procedure architecture described in the previous section, which is why stored procedure–based systems are sometimes referred to as "TP-Lite." On the other hand, systems that make use of true TP monitors are sometimes referred to as "TP-Heavy."

Application servers provide additional valuable services, such as:

Funneling

Like Oracle's shared servers, application servers leverage a pool of shared services across a larger user population. Instead of each user's connecting directly to the database, the client calls a service running under the application server's control. The application servers invoke one of its services; the service interacts with the database.

Connection pooling

The application server maintains a pool of shared, persistent database connections used to interact with the database on behalf of clients in handling their requests. This avoids the overhead of individual sessions for each client.

Load-balancing

Client requests are balanced across the multiple shared servers executing on one or more physical machines. The application servers can direct client service calls to the least-loaded server and can spawn additional shared servers as needed.

Fault-tolerance

The application server acts as a transaction manager; the monitor performs the commit or rollback of the transaction.[*] The underlying database becomes a resource manager, but doesn't control the transaction. If the database server fails while executing some transaction, the application server can resubmit the

---

[*] TP monitors usually control transactions using the X/Open Distributed Transaction Processing standard published by the X/Open standards body. A database that supports the XA interface can function as a resource manager under control of a TP monitor, which acts as a transaction manager.

transaction to a surviving database server, as control of the transaction lies with the application server.

This type of transaction resiliency is a hallmark of the older TP monitors such as Tuxedo, and the newer application servers and standards offer similar features.

Transaction routing

The logic in the middle tier can direct transactions to specific database servers, increasing scalability.

Heterogeneous transactions

Application servers can manage transactions across multiple heterogeneous database servers—for example, a transaction that updates data in Oracle and DB2.

While developing three-tier OLTP systems is complex and requires specialized skills, the benefits are substantial. Systems that use application servers provide higher scalability, availability, and flexibility than the simpler two-tier systems. Determining which architecture is appropriate for an OLTP system requires (among other things) careful evaluation and consideration of costs, available skills, workload profiles, scalability requirements, and availability requirements.

Figure 8-3 illustrates a three-tier system using an application server.

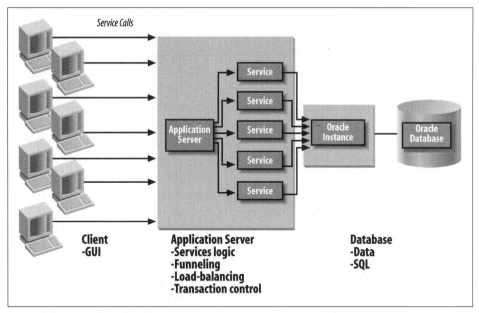

Figure 8-3. Three-tier architecture

Application Servers and Web Servers

The middle tier of web-based systems is usually an application server and/or a web server. These servers provide similar services to the application server previously described, but are more web-centric, dealing with HTTP, HTML, CGI, Java, and Object Request Brokers (ORBs).

J2EE and .NET application servers have evolved a great deal in the last 5 years and are the clear inheritors of the TP monitor legacy for today's N-tier systems. Different companies have different standards and preferences—the proprietary nature of .NET leads some firms to J2EE, while others prefer the tight integration of Microsoft's offerings. A detailed discussion of the relative merits of J2EE and .NET, and application server technology in general, is beyond the scope of this book. Suffice to say that application servers play an extremely important role in today's systems environment and database management personnel need to understand N-tier systems architecture.

Figure 8-4 depicts an N-tier system with a client, web server, application server, and DBMS server:

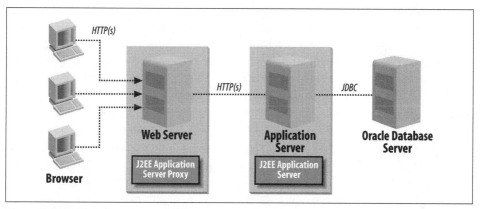

Figure 8-4. An N-tier system

The Grid

Oracle Database 10g is focused on another architecture, grid computing. The actual topology of the grid is not relevant to the discussion in this chapter, because the point of the grid is to provide an extremely simple user interface that transparently connects to a highly flexible source of computing power. In this way, the grid gives IT departments the ability to achieve the benefits of more complex architectures while not imposing undue complexity on users, and OLTP applications are deployed using grid computing resources.

We describe the topology and features of grid computing in some detail in Chapter 14.

Oracle Features for OLTP

Oracle has many features that contribute to OLTP performance, reliability, scalability, and availability. This section presents the basic attributes of many of these features. This section is by no means exhaustive; it's only intended to be an introduction. Please see your relevant Oracle documentation and third-party books for more information.

General Concurrency and Performance

As discussed in Chapter 7, Oracle has implemented excellent support for concurrency and performance in OLTP systems. Some of the key features relevant to OLTP are as follows:

Nonescalating row-level locking
> Oracle locks only the rows a transaction works on and never escalates these locks to page-level or table-level locks. In some databases, which escalate row locks to page locks when enough rows have been locked on a page, contention can result from false lock contention when users want to work on unlocked rows but contend for locks that have escalated to higher granularity levels.

Multiversion read consistency
> Oracle provides statement-level and transaction-level data consistency without requiring read locks. A query is guaranteed to see only the data that was committed at the time the query started. The changes made by transactions that were in-flight but uncommitted at the time the query started won't be visible. Transactions that began after the query started and were committed before the query finishes also won't be seen by the query. Oracle uses rollback segments to reproduce the data as it existed at the time the query started. This capability avoids the unpleasant choice between allowing queries to see uncommitted data (known as dirty reads) or having readers block writers (and vice versa). It also provides a consistent snapshot view of data at a single point in time.

Shared SQL
> The parsing of a SQL statement is fairly CPU-intensive. Oracle caches parsed and optimized SQL statements in the shared SQL area within the shared pool. If another user executes a SQL statement that's cached, the parse and optimize overhead is avoided. The statements must be exactly identical to be reused; no extra spaces, line feeds or differences in capitalization are allowed (see the sidebar). OLTP systems involve a large number of users executing the same application code. These systems provide an ideal opportunity for reusing shared SQL statements.

Stored outlines
> Oracle8*i* added support of execution-plan stability, sometimes referred to as *bound plans*, with stored outlines. The route a SQL statement takes during

execution is critical for high performance. Once application developers and DBAs have tuned a SQL statement for maximum efficiency, they can force the Oracle optimizer to use the same execution plan regardless of environmental changes. This provides critical stability and predictability in the face of software upgrades, schema changes, data-volume changes, and so on. Oracle9*i* added the capability for administrators to edit stored outlines.

With Oracle Database 10*g*, you can select better execution plans for the optimizer to use in conjunction with poorly written SQL to improve OLTP performance without having to rewrite the SQL. The SQL Tuning Advisor performs these advanced optimizations on SQL statements, and can then create an improved SQL Profile for the statement. This profile is used instead of the original optimization plan at runtime.

Scalability

Both the shared server (known as the Multi-Threaded Server prior to Oracle9*i*) and the Database Resource Manager help Oracle support larger or mixed user populations.

Multi-Threaded Server/shared server

Oracle7 introduced the Multi-Threaded Server (MTS, renamed shared server in Oracle9*i* and described in Chapter 2) to allow Oracle to support larger user populations. While shared server and MTS reduced the number of server processes, each client still used its own physical network connection. The resources for network connections aren't unlimited, so Oracle8 introduced two solutions for increasing the capabilities of the actual network socket layer at the operating-system level:

Oracle Net connection pooling
Allows the client population to share a pool of shared physical network connections. Idle clients transparently "time out," and their network connections are returned to the pool to be used by active clients. Each idle client maintains a virtual connection with Oracle and will get another physical connection when activity resumes. With the Oracle security model, authentication is separate from a specific connection, so a single pooled connection can represent different users at different times. Connection pooling is suitable for applications with clients that connect but aren't highly active (for example, email systems).

Oracle Net Connection Manager
Reduces the number of network connections used on the database server. Clients connect to a middle-tier machine running the Oracle Net Connection Manager (CMAN). The Connection Manager multiplexes the traffic for multiple clients into one network connection per Oracle Net dispatcher on the database server. Unlike connection pooling, there is no notion of "time-out" for a client's virtual network connection. The Oracle network topology can include multiple

Bind Variables and Shared SQL

As we've mentioned, Oracle's shared SQL is a key feature for building high-performance applications. In an OLTP application, similar SQL statements may be used repeatedly, but each SQL statement submitted may have different selection criteria contained in the WHERE clause to identify the different sets of rows to operate on. Oracle can share SQL statements, but the statements must be absolutely identical.

To take advantage of this feature for statements that are identical except for specific values in a WHERE clause, you can use bind variables in your SQL statements. The values substituted for the bind variables in the SQL statement may be different, but the statement itself is the same.

Consider an example application for granting raises to employees. The application submits the following SQL:

```
UPDATE emp SET salary = salary * (1 + 0.1)WHERE empno = 123;
UPDATE emp SET salary = salary * (1 + 0.15)WHERE empno = 456;
```

These statements are clearly different; they update different employees identified by different employee numbers, and the employees receive different salary increases. To obtain the benefits of shared SQL, you can write the application to use bind variables for the percentage salary increase and the employee numbers, such as:

```
UPDATE emp SET salary = salary * (1 + :v_incr)WHERE empno = :v_empno;
UPDATE emp SET salary = salary * (1 + :v_incr)WHERE empno = :v_empno;
```

These statements are recognized as identical and would therefore be shared. The application would submit different values for the two variables :v_incr and :v_empno, a percentage increase of 0.1 for employee 123 and 0.15 for employee 456. Oracle substitutes these actual values for the variables in the SQL. The substitution occurs during the phase of processing known as the *bind phase*, which follows the *parse phase* and *optimize phase*. For more details, see the relevant Oracle guide for your development language.

Oracle Database 10g tuning tools can easily spot this type of potential application optimization.

machines running the Connection Manager to provide additional scalability and fault-tolerance.

In terms of scalability, you can think of connection pooling as the middleweight solution and multiplexing via Connection Manager as the heavyweight solution. Figure 8-5 illustrates these two network-scaling technologies.

Connection Manager has become more flexible in Oracle Database 10g, with the added ability to dynamically alter configuration parameters without shutting down Connection Manager and improved access rules to filter CMAN traffic.

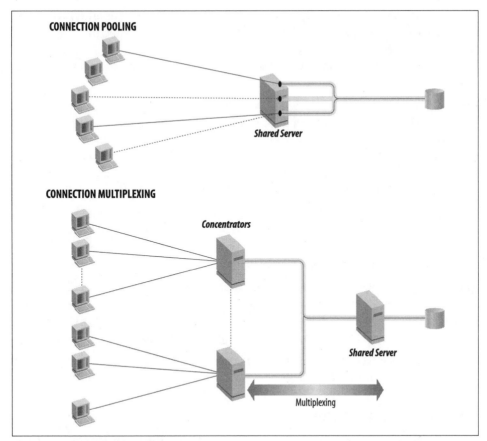

Figure 8-5. Network scaling in Oracle Net

Database Resource Manager

Oracle8*i* introduced the Database Resource Manager (DRM) to simplify and automate the management of mixed workloads in which different users access the same database for different purposes. You can define different consumer groups to contain different groups of users. The DRM allocates CPU and parallelism resources to consumer groups based on *resource plans*. A resource plan defines limits for the amount of a particular computer resource a group of users can use. This allows the DBA to ensure that certain types of users receive sufficient machine resources to meet performance requirements.

For example, you can allocate 80% of the CPU resources to order-entry users, with the remaining 20% allocated to users asking for reports. This allocation prevents reporting users from dominating the machine while order-entry users are working. If the order-entry users aren't using all the allocated resources, the reporting users can use more than their allotted percentage. If the order-entry workload increases, the reporting users will be cut back to respect their 20% allocation. In other words, the order-entry users will get up to 80% of CPU time, as needed, while the users asking for reports will get at least 20% of the CPU time, and more depending on how much the order-entry group is using. With the DRM, you can dynamically alter the details of the plan without shutting down the instance.

Oracle9*i* added a number of significant improvements to the Database Resource Manager. The DRM now allows a DBA to specify the number of active sessions available to a consumer group. Any additional connection requests for the consumer group are queued. By limiting the number of active connections, you can start to avoid the situation where a request comes in that pushes the resource requirements for a group over the limit and affects all the other users in that group.

Oracle9*i* also added to the DRM the ability to proactively estimate the amount of CPU that an operation will require. If an operation looks as if it will exceed the maximum CPU time specified for a resource group, the operation will not be executed, which can prevent inappropriately large operations from even starting.

Finally, since Oracle9*i*, the DRM can also automatically switch a consumer group to another consumer group if that group is active for too long. This feature could be used to automatically switch a consumer group oriented towards short OLTP operations to another group that would be more appropriate for batch operations.

With Oracle Database 10g, you can now define a consumer group by the service name, application, host machine, or operating system user name of a user.

Real Application Clusters

Arguably, the biggest advance in Oracle9*i* was a feature called Real Application Clusters (RAC). Real Application Clusters was a new version of technology replacing Oracle Parallel Server (OPS).

In the first edition of this book, we described OPS as a feature that could be used for improving performance and scalability for certain data warehouse–style applications—applications in which data could be partitioned in logical ways and applications that primarily supported read activity. The reason why OPS was used only in limited cases was the phenomenon known as *pinging*.

In the world of both OPS and RAC, multiple machines access the same database files on shared disk (either physically attached or appearing as physically attached through software). This architecture allows you to add more machines to a cluster of machines, which in turn adds more overall horsepower to the system. But there was a problem with the implementation of this architecture for OPS, stemming from the fact that each machine in a cluster had its own cache. If one machine tried to execute a write operation that required a block in the cache of another machine, that block had to be flushed to the database file on the shared disk—a scenario that was termed a *ping*. This chain of events caused extra disk I/O, which in turn decreased the overall performance of the solution.

The traditional way around this problem was simply to avoid it—to use OPS only when a database would not cause pings with a lot of write operations, or to segregate writes so that they would not require data in use on another node. This limitation required you to carefully consider the type of application to which you would deploy OPS and sometimes forced you to actually modify the design of your application to work around OPS's limitations.

With Real Application Clusters, the problem caused by pings was eliminated. Real Application Clusters fully support the technology known as Cache Fusion. Cache Fusion makes all the data in every cache on every machine in a Real Application Cluster available to every other machine in the cluster. If one machine needs a block that is cached by another machine, the block is directly shipped to the requesting machine, usually over a very high-speed interconnect.

Cache Fusion means that you do not have to work around the problems of pinging. With Real Application Clusters you will be able to see significant scalability improvements for virtually all applications, without any modifications.

Real Application Clusters also deliver all the availability advantages that were a part of OPS. Because all the machines in a Real Application Cluster share the same disk, the failure of a single machine does not mean that the database as a whole has failed. The users connected to the failed machine have to be failed over to another machine in the cluster, but the database server itself will continue to operate.

Oracle also has partnerships with some hardware vendors that are designed to increase the integration of both hardware and database clusters. The goal toward which Oracle and its hardware vendor partners are working is the nirvana of plug-and-play clusters, in which you can add another machine to a cluster by simply plugging it in.

With Oracle Database 10g, this model is extended beyond clusters to grid computing. With this release, Oracle offers all the components you need to use to implement clusters on several operating system platforms as part of the Oracle software stack, including a volume manager and clusterware.

High Availability

From an operational perspective, OLTP systems represent a company's electronic central nervous system, so the databases that support these systems must be highly available. Oracle has a number of features that contribute to high availability:

Standby database
> Oracle provides database redundancy by maintaining a copy of the primary database on another machine, usually at another site. Redo logs from the primary

server are shipped to the standby server and applied there to duplicate the production activity. Oracle8*i* introduced the automated shipping of redo logs to the standby site and the ability to open the standby database for read-only access for reporting.

Oracle9*i* Release 2 introduced the concept of *logical standby*. With a logical standby database the changes are propagated with SQL statements, rather than redo logs, which allows the logical standby database to be used for other database operations.

Transparent Application Failover (TAF)
TAF is a programming interface that enables you to automatically reconnect a user session to another Oracle instance should the primary instance fail.

Advanced Queuing (AQ)
AQ provides a method for asynchronous, or deferred, intersystem communication, allowing systems to operate more independently. Avoiding direct system dependencies can help to avoid "cascading" failures, allowing interconnected systems to continue to operate even if one system fails. AQ is described in more detail in the following section.

Replication
You can use Oracle's built-in replication functionality to provide data redundancy. Changes made by transactions are replicated synchronously or asynchronously to other databases. If the primary database fails, the data is available from the other databases. As of Oracle9*i* Release 2, log-based replication and Advanced Queueing were included as part of Streams.

Real Application Clusters
Real Application Clusters (Oracle Parallel Server prior to Oracle9*i*), increased the scalability of the Oracle database. However, by supporting multiple instances with full access to one database, RAC also provides the highest levels of availability for protection from the failure of a node in a clustered or MPP environment. If one node fails, the surviving nodes provide continued access to the database. With Oracle Database 10g, grid computing deployment further extends availability capabilities.

For a more detailed discussion of high availability, see Chapter 10.

Oracle Advanced Queuing and Streams

Messaging technology has existed for quite some time and is common in OLTP applications. Typical messaging technologies provide a reliable transport layer for shipping messages from one machine to another over a network. Oracle8 introduced Advanced Queuing (AQ) as an integrated database service. Oracle9*i* Release 2 combined AQ with log-based replication in the creation of Oracle Streams.

Oracle AQ provides the benefits of simple messaging products but adds the value of database-resident queues. The information in message queues represents critical business events and should be stored in a reliable, scalable, secure, and recoverable place. Placing the queues in the database extends the core benefits of a database to the queues themselves.

The data that flows through queues represents the ebb and flow of business activity. Analyzing the types and volumes of message traffic can help to identify how different business functions are operating and interacting and this, in turn, can provide valuable insights into the operation of your business. Oracle AQ supports the notion of *message warehousing*, in which the content and details of the queues can be queried and analyzed because they're already in the database. Oracle can dequeue messages but can leave historical data in the queues for subsequent analysis.

Applications can enqueue and dequeue messages as part of a transaction or as a separate event that occurs as soon as the specific enqueue or dequeue statement is issued. Queue actions included in the scope of a transaction are committed or rolled back with that transaction. Should a failure occur, the queue activities are recovered along with the rest of the database activities.

Oracle can propagate messages from one queue to another by providing a routing engine for message traffic. Figure 8-6 illustrates the use of queuing and propagation.

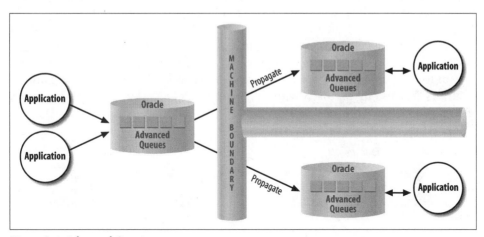

Figure 8-6. Advanced Queuing

Oracle Database 10g makes it easier to implement Streams programmatically, by allowing you to enqueue and dequeue batches of messages and by reducing the amount of coding required to interact with queues.

Advanced Queuing for System Interfaces

Implementing OLTP systems invariably involves interfaces with other systems in the enterprise or in other companies. The effort to design, create, and manage these interfaces is substantial and can easily account for 40 to 60% of the cost of large-scale Enterprise Resource Planning (ERP) implementations. Furthermore, adding other systems to the mix or changing existing systems entails reworking the interfaces, resulting in an increasing and ongoing burden. Oracle is focusing on its Advanced Queuing technology as the foundation for integrating application systems together with the Enterprise Integration Framework.

Oracle's Enterprise Integration Framework is a bundle of services and products intended to help companies solve the integration problem by implementing a "hub-and-spoke" architecture using a combination of messaging, routing, and transformation technologies. Traditionally, you would develop a specific interface between two systems. As you added a third system to the mix, you would have to create more specific interfaces between each of the systems. The more systems you attempt to integrate, the more custom interfaces you would be responsible for developing and the greater the development and maintenance burden would be.

With the Enterprise Integration Framework, individual systems connect to a hub via the spokes, thus avoiding direct system-to-system interfaces. The spokes send and receive messages, while the hub provides routing and transformation services. This reduces the number of interfaces required to connect a set of systems. You don't need a specific interface for every specific system pair. Adding systems to existing systems doesn't require development of many new interfaces. You connect the new system to the hub and leverage the routing and transformation services. Figure 8-7 contrasts the custom approach with the hub-and-spoke approach of the Enterprise Integration Framework.

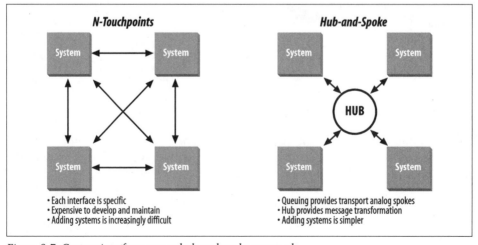

Figure 8-7. Custom interfaces versus hub-and-spoke approach

Oracle and Publish-Subscribe Technology

Oracle8*i* enhanced Advanced Queuing to include publish-subscribe functionality. Applications can subscribe to a message queue by specifying the attributes of messages they're interested in receiving. When another application publishes a message by placing it in a queue, Oracle evaluates the contents of the message to determine which of the subscribing applications are interested and notifies those applications. For example, a shipping application can subscribe to a queue used for orders and specify that only messages for orders with a status of "Ready to Ship" are of interest. As messages representing these orders flow through the queue, the shipping application will receive only the desired messages. This publish-subscribe functionality, coupled with message propagation for routing, provides a very powerful messaging backbone for information flow between systems.

Object Technologies and Distributed Components

In many ways, the greater the amount of information, the more intelligence that can be extracted from it. Integrating information from separate systems can be an enormous task, especially because the complexity of integration increases geometrically as more systems are added to the mix.

While messaging technologies can assist with interfacing different systems, online interaction is often needed as well. For example, if the Human Resources system maintains information about the company's employees (such as the department in which they work and their role), ideally the Purchasing system could access the data in the HR system online at the time purchases are being made. At this point, the Purchasing system could determine the spending limits of the purchaser and to what department the accounting should be tied. In practice, these online interfaces are difficult to build because they require the systems to agree, and remain in agreement, about how to communicate. Each system has proprietary application programming interfaces (APIs) that allow other systems to communicate with them. These specific, and often conflicting, APIs limit the reuse of the functionality within each system.

Object technologies offer one solution: systems communicate by invoking methods on objects instead of by calling specific APIs. For example, if you want to check the department of a user, you make a standard object call to the employee object managed by the HR system.

Oracle8*i* and later versions support a number of object technologies, including:

CORBA
> The Common Object Request Broker Architecture, a multivendor industry standard developed by the Object Management Group (OMG) for object interaction

Java

A popular object-oriented language

EJB

Enterprise JavaBeans, a standard architecture for computing using business components written in Java

CORBA, EJB, and objects are covered in more detail in Chapter 13.

CHAPTER 9

Oracle and Data Warehousing

Although a database is general-purpose software, it provides a solution for a variety of technical requirements, including:

Recording and storing data
Reliably storing data and protecting each user's data from the effects of other users' changes

Reading data for online viewing and reports
Providing a consistent view of the data

Analyzing data to detect business trends
Enables summarizing data and relating many different summaries to each other

The last two solutions are often deployed as a *data warehouse*, part of an infrastructure that provides *business intelligence* for corporate performance management.

Data warehousing and business intelligence implementations are a popular and powerful trend in information technology. There is a very simple motivation behind this trend: businesses gain the ability to use their data in making strategic and tactical decisions. Business intelligence can reveal hidden value embedded in an organization's data stores.

Recognizing the trend, Oracle began adding data warehousing features to Oracle7 in the early 1990s. Additional features for warehousing and business intelligence appeared in subsequent releases, particularly to enable better performance, functionality, scalability, and management. Oracle also developed tools for building and using a business intelligence infrastructure, including data movement and business analyses tools.

A business intelligence infrastructure can enable business analysts to answer the following:

- How does a scenario relate to past business results?
- What knowledge can be gained by looking at the data differently?

- What could happen in the future?
- How can business be changed to positively influence the future?

This chapter introduces the basic concepts, technologies, and tools used in data warehousing and business intelligence. To help you understand how Oracle addresses infrastructure and analyses issues, we'll first spend a little time describing basic terms and technologies.

Business Intelligence Basics

Why build a data warehouse or business intelligence solution? Why is the data in an On-Line Transaction Processing (OLTP) database only part of a business intelligence solution? Data warehouses are often designed with the following in mind:

Strategic analyses discern trends in data, rather than individual facts.
> Data warehouses often are used to create simple reports based on aggregate values culled from enormous amounts of data. If OLTP databases attempted to create these aggregates on the fly they would use a lot of resources, which would impact their ability to process transactions in a timely manner.

The information in a data warehouse is more commonly read-only, with infrequent updates.
> This means that the overhead of transaction control, an important part of a normal OLTP database system, isn't really needed for a data warehouse.

The data used for analyses may not require up-to-the-minute accuracy.
> Because strategic analysis is concerned with trends over time, the data used can be a day, a week, or even a month old, depending on the analysis being done. This means that data in a data warehouse can have some or all of its aggregate values created as part of a batch process offline. However, as warehouses are used for tactical management, near real-time accuracy emerges as a requirement.

The design required for an efficient data warehouse differs from the standard normalized design for a relational database.
> Queries are typically read against a fact table, which may contain summary information using a specific type of schema design called a *star schema*. This design lets you access facts quite flexibly along key dimensions or "look-up" values. (The star schema is described in more detail later, in the section "Data Warehouse Design.") For instance, a data warehouse user may want to compare the total amount of sales, which comes from a fact table, by region, store in the region, and items, all of which can be considered key dimensions.

The Evolution of Business Intelligence

Business intelligence is not a new idea. The use of corporate data for strategic decision making beyond simple tracking and day-to-day operations has gone on for almost as long as computing itself.

Quite early, builders and users of operational systems recognized potential business benefits of analyzing the data in complementary systems. In fact, much of the early growth in personal computers was tied to the use of spreadsheets that performed analyses against data downloaded from the operational systems. Business executives began to direct IT efforts toward building solutions used to obtain a better understanding of business using existing business data. This understanding enabled new business strategies. Many of these early joint initiatives were successful data warehousing projects. Today, data warehouses are used in business areas such as customer relationship management, sales and marketing campaign analysis, product management and packaging, financial analysis, supply chain analysis, and risk and fraud analysis.

In the 1980s, many organizations began using dedicated servers for these applications, which were collectively known as *decision support systems* (DSS). Decision-support queries tended to be particularly CPU and memory intensive and took place in a primarily read-only environment, whereas traditional OLTP was typically I/O intensive with a large number of updates. The characteristics of queries were much less predictable (e.g., more "ad-hoc") than what had been experienced in OLTP systems. This led to the development of data stores for decision support apart from those for OLTP.

When Bill Inmon (whose books are noted in Appendix B) and others popularized the term "data warehouse" in the early 1990s, a formalized common infrastructure for building a solution came into being. Since then, the topology of the data warehouse has continued to evolve, as the next section illustrates.

A Topology for Business Intelligence

Although data warehouses were initially conceived as a large, enterprise-wide source of all information, their topology often now appears as a multi-tier architecture, as shown in Figure 9-1.

The topology shown in Figure 9-1 is the mature result of years of experience. The evolution from a traditional client/server environment to multiple tiers occurred for a variety of reasons. Initial efforts at creating a single warehouse often resulted in "analysis paralysis." Just as efforts to define an enterprise-wide OLTP model often take years (due to cross-departmental politics and the scope of the effort), similar attempts in data warehousing also took much longer than businesses were willing to accept. These efforts were further hampered by the continually changing analysis

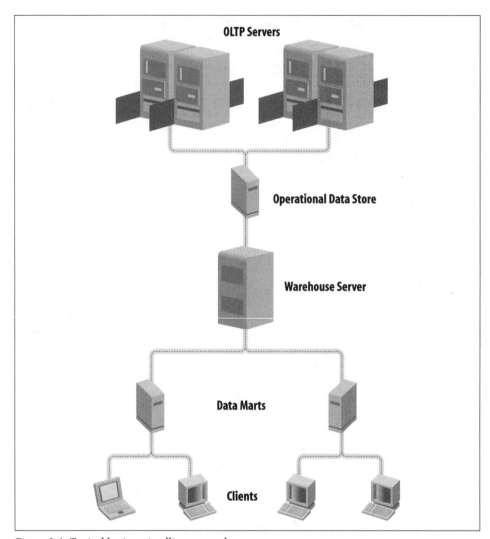

Figure 9-1. Typical business intelligence topology

requirements necessitated by a continually changing marketplace. While the data elements and requirements for operational systems can remain relatively stagnant over time, understanding business trends can be like trying to catch lightning in a bottle.

Consequently, attempts at building such enterprise-wide models in an effort to satisfy everyone often satisfied no one.

Data Marts

When some large-scale, enterprise-only data warehouse efforts ended in dismal failure, frustration and impatience followed. Some people reacted and built department-focused independent *data marts* by extracting data from the appropriate operational source systems. Many data marts were initially quite successful because they fulfilled a specific business need relatively quickly.

However, problems began to surface. There was often no coordination between departments regarding basic definitions, such as "customer." If a senior manager asked the same question of multiple departments, the answers provided by these independent data marts were often different, thus calling into question the validity of any of the marts. Many departments also encountered ongoing difficulty in managing these multiple data marts and in maintaining extractions from operational sources (which were often duplicated across multiple departments).

As decision-support architects took another look at their solutions, they began to realize that it was very important to have a consistent view of the detailed data at an enterprise data warehouse level. They also saw that data marts could solve business problems and provide return on investment in an incremental fashion. Today, most successful implementers simultaneously grow dependent data marts one business solution at a time while growing the enterprise warehouse server in an incremental fashion.

The currently accepted definition of a data mart is simply a subject- or application-specific data warehouse, usually implemented within a department. Typically, these data marts are built for performance and may include a large number of summary tables. Data marts were initially thought of as being small, because not all the detail data for a department or data from other departments need be loaded in the mart. However, some marts get quite large as they incorporate data from outside sources (sometimes purchased) that isn't relevant in other parts of the business.

In some companies, data marts are deployed to meet specific project goals with models optimized for performance for that particular project. Such data marts are retired when the project is completed and the hardware is reused for other projects. As the analysis requirements for a business change, the topology of any particular data warehouse is subject to evolution over time, so developers must be aware of this possibility.

Increasingly, companies interested in costs savings are reexamining the wisdom of having a large number of data marts and are consolidating marts where possible. Recent new database features enabling effective management of different user communities helped to make consolidation possible.

Operational Data Store and Enterprise Warehouse

The *operational data store* (ODS) concept also grew in popularity in the 1990s. The ODS may best be described as a distribution center for current data. Like the OLTP servers, the schema is highly normalized and the data is recent. The ODS serves as a consolidation point for reporting and can give the business one location for viewing current data that crosses divisions or departments. The popularity of the ODS grew in part as a result of companies in the midst of acquisitions and mergers. These organizations often face mixed-application environments. The ODS acts as a staging location that can be used as the source for further transformations into a data warehouse or into data marts.

The warehouse server, or *enterprise data warehouse*, is a multi-subject historical information store usually supporting multiple departments and often serving as the corporate database of record. When an ODS is established, the warehouse server often extracts data from the ODS. When an ODS isn't present, data for the warehouse is directly extracted and transformed from operational sources. External data may also feed the warehouse server.

As noted previously in the data mart discussion, platform consolidation is being examined within these tiers today. The enterprise data warehouse can be the point of consolidation for the ODS and multiple data marts. Although different logical models remain, they are sometimes consolidated to a single platform.

Data Warehouse Design

The database serves as the foundation of the data warehouse: it is the place where the data is stored. But there is more to a data warehouse than simply data—a data warehouse becomes useful only when business users properly use data stored within it. This may seem like a trivial point, but we've seen numerous companies build data warehouses without consulting business users to determine business needs; thus, the database ends up with very few users, little activity, and no business intelligence is gained.

Assuming that your warehouse is well planned and there is a demand for the data, your next challenge will be to figure out how to handle the demand. You will be faced with the need to design your data warehouse to deliver appropriate performance to your users—performance that may initially seem far beyond the capabilities of your system, because the information requested from the data warehouse can involve summaries and comparisons of massive amounts of detailed data.

When you start designing the data warehouse, also remember that a data warehouse is never complete. When the business changes, so too must the data warehouse. Thus, the ability to track changes through metadata stored in a repository often becomes critical in design phases.

Various design tools can provide this capability. Oracle's Warehouse Builder provides a metadata repository and also the capability to import metadata from operational tables and then forward-engineer new schema and tables. A data warehouse designer creates columns for the new tables and builds constraints for the new schema. Maps are then created between source and target columns with appropriate transformations. DML scripts for creation of new tables, and PL/SQL or SQL*Loader scripts for extraction, transformation, and loading (ETL) are automatically generated.

As noted previously, data warehouses historically have had a different set of usage characteristics from those of an OLTP database. One aspect that makes it easier to meet data warehousing performance requirements is the high percentage of read operations. Oracle's locking model, described in detail in Chapter 7, is ideally suited to support data warehouse operations. Oracle doesn't place any locks onto data that's being read, thus reducing contention and resource requirements for situations in which there are a lot of database reads. Oracle is consequently well-suited to act as the repository for a data warehouse. Because locks don't escalate, Oracle is also extremely appropriate for near real-time data feeds into the warehouse in a scenario not unlike some OLTP implementations.

Warehousing usage characteristics also lead to different types of design schema. In OLTP databases, transaction data is usually stored in multiple tables and data items are stored only once. If a query requests data from more than one transaction table, the tables are joined together. Typically, the database query optimizer decides which table to use as the starting point for the join, based on the assumption that the data in the tables is essentially equally important.

A warehouse schema may use a different model. Although Oracle-based data warehouses may be modeled as third normal form (3NF), when business users need an understandable schema to formulate their own ad-hoc queries or analytical processing is required, key transaction data may be more appropriately stored in a central fact table, surrounded by dimension or look-up tables, as shown in Figure 9-2. The fact table can contain summarized data for data items duplicated elsewhere in the warehouse, and dimension tables can contain multiple hierarchies. As companies consolidate their data marts into enterprise data warehouses, many now deploy a variation called a *hybrid schema*, a mixture of third normal form and star schema.

Ralph Kimball, author of the widely read book *The Data Warehouse Toolkit* (see Appendix B for details), is largely credited with discovering that users of data warehouses typically pose their queries in such a manner that the star schema, shown in Figure 9-2, is an appropriate model to use. A typical query might be something like the following:

> Show me how many sales of computers (a product type) were sold by a store chain (a channel) in Wisconsin (a geography) over the past 6 months (a time).

The schema in Figure 9-2 shows a relatively large sales transactions table (called a *fact table*) surrounded by smaller tables (called *dimensions* or *look-up tables*). The query just described is often called *multidimensional*, because several dimensions are included (time is almost always one of them). Because these queries are typical in a data warehouse, the recognition of the star schema by a cost-based optimizer can deliver enormous performance benefits.

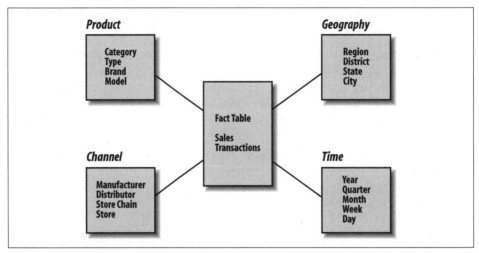

Figure 9-2. Typical star schema

Query Optimization

Oracle first provided the ability to recognize a star schema in the query optimizer in Oracle7 and has focused on making its cost-based query optimizer smarter in response to decision-support queries in subsequent database releases. To further improve optimizer prediction accuracy, in Oracle Database 10g optimizer predictions are compared to actual runtime performance and any errors are subsequently corrected automatically.

How does the optimizer handle a query against a star schema? First, it finds a sales transactions fact table (shown in Figure 9-2) with a lot more entries than the surrounding dimension tables. This is the clue that a star schema exists. As Oracle7 evolved, the optimizer began to produce much smarter plans. The optimizer for a standard relational database typically would have tried to join each of the dimension tables to the fact table, one at a time. Because the fact table is usually very large, using the fact table in multiple joins takes a lot of time.

Cartesian product joins were added to Oracle7 to first join the dimension tables, with a subsequent single join back to the fact table in the final step. This technique works relatively well when there are not many dimension tables (typically six or fewer, as a rule of thumb, to keep the Cartesian product small) and when data is relatively well populated.

In some situations, there are a fairly large number of dimension tables or the data in the fact table is sparse. For joining such tables, a parallel bitmap star join may be selected by the optimizer.

Bitmap Indexes

Bitmap indexes, described in Chapter 4, were first introduced in Oracle7 to speed up the type of data retrieval and joins in data warehousing queries. Bitmap indexes in Oracle are typically considered for columns in which the data has low cardinality. *Cardinality* is the number of different values in an index divided by the number of rows. There are various opinions about what low cardinality actually is. Some people consider cardinality as high as 10% to be low, but remember that if a table has a million rows, that "low" cardinality would mean 100,000 different values in a column!

In a bitmap index, a value of 1 in the index indicates that a value is present in a particular row and 0 indicates that the value is not present. A bitmap is built for each of the values in the indexed columns. Because computers are built on a concept of 1s and 0s, this technique can greatly speed up data retrieval. In addition, join operations such as AND become a simple addition operation across multiple bitmaps. A side benefit is that bitmap indexes can provide considerable storage savings.

Figure 9-3 illustrates the use of a bitmap index in a compound WHERE clause. Bitmap indexes can be used together for even faster performance. The bitmap indexes are essentially stacked together, as a set of punch cards might be. Oracle simply looks for those parts of the stack with all the bits turned on (indicating the presence of the value), in the same way that you could try to stick a knitting needle through the portions of the card stack that were punched out on all of the cards.

In Oracle, star-query performance is improved when bitmap indexes are created on the foreign-keys columns of the fact table that link to the surrounding dimension tables. A parallel bitmap star join occurs in which the bitmaps retrieve only the necessary rows from the fact table and the rows are joined to the dimension tables. During the join, sparseness (i.e., a large quantity of empty values) is recognized inherently in the bitmaps, and the number of dimension tables isn't a problem. This algorithm can also efficiently handle a *snowflake schema*, which is an extension of a standard star schema in which there are multiple tables for each dimension. To further speed queries, Oracle9i added a bitmap join index from fact tables to dimension tables.

Performing queries in parallel also obviously improves performance. Joins and sorts are frequently used to solve decision-support queries. Parallelism is described in Chapter 6. That chapter lists all of the applications that Oracle can perform in parallel (see "What Can Be Parallelized?").

Real Application Clusters

Real Application Clusters, which replaced Oracle Parallel Server as of Oracle9i, further expands parallelism by enabling queries to transparently scale across nodes in clusters or in grids of computer systems.

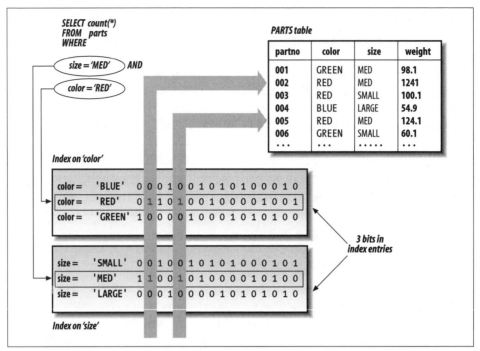

Figure 9-3. Bitmap index operation in a compound WHERE clause

Remember that these Oracle features use the cost-based optimizer and, prior to Oracle Database 10g, you should run statistics periodically (using the ANALYZE statement) on the tables to ensure good performance. Statistics gathering can be done in parallel.

In Oracle Database 10g, statistics gathering can be automatic and populates the Automatic Workload Repository. For example, the Oracle Database 10g SQL Tuning Advisor leverages this information when making tuning recommendations.

Summary Tables

Data within dimensions is usually hierarchical in nature (e.g., in the time dimension, day rolls up to week, which rolls up to month, which rolls up to quarter, which rolls up to year). If the query is simply looking for data summarized at a monthly level, why should it have to sort through more detailed daily and weekly data? Instead, it can simply view data at or above that level of the hierarchy. Formerly, data warehousing performance consultants designed these types of summary tables—including multiple levels of precalculated summarization. For example, all the time periods listed in Figure 9-2 can be calculated on the fly using different groupings of days. However, to speed queries based on a different time series, a data warehouse can have values precalculated for weeks and months and stored in summary tables to which queries can be redirected.

Materialized Views

Oracle8*i* introduced the concept of *materialized views* for the creation of summary tables for facts and dimensions that can represent rollup levels in the hierarchies. A materialized view provides precomputed summary data; most importantly, a materialized view is automatically substituted for a larger detailed fact table when appropriate. The cost-based query optimizer can perform query rewrites to these summary tables and rollup levels in the hierarchy transparently, often resulting in dramatic increases in performance. For instance, if a query can be answered by summary data based on sales by month, the query optimizer will automatically substitute the materialized view for the more granular table when processing the query. A query at the quarter level might use monthly aggregates in the materialized view, selecting the months needed for the quarter(s). There are plans beyond the first release of Oracle Database 10*g* to add query rewrite capabilities with which the optimizer can make use of multiple appropriate materialized views.

Analytics, OLAP, and Data Mining in the Database

Analysis of large data sets is faster when it takes place where the data is stored (e.g. in the database). This section describes the functions and other features available for analysis and data mining in the database.

Functions

Oracle releases dating back to Oracle8*i* have each added more analytic and statistical functions as SQL extensions to the core database. Including new functions added in Oracle Database 10*g* and previous database iterations, these functions now include:

Ranking functions
> Used to compute a record's rank with respect to other records. Functions include RANK, DENSE_RANK, CUME_DIST, PERCENT_RANK, NTILE, and ROW_NUMBER. Hypothetical ranking was an addition to Oracle9*i*.

Windowing aggregate functions
> Used to compute cumulative and moving averages. Functions include SUM, AVG, MIN, MAX, COUNT, VARIANCE, STDDEV, FIRST_VALUE, and LAST_VALUE.

LAG/LEAD functions
Often used to compare values from similar time periods, such as the first quarter of 1999 and the first quarter of 2000.

Reporting aggregate functions
Functions include SUM, AVG, MIN, MAX, COUNT, VARIANCE, STDDEV, and RATIO_TO_REPORT.

Statistical aggregates
Examples include correlation, linear regression, and variance.

Descriptive statistics
Examples include average, standard deviation, variance, min, max, median (via a percentile count), mode, group-by, and roll-up. Oracle Database 10*g* also adds DBMS_STAT_FUNCS for summarizing numerical columns in a table by applying various statistical functions.

Correlations
Examples include Pearson's correlation coefficients, Spearman's and Kendall's.

Crosstabs
Examples include enhancements with % statistics, chi squared, phi coefficient.

Hypothesis testing
Examples include T-test, F-test, One-Way ANOVA, Chi-square, Mann Whitney, Kolmogorov-Smirnov.

Distribution fitting
Examples include normal, uniform, Poisson, exponential, and Weibull.

Pareto analysis
Examples include 80/20 rule and cumulative results table.

OLAP and Data Mining Options

For stored cubes (objects with predefined multidimensional joins), facts, and dimensions in the relational database, Oracle introduced an OLAP Option in Oracle9*i* that is replacing Express Server, a separate Oracle multidimensional OLAP engine. OLAP capabilities provided by the option are accessed through a Java API or directly through SQL. Oracle9*i* also first introduced data mining algorithms in the database accessible via a Java API. These are described more in the "Other Data Warehouse Software" section of this chapter.

Other Capabilities

Oracle Database 10*g* adds the MODEL clause as an extension to the SELECT statement. This clause enables relational data to be treated as multidimensional arrays (much like spreadsheets) and is also used to define formulas for the arrays. Finally, Oracle Database 10*g* also adds support for IEEE floating-point number types, important in many of these calculations.

Database Extensibility and the Data Warehouse

A growing trend in data warehousing is the storage of multiple datatypes within the database. Although we discuss database options in Chapter 13, we'll quickly mention how these options might be useful in data warehousing.

interMedia

The *inter*Media feature opens up the possibilities of including documents, audio, video, and some locator functions in the warehouse. Of these, text retrieval (Oracle Text) is most commonly used in warehouses today. However, the number of companies storing other types of data in warehouses, such as images, is growing. Often, storage of these types of data is driven by a need to provide remote users with access.

Spatial option

The Spatial option is also relevant in a data warehouse in which data is retrieved based on proximity to certain locations. Spatial data includes some type of geographic coordinates. Typically, companies use add-on products in conjunction with Oracle's Spatial option. An example of this option's use for data warehousing is a marketing analysis application that determines the viability of retail outlets at various locations.

XML

Oracle added native XML datatype support to the Oracle9*i* database and XML and SQL interchangeability for searching. Oracle is providing key technology in the development of the XQuery standard, a prototype of which was first made available for Oracle9*i*.

Managing the Data Warehouse

Once you've built a data warehouse topology, you could deploy multiple Oracle databases to implement the data warehouse and its data marts. Enterprise-wide warehouses are more common on Unix servers and are beginning to appear on clustered (RAC) Linux platforms. Smaller data marts are common on Windows and Linux. Many organizations are increasingly consolidating data marts and enterprise data warehouses on the more scalable platforms.

Oracle Enterprise Manager provides a common GUI for managing these multiple instances regardless of the underlying operating system. EM is browser-based with a multiuser repository for tracking and managing the Oracle instances. (EM is discussed in much more detail in Chapter 5.)

In warehousing, in addition to basic management, ongoing tuning for performance is crucial. Enterprise Manager 10*g* supports many of the automated diagnostics and tuning features in Oracle Database 10*g*.

Within the largest warehouses and data marts, you may want to manage or maintain availability to some of the data even as other parts of the database are moved offline. Oracle's Partitioning option enables data partitions based on business value ranges (such as date) or discrete values for administrative flexibility, while enhancing query performance through the cost-based optimizer's ability to eliminate access to non-relevant partitions. As an example, "rolling window" administrative operations are used to add new data and remove old data based on ranges of time. A new partition can be added, loaded, and indexed in parallel, and optionally removed, all without impacting access to existing data.

Range partitioning first became available as an Oracle8 option. Hash partitioning was added to the Oracle8i Partitioning option enabling the spread of data evenly based on a hash algorithm for performance. Hashing may be used within range partitions (composite partitioning) to increase the performance of queries while still maintaining the manageability offered by range partitioning. Oracle9i introduced "List" partitioning—partitions based on discrete values such as geographies. A composite partitioning type of Range-List, such that you can partition by dates within geographies, first appeared in Oracle9i Release 2.

Data Warehouses and Backups

Early data warehousing practitioners often overlooked the need to perform backups. Their belief was that because data for the warehouse was extracted from operational systems, the warehouses could easily be repopulated from those same systems if needed. However, as warehouses grew and the transformations needed to create and refresh them evolved, it became evident that backups of data warehouses were necessary because the transformation process had grown extremely complicated and time-consuming. Today, planning for warehouse availability includes not only an understanding of how long loading will take, but also backup and recovery operations.

Other Data Warehouse Software

A data warehouse isn't necessarily built with a single software product, nor is it simply a database. In addition to the database capabilities we've described, if you're going to build an effective data warehouse topology like the one we've outlined, your software will provide the following functionality:

Extract data from operational data sources
    The extraction process is fairly straightforward but can be significantly optimized, because it typically involves moving large amounts of data.

Transform and/or cleanse data

Because the data in a data warehouse can come from many different sources, the data must frequently be converted into a common format. Because of inherent problems in legacy systems, the original data may also have to be cleansed by eliminating or modifying invalid values.

Transport data from OLTP systems to the data warehouse/marts

As with the extraction process, the transportation process can be optimized for performance.

Provide basic reporting

Basic reporting can give you the same reporting capabilities as a normal database.

Provide OLAP for multidimensional analysis

OLAP tools give you the specialized type of analysis you need to spot business changes and trends. These tools typically provide a way to translate multiple dimensions into the two-dimensional world of a screen and give you the ability to easily rotate those dimensions.

Provide data mining

Data mining is a process in which the data in a data warehouse is modeled against known outcomes, and the models can lead to new business opportunities.

Provide a way to store and retrieve metadata

A metadata repository can be used not only to store the descriptive data, but also to enable extended management services such as versioning and impact analysis.

The following sections provide details on how each of these requirements can be met.

Extraction, Transformation, and Loading

The first three requirements described in the previous list are often handled by what are called ETL tools (for *extraction, transformation, and loading*). Those who are new to data warehousing might want to assume that the data in the operational sources is clean and that transformations can be ignored. Unfortunately, this is rarely the case because the process of understanding the data sources, designing the transformations, testing the loading process, and debugging is often the most time-consuming part of deployment. Transformations generally remove bogus data (including erroneous entries and duplicate entries), convert data items to an agreed-upon format, and filter data not considered necessary for the warehouse. These operations not only improve the quality of the data, but also frequently reduce the overall amount of data, which, in turn, improves data warehouse performance.

The frequency with which the extraction occurs is largely determined by the required timeliness of the data in the warehouse. Most extraction and loading takes place on more of a "batch" basis with a known time delay (typically hourly or daily, but sometimes even weekly or monthly). Many early warehouses were completely refreshed during the loading process. As data volumes grew, this became impractical due to limited time frames available for loading. Today, updates to tables are more common. When a need for near real-time data exists, warehouses can be loaded nearly continuously using a *trickle feed*.

Is Cleanliness Best?

Once the data in the warehouse is "clean," is this version of the true nature of the data propagated back to the originating OLTP systems? This is an important issue for data warehouse implementation. In some cases, a "closed loop" process is implemented whereby updates are provided back to the originating systems. In addition to minimizing some of the cleansing that takes place during future extractions, operational reports thus become more accurate.

Another viable option is to avoid cleansing by improving the quality of the data at the time it's input into the operational system. This can sometimes be accomplished by not allowing a "default" condition as allowable input into a data field. Presenting the data-entry person with an array of valid options, one of which *must* be selected, is often a way to ensure the most consistent and valid responses. Many companies also provide education to the data-entry people at this time, showing them how the data they're keying in will be used and what the significance of it is.

Simple extraction and transportation of data is possible using one of several Oracle database features:

Transparent Gateways and Heterogeneous Services
> Provide a bridge to retrieve data from non-Oracle sources using Oracle SQL to load an Oracle database. Heterogeneous Services provide Open DataBase Connectivity (ODBC) connectivity to non-Oracle relational sources. Gateways can optionally provide a higher level of performance when extracting data from non-Oracle sources.

Transportable tablespaces
> Another feature for data movement, transportable tablespaces enable rapid data movement between Oracle instances without export/import. Metadata (the data dictionary) is exported from the source and imported to the target. The transferred tablespace can then be mounted on the target. Oracle Database 10g introduces cross-platform transportable tablespaces, which can move a tablespace from one type of system (e.g., Solaris) to another (e.g., Linux).

Oracle Streams

Comes bundled with Oracle since Oracle9*i* Release 2. Streams includes Oracle's log-based replication, Advanced Queueing (AQ), and, in Oracle Database 10*g*, transportable tablespaces. It is often used for near real-time data movement. Oracle Database 10*g* adds support for downstream capture, which allows changed data to be collected from log files, eliminating overhead; RMAN and Transportable Tablespaces for instantiation; and now also supports LONG, LONG RAW, and NCLOB datatypes. Oracle Database 10*g* adds an asynchronous change data capture that uses Streams to transport from a source database to a target only changed records.

Data Pump Fast Import/Export

New in Oracle Database 10*g*, and enabled via external table support, Data Pump is a new import/export format. Parallel direct path loading and unloading is supported.

Each of these database features is typically used for high performance data transfers and not (by themselves) for difficult transformations. Oracle Warehouse Builder (OWB) is Oracle's ETL tool used for building maps from extraction sources, through predefined or custom transformations to target tables. OWB can then be used to automatically generate the scripts needed to perform the ETL. More than just an ETL tool, OWB can also be used as a data warehouse design tool and provides a metadata repository. Designs may also be imported from a variety of design tools, such as Oracle Designer, CA's ERwin, and Sybase PowerDesigner.

In most warehouse building, metadata is first imported that describes source tables, including Oracle (via database links) and other RDBMS systems (through ODBC or gateways) and flat files. Target tables are designed or imported, and source metadata is mapped to target metadata, including transformations (see Figure 9-4 for an example). OWB's basic set of transformations include a name and address cleansing operator for use with Oracle partners' libraries and applications that perform "householding," matching, and merging of data.

OWB can then validate the source-to-target mappings. Once validated, you can then generate any of the following:

- DDL, if target tables are to be created
- SQL*Loader control files, for the loading of flat files
- PL/SQL scripts, for ETL from relational sources

Scripts are deployed to, and run at, the target data warehouse, typically scheduled using the Enterprise Manager job scheduler. For more complex scheduling of ETL jobs where certain prerequisites must be met, OWB includes an interface to Oracle Workflow.

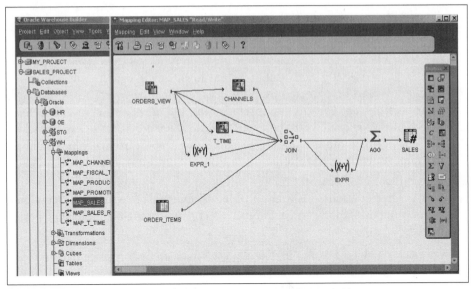

Figure 9-4. Typical Oracle Warehouse Builder source table–to–target table mapping

OWB provides access to a number of other non-Oracle sources. A SAP Integrator provides SQL access to Oracle RDBMS-based SAP tables, and an ABAP code generator builds access to any SAP table on any database, including cluster tables, through a RFC connection.

For high-speed loading of flat files, Oracle SQL*Loader's *direct path load* option provides rapid loading by bypassing the buffer cache and rollback mechanism and writing directly to the datafile. You can run SQL*Loader sessions in parallel to further speed the table loading process (as many warehouses need to be loaded in a limited "window" of time). Many popular extraction tools, including OWB, generate SQL*Loader scripts.

Oracle9*i* first added key ETL functionality in the core database engine including support for external tables, table functions, merge (i.e., insert or update depending on the existence of a data item), multi-table inserts, change data capture, and resumable statements. Today, OWB can be used to leverage this functionality. Additionally, OWB can create trickle feeds through Oracle's AQ, a component of Streams.

Reporting and Ad-Hoc Query Tools

Marketing, financial, and other business analysts are rarely interested in the storage and schema that hold their information. Their interest levels rise when the discussion turns to the tools they'll be using. Business intelligence tools are often evaluated and purchased within individual business areas, sometimes without close IT coordination. Oracle database customers have a choice of Oracle's suite of business intelligence tools or popular independent vendors' products such as Hyperion/Brio,

Business Objects, Cognos, and MicroStrategy. Oracle bundles the business tools it provides in the Oracle Application Server.

Of the tools users need, the least-glamorous but most-often-accessed are reports. Business analysts may wish to avoid reporting software if it requires help from the IT staff, especially if the process of creating and deploying the reports is more time-consuming and less flexible than manipulating the data directly. However, reports appeal to executives within a company because they require no special IT skills or knowledge. The distribution of such reports has been greatly improved as web-based report generation becomes commonplace and the user needs only familiarity with a browser.

Oracle's tool for generating reports, Oracle Reports, has a wizard-based frontend for building reports that can then be deployed to the Web for access as Adobe Acrobat, plain text, or HTML files. With this tool, you can cache reports on a middle-tier server for better performance. The tool also provides some limited drill-down search capabilities, in which a user can ask for more detail about a particular portion of a report.

More sophisticated users need to pose "what-if" questions, such as "what sales volume occurred in the Midwest sub-regions in 2004 and how did sales compare to 2003?" Such users need ad-hoc query tools. Initially developed as client/server tools, many are now web-based and provide similar functionality to the earlier reporting tools. A common theme has been to make these tools much more graphically intuitive. Queries are typically posed by selecting icons that represent tables and items. Users only need be knowledgeable on where their data is stored, and what it represents. The SQL is generated behind the scenes.

Oracle Discoverer, a web-based ad-hoc query tool, provides an easy-to-use frontend for picking and choosing data items around which to build queries and is typically used by business users. Users can generate their own reports and deploy them to the Web as HTML files. Discoverer has a query governor that can predict the amount of time a query will take based on comparisons in records of previous queries kept in the database server. IT can use a separate administrative layer to place limits on the time allowed to perform queries, because an analyst can (either intentionally or accidentally) request incredibly complex and lengthy queries for a particular report. This type of request could result in slow delivery of results and negatively impact overall database performance.

Oracle Discoverer is most often used for querying an Oracle relational database, but ODBC support enables this tool to be used with other databases.

The Portal product, a part of Oracle Application Server, provides an integration point for custom-built business intelligence applications using Oracle Reports, Discoverer, and other tools. It also provides access to a number of other applications and web sites through its interface, and it is highly customizable by users.

OLAP and OLAP Applications Building

As business users become more sophisticated, their questions evolve from "what happened" to "what trends are present and what might happen in the future?" *OLAP tools* provide the ability to handle time-series and mathematical analysis for understanding past trends and forecasting the future.

OLAP initially grew around the early inability of relational databases to effectively handle multidimensional queries (described above in the section "Data Warehouse Design"). The first OLAP tools were packaged with their own data "cubes." Data was downloaded from relational sources.

These separate database engines are called Multidimensional On-Line Analytical Processing engines, or *MOLAP engines*. Examples include Oracle's Express Server and Hyperion Essbase, as well as the Microsoft offering that is part of SQL Server. These MOLAP engines handle queries extremely quickly and work best when the data is not updated frequently (because the cube-generation process takes time).

Today, OLAP tools are used more often with relational databases than MOLAP engines, because star queries are supported to various degrees in many databases and because there is an increased need for very frequently updated data. When used in this fashion, the interaction is called *ROLAP*, which stands for Relational On-Line Analytical Processing. Tools that can work against either relational databases or MOLAP engines are sometimes referred to as *hybrid tools*.

Oracle's OLAP functionality now resides in the Oracle relational database management system (RDBMS). For ROLAP deployment, Oracle Discoverer and other tools can leverage ANSI standard analytic functions built into the database as SQL extensions. Discoverer can also leverage the RDBMS materialized views and an analyzer component provides a frontend to the database OLAP option.

Popular business intelligence tools can also access the OLAP Option, a MOLAP cube within the relational database, via SQL (since Oracle9*i* Release 2). Custom OLAP applications, formerly built via Oracle's Express Objects, are now built using Oracle's JDeveloper and *business intelligence beans*. The Java beans provide prebuilt components for manipulating tables, crosstabs, and graphs, and for building queries and calculations similar to the functionality previously found in Express. JDeveloper generates Java code using these building blocks that map to the Java OLAP API provided by Oracle's OLAP Option. The Oracle Database 10*g* release adds the capability to use XML to describe the OLAP multidimensional data model.

Data Mining

Data mining, an often overused and misunderstood term in data warehousing, is the use of mathematical algorithms to model relationships in the data that wouldn't be apparent by using any other tools. Most companies shouldn't approach data mining unless analysts have met the following criteria:

- An understanding of the quality and meaning of the data in the warehouse
- Business insight gained using other tools and the warehouse
- An understanding of a business issue being driven by too many variables to model outcomes in any other way

In other words, data-mining tools are not a replacement for the analytical skills of data warehouse users.

The data-mining tools themselves can rely on a number of techniques to produce the relationships, such as:

- Extended statistical algorithms, provided by statistical tools vendors, that can highlight statistical variations in the data.
- Clustering techniques that show how business outcomes can fall into certain groups, such as insurance claims versus time for various age brackets. In this example, once a low-risk group is found or classified, further research into influencing factors or "associations" might take place.
- Logic models (if A occurs, then B or C are possible outcomes) validated against small sample sets and then applied to larger data models for prediction.
- Neural networks "trained" against small sets, with known results to be applied later against a much larger set.
- Visualization techniques used to graphically plot variables and understand which variables are key to a particular outcome.

Data mining has been used successfully to solve difficult business problems such as fraud detection and churn in micro-opportunity marketing, as well as in other areas where many variables can influence an outcome. Companies servicing credit cards use data mining to track unusual usage—for example, the unexpected charging to a credit card of expensive jewelry in a city not normally traveled to by the cardholder. Discovering clusters of unusual buying patterns within certain small groups might also drive micro-opportunity marketing campaigns aimed at small audiences with a high probability of purchasing products or services.

A recent trend among relational database providers is tighter integration of data-mining algorithms into the relational database. Oracle's data-mining strategy initially leveraged a traditional client/server version of a product called Oracle Darwin to provide algorithms for modeling associations, neural networks, classification and regression trees, and clusters against Oracle tables or flat files. Oracle began to embed these algorithms in the Oracle9i database. Algorithms now embedded in the database include Naïve Bayes, Associations, Adaptive Bayes Networks, Clustering, Support Vector Machines (SVM), and Nonnegative Matrix Factorization (NMF). The algorithms are accessible via a Java API; however, they may prove most useful when leveraged by Oracle products such as Oracle Personalization, for real-time web site recommendations. New data mining capabilities in Oracle Database 10g include text mining (providing document clustering and classification) and BLAST similarity searches, leveraging the new SVM algorithms (common in genetic research). Data mining applications can be custom built using Oracle's JDeveloper in combination with DM4J. DM4J is used to develop, test, and score the models. It provides the ability to define metadata, tune the generated Java code, view generated XML files, and test application components.

Business Intelligence Applications

Business intelligence applications are prebuilt solutions providing extended reporting and "dashboard-like" interfaces to display business trends. The applications may directly access OLTP applications by leveraging Oracle materialized views, such as Oracle's Daily Business Intelligence, or more traditional data warehouses, such as SAP Business Warehouse and most custom deployment topologies.

The new business intelligence applications from software vendors focus on specific areas of business expertise, such as marketing or financial analysis. These applications include predefined queries, reports, and charts that deliver the kind of information required for a particular type of business analysis while sparing the end user the complexity of creating these objects from scratch.

Oracle ERP Applications Intelligence modules provide a mixture of access into Oracle transactions tables (for Daily Business Intelligence) and into Oracle's Enterprise Data Warehouse (EDW). Access is commonly through prebuilt Oracle Discoverer workbooks containing prepopulated business metadata. Oracle intelligence modules include Financial, Purchasing, Project, Manufacturing, Supply Chain, Marketing, and Human Resources Intelligence. The EDW can leverage customized Oracle Applications Flexfields through an Oracle Applications Integrator available for Oracle Warehouse Builder. It can also be extended to extract and load data from non-Oracle sources through OWB. Oracle also offers other useful applications, including a Balanced Scorecard for measuring and displaying progress toward meeting business objectives and key performance indicators.

The promise of tightly integrated solutions, such as the Intelligence modules, is that they will provide easier-to-deploy solutions with more out-of-the-box functionality. While some customization will probably always be needed, the time required to deploy an initial and useful solution should be substantially reduced.

The Metadata Challenge

On the one hand, *metadata*—or descriptive data about data—is incredibly important. Virtually all types of interactions with a database require the use of metadata, from datatypes of the data to business meaning and history of data fields.

On the other hand, metadata is useful only if the tools and clients who wish to use it can leverage it. One of the great challenges is to create a set of common metadata definitions that allows tools and databases from different vendors to interact.

There have been a number of attempts to reach an agreement on common metadata definitions. In 2000, a standard was ratified that defines a common interface for interchange of metadata implementations. Named the Common Warehouse Metadata Interchange (CWMI) by the Object Management Group (OMG), this standard is based on XML interchange. Oracle was one of the early proponents and developers of the technology in this standard. Oracle has a CWM bridge for exchanging metadata stored in the Oracle Warehouse Builder repository. OWB also includes a metadata viewer for more detailed metadata reports, and a viewer for data lineage and impact analysis diagrams.

Best Practices

Those experienced in business intelligence generally agree that the following are typical reasons why these projects fail:

Failure to involve business users, IT representatives, sponsoring executives, and anyone else with a vested interest throughout the data warehousing process
> Not only do all of these groups provide valuable input for creating a data warehouse, but lack of support by any of them can cause a data warehouse to fail.

Overlooking the key reasons for the data warehouse existence
> During the planning stages, data warehouse designers can lose sight of the forces driving the creation of the warehouse.

Overlooked details and incorrect assumptions
> A less-than-rigorous examination of the environment for a data warehouse can doom the project to failure.

Unrealistic time frames and scope
> As with all projects, starting the creation of a data warehouse with too short a time frame and too aggressive a scope will force the data warehouse team to cut corners, resulting in the mistakes previously mentioned.

Failure to manage expectations
> Data warehouses, like all technologies, are not a panacea. You must make sure that all members of the team, as well as the eventual users of the data warehouse, have an appropriate set of expectations.

Tactical decision-making at the expense of long-term strategy
> Although it may seem overly time-consuming at the start, you must keep in mind the long-term goals of your project, and your organization, throughout the design and implementation process. Failing to do so has two results: it delays the onset of problems, but it also increases the likelihood and severity of those problems.

Failure to leverage the experience of others

There's nothing like learning from those who have succeeded on similar projects. It's almost as good to gain from the experience of others who have failed at similar tasks; at least you can avoid the mistakes that led to their failures.

Successful business intelligence projects require the continuous involvement of business analysts and users, sponsoring executives, and IT. Ignoring this often-repeated piece of advice is probably the single biggest cause of many of the most spectacular failures. Establishing a warehouse has to produce a clear business benefit and return on investment (ROI). Executives are key throughout the process because data warehouse and data mart coordination often crosses departmental boundaries, and funding likely comes from high levels.

Your business intelligence project should provide answers to business problems that are linked to key business initiatives. Ruthlessly eliminate any developments that take projects in another direction. The motivation behind the technology implementation schedule should be the desire to answer critical business questions. Positive ROI from the project should be demonstrated during the incremental building process.

Common Misconceptions

Having too simplistic a view during any part of the building process (a view that overlooks details) can lead to many problems. Here are just a few of the typical (and usually incorrect) assumptions people make in the process of implementing a business intelligence solution:

- Sources of data are clean and consistent.
- Someone in the organization understands what is in the source databases, the quality of the data, and where to find items of business interest.
- Extractions from operational sources can be built and discarded as needed, with no records left behind.
- Summary data is going to be adequate, and detailed data can be left out.
- IT has all the skills available to manage and develop all the necessary extraction routines, tune the database(s), maintain the systems and the network, and perform backups and recoveries in a reasonable time frame.
- Development is possible without continuous feedback and periodic prototyping involving analysts and possibly sponsoring executives.
- The warehouse won't change over time, so "versioning" won't be an issue.
- Analysts will have all the skills needed to make full use of the warehouse or the warehouse tools.

- IT can control what tools the analysts select and use.
- The number of users is known and predictable.
- The kinds of queries are known and predictable.
- Computer hardware is infinitely scalable, regardless of design.
- If a business area builds a data mart independently, IT won't be asked to support it later.
- Consultants will be readily available in a pinch to solve last-minute problems.
- Metadata is not important, and planning for it can be delayed.

Effective Strategy

Most software and implementation projects have difficulty meeting schedules. Because of the complexity in business intelligence projects, they frequently take much longer than the initial schedule, which is exactly what an executive who needs the information to make vital strategic decisions doesn't want to hear! If you build in increments implementing working prototypes along the way, the project can begin showing positive ROI, and changes in the subsequent schedule can be linked back to real business requirements, not just to technical issues (which executives don't ordinarily understand).

You must avoid scope creep and expectations throughout the project. When you receive recommended changes or additions from the business side, you must confirm that these changes provide an adequate return on investment or you will find yourself working long and hard on facets of the warehouse without any real payoff. The business reasoning must be part of the prioritization process; you must understand why trade-offs are made. If you run into departmental "turf wars" over the ownership of data, you'll need to involve key executives for mediation and guidance.

The pressure of limited time and skills and immediate business needs sometimes leads to making tactical decisions in establishing a data warehouse at the expense of a long-term strategy. In spite of the pressures, you should create a long-term strategy at the beginning of the project and stick to it, or at least be aware of the consequences of modifying it. There should be just enough detail to prevent wasted efforts along the way, and the strategy should be flexible enough to take into account business acquisitions, mergers, and so on.

Your long-term strategy must embrace emerging trends in warehousing such as web deployment and the need for high-availability solutions. The rate of change and volume of products being introduced sometimes makes it difficult to sort through what is real and what is hype. Most companies struggle with keeping up with the knowledge curve. Traditional sources of information include vendors, consultants, and data-processing industry consultants, each of which usually has a vested interest in selling something. The vendors want to sell products; the consultants want to sell skills they have "on the bench"; and IT industry analysts may be reselling their favorable reviews of vendors and consultants to those same vendors and consultants. Any single source can lead to wrong conclusions, but by talking to multiple sources, some consensus should emerge and provide answers to your questions.

The best way to gain insight is by discussing business intelligence projects with similar companies—at least at the working prototype stage—at conferences. Finding workable solutions and establishing a set of contacts to network with in the future can make attendance at these conferences well worth the price (and may even be more valuable than the topics presented).

CHAPTER 10

Oracle and High Availability

The data stored in the databases of your organization's computer systems is extremely valuable. In many cases, this data represents your organization's most valuable asset. Protecting this asset is crucial for any Oracle site.

As a DBA, system administrator, or system architect, you'll probably have to use a variety of options and techniques to ensure that your data is adequately protected from a catastrophe. Of course, implementing proper backup operations is the foundation of any disaster-prevention strategy, but there are other ways to avoid a variety of disasters, from simple disk failures to a complete failure of your primary site.

Computer hardware is, by and large, extremely reliable, which may make it tempting for you to postpone thinking about disaster recovery. Most software is also very reliable, and the Oracle database protects the integrity of its data even in the event of a software failure. However, components and software will, at times, fail, and the more components are involved, the greater the likelihood of a disaster.

The difference between an inconvenience and a disaster is the presence or absence of adequate recovery plans, so it's best to understand all of the options available with Oracle so you can choose the best approach for your particular site.

With Oracle, you can guarantee that your precious data is highly available. Some of the types of high-availability features are part of the Oracle software, such as Oracle's automatic crash recovery and the Real Application Clusters option. Other features are available from third-party vendors, such as hardware failover solutions and some backup managers. Finally, some of the most important features of a high-availability solution are dependent on implementing appropriate procedures to safeguard your data. This chapter covers all three aspects of high availability.

What Is High Availability?

Before we can begin a discussion of how to ensure a high level of availability for your data, you need to understand the exact meaning of the term *availability*.

Availability can mean different things for different organizations. For this discussion, we'll consider a system to be available when that system is both *up* (which means that the database can be accessed by users) and *working* (which means that the database is delivering the expected functionality to users with the expected performance).

Businesses have always depended on their data being available. With the expansion of the user base that has come with increased use of the Web, database failures can have an even more dramatic impact on business. Failure of web-based systems with links outside a company's employees are, unfortunately, immediately visible to the outside world and can seriously affect the company's financial health as well as its image and the loyalty of its customers and partners. Consider the Internet service offered by UPS and FedEx to share package status and tracking with their customers. As customers come to depend heavily on a service offered over the Web, interruptions in that service can cause these same customers to move to competitors.

In addition, the demands posed by integrating multiple systems means a single failure can cause entire supply chains to become unavailable.

To implement systems that are highly availabile, you must include techniques to avoid downtime, such as redundant hardware, as well as techniques to allow recovery from disasters, such as implementing the appropriate backup routines.

Measuring and Planning Availability

Most organizations automatically assume that they need 24/7 availability, meaning that the system must be available 24 hours a day, 7 days a week. Quite often, this requirement is stated with little examination of the business functions the system will support. With the perceived cost of technology components on the decline and their reliability on the increase, most users and a fair number of IT personnel feel that achieving very high levels of availability should be simple and cheap. Many of us leave our PCs running all the time, and many people have not experienced the joy of losing their hard drives or having their power supplies fail, at least recently.

Unfortunately, while some components are certainly becoming cheaper and more reliable, component availability doesn't equate to system availability. The complex layering of hardware and software in today's two- and three-tier systems introduces multiple interdependencies and points of failure. Achieving very high levels of availability for a system with varied and interdependent components is not necessarily either simple or inexpensive.

To provide some perspective, consider Table 10-1, which translates the percentage of system availability into days, minutes, and hours of annual downtime based on a 365-day year.

Table 10-1. *System availability*

% availability	System downtime per year		
	Days	Hours	Minutes
95.000	18	6	0
96.000	14	14	24
97.000	10	23	48
98.000	7	7	12
99.000	3	16	36
99.500	1	20	48
99.900	0	9	46
99.990	0	1	53
99.999	0	0	5

Large-scale systems that achieve over 99% availability typically cost well into the millions of dollars to design and implement, with high ongoing operational costs as well. Marginal increases in availability require large incremental investments in all system components. Moving from 95% to 99% availability is likely to be very costly, while moving from 99% to 99.99% will probably cost even more.

Another key aspect of measuring availability is the definition of *when* the system must be available. A required availability of 99% of the time during normal working hours from 8 a.m. to 5 p.m. is very different from 99% availability based on a 24-hour day. In the same way that you must carefully define your required level of availability, you must also consider the hours during which availability is measured. For example, a lot of companies still typically take orders during business hours. The cost of a down order-entry system is very high during the business day. However, the cost of downtime drops after 5 p.m. This factor points to opportunities for scheduled downtime after hours that will, in turn, help reduce unplanned failures during business hours. At the other end of the spectrum, consider web-based and multinational companies, whose global reach implies that the business day never ends.

The often casually stated default requirement that a system be available 24/7 must be put in the context of the high costs required. Even an initial examination of the complexity and cost of very high availability will often lead to more realistic goals and associated budgets for system availability.

The costs of achieving high availability are certainly justified in some cases. It may cost a brokerage house millions of dollars an hour for each hour that their key systems are down, while a less demanding business, such as catalog sales, may lose only thousands of dollars an hour, based on a less efficient manual system that acts as a stopgap measure. But, regardless of the cost of lost business opportunity, an unexpected loss of availability can cut into the productivity of employees and IT staff alike.

Causes of Unplanned Downtime

There are many different causes of unplanned downtime. You can prevent some very easily, while others require significant investments in site infrastructure, telecommunications, hardware, software, and skilled employees. Figure 10-1 summarizes some of the more common causes of system failures.

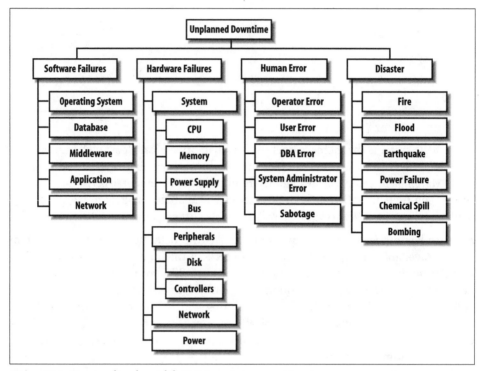

Figure 10-1. Causes of unplanned downtime

When creating a plan to guarantee the availability of your application, you should make a point of considering all the items shown in this chart as well as other potential causes of system interruption that are specific to your own circumstances. As with all planning, it's much better to consider all options, even if you quickly dismiss them, than to be caught off guard when an unexpected event occurs.

System Availability Versus Component Availability

A complete system is composed of various hardware, software, and networking components operating as a technology *stack*. Ensuring the availability of individual components doesn't necessarily guarantee system availability. Different strategies and solutions exist for achieving high availability for each of the system components. Figure 10-2 illustrates the technology stack used to deliver a potential system.

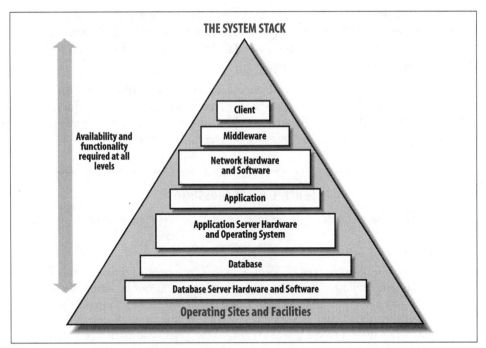

Figure 10-2. Components of a system

As this figure shows, a variety of physical and logical layers must cooperate to deliver an application. Some systems may involve fewer components; for example, a two-tier client/server system would not have the additional application server components.

Failures in the components above the database can effectively prevent access to the database even though the database itself may be available. The database server and the database itself serve as the foundation for the stack. When a database fails, it immediately affects the higher levels of the stack. If the failure results in lost or corrupted data, the overall integrity of the application may be affected.

The potential threats to availability span all the components involved in an application system, but in this chapter we'll examine only availability issues relating specifically to the database.

System Crashes

The abrupt failure of the server machine running the database is one of the most common causes of unplanned downtime. The server may crash because of hardware problems, such as the failure of a power supply, or because of software problems, such as a process that begins to consume all the machine's CPU resources. Even if the underlying server platform is fine, the Oracle instance itself can fail. Whatever the cause of the crash, the effect on Oracle is the same—the instance cannot deliver its promised functionality. Remember that when an Oracle database crashes, it's the instance that crashes, not the database, as described in Chapter 2. Even when a system crashes, the crash will not imperil any data that's already safely stored within the disk files used by the Oracle database.

The impact of the crash will depend on the activity in progress at the time of the crash. Any connected sessions will no longer have a server process to which to talk. All active queries and transactions will be abruptly terminated. The process of cleaning up the resulting mess is called *instance recovery* or *crash recovery*.

Telltale Error Messages

The following two error messages are often good indicators that an Oracle instance is down:

```
ORA-03113:  End-of-file on communication channel
```

This message is usually received by clients that try to resubmit an operation that failed due to an instance failure. The message is somewhat cryptic but becomes clear if you interpret it very literally. Oracle works using a pipe to communicate between the client application and its associated server process in the Oracle instance. When the instance fails, the client's server process ceases to exist, so there is no one listening on the other end of the pipe. The communication channel between the client and the server is no longer valid.

```
ORA-01034:  Oracle not available
```

This terse message means that when the client requested a connection to the Oracle instance, the instance was not there. Clients that try to connect to a failed instance will typically get this message. The client can connect to the Listener, but when the Listener attempts to hand the client off to the requested Oracle instance, the ORA-01034 condition results.

What Is Instance Recovery?

When you restart an Oracle instance after a failure, Oracle detects that a crash occurred using information in the control file and the headers of the database files. Oracle then performs instance recovery automatically and uses the online redo logs to guarantee that the physical database is restored to a consistent state as it existed at the time of the crash. This requires two actions:

- All committed transactions will be recovered.
- In-flight transactions will be rolled back or undone.

Note that an in-flight transaction might be one that a user didn't commit or one that was committed by the user but not confirmed by Oracle before the system failure. A transaction isn't considered committed until Oracle has written the relevant details of the transaction to the current online redo log and has sent back a message to the client application confirming the committed transaction.

Phases of Instance Recovery

Instance recovery has two phases: rollforward and rollback.

Recovering an instance requires the use of the redo logs, described in Chapter 2. The redo logs contain a recording of all the physical changes made to the database as a result of transactional activity, both committed and uncommitted.

The checkpoint concept, also introduced in Chapter 2, is critical to understanding crash recovery. When a transaction is committed, Oracle writes all associated database block changes to the current online redo log. The actual database blocks may have already been flushed to disk, or may be flushed at some later point. This means that the online redo log can contain changes not yet reflected in the actual database blocks stored in the datafiles. Oracle periodically ensures that the data blocks in the datafiles on disk are synchronized with the redo log to reflect all the committed changes up to a point in time. Oracle does this by writing all the database blocks changed by those committed transactions to the datafiles on disk. This operation is called a *checkpoint*. Completed checkpoints are recorded in the control file, datafile headers, and redo log.

Rollforward

At any point in time, the online redo logs will be ahead of the datafiles by a certain amount of time or number of committed transactions. Instance recovery closes this gap and ensures that the datafiles reflect all committed transactions up to the time the instance crashed. Oracle performs instance recovery by rolling forward through the online redo log and replaying all the changes from the last completed checkpoint to the time of instance failure. This operation is called the *rollforward* phase of instance recovery.

While implementing rollforward recovery, Oracle reads the necessary database blocks into the System Global Area and reproduces the changes that were originally applied to the blocks. This process includes reproducing the undo or rollback information, in addition to the data changes. Rollback segments are composed of extents and data blocks just like tables, and all changes to rollback segment blocks are part of the redo for a given transaction. For example, suppose that a user changed an employee name from "John" to "Jonathan". As Oracle applies the redo log, it will read the block containing the employee row into the cache and redo the name change. As part of recovering the transaction, Oracle will also write the old name "John" to a rollback segment, as was done for the original transaction.

When the rollforward phase is finished, all the changes for committed and uncommitted transactions have been reproduced. The uncommitted transactions are in-flight once again, just as they were at the time the crash occurred. This leads to the next logical phase of instance recovery—rollback. But before we discuss rollbacks themselves, we need to look at how Oracle uses checkpoints and how the timing of checkpoints can affect recovery time.

Fast-start fault recovery and bounded recovery time

Checkpoints cause an increase in I/O as the database writer flushes all the database blocks to disk to bring the datafiles up to the time of the checkpoint. Prior to Oracle8, DBAs controlled the checkpoint frequency using initialization file parameters and the size of the redo log files. The relevant initialization file parameters are:

LOG_CHECKPOINT_INTERVAL
> The number of redo log blocks (operating system blocks) written between checkpoints.

LOG_CHECKPOINT_TIMEOUT
> The number of seconds between checkpoints. A 0 value disables time-based checkpoints.

Oracle performs a checkpoint whenever a log switch occurs, regardless of the values used for these parameters.

Reducing the checkpoint interval or timeout can result in smaller amounts of data between checkpoints. This reduced data can lead to faster recovery times, but can also introduce the overhead of more frequent checkpoints and their associated disk activity. For additional details about the subtleties of these parameters, see the section "Managing the Online Redo Log" in the appropriate backup and recovery documentation.

A common strategy for minimizing the number of checkpoints is to set these initialization file parameters so that checkpoints occur only with log switches. For example, a DBA might set LOG_CHECKPOINT_TIMEOUT to 0 and LOG_CHECKPOINT_INTERVAL to a value higher than the size of the redo log file. These settings result in applying a minimum of one redo log file's worth of redo in the event of a crash, which can result in unacceptably long recovery times.

Oracle8i introduced an initialization file parameter that provides a simpler and more accurate way to control recovery times: FAST_START_IO_TARGET. The bulk of recovery activity involves performing I/O for reading database blocks into the cache so that redo can be applied to them. This parameter sets a target ceiling on how many database blocks Oracle will have to read in applying redo information. Oracle will dynamically vary the checkpoint frequency in an attempt to limit the number of blocks that will need to be read for recovery to the value of this parameter. This variance will, in turn, more effectively limit the associated recovery time without setting checkpoint rates to a fixed value that isn't valid for different workloads.

Oracle9*i* further sped this recovery process. Beginning at the last checkpoint, the redo log is scanned for data blocks that contain unsaved changes and need to be recovered. In the subsequent scan, changes are applied only where needed. Because the subsequent scan is a sequential read and reading unnecessary blocks (random I/O) is eliminated, the recovery time is reduced.

Oracle9*i* also introduced a fast-start time-based recovery feature. DBAs can specify a target for recovery time in seconds (in the FAST_START_MTTR_TARGET initialization parameter, where MTTR stands for Mean Time to Recover) in order to meet Service Level Agreements and other requirements. The database will automatically determine values for FAST_START_IO_TARGET and LOG_CHECKPOINT_INTERVAL. Estimated MTTR values are calculated and placed in V$INSTANCE_RECOVERY, thereby providing a means for real-world calibration and more accurate estimates over time.

Rollback

The rollforward phase re-creates uncommitted transactions and their associated rollback information. These in-flight transactions must be rolled back to return to a consistent state.

In Oracle releases prior to Version 7.3, the database isn't available until all uncommitted transactions had been rolled back. Although a DBA can control the checkpoint frequency and therefore control the time required for the rollforward phase of instance recovery, the number of uncommitted transactions at the time of the crash can vary tremendously and cannot really be accurately controlled or predicted. In a busy OLTP system, there are typically a fair number of in-flight transactions requiring rollback after a crash. This situation led to variable and unpredictable times for crash recovery. The solution to this problem, *deferred rollback*, was introduced in Oracle 7.3.

Deferred rollback

In Version 7.3 and later, Oracle opens the database after the rollforward phase of recovery and performs the rollback of uncommitted transactions in the background. This process reduces database downtime and helps to reduce the variability of recovery times by deferring the rollback phase.

But what if a user's transaction begins working in a database block that contains some changes left behind by an uncommitted transaction? If this happens, the user's transaction will trigger a foreground rollback to undo the changes and will then proceed when rollback is complete. This action is transparent to the user—he doesn't receive error messages or have to resubmit the transaction.

Fast-start rollback

Oracle8*i* further optimized the deferred rollback process by limiting the rollback triggered by a user transaction to the block in which the transaction is interested. For example, suppose there is a large uncommitted transaction that affected 500 database blocks. Prior to Oracle8*i*, the first user transaction that touches one of those 500 blocks will trigger a foreground rollback and will absorb the overhead of rolling back the entire transaction. Leveraging fast-start rollback, the user's transaction will roll back only the changes to the block in which it's interested. New transactions don't have to wait for the complete rollback of large uncommitted transactions.

Protecting Against System Crashes

There are a variety of approaches you can take to help protect your system against the ill effects of system crashes, including the following:

- Providing component redundancy
- Using Real Application Clusters/Oracle Parallel Server
- Using Transparent Application Failover software services

Component Redundancy

As basic protection, the various hardware components that make up the database server itself must be fault-tolerant. *Fault-tolerance*, as the name implies, allows the overall hardware system to continue to operate even if one of its components fails. This feature, in turn, implies redundant components and the ability to detect component failure and seamlessly integrate the failed component's replacement. The major system components that should be fault-tolerant include the following:

- Disk drives
- Disk controllers
- CPUs
- Power supplies
- Cooling fans
- Network cards
- System buses

Disk failure is the largest area of exposure for hardware failure, because disks have the shortest times between failure of any of the components in a computer system. Disks also present the greatest variety of redundant solutions, so discussing that type of failure in detail should provide the best example of how high availability can be implemented with hardware.

Disk redundancy

Disk failure is the most common cause of system failure. Although the mean time to failure of an individual disk drive is very high, the ever-increasing number of disks used for today's very large databases results in more frequent disk failures. Protection from disk failure is usually accomplished using RAID technology. The term RAID (Redundant Array of Inexpensive Disks) originated in a paper published in 1987 by Patterson, Gibson, and Katz at the University of California. (RAID also means Redundant Array of Independent Disks.) The use of redundant storage has become common for systems of all sizes and types for two primary reasons: the real threat of disk failure and the proliferation of packaged, relatively affordable RAID solutions.

RAID technology uses one of two concepts to achieve redundancy:

Mirroring
> The actual data is duplicated on another disk in the system.

Striping with parity
> Data is striped on multiple disks, but instead of duplicating the data itself for redundancy, a mathematical calculation termed *parity* is performed on the data and the result is stored on another disk. You can think of parity as the sum of the striped data. If one of the disks is lost, you can reconstruct the data on that disk using the surviving disks and the parity data. The lost data represents the only unknown variable in the equation and can be derived. You can conceptualize this as a simple formula:
>
> $$A + B + C + D = E$$
>
> in which A–D are data striped across four disks and E is the parity data on a fifth disk. If you lose any of the disks, you can solve the equation to identify the missing component. For example, if you lose the B drive you can solve the formula as
>
> $$B = E - A - C - D.$$

There are a number of different disk configurations or types of RAID technology, which are formally termed *levels*. The basics of RAID technology were introduced in Chapter 6, but Table 10-2 summarizes the most relevant levels of RAID in a bit more detail, in terms of their cost, high availability, and the way Oracle uses each RAID level.

Table 10-2. RAID levels relevant to high availability

Level	Disk configuration	Cost	Comments	Oracle usage
0	Simple striping, no redundancy	Same cost as unprotected storage.	Also referred to as JBOD (Just a Bunch of Disks). The term RAID-0 is used to describe striping, which increases read and write throughput. However, this is not really RAID, as there is no actual redundancy.	Striping simplifies administration for Oracle datafiles. Suitable for all types of data for which redundancy isn't required.

Table 10-2. RAID levels relevant to high availability (continued)

Level	Disk configuration	Cost	Comments	Oracle usage
1	Mirroring	Twice the cost of unprotected storage.	Same write performance as a single disk. Read performance may improve through servicing reads from both copies.	Lack of striping adds complexity of managing a larger number of devices for Oracle. Often used for redo logs, because the I/O for redo is typically relatively small sequential writes. Striped arrays are more suited to large I/Os or to multiple smaller, random I/Os.
0+1	Striping and mirroring	Twice the cost of unprotected storage.	Best of both worlds— striping increases read and write performance and mirroring for redundancy avoids "read-modify-write" overhead of RAID-5.	Same usage as RAID-0, but provides protection from disk failure.
5	Striping with rotating or distributed parity	Storage capacity is reduced by 1/N, where N is the number of disks in the array. For example, the storage is reduced by 20%, or 1/5 of the total disk storage, for a 5-disk array.	Parity data is spread across all disks, avoiding the potential bottleneck found in some other types of RAID arrays. Striping increases read performance. Maintaining parity data adds additional I/O, decreasing write performance. For each write, the associated parity data must be read, modified, and written back to disk. This is referred to as the "read-modify-write" penalty.	Cost-effective solution for all Oracle data except redo logs. Degraded write performance must be taken into account. Popular for data warehouses as they involve mostly read activity. However, write penalties may slow loads and index builds. Often avoided for high-volume OLTP due to write penalties. Some storage vendors, such as EMC, have proprietary solutions (RAID-S) to minimize parity overhead on writes.

Figure 10-3 illustrates the disk configurations for various RAID levels.

Automatic Storage Management

Oracle Database 10g includes a new capability called Automatic Storage Management (ASM), which provides striping and mirroring for many types of disks, including JBOD, as described earlier. You can specify groups of disks, and designate a failover group to be used in the result of a disk failure. ASM includes the ability to detect disk "hot spots" and redistribute data to avoid disk bottlenecks, as well as the capability of adding disks to a disk group without any interruption in service.

ASM is designed both to simplify disk management and to allow you to use cheaper disk systems and still obtain higher levels of reliability and performance.

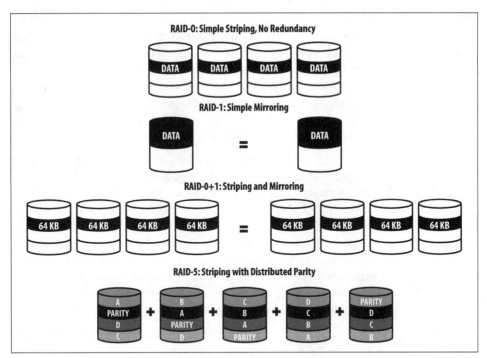

Figure 10-3. RAID levels commonly used with an Oracle database

---

Which RAID Levels Should You Use with Oracle?

Some people say that you should never use RAID-5 for an Oracle database because of the degraded write performance of this level of RAID. RAID-1 and RAID-0+1 offer better performance, but double the cost of disk storage. RAID-5 offers a cheaper and reasonable solution, provided that you can meet performance requirements despite the extra write overhead for maintaining parity data. Use these generic guidelines to help determine the appropriate uses of different RAID levels:

- Use RAID-1 for redo log files
- Use RAID-5 for database files, provided that the write overhead is acceptable
- Use RAID-1 or RAID-0+1 for database files if RAID-5 write overhead is unacceptable

---

Simple Hardware Failover

Oracle recovers automatically from a system crash. This automatic recovery protects the integrity of the data, which is the most essential feature of any relational database, but it also results in downtime as the database recovers from a crash. When a hardware failure occurs, the ability to quickly detect a system crash and initiate recovery is crucial to minimizing the associated downtime.

When an individual server fails, the instance running on that node fails as well. Depending on the cause, the failed node may not return to service quickly, or the failure may not be detected immediately by a human operator. Either way, companies that wish to protect their systems from the failure of a node typically employ a cluster of machines to achieve simple hardware failover. *Failover* is the ability of a surviving node in a cluster to assume the responsibilities of a failed node. Although failover doesn't directly address the issue of the reliability of the underlying hardware, automated failover can reduce the downtime from hardware failure.

The concept is very simple: a combination of software and hardware "watches" over the cluster. Typically, this monitoring is done by regularly checking a "heartbeat," which is a message sent between machines in the cluster. If Machine A fails, Machine B will detect the failure through the loss of the heartbeat and will execute scripts to take over control of the disks, assume Machine A's network address, and restart the processes that failed with Machine A. From an Oracle database perspective, the entire set of events is identical to an instance crash followed by an instance recovery. The instance uses the control files, redo log files, and database files to perform crash recovery. The fact that the instance is now running on another machine is irrelevant—the various Oracle files on disk are the key.

Most failover solutions include software that runs on the machine to monitor specific processes, such as the background processes of the Oracle instance. If the primary node itself has not failed but some process has, the monitoring software will detect the failure of the process and take some action based on scripts set up by the system administrator. For example, if the Oracle instance fails, the monitoring software may attempt to restart the Oracle instance three times. If all three attempts are unsuccessful, the software may initiate physical hardware failover, transferring control to the alternate node in the cluster.

Figures 10-4 and 10-5 illustrate the process of implementing a simple failover.

Outage duration for hardware failover

The time for failover to take effect, and therefore the length of the associated database downtime, depends on the following intervals:

Time for the alternate node to detect the failure of the primary node
> The alternate node monitors the primary node using a heartbeat mechanism. The frequency of this check is usually configurable—for example, every 30 seconds—providing control over the maximum time that a primary node failure will go undetected.

Time for the alternate node to execute various startup actions
> The time needed for such actions (e.g., assuming control of the disks used to store the Oracle database) may vary by system and should be determined through testing. One important consideration is the time required for a filesystem check. The larger the database, the larger the number of filesystems that

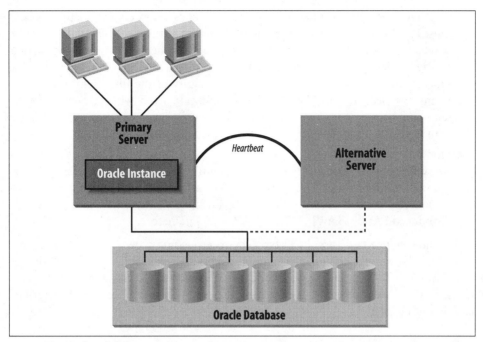

Figure 10-4. Before failover

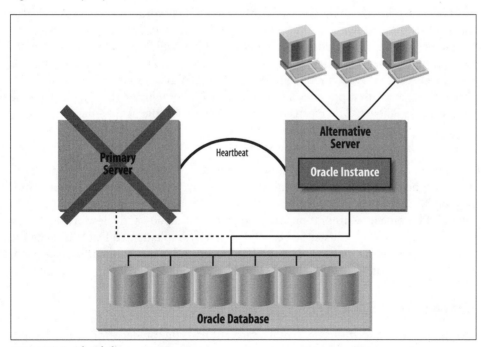

Figure 10-5. After failover

may have been used. When the alternate node assumes control of the disks, it must check the state of the various filesystems on the disks. This time can be reduced by using a journaled filesystem, such as the one provided by Veritas Software (*http://www.veritas.com*). This software essentially uses a logging scheme similar to Oracle's to protect the integrity of the filesystem, thus eliminating the need for a complete filesystem check. Even with journaled filesystems, disk takeover can easily take several minutes, particularly on a busy system with high levels of disk activity.

Time for Oracle crash recovery

As we mentioned, you can effectively control this time period using checkpoints. Oracle provides a simple way to control recovery times using the initialization parameter FAST_START_IO_TARGET and the more recently introduced FAST_START_MTTR_TARGET parameter.

When the instance fails, users will typically receive some type of error message and will typically attempt to log in again. Application developers can deal with this sequence of failover events with generic or specific error handling in their applications, or they can use the Transparent Application Failover functionality described later in this chapter.

Failover and operating system platform

Failover capability has long been available in the Unix world; more recently, it was introduced to Windows with the availability of Microsoft Cluster Server clustering technology. The Unix vendors typically offer a simple failover solution consisting of two machines, an interconnect between the machines, and the required software. No additional software is required from Oracle. In the Windows arena, Oracle includes Fail Safe, software that provides a GUI interface for configuring the Oracle database for hardware failover. The mechanics of the failover are the same—the GUI is simply an administrative convenience. Configuration wizards may also be used to enable failover in the Oracle Application Server middle tier.

Oracle offered a failover solution for Windows NT with Oracle7 even before Microsoft had delivered its clustering solution. Early versions of Fail Safe were available on NT hardware from vendors with clustering and failover experience, such as Digital Equipment Corporation (subsequently Compaq and now HP). When Microsoft delivered its Cluster Server, Oracle simply implemented Fail Safe using the Cluster Server interfaces instead of the hardware vendor interfaces previously used. Fail Safe can be configured for clusters of up to four nodes.

Real Application Clusters

Oracle first introduced Oracle Parallel Server (OPS), the predecessor to Real Application Clusters (RAC), in 1989 on Digital Equipment Corporation's VAX clusters running the VMS operating system. OPS became available in the Unix environment in 1993. Oracle now offers Real Application Clusters on virtually every commercially available cluster or Massively Parallel Processing (MPP) hardware configuration.

At first glance, Real Application Clusters may look similar to the clustered solutions described earlier in the "Simple Hardware Failover" section. Both failover and Real Application Clusters involve clustered hardware with access to disks from multiple nodes. The key difference is that Real Application Clusters uses multiple Oracle instances that provide concurrent access to the same database. With simple hardware failover only one node has an active instance, but with Real Application Clusters each node is an active Oracle instance. Clients can connect to any of the instances to access the same database.

Because each Oracle instance runs on its own node, if a node fails, the instance on that node also fails. The overall Oracle database remains available from the surviving instances still running on other working nodes.

Figure 10-6 illustrates Real Application Clusters on a cluster.

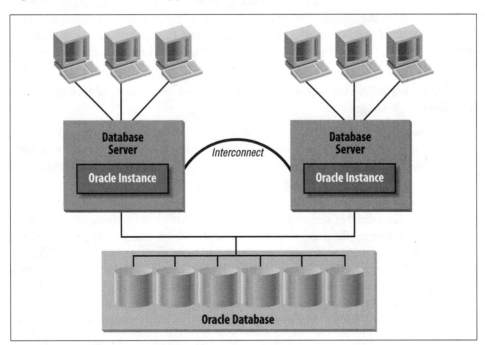

Figure 10-6. Oracle Real Application Clusters on a cluster

Real Application Clusters and hardware failover

Which technology achieves better availability, Real Application Clusters or simple hardware failover capability? The Real Application Clusters option can typically provide higher levels of availability than simple hardware failover, as we explain in the remainder of this section. This option can also provide additional flexibility for scaling the application across multiple machines, although it does require more sophisticated system and database administration skills. Simply put, if the higher availability and flexibility of Real Application Clusters doesn't justify the additional expense and complexity, the use of a simple hardware failover solution is probably a more appropriate choice.

While the Real Application Clusters option is an add-on to your Oracle database license, it is not a separate database product. Although it supports Oracle instances across multiple nodes, it is based on and uses the same core Oracle database product. Installing Real Application Clusters adds code to the Oracle executable but doesn't replace the core database program.

Real Application Clusters increases availability by enabling avoidance of complete database blackouts. With simple hardware failover, the database is completely unavailable until node failover, instance startup, and crash recovery are complete. With Real Application Clusters, clients can connect to a surviving instance any time. Clients may be able to continue working with no interruption, depending on whether the data they need to work on was under the control of the failed instance. You can think of the failure of a Real Application Clusters instance as a potential database "brownout," as opposed to the guaranteed blackout caused by hardware failover.

Some other key differences between hardware failover and Real Application Clusters include the following:

- The Real Application Clusters option avoids the various activities involved in disk takeover: mounting volumes, validating filesystem integrity, opening Oracle database files, and so on. Not performing these activities can significantly reduce the time required to achieve full system availability.

- The Real Application Clusters option doesn't require the creation and maintenance of the complex scripts typically used to control the activities for hardware failover. For example, there is no need to script which disk volumes will be taken over by a surviving node. The automatic nature of Real Application Clusters avoids the complex initial system administration to set up the failover environment, as well as the ongoing administration needed as additional disk volumes are used. In fact, adding disk volumes to your database but forgetting to add the volumes to the various failover scripts can cause a hardware failover solution to fail itself!

In a simple two-way cluster used for hardware failover, both machines should have equal processing power and should be sized so that each can handle the entire workload. This equivalence is clearly required because only one node of the cluster is used at any point for the entire workload. If one node fails, the other should be capable of running the same workload with equal performance.

With Real Application Clusters, you can use both nodes of the cluster concurrently to spread the workload, reducing the load on one machine or node. You must still make sure that each machine will be powerful enough to adequately handle the entire workload (albeit at a reduced performance level) to meet basic business requirements when a node is not available.

Of course, using Real Application Clusters to spread the workload over several machines will result in a lower percentage of each machine's resources being used in normal operating conditions, which is typically more expensive than using fully utilized machines. Each machine in the cluster must devote some overhead to maintaining its role in the cluster, although Oracle claims that this overhead may reduce overall machine throughput by only as little as 10–15%. You will have to weigh the benefits of carrying on without any performance degradation in the event of a node failure versus the cost of buying more powerful machines. The economics of your situation may dictate that a decrease in performance in the event of a node failure is more palatable than a larger initial outlay for larger systems.

Using Real Application Clusters for scalability is a bit more complex than it is for high availability, but much of the complexity of tuning and programming has been removed since Oracle9i. Deployment has been simplified with Oracle Database 10g through the introduction of integrated clusterware. You can learn more about Real Application Clusters scalability in Oracle documentation and in Chapter 8 of this book.

Node failure and Real Application Clusters

The database instances provide protection for each other—if an instance fails, one of the surviving instances will detect the failure and automatically initiate Real Applications Clusters recovery. This type of recovery is different from the hardware failover, discussed previously. No actual "failover" occurs—no disk takeover is required, because all nodes already have access to the disks used for the database. There is no need to start an Oracle instance on the surviving node or nodes, because Oracle is already running on all the nodes. The Oracle software performs the necessary actions without using scripts; the required steps are an integral part of Real Application Clusters software.

The phases of Real Application Clusters recovery are the following:

Cluster reorganization
> When an instance failure occurs, Real Application Clusters must first determine which nodes of the cluster remain in service. Oracle9i introduced a disk-based heartbeat in which each database group member votes on what members are part of the current group. Based on arbitration, a correct current group configuration is established. The time required for this operation is very brief.

Lock database rebuild

The lock database, which contains the information used to coordinate Real Application Clusters traffic, is distributed across the multiple active instances. Therefore, a portion of that information is lost when a node fails. The remaining nodes have sufficient redundant data to reconstruct the lost information. Once the cluster membership has been determined, the surviving instances reconstruct the lock database. The time for this phase depends on how many locks must be recovered, as well as whether the rebuild process involves a single surviving node or multiple surviving nodes. Oracle speeds the lock remastering process by allowing optimization of lock master locations in the background while users are accessing the system. In a two-node cluster, node failure leaves a single surviving node that acts as a dictator and processes the lock operations very quickly.

Instance recovery

Once the lock database has been rebuilt, the redo logs from the failed instance perform crash recovery. This is similar to single-instance crash recovery—a rollforward phase followed by a nonblocking, deferred rollback phase. The key difference is that the recovery isn't performed by restarting a failed instance. Rather, it's performed by the instance that detected the failure.

While Real Application Clusters recovery is in progress, clients connected to surviving instances remain connected and can continue working. In some cases users may experience a slight delay in response times, but their sessions aren't terminated. Clients connected to the failed instance can reconnect to a surviving instance and can resume working. Uncommitted transactions will be rolled back and will have to be resubmitted. Queries that were active will also have been terminated and will require resubmission. A very powerful feature, Transparent Application Failover (TAF) can be used to automatically continue query processing on a surviving node without requiring users to resubmit their queries. You can also use TAF to resubmit transactions without user intervention.

Parallel Fail Safe / RACGuard

Oracle Parallel Fail Safe was renamed RACGuard in Oracle9*i* and integrated into the core RAC product in Oracle Database 10*g*. Prior to Oracle Database 10*g*, it was a feature in Real Application Clusters that leveraged the clustering technology of systems vendors. It supported such features as:

- Automated, fast, and bounded recovery times from Oracle instance crashes
- Automatic capture of diagnostic data
- Guaranteed primary and secondary configuration
- Support for features such as Transparent Application Failover (described in the next section)

- Client preconnection to secondary instances to speed reconnection

Oracle Transparent Application Failover

Oracle introduced the Transparent Application Failover (TAF) capability in the first release of Oracle8. As the name implies, TAF provides a seamless migration of users' sessions from one Oracle instance to another. You can use TAF to mask the failure of an instance for transparent high availability or to migrate users from an active instance to a less active one. Figure 10-7 illustrates TAF with Real Application Clusters.

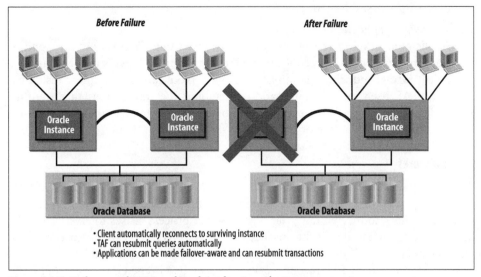

Figure 10-7. Failover with TAF and Real Application Clusters

As shown in this figure, TAF can automatically reconnect clients to another instance of the database, which provides access to the same database as the original instance. The high-availability benefits of TAF include the following:

Transparent reconnection

Clients don't have to manually reconnect to a surviving instance. You can optimally reconfigure TAF to preconnect clients to an alternate instance in addition to their primary instance when they log on. Preconnecting clients to an alternate instance removes the overhead of establishing a new connection when automatic failover takes place. For systems with a large number of connected clients, this preconnection avoids the overhead and delays caused by flooding the alternate instance with a large number of simultaneous connection requests.

Automatic resubmission of queries

TAF can automatically resubmit queries that were active at the time the first instance failed and can resume sending results back to the client. Oracle will re-execute the query as of the time the original query started. Oracle's read consistency will therefore provide the correct answer regardless of any activity since the query began. However, when the user requests the "next" row from a query, Oracle will have to process through all rows from the start of the query until the requested row, which may result in a performance lag.

Callback functions

Oracle8*i* enhanced TAF by enabling the application developer to register a "callback function" with TAF. Once TAF has successfully reconnected the client to the alternate instance, the registered function will be called automatically. The application developer can use the callback function to reinitialize various aspects of session state as desired.

Failover-aware applications

Application developers can leverage TAF by writing "failover-aware" applications that resubmit transactions that were lost when the client's primary instance failed, further reducing the impact of failure. Note that unlike query resubmission, TAF itself doesn't automatically resubmit the transactions that were in-flight. Rather, it provides a framework for a seamless failover that can be leveraged by application developers.

How TAF works

TAF is implemented in the Oracle Call Interface (OCI) layer, a low-level API for establishing and managing Oracle database connections. When the instance to which a client is connected fails, the client's server process ceases to exist. The OCI layer in the client can detect the absence of a server process on the other end of the channel and automatically establish a new connection to another instance. The alternate instance to which TAF reconnects users is specified in the Oracle Net configuration files, which are described in the Oracle Net documentation.

Because OCI is a low-level API, writing programs with OCI requires more effort and sophistication on the part of the developer. Fortunately, Oracle uses OCI to write client tools and various drivers, so that applications using these tools can leverage TAF. Support for TAF in ODBC and JDBC drivers is especially useful; it means that TAF can be leveraged by any client application that uses these drivers to connect to Oracle. For example, TAF can provide automatic reconnection for a third-party query tool that uses ODBC. To implement TAF with ODBC, set up an ODBC data source that uses an Oracle Net service name that has been configured to use TAF in the Oracle Net configuration files. ODBC uses Oracle Net and can therefore leverage the TAF feature.

TAF and various Oracle configurations

Although the TAF-Real Application Clusters combination is the most obvious combination for high availability, TAF can be used with a single Oracle instance or with multiple databases, each accessible from a single instance. Some possible configurations are as follows:

- TAF can automatically reconnect clients back to their original instances for cases in which the instance failed but the node did not. An automated monitoring system, such as the Oracle Enterprise Manager, can detect instance failure quickly and restart the instance. The fast-start recovery features in Oracle enable very low crash recovery times. Users that aren't performing heads-down data entry work can be automatically reconnected by TAF and might never be aware that their instance failed and was restarted.

- In simple clusters, TAF can reconnect users to the instance started by simple hardware failover on the surviving node of a cluster. The reconnection cannot occur until the alternate node has started Oracle and has performed crash recovery.

- When there are two distinct databases, each with a single instance, TAF can reconnect clients to an instance that provides access to a different database running in another data center. This clearly requires replication of the relevant data between the two databases. Oracle fortunately provides automated support for data replication, which is covered in the later section entitled "Complete Site Failure."

Recovering from Disasters

Despite the prevalence of redundant or protected disk storage, media failures can and do occur. In cases in which one or more Oracle datafiles are lost due to disk failure, you must use database backups to recover the lost data.

There are times when simple human or machine error can also lead to the loss of data, just as a media failure can. For example, an administrator may accidentally delete a datafile, or an I/O subsystem may malfunction, corrupting data on the disks. The key to being prepared to handle these types of disasters is implementing a good backup and recovery strategy.

Developing a Backup and Recovery Strategy

Proper development, documentation, and testing of your backup and recovery strategy is one of the most important activities in implementing an Oracle database. You must test every phase of the backup and recovery process to ensure that the entire process works, because once a disaster hits the complete recovery process *must* work flawlessly.

Some companies test the backup procedure but fail to actually test recovery using the backups taken. Only when a failure requires the use of the backups do companies discover that the backups in place were unusable for some reason. It's critical to test the entire cycle from backup through restore and recovery.

Taking Oracle Backups

Two basic types of backups are available with Oracle:

Hot backup
> The datafiles for one or more tablespaces are backed up while the database is active.

Cold backup
> The database is shut down and all the datafiles, redo log files, and control files are backed up.

With a hot backup, not all of the datafiles must be backed up at once. For instance, you may want to back up a different group of datafiles each night. You must be sure to keep backups of the archived redo logs that date back to your oldest backed-up datafile, because you'll need them if you have to implement rollforward recovery from the time of that oldest datafile backup.

Some DBAs with very large databases back up the various datafiles over several runs. Some DBAs back up the datafiles that contain data subject to frequent changes more frequently (for example, daily), and back up datafiles containing more static data less often (for example, weekly). There are commands to back up the control file as well; this should be done after all the datafiles have been backed up.

If the database isn't archiving redo logs (this is known as running in NOARCHIVELOG mode and is described in Chapter 2), you can only take complete cold backups. If the database is archiving redo logs, it can be backed up while running.

Regardless of backup type, you should also back up the *INIT.ORA* or *SPFILE* file and password files—these are key files for the operation of your Oracle database. While not required, you should also back up the various scripts used to create and further develop the database. These scripts represent an important part of the documentation of the structure and evolution of the database.

For more information about the different types of backups and variations on these types, please refer to your Oracle documentation as well as the third-party books listed in Appendix B.

Using Backups to Recover

Two basic types of recovery are possible with Oracle, based on whether or not you are archiving the redo logs:

Complete database recovery

If the database did not archive redo logs, only a complete cold backup is possible. Correspondingly, only a complete database recovery can be performed. You restore the database files, redo logs, and control files from the backup. The database is essentially restored as of the time of the backup. All work done since the time of the backup is lost and a complete recovery must be performed even if only one of the datafiles is damaged. The potential for lost work, coupled with the need to restore the entire database to correct partial failure, are reasons most shops avoid this situation by running their databases in ARCHIVELOG mode. Figure 10-8 illustrates backup and recovery for a database without archived redo logs.

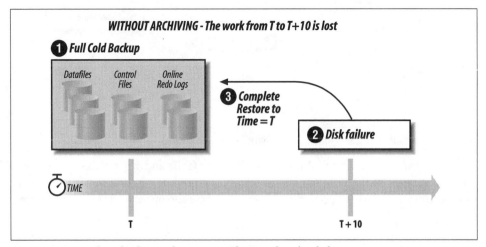

Figure 10-8. Database backup and recovery without archived redo logs

Partial or targeted restore and rollforward recovery

When you're running the Oracle database in ARCHIVELOG mode, you can restore only the damaged datafile(s) and can apply redo log information from the time the backup was taken to the point of failure. The archived and online redo logs reproduce all the changes to the restored datafiles to bring them up to the same point in time as the rest of the database. This procedure minimizes the time for the restore and recovery operations. Partial recovery like this can be done with the database down. Alternatively, the affected tablespace(s) can be placed offline and recovery can be performed with the rest of the database available. Oracle9i improved the granularity of the recovery process by also enabling restore and recovery of individual data blocks instead of providing restore and recovery only of entire datafiles. Figure 10-9 illustrates backup and recovery with archived redo logs.

Obviously, the redo logs are extremely important. Oracle first enabled analysis of these files through the LogMiner tool in Oracle8i. Since Oracle9i, the LogMiner is

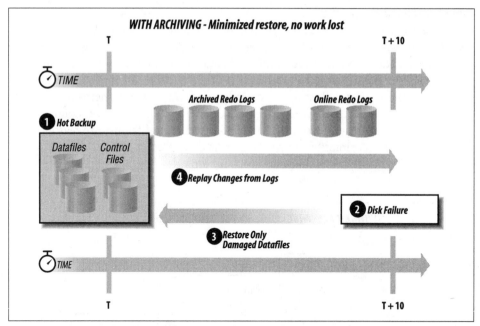

Figure 10-9. Database backup and recovery with archived redo logs

accessible through an Oracle Enterprise Manager GUI, and it provides log analysis for all datatypes. If the redo log has become corrupted, the LogMiner can now read past corrupted records as desired in order to analyze the impact on transactions after the corruption.

Read-Only Tablespaces

Oracle 7.3 introduced read-only tablespaces. Using the ALTER TABLESPACE statement in SQL, you can mark a tablespace as read-only. No changes are possible to the objects stored in a read-only tablespace. You can toggle a tablespace between read/write and read-only states as you wish.

Once a tablespace is in read-only mode, it can be backed up once and doesn't have to be backed up again, because its contents cannot change unless it's placed in read/write mode. Marking a tablespace as read-only allows entire sections of a database to be marked read-only, backed up once, and excluded from regular backups thereafter.

If a datafile of a read-only tablespace is damaged, you can restore it directly from the backup without any recovery. Because no changes were made to the datafiles, no redo log information needs to be applied. For databases with significant static or historical data, this option can significantly simplify and streamline backup and restore operations.

Read-only tablespaces, combined with Oracle's ability to partition a table on a range or list of column values (for example, a date) provide powerful support for the rolling windows common to data warehouses (described in Chapter 9). Once a new month's data is loaded, indexed, and so on, the relevant tablespaces can be marked read-only and backed up once, removing the tablespaces datafile(s) from the cycle of ongoing backup and significantly reducing the time required for those backup operations.

Point-in-Time Recovery

Oracle 7.3 introduced point-in-time recovery (PITR) for the entire database. Point-in-time recovery allows a DBA to restore the datafiles for the database and apply redo information up to a specific time or System Change Number (SCN). This limited type of recovery is useful for cases in which an error occurred—for example, if a table was dropped accidentally or a large number of rows were deleted incorrectly. The DBA can restore the database to the point in time just prior to the event to undo the results of the mistake.

A difficulty with database-level point-in-time recovery is that the entire database has to be restored. In response to this limitation, Oracle8 introduced point-in-time recovery at the tablespace level within the database. Point-in-time recovery based on a tablespace allows a DBA to restore and recover a specific tablespace or set of tablespaces to a particular point in time. Only the tablespace(s) containing the desired objects need to be recovered. This is a very useful improvement given the ever-increasing size of today's databases.

You should use this tablespace feature carefully, because objects in one tablespace may have dependencies, such as referential integrity constraints, on objects in other tablespaces. For example, suppose that Tablespace1 contains the EMP table and Tablespace2 contains the DEPT table, and a foreign key constraint links these two tables together for referential integrity. If you were to recover Tablespace2 to an earlier point than Tablespace1, you might find that you had rows in the EMP table that contained an invalid foreign key value, because the matching primary key entry in the DEPT table had not been rolled forward to the place where the primary key value to which the EMP table refers had been added.

Flashback

Oracle9i introduced a new recovery option called *flashback*, which was designed to help to recovery from user errors.

The concept behind flashback recovery is simple. You can execute a query against the database as of a particular time or system change number (SCN). Oracle delivers the result set as it would have appeared if the query were run at that time, using the undo log information segments to reconstruct the data, which can then be used to correct the results of the errant action.

Oracle Database 10*g* includes a much wider range of flashback options, including:

FLASHBACK DATABASE
> Returns (rolls back) the entire database to a particular point in time. Can be used instead of point-in-time recovery in some situations.

FLASHBACK TABLE
> Returns a specific table to a specific point in time.

FLASHBACK TRANSACTION
> Returns all the changes made by one specific transaction.

FLASHBACK DROP
> Rolls back a drop operation. When an object is dropped, it is placed in a Recycle Bin, so a user can simply un-drop the object to restore it.

SELECT Flashback clauses
> New clauses in the SELECT statement return all the versions of rows (i.e., show changes to the rows) in a particular query over a span of time.

Recovery Manager

Recovery Manager (RMAN) debuted with Oracle8 and provides server-managed backup and recovery. RMAN includes the ability to perform and track backup and recovery operations. RMAN does the following:

- Backs up one or more datafiles to disk or tape
- Backs up archived redo logs to disk or tape
- Restores datafiles from disk or tape
- Restores and applies archived redo logs to perform recovery
- Automatically parallelizes both the reading and writing of the various Oracle files being backed up

RMAN performs the backup operations and updates a catalog, which is stored in an Oracle database with the details of what backups were taken and where they were stored. You can query this catalog for critical information, such as datafiles that have not been backed up or datafiles whose backups have been invalidated through NOLOGGING operations performed on objects contained in those datafiles.

RMAN also uses the catalog to perform incremental backups. RMAN will back up only database blocks that have changed since the last backup. When RMAN backs up only the individual changed blocks in the database, the overall backup and recovery time can be significantly reduced for databases in which a small percentage of the data in large tables changes. With Oracle Database 10*g*, RMAN can apply incremental backups to an image backup of the database; it also provides enhanced performance for incremental backups.

Another major advantage RMAN offers is to make it simpler to perform hot or online backups. RMAN also reduces the overhead required to make online backups.

Prior to RMAN (in Oracle7), you took hot backups by issuing ALTER TABLESPACE BEGIN BACKUP statements for the tablespace whose datafiles were to be backed up; you backed up the datafiles using operating system commands and issuing ALTER TABLESPACE END BACKUP statements. Oracle continued to write blocks to the datafiles while they were being backed up, and there was no restriction on user activity. This meant that the datafile backups could contain blocks from different points in time, because the backup process itself occurred over time and blocks were being written to the datafiles during this time.

Consider the following example. The operating system process reading the datafile reads the first operating system block within an Oracle block composed of two operating system blocks and writes it to tape at Time T. At T+1, Oracle updates the database block in the datafile. Both operating system blocks in the datafile on disk are now consistent as of Time T+1. The operating system process for the backup then reads and backs up the second operating system block as of T+1. The datafile backup now contains a "fuzzy" database block. The two operating system blocks that make up the Oracle block in the backup are from different points in time—the first operating system block is as of Time T, and the second is as of Time T+1.

To address this potential inconsistency, Oracle7 backups automatically included extra redo information to correct this situation for any tablespace for which an ALTER TABLESPACE BEGIN BACKUP had been issued. In Oracle Database 10*g*, you can issue a single ALTER DATABASE statement to put all of the tablespaces in a database into hot backup mode.

RMAN is an Oracle process in Oracle8 and more recent releases that reads and writes Oracle blocks, not operating system blocks. While RMAN is backing up a datafile Oracle blocks can be written to it, but RMAN will read and write in consistent Oracle blocks, not operating system blocks within an Oracle block. This removes the possibility of fuzzy Oracle blocks in the datafile backups and therefore removes the need for the ALTER TABLESPACE statements and the additional redo.

In Oracle Database 10*g*, RMAN is used to support automated disk-based backup. Disk-based strategies have an advantage over tape: they enable random access to any data such that only changes need be backed up or recovered. RMAN can be set up to run a backup job to disk at a specific time. RMAN will manage the deletion of backup files that are no longer necessary. Future releases promise to integrate these automatic backups with a maintenance window of time, which can minimize the impact of backup operations by running them when resources are readily available.

Complete Site Failure

Protection from the complete failure of your primary Oracle site poses significant challenges. Your company must carefully evaluate the risks to its primary site. These risks include physical and environmental problems as well as hardware risks. For example, is the data center in an area prone to floods, tornadoes, or earthquakes? Are power failures a frequent occurrence? Previous versions of this book treated events such as "a terrorist attack or an airplane crash into the data center" as remote possibilities, but, unfortunately, these scenarios no longer seem so implausible.

Protection from primary site failure involves monitoring of and redundancy controls for the following:

- Data center power supply
- Data center climate control facilities
- Database server redundancy
- Database redundancy
- Data redundancy

The first three items on the list are aimed at preventing the failure of the data center. Data server redundancy, through simple hardware failover or Real Application Clusters, provides protection from node failure within a data center but not from complete data center loss.

Should the data center fail completely, the last two items—database redundancy and data redundancy—provide for disaster recovery.

Emerging Technologies: Clusters Across a Distance

Some vendors are now offering clustering solutions that allow the nodes of the cluster to be separated by enough distance to allow one node to survive the failure of the data center that contains the other node. In fact, it is anticipated that many grid computing deployments will occur this way in the future. The clustering of nodes separated by a few kilometers is becoming possible using sophisticated interconnect technologies that can function over greater distances. The disks are mirrored with a copy at each site to allow each site to function in the event of a complete failure of the other site.

These solutions are intriguing because they can provide data server redundancy and data center redundancy in a single solution. If one node (or the data center containing it) fails, the node in the other data center provides failover.

Oracle Data Guard: Standby Database for Redundancy

Oracle's physical standby database functionality was introduced in Oracle 7.3 to provide database redundancy. In Oracle9*i*, this concept was extended to include

---

support for a logical standby database. The enhanced feature set is called Oracle Data Guard.

The concept of a physical standby database is simple—keep a copy of the database files at a second location, ship the redo logs to the second site as they are filled, and apply them to the copy of the database. This process keeps the standby database "a few steps" behind the primary database. If the primary site fails, the standby database is opened and becomes the production database. The potential data loss is limited to the transactions in any redo logs that have not been shipped to the standby site. Figure 10-10 illustrates the standby database feature.

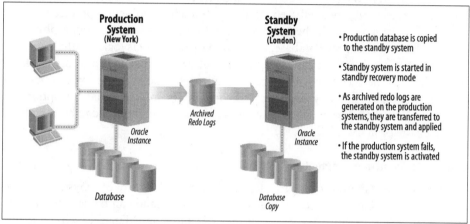

Figure 10-10. Standby database

The physical standby database can be opened only for read-only access. You can use read-only access to offload reporting, such as end-of-day reports, from the primary server to the standby server. The ability to offload reporting requests provides flexibility for reporting and queries and can help performance on the primary server while making use of the standby server.

While the standby database is being used for reporting, the archived redo information from the primary site couldn't be applied prior to Oracle Database 10g. Recovery can continue when the standby database is closed again. This factor has important implications for the time it will take to recover from an outage with the standby database. If the primary site fails while the standby database is open for reporting, the archived redo information from the primary site that accumulated while the standby database was querying must be applied before the standby is brought online. This application of archived redo information increases the duration of the outage. You'll need to weigh the benefits of using the standby database for reporting against the recovery time and the duration of the outage should a failure occur while archived redo information is not being applied at the standby. Oracle Database 10g introduces a real-time feature enabling redo data to be applied at the standby as soon as it is received.

Once a standby database is opened for read/write access, as opposed to read-only access, it can no longer be used as a standby database and you cannot resume applying archived redo information later. The standby database must be "re-cloned" from the primary site if it is opened accidentally in read/write mode.

Logical standby database

Oracle Data Guard also offers a logical standby database capability. With this capability, the standard Oracle archive logs are transformed into SQL transactions, and these are applied to an open standby database. The logical standby database is different physically from the primary standby database and can be used for different tasks. For example, the primary database might be indexed for transaction processing while the standby database might be indexed for data warehousing. Although physically different from the primary database, the secondary database is logically the same and can take over processing in case the primary fails. As archive logs are shipped from the primary to the secondary, undo records in the shipped archive log can be compared to the logical standby undo records to guard against potential corruption. As of Oracle Database 10g, you can instantiate the logical standby database without quiescing the primary.

Oracle Data Guard management

The Oracle Data Guard broker provides monitoring and control for physical and logical standby databases and components. A single command can be used to perform failover. Oracle Enterprise Manager provides a Data Guard Manager GUI for setting up, monitoring, and managing the standby database.

The Oracle Database 10g Data Guard broker adds support for creating and managing configurations containing RAC primary and standby databases. The Data Guard broker leverages the Cluster Ready Services in Oracle Database 10g.

Possible Causes of Lost Data with a Physical Standby Database

There is a possibility that you will lose data, even if you use a physical standby database. There are three possible causes of lost data in the event of primary site failure:

- Archived redo logs have not been shipped to the standby site
- Filled online redo logs have not been archived yet
- The current online redo log is not a candidate for archiving until a log switch occurs

These three potential problems are addressed in different ways, as described in the following sections.

Copying archived redo logs to a standby site

Prior to Oracle8*i*, copying of archived redo logs from the primary to the standby site was not automated. You were free to use any method to copy the files across the network. For example, you could schedule a batch job that copies archived logs to the standby site every *N* minutes. If the primary site fails, these copies would limit the lost redo information (and therefore the lost data) to a maximum of *N* minutes of work.

Oracle8*i* first provided support for the archiving of redo logs to a destination on the primary server as well as on multiple remote servers. This feature automates the copying and application of the archived redo logs to one or more standby sites. The lost data is then limited to the contents of any filled redo logs that have not been completely archived, as well as the current online redo log. Oracle also automatically applies the archived redo logs to the standby database as they arrive.

Oracle9*i* added the option to specify zero data loss to a standby machine. In this mode, all changes to a local log file are written synchronously to a remote log file. This mode guarantees that switching over to the standby database will not result in any lost data. As you might guess, this mode may impact performance, as each log write must also be completed to a remote log file. Oracle provides an option that will only wait to write to a remote log for a specified period of time, so that a network failure will not bring database processing to a halt.

Unarchived redo information and the role of geomirroring

If you cannot allow primary site failure to result in the loss of *any* data, and do not choose to use the zero data loss option of Data Guard, the solution is to mirror all redo log and control file activity from the primary site to the standby site.

You can provide this level of reliability by using a remote mirroring technology sometimes known as *geomirroring*. Essentially, all writes to the online redo log files and the control files at the primary site must be mirrored synchronously to the standby site. For simplicity, you can also geomirror the archived log destination, which will duplicate the archived logs at the remote site, in effect copying the archived redo logs from the primary to the standby site. This approach can simplify operations; you use one solution for all the mirroring requirements, as opposed to having Oracle copy the archived logs and having geomirroring handle the other critical files.

Geomirroring of the online redo logs results in every committed transaction being written to both the online redo log at the primary site and the copy of the online redo log at the standby site. This process adds some time to each transaction for the mirrored write to reach the standby site. Depending on the distance between the sites and the network used, geomirroring can hamper performance, so you should test its impact on the normal operation of your database.

Geomirroring provides the most complete protection against primary site failure and, accordingly, it's a relatively expensive solution. You will need to weigh the cost of the sophisticated disk subsystems and high-speed telecommunication lines needed for nonintrusive geomirroring against the cost of losing the data in any unarchived redo logs and the current online redo log. See Appendix B for where to find more information about geomirroring.

Data Redundancy Solutions

Redundant data is another option for dealing with primary site failure. Implementing a redundant data approach differs from using a standby database, which duplicates the entire primary database. Data redundancy is achieved by having a copy of your critical data in an entirely separate Oracle database with a different structure. The data, not the database itself, is redundant. If the primary site fails, users can continue working using the redundant data in the secondary database.

Oracle provides automated synchronous and asynchronous data-replication features to support data redundancy. For simplicity, in the following sections we'll examine replication using a simple two-site example—a primary and a secondary. Oracle can, however, perform *N*-way or multimaster replication involving more than two sites with all sites replicating to all others.

Data Replication: Synchronous and Asynchronous

Whenever you have a data replication scenario, you always have a primary site, from which the replication originates, and a secondary site, which is the recipient of the data replication. (In a multimaster scenario, you can have more than one master site, and a single machine can be a master site for one replication plan and a secondary site for another.) When you design your replication plan, you must consider the degree to which data at the secondary site can differ for a period of time from the data at the primary site. This difference is referred to as *data divergence*. When you implement replication, Oracle generates triggers on all specified tables. These triggers are fired as part of the primary site transactions. The triggers either update the secondary site's data as part of the same transaction (*synchronous replication*) or place an entry in a deferred transaction queue that will be used later to update the secondary site (*asynchronous replication*).

Key considerations in setting up a replication environment include the following:

Tolerance for data divergence
> The smaller the data divergence, the more individual replication actions will have to be performed. You will reduce the resources needed to implement the replication by increasing the data divergence.

Performance requirements

Because replication requires resources, it can have an impact on performance. However, Oracle Database 10g allows Oracle Streams to capture change data from log files, which greatly reduces the performance impact of replication on an active database.

Network bandwidth

Because replication uses network bandwidth, you have to consider the availability of this resource.

Distance between sites

The more distance between sites, the longer the physical transfer of data will take and the longer each application will take.

Site and network stability

If a site or a network goes down, all replications that use that network or are destined for that site will not be received. When either of these resources comes back online, the stored replication traffic can have an impact on the amount of time it takes to recover the site.

Experience level of your database administrators

Even the most effective replication plan can be undone by DBAs who aren't familiar with replication.

Figure 10-11 illustrates synchronous and asynchronous replication.

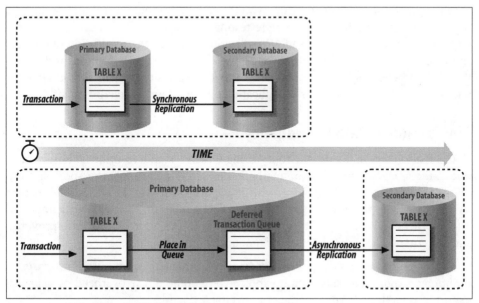

Figure 10-11. Oracle replication for redundant data

Synchronous, or *real-time*, *replication* can be used when there is no tolerance for data divergence or lost data. The data at the secondary site *must* match the primary site at all times and reflect all committed transactions. Each transaction at the primary site will fire triggers that call procedures at the secondary site to reproduce the transaction. Synchronous replication uses distributed transactions that will add overhead to every transaction at the primary site. Whether or not this additional overhead is acceptable will clearly depend on your specific requirements. Synchronous replication introduces system interdependencies—the secondary site and the network connecting the sites must be up or the primary site will not be able to perform transactions.

You can also use *asynchronous*, or *deferred*, *replication* to provide redundant data. With asynchronous replication, transactions are performed at the primary site and replicated some time later to the secondary site. Until the deferred transaction queue is "pushed" to the secondary site, replicating the changes, the data at the secondary site will differ from the primary site data. If the primary database is irrevocably lost, any unpushed transactions in the deferred queue will also be lost.

The extent of the data divergence and potential data loss resulting from the divergence is a very important consideration in configuring asynchronous replication. In addition, asynchronous replication allows the primary site to function when the network or the secondary site is down, while synchronous replication requires that the secondary site be available. Asynchronous replication adds overhead to transactions at the primary site, so once again, you'll need to carefully consider throughput requirements and perform appropriate testing. Typically, asynchronous replication adds less overhead than synchronous replication, because the replication of changes can be efficiently batched to the secondary site. However, asynchronous replication will still add overhead to the operation of the primary site, so you should consider and test the effect of both types of replication on your database environment.

Old-Fashioned Data Redundancy

You can also achieve data redundancy using Oracle's standard utilities. Historically, one of the most common backup methods for Oracle was simply to export the contents of the database into a file using the Oracle Export utility. This file could then be shipped in binary form to any platform Oracle supports and subsequently imported into another database with Oracle's Import utility. This approach can still provide a simple form of data redundancy if the amount of data is manageable.

Oracle 7.3 introduced a *direct path export* feature that runs about 70% faster than a traditional export. The direct path export avoids some of the overhead of a normal export by directly accessing the data in the Oracle datafiles.

You can also improve the performance of an import with some planning. An import is essentially a series of INSERT statements, so you can optimize the insert process by inserting the data into a table without indexes and then adding the indexes after the table is built. The time and resources needed to perform large exports and imports may make this an appropriate option.

Another export solution is to unload data from the desired tables into simple flat files by spooling the output of a SELECT statement to an operating system file. You can then ship the flat file to the secondary site and use Oracle's SQL*Loader utility to load the data into duplicate tables in the secondary database. For cases in which a significant amount of data is input to the primary system using loads, such as in a data warehouse, a viable disaster-recovery plan is simply to back up the load files to a secondary site on which they will wait, ready for reloading to either the primary or secondary sites should a disaster occur.

Oracle Database 10*g* further speeds this process through introduction of the new Data Pump, a higher-speed export/import.

While these methods may seem relatively crude, they can provide simple data redundancy for targeted sets of data. Transportable tablespaces can also be used to move entire tablespaces to a backup platform. Oracle Database 10*g* lets you transport tablespaces from one type of system to another, which increases their flexibility for implementing redundancy, moving large amounts of data, and migrating to another database platform.

Export/Import, Standby Database, or Replication?

All the choices we've discussed in this chapter offer you some type of protection against losing critical data—or your entire database. But which one is right for your needs?

To quote the standard answer to so many technical questions, "It depends:"

- Export/Import, whether in its original form or in the Oracle Database 10*g* Data Pump, provides a simple and proven method, but the overhead involved with this method typically leaves larger time periods where data is lost in the event of a failure.

- Transportable tablespaces can provide the same functionality with better performance, but are less granular.

- A physical standby database typically leaves smaller data gaps or, in the case since introduction of Oracle9*i* zero-data loss, no data gap; however, this solution does require the expense of redundant hardware.

- Replication also requires redundant hardware and ensures consistent and complete data on both the primary and backup server, but this solution is the most resource-intensive of all.

You should carefully balance the cost, both in extra hardware and performance, of each of these solutions, and balance them against the potential cost of a database or server failure. Of course, any one of these solutions is infinitely more valuable than not implementing any of them and simply hoping that a disaster never happens to you.

CHAPTER 11

Oracle and Hardware Architecture

In Chapter 2 we discussed the architecture of the Oracle database, and in Chapter 6 we described how Oracle uses hardware resources. Although Oracle operates in the same way on many hardware platforms, different hardware architectures can ultimately determine the specific scalability, performance tuning, management, and reliability options available to you. Over the years, Oracle has developed new features to address specific platforms and, with Oracle Database 10g, continues this process with a commitment to grid computing. This chapter discusses the various hardware architectures to provide a basis for understanding how Oracle leverages each of these platforms.

This chapter explains the following hardware systems and how Oracle takes advantage of the features inherent in each of the platforms:

- Uniprocessors
- Symmetric Multiprocessing (SMP) systems
- Clusters
- Massively Parallel Processing (MPP) systems
- Non-Uniform Memory Access (NUMA) systems
- Grid computing

We'll also discuss the use of different disk technologies and how to choose the hardware system that's most appropriate for your purposes.

System Basics

Any discussion of hardware systems begins with a review of the components that make up a hardware platform and the impact these components have on the overall system. You'll find the same essential components under the covers of any computer system:

- One or more CPUs, which execute the basic instructions that make up computer programs
- Memory, which stores recently accessed instructions and data
- An input/output (I/O) system, which typically consists of some combination of a disk, a diskette, and tape controllers for pulling data and programs off physical media or network controllers for connecting the system to other systems on the network.

The number of each of these components and the capabilities of the individual components themselves determine the ultimate cost and scalability of a system. A machine with four processors is typically more expensive and capable of doing more work than a single-processor machine; new versions of components, such as CPU chips, are typically faster and more expensive than older versions.

 Typically, in the fast moving world of chip development, computers with a smaller number of processors are able to integrate new chips more rapidly than machines with larger numbers of CPUs.

In decision-support or data warehousing systems, CPU and memory are often the performance-limiting components. In online transaction processing (OLTP) systems, I/O is often the most critical component.

Each component has a latency cost and capacity associated with it. The *latency cost* of a component is the amount of latency the use of that component introduces into the system—in other words, how much slower each successive level of a component is than its previous level (e.g., Level 2 versus Level 1; see Table 11-1).

The CPU and the Level 1 (L1) memory cache on the CPU have the lowest latency, as shown in Table 11-1, but also the least capacity. Disk has the most capacity but the highest latency.

 There are several different types of memory: an L1 cache, which is on the CPU chip; an L2 (Level 2) cache, which is on the same board as the CPU; and main memory, which is the remaining memory on the machine.

Table 11-1. Typical sizes and latencies of system components

Element	Typical storage capability	Typical latency
CPU	None	10 nanoseconds
L1 cache (on CPU)	10s to 100s of KBs	10 nanoseconds
L2 cache (on same board)	100s of KBs to MBs	40–60 nanoseconds
Main memory	MBs to 10 GBs	200–400 nanoseconds
Disk	GBs to TBs	10–15 million nanoseconds (10–15 milliseconds)

An important part of tuning any Oracle database involves reducing the need to read data from sources with the greatest latency (e.g. disk) and, when a disk must be accessed, ensuring that there are as few bottlenecks as possible in the I/O subsystem. As a program (or the Oracle database a program uses) accesses a greater percentage of its data from memory rather than disk, the overall latency of the system is correspondingly decreased. For more information about some of these tuning issues, see Chapter 6.

Uniprocessor Systems

Uniprocessor systems, like the one shown in Figure 11-1, are the simplest systems in terms of architecture. Each of these systems (typically a standard personal computer) contains a single CPU and a single I/O channel and is made entirely with industry-standard components. They are most often used as single-user stand-alone machines; for example, for database development or as client machines in a network. Some uniprocessor machines are also used as small servers for databases. Versions of this architecture made with more exotic RISC-based CPUs are typically used as engineering, scientific, or graphics workstations today.

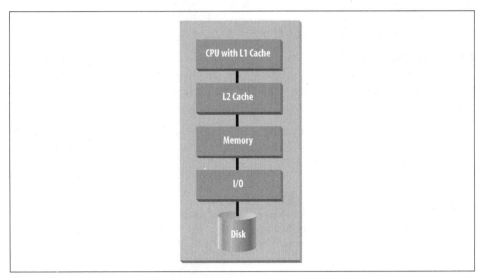

Figure 11-1. Typical uniprocessor system

Until the 1990s, uniprocessor systems were frequently used as servers because of their low price and the limited ability of relational databases to fully utilize other types of systems. However, Oracle evolved to take advantage of systems containing multiple CPUs through improved parallelism and more sophisticated optimization. At the same time, the price points of Symmetric Multiprocessing (SMP) systems (described in the next section) have plummeted dramatically, making SMP systems the database hardware servers of choice.

Although there is only a single processor in a uniprocessor system, the server operating systems used by these systems now support multiple threads. Each thread can be used to support a concurrent process, which can execute in parallel. By default, the PARALLEL_THREADS_PER_CPU parameter in the initialization file is set at 2 for most platforms on which Oracle runs. Oracle can further determine the degree of parallelism based on parameters set in the initialization file or using the adaptive degree of parallelism feature. This adaptive multiuser feature makes use of algorithms that take into account the number of threads. Additional tuning parameters can also affect parallelism. For more information about the parallel thread capability of Oracle, see Chapter 6.

Symmetric Multiprocessing Systems

One of the limiting factors for a uniprocessor system is the ultimate speed of its processor—all applications have to share this one resource. Symmetric Multiprocessing (SMP) systems were invented in an effort to overcome this limitation by adding CPUs to the memory bus, as shown in Figure 11-2.

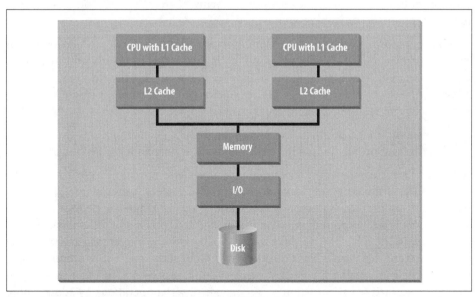

Figure 11-2. Typical Symmetric Multiprocessing (SMP) system

Each CPU has its own memory cache. Data resident in the cache of one CPU is sometimes needed for processing by a second CPU. Because of this potential sharing of data, the CPUs for such machines must be able to "snoop" the memory bus to determine where copies of data reside and whether the data is being updated. This snooping is managed transparently by the operating system that controls the SMP system, so either Oracle Standard Edition or Enterprise Edition can be used on these platforms.

SMP platforms have been available since the 1980s as midrange platforms, primarily as Unix-based machines. Today, there is a category of entry-level servers featuring Intel-based CPUs, although Itanium based systems now offer CPU performance challenging other 64-bit CPUs. The most popular operating systems in this category are Windows and Linux.

SMP servers that can scale to larger sizes from HP, IBM, and Sun feature variations on this basic design. For example, SMP systems might include Reduced Instruction Set Chips (RISC) for CPUs or larger Itanium configurations, a larger L2 cache, faster memory bus and/or multiple higher speed I/O channels. Each enhancement is intended to remove potential bottlenecks that can limit performance. Unix is the most common operating system used in Oracle implementations on high-end SMP servers.

The number of CPUs on SMP was historically limited by scalability of the system (memory) bus. As more CPUs were added to the bus, the bus itself could be saturated with traffic between CPUs attached to the bus.

Systems featuring 64-bit CPUs can handle large amounts of data more efficiently than previous 32-bit CPUs; they support as many as over 70 CPUs on a single system with hundreds of gigabytes of memory.

Of course, the database must have parallelization features to take full advantage of the SMP architecture. Oracle operations such as query execution and other DML activity and data loading can run as parallel processes within the Oracle server, allowing Oracle to take advantage of the benefits of multiprocessor systems. Oracle, like all software systems, benefits from parallel operations, as shown by "Amdahl's Law":

Total execution time = (parallel part / number of processors) + serial part

Amdahl's Law, formulated by mainframe pioneer Gene Amdahl in 1967 to describe performance in mixed parallel and serial workloads, clearly shows that moving an operation from the serial portion of execution to a parallel portion provides the performance increases expected with the use of multiple processors. In the same way, the more serial operations that make up an application, the longer the execution time will be because the sum of the execution time of all serial operations can offset any performance gains realized from the use of multiple processors. In other words, you cannot speed up a serial operation or a sequence of serial operations by adding more processors.

Each subsequent release of Oracle has added more parallelized features to speed up the execution of queries as well as the tuning and maintenance of the database. For a list of Oracle operations that can be parallelized, see the section "What Can Be Parallelized?" in Chapter 6.

Oracle's parallel operations take advantage of available CPU resources. If you're working with a system on which the CPU resources are already being completely consumed, this parallelism will not help improve performance; in fact, it could even hurt performance by adding the increased demands for CPU power required to manage the parallel processes. However, with the shared multi-threaded servers and Oracle Net concentrators (discussed in Chapter 2) parallelization may make more sense, because there will be more CPU power available per Oracle connection.

Clusters

Clustered systems have provided a high-availability, high-scalability solution since initially appearing in the 1980s in the DEC VAXcluster configuration. Clusters can combine all the components of separate machines, including CPUs, memory, and I/O subsystems, into a single hardware entity. However, clusters are typically built by using shared disks linked to multiple "nodes" (computer systems). An interconnect between systems provides a means of exchanging data and instructions without writing to disk (see Figure 11-3). Each system runs its own copy of an operating system and Oracle instance. Grids, described later in this chapter, are typically made up of a few very large clusters.

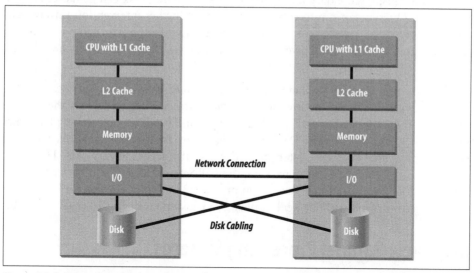

Figure 11-3. Typical cluster (two systems shown)

Oracle's support for clusters dates back to the VAXcluster. Oracle provided a sophisticated locking model so that the multiple nodes could access the shared data on the disks. Clusters required such a locking model, because each machine in the cluster had to be aware of the data locks held by other, physically separate machines in the cluster.

Today, that Oracle solution has evolved into Real Application Clusters or RAC (replacing the Oracle Parallel Server (OPS) that was available prior to Oracle9*i*). RAC is most frequently used for Windows, Linux, or Unix-based clusters. Oracle provides an integrated lock manager that mediates between different servers, or nodes, that seek to update data in the same block.

Real Application Clusters introduced full support of Cache Fusion; with Cache Fusion, locks are maintained in memory without frequent writing to disk. Cache Fusion is different from the standard locking mechanisms that are described in Chapter 7, in that it applies to blocks of data, rather than rows. The mediation is necessary because two different nodes might try to access different rows in the same physical block, which is the smallest amount of data that can be used by Oracle.

Cache Fusion greatly increased performance for read/write operations in Oracle8i OPS and added write/write operations to Cache Fusion in Oracle9i RAC. Oracle Database 10g further speeds performance by leveraging Infiniband networks through support of SDP (Sockets Direct Protocol) and asynchronous I/O protocols, lighter weight transports than used in previous, traditional TCP/IP-based RAC implementations.

Prior to Real Application Clusters, you could configure clusters to deliver higher throughput or greater availability for the system. In the high-availability scenario, if a single node fails, a secondary node attached to the shared disk can get access to the same data. Queries can run to completion without further intervention through client failover, first appearing in Oracle8. Real Application Clusters, due to its increased performance, can deliver both availability and scalability, as each node in a cluster acts as a failover for all the other nodes in the cluster.

Real Application Clusters are being used more frequently in commodity server environments, where clusters of low-priced servers are seeking to deliver the performance of more expensive SMP machines. For simple failover on entry platforms, Oracle also bundles Fail Safe. Data is not shared by the two systems in a Fail Safe configuration, and a second system provides standby access to this data. However, because concurrent access isn't provided, the Fail Safe solution doesn't offer the scalability that Real Application Clusters can provide. The use of clusters for high availability (both with and without Real Application Clusters) is discussed in Chapter 10.

Massively Parallel Processing Systems

Clusters historically have been limited in the throughput they can deliver by the number of shared disk connections possible, because the disks have to be linked physically to each system. Recent advances in serial and fiber channel disk technology have raised disk performance and capacity. But this increased capability has also raised issues of management complexity, because each node introduces another discrete copy of the operating system. With Real Application Clusters, managing the multiple Oracle instances that make up the cluster is essentially the same as managing a single instance, but the multiple machines and the underlying operating systems still make for a greater management burden.

Oracle Database 10g also introduces Automatic Storage Management (ASM), which helps to manage large amounts of disk space; see the discussion in Chapter 5.

Massively Parallel Processing (MPP) systems appeared in the early 1990s to address these limitations. Unlike clusters, the disks in an MPP environment are not shared across multiple nodes, except for high-availability configurations, so the architecture is sometimes called "shared nothing" (shown in Figure 11-4). A special console provides additional operating system–management tools to make management of the many operating system copies appear to be more transparent.

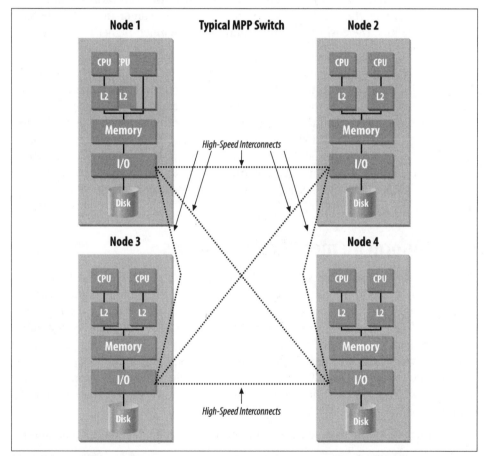

Figure 11-4. Massively Parallel Processing (MPP) configuration (four SMP nodes shown)

In a typical MPP configuration multiple nodes reside in a single cabinet, but MPP configurations can grow to a series of cabinets with hundreds of nodes. The nodes are linked together via a high-speed switch and may be further linked to other cabinets of nodes via cables that physically connect the switch to the other cabinets. The switch provides each of the nodes with multiple interconnects to adjacent nodes. As nodes are added additional paths are enabled between the nodes, and the total throughput possible by the switch continues to scale with the connections. Individual nodes can be single processor or SMP. Oracle Real Application Clusters can use either configuration, although SMP nodes can be utilized for additional parallelism against data residing on a local node and are becoming the default.

The overall performance is a function of the power of individual nodes, the total number of nodes, the throughput offered by the switch, and the distribution of data. For example, in a business intelligence query, a 64-way SMP platform could outperform an MPP platform with 16 4-way SMP nodes, because these types of queries are usually CPU-bound and MPP interconnects are slower than an SMP memory bus. The tradeoff is that the MPP configuration can be much larger than a single SMP platform (although the cost of the MPP solution can be much higher than that of an SMP system).

The most common implementation of Oracle on MPP utilizes the IBM RS/6000 SP. Prior to including a cluster file system with Oracle Database 10g, Oracle RAC relied on a version of IBM AIX for the SP that included the Virtual Shared Disk (VSD). This software enabled the disk on the SP to appear as a shared disk, even though the disk is directly connected to an individual node. Today, the SP is much less popular, even among IBM customers. Scalability of IBM's 64-bit SMP nodes led to increased deployment of small SMP clusters built from IBM's Regatta class servers (e.g. the p690 and later) and the high-speed switch technology created for the SP as an interconnect.

Non-Uniform Memory Access Systems

Non-Uniform Memory Access (NUMA) computers, introduced in the mid-1990s, provide even greater throughput than SMP by linking multiple SMP components via distributed memory, as shown in Figure 11-5. Like MPP and clusters, these systems provide scaling of memory and I/O subsystems in addition to CPUs. A key difference is the single operating system copy that manages the entire platform and a directory-based cache coherency scheme to keep data synchronized. Memory access between nodes is in the hundreds of microseconds, which is much faster than going to disk in MPP or cluster configurations, and only slightly less swift than local memory bus speeds in a single SMP system.

This enables NUMA to have some major advantages over MPP and cluster solutions:

- Parallel versions of applications don't need to be developed or certified to run on these machines (although additional performance gains may be realized when such applications can be tuned for NUMA).

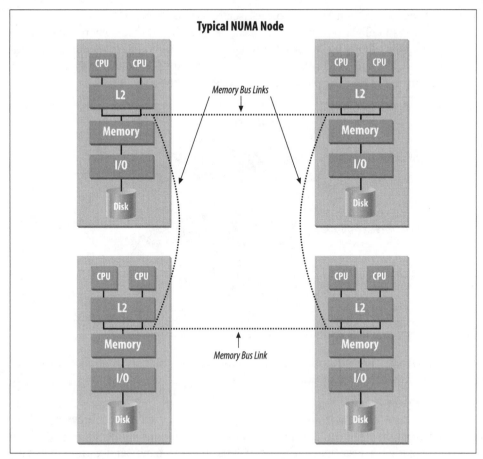

Figure 11-5. *Non-Uniform Memory Access (NUMA) configuration*

- Management is much simpler on NUMA systems than on clusters because there is only one copy of the operating system to manage and only one database instance is typically deployed.

Oracle has developed on multiple NUMA platforms to provide highly tunable Oracle versions that can take advantage of the benefits offered. Today, Hewlett Packard Superdome and HP/Compaq AlphaServer (GS-320) and are examples of NUMA systems with demonstrated scalability in production databases that scale into the tens of terabytes.

Grid Computing

The "*g*" in Oracle Database 10*g* signifies Oracle's focus on enabling grid computing with this database release. *Grids* are simply pools of computers that provide needed resources for applications on an as-needed basis. The goal is to provide computing resources that transparently scale to the user community, much as an electrical utility company can deliver power to meet peak demand by accessing energy from other power providers' plants via a power grid. Computing grids enable this dynamic provisioning of CPU and data resources (shown in Figure 11-6). Oracle Database 10g with RAC form the foundation for the provisioning of these resources.

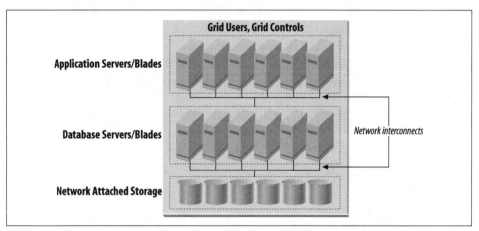

Figure 11-6. Sample grid configuration, including computer blades and cluster

Oracle Database 10g adds several important features that enable the delivery of resources when needed via a grid:

Dynamic Service Provisioning

This feature automatically allocates and reallocates server resources based on configuration and failover rules. Service requests are automatically routed to the server with the least load. If a server fails, the surviving services are automatically reallocated to the available servers.

Web services

Web services are also an inherent part of the grid landscape, because applications running on the grid want to use the same type of transparent access to components (or services) that users have to applications. New database web services provide support for queries, messaging, and DML, can access Java and PL/SQL, and can provide full XML support.

Rolling upgrades

Oracle Database 10g facilitates the management of large numbers of nodes through rolling upgrades. A rolling upgrade allows you to bring down some of the nodes in the grid, upgrade their software, and then bring them back online as part of the grid. You can then repeat this procedure with the other nodes. The end result is that you can achieve a complete upgrade of your Oracle database software without having to bring down the database.

Automatic Storage Management

The ASM system also enables management of large numbers of nodes by implementing automatic data rebalancing across disks, as well as easy addition of new disks to the overall pool of storage.

Enterprise Manager

Enterprise Manager 10*g* is designed to manage a grid infrastructure from a central location, including RAC databases, storage, Oracle Application Servers, and network services.

Disk Technology

The discussion of hardware architectures and performance in this chapter so far has centered on ways of increasing performance by increasing available system resources such as CPUs, memory, and I/O subsystems and on parallelism that can take advantage of these resources.

Another classic way to increase hardware performance is to tune for I/O, which includes tuning for disk layout. Because disk access has the greatest latency, the main focus of I/O tuning is typically keeping what has been retrieved from disk in memory. The actual performance of retrieving that data from disks can also be improved by spreading the data evenly across multiple disks and by making sure there are enough disk controllers to transfer the data from disk onto the I/O bus and into memory. As noted previously, Oracle Database 10*g* now includes automatic data rebalancing across disks, greatly simplifying the day-to-day management. However, working with your hardware vendor regarding disk controller selection and configuration is still important.

Disk Deployment Strategies

Disks have typically been directly attached to systems—more expensive systems offer fastest disk controllers and I/O. Disks are also configured in a variety of ways for redundancy, eliminating the possibility of single points of disk failure resulting in loss of access to data. As network bandwidth improved, deployments that include Network Attached Storage (NAS) and Storage Area Networks (SAN) have appeared as cost-effective alternatives.

Disk is commonly deployed in arrays, the industry standard being RAID (Redundant Array of Inexpensive/Independent Disks). You can use RAID as a part of any of the configurations we've discussed to provide higher performance and reliability. RAID disk arrays were introduced in Chapter 6 and discussed in the context of their use in high-availability scenarios in Chapter 10. Please refer to those chapters for more information about RAID disk arrays. In addition, Oracle Database 10*g*'s Automatic Storage Management (ASM) capabilities can deliver much of the functionality of a RAID array, such as striping and mirroring, with a collection of commodity disks. ASM is further described in Chapter 5.

Keep in mind that newer higher capacity drives may allow you to store more and more data cheaply, but may not provide the access paths (e.g. spindles) necessary for demanding multiuser query performance. Proper disk configuration is a balance of capacity, availability, and performance considerations that meet your business application needs.

Oracle9*i* introduced table compression in the database as a means of decreasing disk storage requirements. Duplicate values in a data block are eliminated because values that are duplicated are stored in a symbol table at the beginning of the block, and all additional occurrences are replaced with a short reference to the symbol table. Compression ratios vary, but typical reductions observed in storage required in real implementations is about half that of uncompressed data.

In addition to reducing disk storage, compressed data can also be advantageous to query speed when it fits entirely into cache (instead of requiring disk access). Loading data as compressed can take about twice as long, so many companies load new data uncompressed in a partition, then compress that partitioned data as it ages.

Which Platform Deployment Solution?

In a world in which there was no limit to the amount of money you could spend on hardware, you could make a simple decision about the most appropriate hardware: simply choose the level of throughput and reliability you need, and go buy it! Unfortunately, we have yet to discover the location of this kind of world, so your choice of a hardware solution will often be a compromise.

Platform Comparison

The most commonly implemented hardware platform for an Oracle server is the SMP system, which strikes a nice balance between power and price. SMP systems are popular for the following reasons:

- SMP systems offer more and simpler scalability options for the future than uniprocessor systems.
- 64-bit processors and operating systems with large memory support enable SMP systems to handle the needs of very large (even multi-terabyte) databases.
- SMP systems have a single operating system and a single Oracle instance to manage and maintain, unlike clusters, MPP, or a grid environment.
- Far more applications are certified to run on SMP systems than clusters, MPP, and grid configurations.
- SMP systems are sometimes less expensive than NUMA, clusters, MPP, or grid configurations in similar CPU configurations because memory and I/O subsystems are not duplicated to the same degree.

This is not to say that other configurations should not be considered. Certainly, if scalability demands exceed the capabilities of SMP machines, clusters or a grid may provide the only viable solution. Clusters can prove cheaper through use of "commodity" systems in RAC configurations. With careful planning and an enterprise-computing management style, such configurations do provide powerful and highly available solutions.

NUMA offers an interesting alternative approach. At this point, HP platforms host some of the largest Oracle based implementations, scaling to databases in the tens of terabytes of data with more than 1,000 concurrent query processes.

Table 11-2 provides a comparison of the relative strengths of the different deployment platforms for price, availability, manageability, and scalability.

Table 11-2. Relative strengths of deployment platforms

Ranking	Scalability	Manageability	Availability	Price
Best	Grid	Uniprocessor	Grid	Uniprocessor
	Cluster, MPP	SMP	Cluster, MPP	Grid, cluster
	NUMA	NUMA	NUMA	SMP
	SMP	Grid, MPP	SMP	NUMA
Worst	Uniprocessor	Cluster	Uniprocessor	MPP

You should select a storage technology based on your performance and recovery requirements and budget. In general, more expensive solutions offer better performance and more flexible availability options.

Approaches to Choosing Platforms

When selecting a solution for deployment, most organizations choose systems that will meet anticipated performance and scalability needs for the near future, taking into account management and availability requirements. However, there are two additional approaches to be considered.

First is the truism with which we're all familiar—the longer you wait, the cheaper computer hardware (and related components) get. According to Moore's Law, credited by Intel to Gordon Moore in 1965 (and proven many times over since then), each chip will double in capacity every 18–24 months, each time providing huge leaps in performance.

This continual reduction in price and increase in performance characteristics is an ongoing fact of life in the computer hardware industry. But how can you use this fact in planning deployment strategies for your organizational system architecture?

Buy what you need, when you need it, and plan for the obsolescence of hardware by recycling it into the organization when it no longer meets the needs of an individual application. For example, today's departmental server may turn into tomorrow's web listener. As another example, grid deployment enables you to continue to leverage older hardware as part of the existing computing solution.

Second, remember to consider the effect of hardware upgrades, particularly CPU upgrades in non-grid solutions. SMP systems and nodes require that all CPUs be identical, so if you upgrade one you will have to upgrade all of them. At some point the vendor will recommend a new system anyway because other internal features (e.g., memory and I/O bus technologies) will have been improved, partly to match the increased capabilities of the new CPUs.

Grid technology is tempting to consider because new machine types can be added to the grid as they become available. The self-tuning aspects of Oracle Database 10g make grid computing more practical by eliminating difficult manual tuning efforts that formerly needed to take into account variations in systems.

CHAPTER 12

Distributed Databases
and Distributed Data

Data in large and mid-sized companies frequently resides on multiple servers. The data might be distributed across various-sized servers running a mix of operating systems for a number of reasons, including scalability, performance, access, and management. As a result, the data needed to answer business questions may not reside on a single local server. The user may need to access data on several servers simultaneously, or the data required for an answer may need to be moved to a local server. Inserts, updates, or deletions of data on these distributed servers may also be necessary.

There are two basic ways to deal with data in distributed databases: as part of a single distributed entity in which the distributed architecture is transparent, or by using a variety of replication techniques to create copies of the data in more than one location. This chapter will examine both of these options and the technologies associated with each solution. Several of the technologies described here can be used in combination with Oracle Application Server components to integrate data from several sources (for example, to facilitate document exchange). This combination of Oracle technology solutions is sometimes referred to as the Oracle Enterprise Integration framework.

Grid computing introduces a new third solution to widely distributed data—a single database deployment model leveraging Oracle's Real Application Clusters and Application Server services. As might be expected, capabilities introduced earlier for distributed data play a part in this solution, particularly Oracle Streams, as described later in this chapter.

Accessing Multiple Databases as a Single Entity

Users sometimes need to query or manipulate data that resides in multiple Oracle databases or in a mixture of Oracle and non-Oracle databases. This section describes a number of techniques and architectures you can use to enable these capabilities in a distributed environment.

Distributed Data Access Across Multiple Oracle Databases

For many years, Oracle has offered access to distributed data residing on multiple Oracle database servers on multiple systems or *nodes*. Users don't need to know the location of the data in distributed databases. Data is accessed by table name, physical location, network protocol, and operating system, in a manner transparent to users. A distributed database residing on multiple database servers can appear to users to be a single logical database.

Developers can create connections between individual databases by creating database links in SQL. These connections form a distributed database. For example, the statement:

```
CREATE PUBLIC DATABASE LINK employees.northpole.bigtoyco.com
```

creates a path to a remote database of that name containing Bigtoyco's North Pole employees. Any application or user attached to a local employees database can access the remote North Pole database by using the global access name (employees. northpole.bigtoyco.com) in SQL queries, inserts, updates, deletions, and other statements. Oracle Net (previously known as Net8 or SQL*Net) handles the interaction with any network protocols used to communicate with the remote database.

Let's look briefly at how queries and updates issued for distributed Oracle databases differ from those issued for a single Oracle database. When using distributed data in a query, your primary concern is to properly optimize the retrieval of data for a query. Queries in a single Oracle database are optimized for performance, most frequently using the cost-based optimizer, as discussed in Chapter 4. Oracle7 added global cost-based optimization for the improvement of query performance across distributed databases as well. For example, the cost-based optimizer considers indexes on remote databases when choosing a plan, whereas the rule-based optimizer does not. The cost-based optimizer also considers statistics on remote databases. Improvements to the Oracle8*i* optimizer included optimizing for join and set operations to be performed on the nodes offering the best performance and also minimizing the amount of data sent between systems. For these reasons, the cost-based optimizer is more frequently recommended and used for distributed databases.

When a user wants to write data back to a distributed database, the issue becomes a bit more complicated. As we've mentioned before, a transaction is an atomic logical unit of work that typically contains one or more SQL statements. These statements write data to a database and must either be committed or rolled back as a unit. Distributed transactions can take place across multiple database servers. When distributed transactions are committed via the SQL COMMIT statement, Oracle uses a two-phase commit protocol to ensure transaction integrity and consistency across multiple systems. This protocol is further described in the "Two-Phase Commits" section of this chapter.

Access to and from Non-Oracle Databases

Oracle's Transparent Gateways (illustrated in Figure 12-1) are Oracle software products that provide users with access to non-Oracle databases via Oracle SQL. Oracle SQL is automatically translated into the SQL of the target database, allowing applications developed for Oracle to be used against non-Oracle databases. Native SQL of the target database can also be transmitted directly. Oracle datatypes such as NUMBER, CHAR, and DATE are converted into the datatypes of the target. Oracle data dictionary views are provided for target data store objects. As with Oracle databases, heterogeneous databases can be linked to Oracle through database links to create a distributed database. The gateways can be deployed in a two-tier architecture in the Oracle database or in a middle tier (Oracle Application Server).

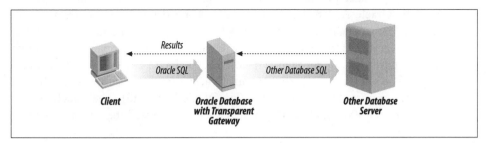

Figure 12-1. Typical configuration and use of Transparent Gateways

There are four basic types of database connectivity provided:

Open Database Connectivity
> Generic ODBC and OLE DB interfaces are free and are bundled with the Oracle database. Open Systems Gateways provide access to Informix, Microsoft SQL Server, Sybase, and other databases on Unix and Windows platforms. These interfaces and gateways leverage Heterogeneous Services included in the Oracle database, which determine optimal SQL strategies for the remote site. Additionally, Oracle's OLAP Option for Oracle Database 10g provides OLE DB for OLAP (ODBO) enabling access from a variety of analysis tools.

Transparent Gateways
> Transparent Gateways exist for dozens of non-Oracle data stores. Mainframe Integration Gateways provide access to DB2 on mainframes. Enterprise Integration Gateways provide access to IBM AS/400 and via IBM Distributed Relational Database Architecture (DRDA) connections. Finally, Oracle offers the EDA/SQL Gateways for a number of other sources. Transparent Gateways performance improved in Oracle8 by moving Heterogeneous Services from the Transparent Gateways layer into the database kernel. Performance was further improved in the Oracle8i release with the introduction of multi-threading for these services and in Oracle9i with multi-threaded agent support. Oracle Database 10g adds support for remote functions in non-Oracle databases embedded in SELECT statements.

Procedural Gateways

Procedural Gateways implement remote procedure calls (RPCs) to applications built on non-Oracle data stores. The Gateway for APPC, the standard IBM protocol for RPCs, is used when Oracle applications need procedural access to applications built on CICS, DB2, IMS, VSAM, and other data stores on the mainframe and applications that use SNA LU6.2 to communicate to the mainframe. The Oracle Procedural Gateway for IBM MQSeries allows Oracle-based applications to exchange messages with applications that communicate via MQSeries message queues. Both are included with the Oracle Enterprise Integration Gateways.

Access Manager

An Access Manager provides access to Oracle from non–Oracle based applications. The Oracle Access Manager for AS/400 resides on the AS/400 and provides AS/400 applications written in RPG, C, or COBOL access to Oracle running on any platform. You can access Oracle from these applications through ANSI-standard SQL or through Oracle DML or DDL. Because PL/SQL is also supported, AS/400 applications can call Oracle stored procedures. TCP/IP and LU6.2 are supported for connectivity (via Oracle Net/Net8). The Oracle Access Manager for AS/400 is included with the Oracle Enterprise Integration Gateways.

Two-Phase Commits

One of the biggest issues associated with the use of distributed databases is the difficulty of guaranteeing the same level of data integrity for updates to distributed databases. Because a transaction that writes data to multiple databases must depend on a network for the transmission of information, it is inherently more susceptible to lost information than a single Oracle instance on a single machine. And because a transaction must guarantee that all writes occur, this increased instability could adversely affect data integrity.

The standard solution for this problem is to use two message-passing phases as part of a transaction commit; hence, the protocol used is referred to as a *two-phase commit*. The main database first polls each of the participants to determine if they are ready; if they are, the transactional updates are tentatively sent to them. In the second phase, if all the participants are in agreement that the messages have properly been received, the changes are committed. If any of the nodes involved in the transaction cannot verify receipt of the changes, the transactions are rolled back to their original state.

For example, if a transaction is to span databases on machines A, B, and C, in the first phase of the commit operation each of the databases is sent the appropriate transactional update. If each of these machines acknowledges that it has received the update, the second phase of the update executes the COMMIT statement.

You can compare this approach with a single-phase update in which the COMMIT statement is sent along with the transactional update information. There is no way of knowing whether the update ever reached all the machines, so any sort of interruption in the delivery of the update to any of the machines would cause the data to be in an inconsistent state. When a transaction involves more than one machine, the possibility of the loss of an update to one of the machines increases greatly, which, in turn, mandates the use of the two-phase commit protocol. Of course, because the two-phase commit protocol requires more messaging to be passed between machines, a two-phase commit can take longer than a standard commit; however, the corresponding gain in all-important data integrity more than makes up for the decrease in performance.

Transaction Processing Monitors

In 1991, X/Open defined an open systems standard interface through which transaction processing (TP) monitors could communicate with XA-compliant resource managers (the role of the Oracle RDBMS and other XA-compliant databases in the X/Open model). Several popular TP monitors that support XA have appeared, including BEA Tuxedo and IBM's CICS and Encina (primarily used on IBM AIX or Windows and bundled today in IBM TXSeries within WebSphere).

Oracle added an Oracle Manager for Microsoft Transaction Server (MTS) to Oracle8i for Windows NT. With this option, Oracle can provide a database solution where MTS works as an application server for COM-based distributed applications. Further enhancements in Oracle9i enabled the database to participate as a transaction resource manager in MTS environments and, in Release 2 of Oracle9i, added .NET support, enabling .NET transactional applications to use Oracle as a resource manager.

We have mentioned TP monitors in previous chapters in connection with their role in online transaction processing. Among their other duties, TP monitors assure that transactions between multiple applications and resources complete properly. As noted previously, Oracle provides its own two-phase commit protocol for distributed transactions, one of the early primary uses of a TP monitor. Standalone TP monitors are used less frequently today for workload management (see Figure 12-2), as this capability is now built into middle-tier applications. Examples of why TP monitors might still be used with Oracle databases include:

- Migration of legacy applications (usually originally written using CICS and COBOL for a mainframe) to CICS on Unix or Windows NT
- Two-phase commits between Oracle and other XA-compliant databases
- Three-tier implementations for ActiveX/DCOM applications deployed on Windows platforms (using MTS)

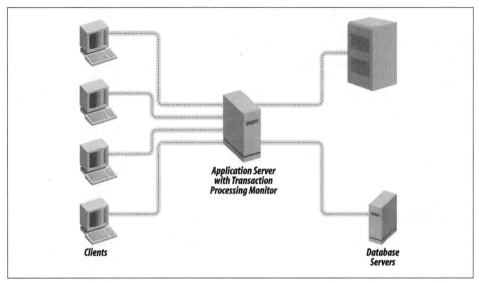

Figure 12-2. Application server with TP monitor

Moving Data Between Distributed Systems

The previous section discussed the use of multiple database servers acting together as part of a single logical database for users. The following situations call for the contents of a database to be duplicated and moved between systems:

- When data available locally eliminates network bandwidth issues or contention for system resources

- When mobile database users can take their databases with them and operate disconnected from the network

- When redundant databases can help to deliver higher levels of reliability, as each database can be used as a backup for other databases

The biggest issue facing users of multiple identical or similar databases is how to keep the data on all of the servers in sync as the data is changed over time. As a user inserts, updates, or deletes data on one database, you need to have some way to get this new data to the other databases. In addition, you will have to deal with the possible data-integrity issues that can crop up if the changes introduced by distributed users contend with each other.

Oracle offers a number of strategies to address this situation. The following sections discuss techniques for data and table movement among distributed systems.

Advanced Replication

The copying and maintaining of database tables among multiple Oracle databases on distributed systems is known as *replication*. Changes that are applied at any local site are propagated automatically to all of the remote sites. These changes can include updates to data or changes to the database schema. Replication is frequently implemented to provide faster access for local users at remote sites or to provide a disaster-recovery site in the event of loss of a primary site. Oracle's Advanced Replication features support both asynchronous replication and synchronous replication. Oracle also supports heterogeneous replication with DB2 through its Replication Services, bundled in the Mainframe Integration Gateways.

Replication continues to evolve. Oracle8 moved execution of replication triggers to the database kernel and enabled automatic parallelization of data replication to improve performance. Oracle8*i* added replication triggered by changes to selected rows or columns of a table. Oracle9*i* replication added support for object datatypes and multi-tier updateable materialized views. Release 2 of Oracle9i added log-based replication via Oracle Streams (described later in this chapter).

Asynchronous replication is the storage of changes locally for later forwarding to a remote site. Some types of asynchronous replication include read-only snapshots replicated from a single updateable master table and updateable snapshots that, although disconnected, can also be updated.

In the Standard Edition of Oracle, you can have only one master site, which replicates changes to its child sites. In the Enterprise Edition, multiple master sites can exist and updates can take place at any of these sites. The updates to these sites must be *synchronized*, meaning that an update is not completed until all of the target sites have been updated; otherwise, conflicts can remain unresolved. Conflicts can occur when more than one site updates the same data element during the same replication interval. Changes are propagated using deferred remote procedure calls (RPCs) based on events or at points in time when connectivity is available or communications costs are minimal.

Several conflict-resolution routines provided with Enterprise Edition can be automatically used to resolve replication conflicts. An administrator can simply choose which conflict-resolution strategy he wishes to use for a particular replication. For updates that may affect a column or groups of columns, standard resolution choices include the following:

Overwrite and discard value
> Used when there is a single master (originating) site for new values to update current values at destination sites.

Minimum and maximum value
> Minimum compares the new value at the originating site and the current value at the destination and applies the new value only if it is less than the current value.
>
> Maximum compares the new value at the originating site and the current value at the destination and applies the new value only if it is greater than the current value.

Earliest and latest timestamp value (with designation of a column of type DATE)
> Earliest dictates that when there are multiple new values, the value used for updates will be in the row with the earliest timestamp.
>
> Latest dictates that when there are multiple new values, the value used for updates will be in the row with the latest timestamp.

Additive and average value for column groups with single numeric columns
> Additive takes the difference of new and old values at the originating site and adds them to the current value at the destination site.
>
> Average takes the current value at the destination and the new value at the originating site, divides by 2, and applies the new value.

Priority groups and site priority
> When priority levels are assigned to columns and multiple new values occur, columns with a lower priority will be updated by columns with a higher priority.

Also available for use are built-in uniqueness conflict-resolution routines, which will resolve conflicts that result from the distributed use of primary key and unique constraints. The built-in routines include the following:

Append site name to duplicate value
> Appends the global database name of the originating site to the replicated column

Append sequence to duplicate value
> Appends a generated sequence number to the column value

Discard duplicate value
> Discards the row at the originating site that causes errors

You can also write your own custom conflict-resolution routines and assign them if your business requirements are not addressed by the standard routines.

Managing advanced replication

You can manage replication through Oracle's Replication Manager, which is launched from the Oracle Enterprise Manager. Administrators can configure database objects that need to be replicated, schedule replication, troubleshoot error conditions, and view the deferred transaction queue at each location through this central interface. A deferred transaction queue is a queue holding transactions that will be replicated (and applied) to child sites.

For example, to set up a typical multimaster replication, you must first define master groups and tables and objects to be replicated in each of the databases.

The Replication Manager wizard, which is part of the Oracle Enterprise Manager Java version, then defines and sets up how replication will occur. You first define a connection to the master definition site, then create one or more master groups for replicating tables and objects to the multiple master sites. Next, you assign conflict-resolution routines for replicated tables in each master group. Finally, you grant appropriate access privileges to users of applications that access the data at the multiple sites.

Transportable Tablespaces

Transportable tablespaces are a way to speed up the distribution of complete tablespaces between multiple databases. Transportable tablespaces were introduced with Oracle8*i* Enterprise Edition to rapidly copy and distribute tablespaces among database instances. Previously, tablespaces needed to be exported from the source database and imported at the target (or unloaded and loaded). Transportable tablespaces enable copies to be moved simply through the use of file transfer commands such as *ftp*. Before you copy and move a copy of the tablespace, you should make the tablespace read-only to avoid inadvertently changing it. Data dictionary information needs to be exported from the source prior to transfer, then imported at the target.

Some of the most popular reasons to use transportable tablespaces include:

- Rapid copying of tablespaces from enterprise data warehouses to data marts
- Copying of tablespaces from operational systems to operational data stores for use in consolidated reporting
- Publishing of tablespaces for distribution on CD-ROM
- Use of backup copies for rapid point-in-time tablespace recovery

Prior to Oracle9*i*, Oracle block sizes needed to be the same and, prior to Oracle Database 10*g*, platform operating systems needed to be the same for both Oracle instances in order to use this feature. Oracle Database 10*g* introduces transportable tablespaces that can be used across different platforms.

Advanced Queuing

In the 1980s, *message-oriented middleware* (MOM) gained popular usage. MOM uses *messages* to transmit information between systems. It doesn't require the overhead of a two-phase commit because the MOM itself guarantees the delivery of all messages. Products such as IBM's MQSeries store control information (message destination, expiration, priority, and recipients) and the message contents in a file-based queue.

Delivery is guaranteed in that the message will remain in the queue until the destination is available and the message is forwarded.

Oracle's Advanced Queuing (AQ) facility, first introduced with Oracle8 Enterprise Edition, provides a complete queuing environment by storing the queue in the Oracle relational database. Advanced queues are Oracle database tables that support queuing operations—in particular, *enqueue* to create messages and *dequeue* to consume them. These messages, which can either be unstructured (raw) or structured (as Oracle objects, which are described in Chapter 13), correspond to rows in a table. Messages are stored in normal queues for normal message handling or in exception queues if they cannot be retrieved for some reason.

Queue Creation and Management

Queues are created through PL/SQL statements or the Java API. Oracle9*i* introduced several new AQ capabilities:

- XML-based messaging over HTTP enables support across firewalls; requests may be through the XML-based Internet Document Access Protocol (*i*DAP).
- AQ policies and services can be defined using Dynamic Services.
- AQ agents can be defined in and managed through the Oracle Internet Directory (OID).

An administrator creates a queue by following these steps:

1. Create a queue table.
2. Create and name the queue.
3. Specify the queue as a normal queue or an exception queue.
4. Specify how long messages remain in the queue: indefinitely, for a fixed length of time, until a particular time elapses between retries, or based on the number of retries.

Queues can be started and stopped by the administrator, who also grants users the privileges necessary for using the queue and revokes those privileges when necessary.

Producers of messages specify a queue name, enqueue options, message properties, and the payload to be put into the queue, which is then handled by a producer agent. Consumer agents listen for messages in one or more queues that are then dequeued so users can use the contents. Notification of the existence of messages in the queue can occur via OCI callback registration or through a listen call that can be used by applications to monitor for messages in multiple queues.

Because messages are stored in queues in the database, a number of message-management features are available. End-to-end tracking is enabled because each message carries its history with it, including location and state of the message, nodes visited, and previous recipients. Messages that don't reach subscribers within a defined lifetime are moved to the exception queue, from which they can be traced. Messages that successfully reach subscribers may be retained after consumption for additional analysis, including enqueue and dequeue times. As messages may be related (for example, one message might be caused by the successful execution of two other messages), retaining the messages can be useful in tracking sequences.

Queue management through Oracle Enterprise Manager Java version includes the following tasks:

- Creating, dropping, starting, and stopping queues
- Adding and removing subscribers
- Scheduling message propagation from local to remote queues
- Displaying queue statistics, including the average queue length, the number of messages in the wait state, the number of messages in the ready state, and the number of expired messages

Since Oracle9*i*, AQ has included a built-in message transformation for PL/SQL and XSLT. A messaging gateway is also available for propagation to other systems, such as MQSeries and TIBCO.

Publish-and-Subscribe Capabilities

Oracle8*i* Enterprise Edition introduced publish-and-subscribe capabilities to Advanced Queuing. As illustrated in Figure 12-3, a *publisher* puts a message onto a queue, while a *subscriber* receives messages from a queue. The publisher and subscriber interact separately with the queue, and neither party needs to know of the existence of the other. Publishers decide when, how, and what to publish, while subscribers express an interest. Messages can be published and subscribed to based on the name of a subject or on its content (through filtering rules). Asynchronous notification is enabled when subscribers register callback functions.

You can use Advanced Queuing and its publish-and-subscribe features for additional notification of database events that, in turn, improve the management of the database or business applications. Database events such as DML (inserts, updates, deletions) and system events (startup, shutdown, and so on) can be published and subscribed to. As an example, an application may be built to automatically inform a subscriber when a shipment occurs to certain highly valued customers; the subscriber would then know that she should begin to track the shipment's progress and alert the customer that it's in transit.

Oracle Streams

Oracle9*i* Release 2 introduced Oracle Streams, a method of sharing data and events within a database or between databases. Streams enables the propagation of changes via a capture-and-apply process. Changes can be propagated between Oracle instances, from Oracle instances to non-Oracle instances (via Transparent Gateways),

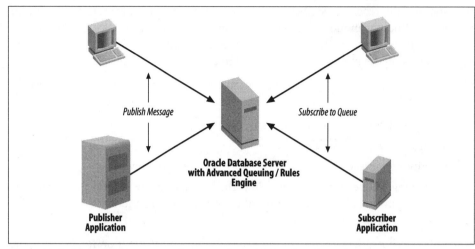

Figure 12-3. Advanced Queuing configuration for publish-subscribe applications

and from non-Oracle databases to Oracle (via messaging gateways). Streams leverages log-based procedures during change capture and queuing procedures as part of the staging. User-supplied "apply" rules define consumption.

Changes are captured from the source database redo log via a background database process into a logical change record (LCR). LCR and user message events are enqueued (staged) in a Streams queue. Events are propagated from source to target queues and then, via a background process, dequeued in the target database and applied. Oracle Database 10*g* adds new capabilities for the downstream capture of changes and for the enqueue /dequeue of messages in batch.

Oracle Streams is typically managed through the Java version of Oracle Enterprise Manager. In Oracle Database 10*g*, Streams can be configured to provide new message notification via email, HTTP, and PL/SQL. For migration from Advanced Replication to Streams, Oracle Database 10*g* provides a migration tool.

Oracle Streams and Grid Computing

Oracle Streams provides key functionality in Oracle Database 10*g* grid computing implementations. By its nature, grid computing can consist of widely distributed data, users, and platforms. Streams enables the movement of data when and where it is needed, as well as message sharing, notification or invocation of user procedures on events, message and database change subscriptions, and interoperation with other platforms. Oracle Database 10*g* streamed databases can offload processing to replica databases by creating operational data stores, or can create replicas and apply changes from replicas or data transformations to the production database. (Grid computing is described in more detail in Chapter 14.)

The use of Streams also plays a role in database migrations to grid computing and Oracle Database 10g. A single command begins the migration process. During this process, Streams captures changes on the source database that are then applied to the target as migration nears completion.

CHAPTER 13

Extending Oracle Datatypes

You can use traditional datatypes, such as those described in Chapter 4, to represent a portion of the information that your organization needs to store and manage. Introduction of the XML datatype (described in Chapter 4) and XML features (described in Chapter 14) have extended Oracle to also function as an "XML database." Oracle also provides datatypes that are specifically designed to provide optimal storage, performance, and flexibility for other specific types of data; these datatypes are the focus of this chapter.

Real-world information used in business, such as purchase orders, claims forms, shipping forms, and so on, may sometimes be best represented as object types, which are more complex than the simple atomic datatypes discussed in Chapter 4. Data that includes a timestamp may be better manipulated as a time series. Location-oriented data may best be represented using spatial coordinates. Documents, images, video clips, and audio clips have their own special requirements for storage and retrieval.

Oracle has extended the functionality of its basic relational database engine to support the storage and manipulation of these nontraditional datatypes through the introduction of additional features and options. Oracle has also extended the types of data, the SQL that manipulates it, and the basic Oracle service framework so that you can modify the data and extend its capabilities even further.

Object-Oriented Development

An object-oriented approach to software development shifts the focus from building computing procedures that operate on sets of data to modeling business processes. Building software components that model business processes with documented interfaces makes programming more efficient and allows applications to offer more flexible deployment strategies. It also makes applications easier to modify when business conditions change. In addition, because the modeling reflects real business use, application performance may improve as objects are built that don't require excessive manipulation to conform to the real-world behavior of the business processes they represent.

Oracle chose to take an evolutionary approach to object technology by allowing *data abstraction*, or the creation of such user-defined datatypes as objects and collections as extensions to the Oracle relational database. The Objects and Extensibility features, included with the database since Oracle8*i*, position Oracle as an object-relational database.

Support of the Java language in Oracle8*i* and Oracle9*i* complements this approach. The JVM (formerly JServer) feature is a Java Virtual Machine integrated with the database. It supports the building and running of Java components, as well as Java stored procedures and triggers, in the server.

The Promise of Object Orientation

Although a number of object-oriented approaches and technologies have been introduced since the 1980s, many of the promised improvements in software development efficiency haven't been realized. One of the reasons that these productivity improvements have failed is the difficulty many developers have had in making the adjustment to building reusable components. In addition, the need to learn new languages (such as C++) and technologies (object-oriented databases, CORBA, DCOM, and .NET) has slowed the adoption of object-oriented development. However, developers are becoming more familiar with these techniques and skills as Java moves into the mainstream of development. Interestingly, Oracle leverages many of these object features itself in development of new database capabilities.

One of the other factors limiting the growth of object-oriented development has been the work needed to adapt existing data to meet the new requirements of the object-oriented world. Oracle's evolutionary approach has made this particular transition easier to deal with.

Object-Relational Features

This section describes the major object-relational features available in Oracle.

Objects in Oracle

Objects created in Oracle are reusable components representing real-world business processes. The objects created using the database Objects and Extensibility features occupy the same role as the table in a standard relational model: the object is a template for the creation of individual "instances" of the object, which take the same role as rows within a table. An object is "instantiated" using Oracle-supplied "constructors" in SQL or PL/SQL.

An *object* consists of a name, one or more attributes, and methods. *Attributes* model the structure and state of the real-world entity, while *methods* model the operations of the entity. Methods are functions or procedures, usually written either in PL/SQL or Java or externally in a language such as C. Methods make up the interface between an object and the outside programming environment. Each method is identified by the name of the object that contains the method and a method name. Each method can have one or more *parameters*, which are the vehicles for passing data to the method from the calling application.

For example, a purchase order can be represented as an object. Attributes can include a purchase order number, a vendor, a vendor address, a ship-to address, an item number, a quantity, and a price. You can use a method to add an item to the purchase order, delete an item from the purchase order, or return the total amount of the purchase order.

You can store objects as rows in tables or as values in columns. Each row object has a unique object identifier (OID) created by Oracle. Row objects can be referred to from other objects or relational tables. The REF datatype represents such references. For column objects, Oracle adds hidden columns for the object's attributes.

Object views provide a means of creating virtual object tables from data stored in the columns of relational tables in the database. They can also include attributes from other objects. Object views are created by defining an object type, writing a query defining the mapping between data and tables containing attributes for that type, and specifying a unique object identifier. When the data is stored in a relational table, the unique identifier is usually the primary key. This implementation means that you can use object programming techniques without converting existing relational tables to object-relational tables. The trade-off when using this approach is that performance may be less than optimal, because the data representing attributes for an object may reside in several different tables. Hence, it may make sense to convert the relational tables to object tables in the future.

Objects that share the same methods are said to be in the same datatype or *class*. For example, internal and external purchase orders can be in the same class as purchase orders. *Collection types* model a number of objects of the same datatype as varying arrays (VARRAYs) if the collection of objects is bounded and ordered or as nested tables if the collection is unbounded and unordered. If a collection has fewer than 4,000 bytes, it is stored as part of the database table; if it is larger, it is stored as a *binary large object*, or BLOB. Nested table rows are stored in a separate table identified through a hidden NESTED_TABLE_ID by Oracle. Typically, VARRAYs are used when an entire collection is being retrieved and nested tables are used when a collection is being queried, particularly if the collection is large and only a subset is needed.

An application can call object methods through SQL, PL/SQL, Pro*C/C++, Java, OCI, and the Oracle Type Translator (OTT). The OTT provides client-side mappings to object types by generating header files containing C structure declarations and indicators. Developers can tune applications by using a client-side object cache to improve performance.

Inheritance, or the use of one class of objects as the basis for another, more specific class, is one of the most powerful features of object orientation. The child class inherits all the methods and attributes of the parent class and also adds its own methods and attributes to supplement the capabilities of the parent class. The great power of inheritance is that a change in a parent class automatically ripples down to the child classes. Object orientation supports inheritance over many levels of parent, child, and grandchild classes.

Polymorphism describes the ability of a child class to supersede the operation of a parent method by redefining the method on its own. Once a method has been replaced in a child class, subsequent changes to the method in the parent class don't ripple down to the child class or its descendants. In the purchase order example, as shown in Figure 13-1, purchase orders from contracted and noncontracted suppliers inherit the methods and attributes of external purchase orders. However, the procedure for placing the order can exhibit polymorphism because additional approvals may be required for ordering from noncontracted suppliers.

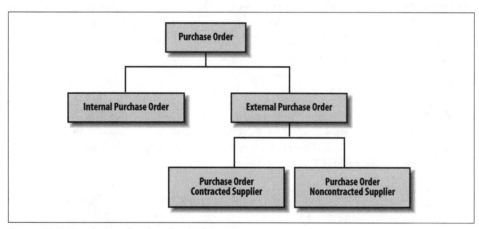

Figure 13-1. Purchase order class hierarchy

Inheritance and polymorphism were not supported in Oracle8*i* objects, although the Oracle8*i* database could act as persistent storage for objects, and an application interface in an object-oriented language such as C++ or Java could add these features to the client-side implementation of objects. Oracle9*i* added SQL type inheritance to the database, as well as object view hierarchies, type evolution, generic and transient datatypes, function-based indexes for type method functions, and multi-level collections. Oracle Database 10*g* adds support for remote access to object types.

Other extensibility features

Several other extensibility features are included in the Objects and Extensibility features. These include:

- The ability to create new index types by defining the structure of the index
- The ability to store the index data inside or outside the Oracle database
- The ability to create user-defined operators for use in standard SQL statements
- An interface to the cost-based optimizer to extend support for user-defined object types and indexes

The use of object-relational features is most common today among software developers who are building database extensions. Oracle itself has made use of these features in the creation of many of the database features—for example, in the Spatial and *inter*Media capabilities.

Java's Role

Java has gained wide acceptance as an application language, particularly for building web-based applications, due to its portability and availability on a wide variety of platforms. For Java developers wanting to use the Oracle database as a backend to their applications, Oracle offers support for the two common approaches to accessing the database from a Java program: JDBC and SQLJ. Both of these approaches are based on industry-standard application program interfaces (APIs):

SQLJ
    An industry standard typically used when static SQL statements have been embedded into a Java program. SQLJ is similar to other Oracle precompilers in that Java source files are created with calls to the SQLJ runtime (as well as to additional profile files). The Java source code is then compiled, and the application is run with the SQLJ runtime library.

JDBC
    Used when the SQL is dynamic, or when a developer wants explicit control over interactions with the database.

SQLJ and JDBC can be mixed in the same program when some SQL is static and other SQL is dynamic.

The Oracle JDBC driver includes the ORACLE.SQL package that contains Java classes representing all the Oracle SQL datatypes. These datatypes include all the numeric types, CHAR, VARCHAR, VARCHAR2, DATE, RAW, ROWID, CLOB, BLOB, BFILE, REF, object types, and collections (VARRAYs or nested tables). This interface allows the use of the Oracle object-relational features (see the earlier section "Objects in Oracle") within Java code. Java applets can communicate with the database via the Oracle Net/Net8 protocol (which is separately deployed to the client machines) or in a "thin version" that uses TCP/IP directly.

The thick driver requires the installation of the Oracle Net software on the client machines, while the thin driver doesn't. The Java applet receives additional Java classes that mimic the Oracle Net protocol. Typically, you would install Oracle Net and use the thick driver on middle-tier application servers to communicate with Oracle, because there are relatively few of these servers. The thin driver is more common for browser-based applications, because installing software on the machines with the browsers negates the thin client advantages.

The Oracle JVM in Oracle9*i* (JServer in Oracle8*i*) introduced additional component- and object-based development options. Oracle9i and subsequent versions feature a tightly integrated Java Virtual Machine (hence the JVM name) and support for Java stored procedures in the database; these enable component-based development to take place through the use of Enterprise JavaBeans (EJBs) and Common Object Request Broker Architecture (CORBA) objects.

Enterprise JavaBeans

Server-side Java components are referred to as Enterprise JavaBeans, or EJBs, in contrast to client-side reusable interface components, which are referred to as simply JavaBeans. You can deploy EJBs in the database server or with the Oracle Application Server. The tight integration of the Java Virtual Machine in the database makes use of database System Global Area (SGA) memory-management capabilities to provide EJB server scalability beyond what would be expected in most JVM implementations. For example, each client within the JVM requires only about 50–150 KB of memory for session state.

CORBA programmers can develop business logic as CORBA objects and then deploy them in Oracle. However, most organizations are far more likely to have developers with a Java programming background who will program using EJBs. EJBs are programmed at a higher level of abstraction than CORBA objects, so the CORBA level is hidden from the programmer. Furthermore, EJBs are portable across a range of JVMs.

In its initial release, Oracle8*i* supported the *session bean*, which is an EJB created by a specific call from the client that usually exists only during a single client/server session. Session beans may be *stateless*, allowing the EJB server to reuse instances of the bean to service clients, or *stateful* (i.e., bound to clients directly). Database cache information maintained by stateful session beans is synchronized with the database when transactions occur by using JDBC or SQLJ. *Entity Java beans*, also known as *persistent beans* (because they remain in existence through multiple sessions), were not supported in Oracle8*i* but are supported in Oracle9*i* and subsequent database JVMs.

Extensibility Features and Options

Oracle's extensibility features and options extend SQL to perform tasks that can't otherwise be easily programmed in a relational database. These include manipulation of time-series data, multimedia, and spatial data. These features are typically used by application developers but are sometimes bundled with applications sold by Oracle partners.

Oracle Time Series

A *time series* is a set of data in which each entry contains a timestamp. Such data is typically used in financial and trading applications and is often obtained from data-collection devices. In general, tables with time-series data don't contain a lot of columns but do contain many rows of data (perhaps representing a long history). A common example of a time series is the daily reporting of a stock's highs and lows, opens and closes, and volumes, as shown in Table 13-1.

Table 13-1. Typical historical time series of stock trading data

Symbol	Timestamp	Open	Close	High	Low	Volume
BIGCO	03-01-1999	30.125	29.75	30.50	29.50	285,000
BIGCO	03-02-1999	30.00	29.50	30.00	28.50	290,000
BIGCO	03-03-1999	29.25	30.125	30.50	29.00	275,000
BIGCO	03-04-1999	30.00	30.50	31.125	30.00	285,000
BIGCO	03-05-1999	30.25	31.125	32.00	30.00	310,000
BIGCO	03-08-1999	31.00	30.25	31.50	29.75	295,000
BIGCO	03-09-1999	30.50	31.00	30.50	32.125	300,000

Time-series functions for analyzing this data were first introduced as a separate option in Oracle8. Today, time-series data can be analyzed using SQL analytic functions that are included with the Oracle database, and the separate option no longer exists. The SQL analytic functions are further described in Chapter 9.

Oracle interMedia and Oracle Text

Oracle *inter*Media has been included with the database since Version 8.1.6 of Oracle8*i*. In Oracle9*i*, the product's text features became known as Oracle Text. These features were available as options in previous versions of Oracle:

- The Text Management feature was formerly known as the ConText option.

- The Locator feature evolved from the Spatial option and supports the location queries and the geocoding described later, in the "Oracle Spatial" section.

- Image storage and manipulation features were formerly bundled in the Image option.

Additionally, the product extensions enable the storage and manipulation of audio and video clips. Oracle has positioned Oracle *inter*Media and Oracle Text as being useful features for applications that typically include multiple media types because the features integrate all of these key datatypes and their associated functions.

Oracle *inter*Media and Oracle Text utilize a number of underlying database storage options, which are described in Table 13-2.

Table 13-2. Storage options for Oracle interMedia and Oracle Text

Type	Storage options
Text/images	VARCHAR2
	BLOB
	CLOB
	VARCHAR
	CHAR
	LONG
	LONG RAW
	Object attribute
	Master-detail stores (in which the master table identifies the text or image and the detail table contains the content)
	BFILEs
	URLs that point to content
Audio and video clips	BLOB
	BFILE
	URLs that point to content
Locator ordinates	VARRAYs

Oracle Database 10*g* has been enhanced to store large documents of up to 128 terabytes in LOBs.

Oracle *inter*Media and Oracle Text support a number of commonly used formats:

- Documents can be indexed while stored in formats such as ASCII, Microsoft Word, Excel, PowerPoint, WordPerfect, HTML, XML, and Adobe Acrobat (PDF).

- Audio formats supported include AU, AIFF, AIFF-C, WAV, MPEG1, MPEG2, and MPEG4.

- Video formats supported include Apple QuickTime 3.0, AVI, video MPEG formats (MPEG and MP4), and Real Networks Real video format (RMFF).

- Image formats supported include BMPF, CALS, FPIX, GIFF (GIF), JFIF (JPEG), PBMF, PGMF, PPMF, PPNF, PCXF (PCX), PICT, PNGF, RPIX, RASF, TGAF, TIFF, and WBMP. Image compression formats supported include ASCII encoding, BMPRLE, DEFLATE, DEFLATE-ADAM7, FAX3, FAX4, GIFLZW,

GIFLZW-INTERLACED, HUFFMAN3, JPEG, JPEG-PROGRESSIVE, LZW, LZWHDIFF, NONE, PACKBITS, PCXRLE, RAW, SUNRLE, and TARGARLE.

With Oracle's text-management capabilities, you can identify the strongest theme (or *gist*) of a document and generate document summaries based on that theme. Oracle Database 10*g* additions include theme (NEAR) proximity searching and the ability to determine the character set and language of documents with unknown content. Searching capabilities include full-text searches for word and phrase matching, theme searches, and mixed searches for both text and non-text data. Oracle Database 10*g* adds native indexing columns of type XMLType using Oracle Text. Typical users of Oracle text management are news services that publish news items to interested users via the Web. Oracle Database 10*g* includes an algorithm for determining popularity rankings of web pages and content.

Oracle Database 10*g* adds an easy custom text application building interface through JDeveloper with a text application generator, a catalog search application generator wizard, and a classification training set wizard.

Oracle9*i* introduced Ultra Search, a prebuilt application built upon Text for performing searches. Today, Ultra Search is included with the Oracle database, Oracle Application Server, and Oracle Collaboration Suite. Ultra Search can search and locate text in Oracle databases, other ODBC-accessible databases, Oracle Portal repositories, IMAP mail servers, HTML documents available from web servers, and other files. Using a *crawler* to index documents, this index of documents residing in the different servers is then stored in an Oracle database. Oracle Application Server users can access Ultra Search through a portlet. Applications builders can invoke Ultra Search using PL/SQL or Java procedures and use the APIs to make crawler results "searchable." Collaboration Suite leverages Ultra Search in searches of its Mail and Files components. Searches in Oracle Files use the Files fulltext index; thus, crawling to build an index is not needed in this component.

Image support in the Oracle database includes conversion among image and compression formats, access to raw pixel data, and support for basic image-manipulation functions such as scaling and cropping.

Clients can access audio and video files through Java Media Framework (JMF) players. (Java Advanced Imaging in Oracle9*i* and more recent releases also provides image support through JMF.) Streaming servers such as the Real Networks Server can also deliver audio and video content on demand.

You can also access images, audio, and video stored in Oracle and *inter*Media through C++, Java, OCI, or PL/SQL. Oracle Database 10*g* image object types support the SQL/MM Still Image standard, ISO/IEC 13249-5 SQL. Also added in Oracle Database 10*g* is support for the Sun Microsystems Java Advanced Imaging (JAI) package for storing and processing content. Audio, video, and images stored using *inter*Media might also be included as part of a web site using a variety of web-authoring tools, including the Portal in the Oracle Application Server, Symantec Visual Page, Microsoft FrontPage, Macromedia Dreamweaver, and Ultradev.

Oracle Spatial Option

Spatial data is data that contains location information. The Oracle Spatial option provides the functions and procedures that allow spatial data to be stored in an Oracle database and then accessed and analyzed according to location comparisons.

An example of using spatial query functions to combine spatial and standard relational conditions would be to "find all homes within two square miles of the intersection of Main Street and First Avenue in which the residents' income is greater than $100,000, and show their location." This query might return a list of home addresses or, when used with a Geographic Information System (GIS), plot the home locations on a map, as shown in Figure 13-2. Geocoding matches references such as addresses, phone numbers (including area codes), and postal codes (with longitude and latitude), which are then stored in the database.

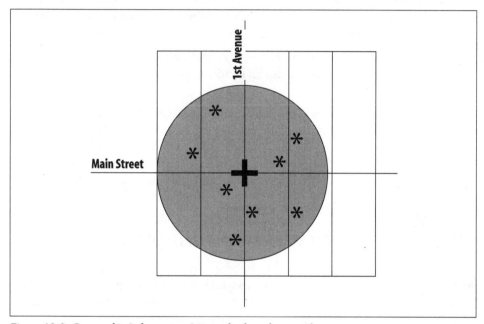

Figure 13-2. Geographic Information System display of a spatial query

Multiple geometric forms are supported by the Oracle Spatial option to represent many different types of spatial data, including points and point clusters, lines and line strings, polygons and complex polygons with holes, arc strings, line strings, compound polygons, and circles. You can determine the interaction of these features through the use of operators such as touch, overlap, inside, and disjoint.

Data that shares the same object space and coordinates but represents different characteristics (such as physical and economic) is often modeled in *layers*. Each layer is divided into tiles representing smaller subareas within the larger area. A representation of this tile is stored with a spatial index that provides for quick lookups of multiple characteristics in the same tile. The Spatial option uses these representations to rapidly retrieve data based on spatial characteristics. For example, you can perform a query against a physical area to examine where pollutants, minerals, and water are present. Each of these characteristics is likely to be stored in a separate layer, but they can be quickly mapped to their common tiles. The designers of these spatial-based databases can increase the resolution of the maps by increasing the number of tiles representing the geography.

The Spatial option fully leverages Oracle's object features through the use of a *spatial object type* that represents single- or multi-element geometries. Spatial coordinates are stored in VARRAYs.

Oracle Database 10g introduces the GeoRaster for storing, indexing, querying, analyzing, and delivering raster image data, associated Spatial vector geometry data, and metadata. This feature enables storage of multidimensional grid layers and digital images in an object-relational schema that are referenced to coordinate systems.

Oracle Database 10g also introduces topology and network management, enabling manipulation of data-describing nodes and edges in a topology or network or manipulation of faces in a topology.

In the real world, most spatial implementations in business aren't custom-built from SQL, but instead utilize purchased GIS solutions that are built on top of databases. Many of these GIS providers include Oracle Spatial technology as part of their product bundles. With the Oracle Database 10g release, you can also use newly introduced spatial analysis and mining subprograms in Oracle Data Mining option applications.

Using the Extensibility Framework in Oracle

Oracle allows users to extend the basic functionality of the database. Oracle's extensibility framework provides entry points in which developers can add their own features to the existing feature set. By using this framework you can do the following:

Add new relational or set operators for use in SQL statements
> These new operators can be useful when working with extended datatypes, such as multimedia or spatial data. You can create relational operators that relate specifically to a particular datatype, such as the relational operator CLOSER TO, which you can use in SQL statements that access spatial data.

Create cooperative indexing
> Cooperative indexing is a scheme in which an external application is responsible for building and using an index structure that you can use with complex datatypes. The indexes created are known as *domain indexes*.

Extend the optimizer

If you use extended indexes, user-defined datatypes, or other features, you can extend the statistics-collection process or define selectivity and cost functions for these extended features. The cost-based optimizer can then use these to choose an appropriate query plan.

Add cartridge services

These are services used by Oracle database extensions (such as the spatial capabilities) providing memory management, context management, parameter management, string and number manipulation, file I/O, internationalization, error reporting, and thread management. These services are available to software developers to provide a means to create uniform integration of extensions with the Oracle database.

With these features, the extensibility framework enables you or a third-party software developer to integrate additional functionality into the main Oracle database while still using the core features of the database, such as security management, backup and recovery, and the SQL interface.

CHAPTER 14

Network Deployment Models

The previous chapters of this book focused on the features and architecture of the Oracle database. This chapter steps beyond the confines of specific features to look at the different deployment architectures that have been a focus of the last three Oracle releases.

This book is now in its third edition. We wrote the first edition about Oracle8 and Oracle8*i*, and added Oracle9*i* coverage to the second edition. In that second edition, we entitled this chapter "Oracle and the Web," recognizing that the capabilities of the Oracle database were being expanded beyond its traditional role—indeed, the database was becoming one of the pillars of an overall Internet platform solution.

With the release of Oracle Database 10*g*, Oracle Corporation is promoting another deployment architecture, the emerging concept known as *grid computing*. This chapter looks at how the Internet and its associated architecture—with its expanded scope and adherence to standards—have impacted the Oracle database over the past few years. It also provides a brief overview of an important complementary part of the "Oracle platform," Oracle Application Server. Finally, the chapter describes how grid computing fits into this evolution.

This new version of this final chapter reflects the state of the Oracle platform with the release of Oracle Database 10*g*, with less emphasis on some of the functionality that went exclusively toward supporting previous versions of the Oracle platform.

The Impact of the Internet

The late 1990s saw an explosion in the world of information technology brought on by the Internet. Although many of the financial highfliers who sought to capitalize on this sea change have fallen by the wayside, the impact of the Internet on the overall landscape and topology of computing has had a lasting effect.

In brief, the Internet tore down corporate IT walls and replaced them with firewalls. Prior to the Internet, real-time information was shared only within the confines of a particular organization—sharing was accomplished essentially through exporting information. The Internet supplied a way for organizations to use their information resources to directly interact with their customers and suppliers.

This massive expansion of scope brought about a number of significant changes, including:

- A new set of standards, including HTTP transport, HTML display, URLs for location, SSL for security, and LDAP for external directories.

- A set of new programming languages, including several different types of server scripting languages, such as JSPs and ASPs, as well as the corresponding growth of the Java environment.

- An even greater emphasis on sharing and integrating information, which was required as individual users needed to access all types of information. Portals and advanced integration standards and technologies seek to address this area of change.

Oracle's entire product line changed to meet the challenge of the Internet. The Oracle database got a new letter in its name, a new product stack sprang up to complete the "Oracle platform" (Oracle Application Server), and Oracle's existing management product, Enterprise Manager, dramatically expanded its focus.

The next few sections of this chapter look at the impact of these new deployment architectures on the Oracle database, on the Oracle Application Server, and on Enterprise Manager.

The Oracle Database and the Internet

There are several areas of functionality in the Oracle database that relate, either directly or more peripherally, to using the database in connection with the Internet. For example, you can:

- Access an Oracle database through a web server, which is included with the product

- Use Internet-era standards, such as the Java programming environment or XML-formatted information

- Use a new development tool in Oracle Database 10g to build browser-based applications

Oracle HTTP Server

Oracle HTTP Server (OHS) is a web server that is included with the Oracle database. The Oracle HTTP Server is essentially the same HTTP server that is included as part of Oracle Application Server. Based on the Apache web server, it has different *mods* that support different types of functionality.

The version of Apache used in OHS is 1.3.*x*, where *x* is the latest released Apache version. For Oracle Database 10*g*, the version is 1.3.28.

Before Oracle Database 10*g*, OHS came as an integrated part of the database. Oracle Database 10*g* includes a standalone version of OHS, which has only some modules (*mods*)—for example, *mod_plsql*, *mod_cgi*, *mod_perl*, and others. (Previous versions of Oracle came with a version of OHS that included a larger number of *mods*.) The standalone version comes on a separate CD-ROM and is installed separately.

The *mod* most directly related to the Oracle database is *mod_plsql*, which provides a connection to the PL/SQL engine within the Oracle database. This module allows a user to call an Oracle PL/SQL procedure in the database.

When a user calls an Oracle procedure, OHS uses two types of configuration information:

- A Data Access Descriptor (DAD), which defines the Oracle database and username/password combination used to access the database
- Some form of pass-through identifier, which routes the call to a PL/SQL procedure

The connection to the database is established through the DAD, which identifies the target database and either uses a specific username and password combination or prompts the user for a username and password. Each PL/SQL agent is associated with a DAD, and each DAD can be associated with several agents.

OHS is configured to listen on a particular port. Requests come in the form of URLs consisting of the name of the server, the port number of the server, the name of the PL/SQL agent that will service the request, and the name of the stored procedure that is to be executed. For instance, suppose that the server name is homeserver, the PL/SQL agent that is to service the request is netu, and the listener is listening on port 4000. A request for a stored procedure called return_time would look like the following:

```
http://homeserver:4000/netu/return_time
```

If this stored procedure accepts parameters, those parameters can be included in the standard URL syntax following the name of the procedure. Of course, this stored procedure would be designed to return HTML code in response to this call.

Standards Support

The Internet era has popularized a new set of standards. The Oracle database provides functionality to support most of these standards, such as the HTTP server mentioned in the previous section. Two standards have a significant amount of support—Java and XML.

Java in the database

The Oracle database includes its own Java Virtual Machine, called the Oracle JVM (formerly known as JServer). Java programs can be developed with any standard Java tool. You can load either the Java source code or the "compiled" version of the Java program in its *.class* format into the database.

The Oracle JVM runs in the same process space as the standard Oracle database and can directly access the information in the database buffers, which can help to improve the performance of data access through Java. It runs as part of a database session, so there is no need to establish an explicit connection to the Oracle server. Because it's part of the Oracle server, the Oracle JVM uses the same security and authentication methods as its host database.

The Oracle JVM Accelerator included with Oracle is a native code compiler that can deliver performance for Java binaries that's close to the performance of compiled C code. It operates by converting Java binaries into specialized C programs, which are then compiled into native libraries. Oracle claims that the garbage collection process (an integral part of a Java Virtual Machine) implemented in the Oracle JVM also provides better performance than most other Java virtual machines.

Enterprise JavaBeans, or EJBs, are a type of Java program that can be run on a server machine within the context of an EJB transaction server. The EJB transaction server provides system-wide services for all EJBs, such as transaction and state management and communication with other EJB servers. The EJB server implemented by Oracle can use some of the internal management capabilities of the Oracle database server, such as those in the shared server. Oracle includes automated tools to load and publish EJBs, which makes them easier to use with Oracle.

PL/SQL and Java. PL/SQL procedures can be called from any Oracle JVM application through the SQLJ interface embedded in the server (the next section describes SQLJ). However, you have to "publish" the top-level Java methods; publishing creates, in effect, a PL/SQL interface for the methods and thus makes them available to PL/SQL procedures. Once the wrapper is created, you can use the Java application just as you would any other PL/SQL procedure—even as part of a standard SQL statement.

With Oracle Database 10g, you can call Java procedures in the database directly, without the need for a PL/SQL wrapper.

 By now, there have been two major releases since Java was introduced in the Oracle database, so it is probably safe to assume that both PL/SQL and Java will continue to exist as procedural languages that can be run inside the Oracle database.

The JPublisher tool, which comes as a part of Oracle8*i* and beyond, is used to create the interface between user-defined datatypes and Java wrapper classes. This capability allows you to extend the object-relational datatypes you may have already created with Oracle to the Java environment, or to create user-defined datatypes that can act as persistent storage for the Java objects you use in your Java applications.

JDBC and SQLJ: Java's 3GL interfaces. Oracle includes two application programming interfaces to data from the Java environment: JDBC and SQLJ. JDBC is a fairly low-level interface that gives Java developers complete control over the interaction between Java applications and data in the Oracle database. JDBC is the functional equivalent of existing APIs such as ODBC. Like ODBC, JDBC is a vendor-independent API.

The JDBC interface is standard, but Oracle offers it in three flavors:

A thin client, 100% Java version
     This version is compact (150 KB compressed) and ideal for clients that use only Java.

A slightly fatter client version that is based on the Oracle Call Interface (OCI)
     This version requires some form of Oracle networking software that supports OCI.

The in-database JDBC driver (JDBC KPRB)
     Java code uses the JDBC KPRB (Kernel Program Bundled) version to access SQL on the same server.

The OCI version of the JDBC interface is a little faster than the pure Java version, so it is most appropriate for use in places like a middle-tier component. The server-side JDBC driver is used for Java stored procedures that run inside the Oracle server.

Oracle also includes the SQLJ interface. SQLJ is a Java library that lets developers use embedded SQL statements in their Java applications. The SQLJ interface works like the Pro* interfaces that already exist for other 3GL languages, such as Pro*C and Pro*COBOL, but unlike these interfaces, SQLJ is an industry standard. You can simply insert SQL statements into your Java code, and the SQLJ translator will translate those calls into their underlying JDBC equivalents.

There are a couple of significant differences between JDBC and SQLJ. Because JDBC simply submits SQL statements as strings, any problems with your SQL syntax won't be found until they are detected by the Oracle database at runtime. With SQLJ, the translator parses the SQL statements and returns errors. On the other hand, SQLJ can be used only for static SQL statements, while JDBC can submit dynamically constructed SQL statements. Much of the flexibility built with dynamic SQL statements can be implemented using bind variables, but there may be times when you need to use the JDBC interface. You can easily mix and match SQLJ and JDBC in your Java application, but the presence of any SQLJ code will require the use of the translator.

XML

XML is a kind of evolutionary standard. It is a text-based markup language, like HTML, but it can be extended to describe a virtually unlimited number of datatypes and structures. Because of this flexibility, it has become a popular standard format for data storage and exchange.

The Oracle database supports a variety of XML standards. It also provides the functionality of a complete XML database, XML DB, as part of the Oracle database. See the later section describing XML DB.

XML standards. Oracle includes a number of features that support XML, such as its XDK (or XML development kit) for Java, C, C++, and PL/SQL. The XDK lets developers send, receive, and interpret XML data from applications written in their respective languages. From Oracle9i on, the XDK also supports the XML schema standard for defining the datatypes for a particular XML document, which replaces the old method of using Document Type Definitions (DTDs). Since Oracle9i, all versions of the XDK also include two JavaBeans (or components), the DBAccess Bean and the DBView Bean, that make it easier for developers to define access to and view XML data stored in the database.

Oracle9i also provided these XML-related features:

XML class generators for Java and C++
Create classes from XML schema definitions.

XML SQL utility
Supports reading and writing XML data to and from the database using SQL. You can also get most of this functionality by using the DBMS_XMLGEN built-in package.

XSQL servlet
Generates XML documents from one or more SQL queries and uses XSL stylesheets to format the results. This servlet can also be used to insert, update, and delete data using XML.

The Oracle9i release included the new XMLType datatype, which we described in Chapter 4. This datatype allows native storage of XML documents in the Oracle9i and later database versions.

Oracle Database 10g continues the improvement in XML support by adding the ability to use multibyte character sets with XML for internationalization.

XML DB. XML DB is a term for a group of XML features that were introduced as part of Release 2 of Oracle9i. XML DB consists of four key areas:

XMLType
Described in Chapter 4, the XMLType datatype indicates to the Oracle database that the contents are XML data, so that specific XML operations, such as XPath-based searches and updates, can be performed on it.

Support for XMLSchema

An XMLSchema is a description of the specific contents and types in an XML document, and can be used as a constraint for an XMLType column. Oracle can also use the information contained in an XMLSchema to automatically shred documents into a series of objects and store them in the database with no loss of information. Oracle XML DB is then able to use the information contained in the XMLSchema to optimize XPath-based queries and updates over the content of XML documents stored in the database.

XML DB repository

The XML DB repository allows a URL to be used to locate an XML document, or to define relationships between XML documents stored in the Oracle database. The XML DB repository includes a hierarchical index that allows a URL-based access to be as efficient as a primary-key based access. The repository also includes support for HTTP, FTP, and WebDAV protocols, which are used by many popular applications—for example, Windows Explorer, Internet Explorer, Microsoft Office, and XML editors such as Corel's XMetaL—to access content stored in the Oracle database without requiring Oracle software on the client.

SQL/XML

SQL/XML provides a standardized method for generating XML documents directly from a SQL statement.

Simplified HTML Applications Development

Oracle offers a wide set of development tools, which we described in Chapter 1. Oracle Database 10g includes a new development tool specifically designed to create and run applications in a browser environment, HTML DB.

HTML DB harks back to the days of WebDB, which provided a way to develop HTML-based applications. Like WebDB, HTML DB gives you a series of browser-based wizards that help you create standard application components.

HTML DB uses the concept of a *workflow* as the organizing principle for sets of these components. The workflow provides a menu interface, typically using tabs, as shown in Figure 14-1.

Within a workflow, you create various pages, which implement specific pieces of functionality, such as reports or data entry or a tree structure used for hierarchical browsing. You can link different pages together within a workflow.

HTML DB lets you provide security for pages and workflows to limit access to HTML DB pages. Workflows and pages have templates that control their look and feel.

Two other aspects of HTML DB provide functionality of interest to DBAs as well as developers:

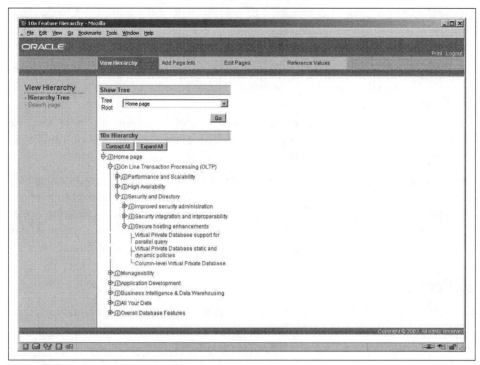

Figure 14-1. An HTML DB application

SQL Workshop
> This portion of the product has a graphical, browser-based interface for all aspects of SQL, from queries to data definition.

Data Workshop
> This portion of the product gives you the ability to import data from text or from XML or Excel spreadsheets, and to export data directly to text or XML formats.

Oracle Application Server

Oracle Application Server 10*g* (AS), which, prior to Oracle Database 10*g*, was known as Oracle *i*AS, is the other major component of the "Oracle platform." The whole field of application servers is significantly less mature than that of relational databases. Consequently, there is less agreement across different vendor offerings as to what functionality constitutes an application server.

Oracle's focus and strategy is based around servicing the leading enterprise database—Oracle. Some of the functionality in AS is also provided as part of the Oracle database, such as the basic web server and the ability to implement browser-based applications. Other components, such as Oracle Portal, compete with other vendors' application servers or niche products.

Oracle Application Server is intended to complement and extend the Oracle database to handle all IT requirements. With Oracle Database 10g, there has been increased integration between the two products in two significant ways:

- Enterprise Manager, which we have discussed throughout this book, now manages AS as well as the Oracle database. The new version is known as Enterprise Manager 10g.

- AS can now automatically recognize the failure of a node in an Oracle database without having to wait for an IP timeout. This allows the application running in AS to take corrective action more rapidly, hiding the failure from a user.

We can't hope to do justice to AS in this brief section, especially considering how the product's functionality has grown over time. For a much fuller overview of the concepts and architecture of AS, see the companion book, *Oracle Application Server 10g Essentials*, available from O'Reilly & Associates later in 2004; that book will provide the same type of coverage for AS that this volume does for the database.

Editions

Oracle Application Server comes in three separate editions for Oracle Database 10g:

Java Edition
> Contains the HTTP Server, Java Containers for J2EE, JDeveloper, Toplink, and Enterprise Manager

Standard Edition
> Contains everything in the Java Edition as well as Portal, single sign-on capabilities, and the Content Management SDK

Enterprise Edition
> Contains everything in Standard Edition, with these additional components:
> - Web Cache
> - Integration platform
> - Oracle Internet Directory
> - Oracle Application Server Certificate Authority
> - Discoverer
> - Reporting and Forms services
> - Personalization
> - Wireless

In Oracle Application Server 10g, clickstream intelligence and the database cache are no longer supported as part of the product.

The pricing structure in place as of this writing offers Java Edition for $5,000 per CPU, with Standard Edition and Enterprise Edition each available for a higher price.

Please keep in mind that packaging and pricing are the exclusive realm of Oracle Corporation and can be changed at any time.

Installation

You can see from the brief list of functionality in the previous section that Oracle Application Server is a broad product. You can configure AS as part of the installation process to provide different types of functionality, including J2EE server, Web Cache, Portal, Wireless, Business Intelligence, and Forms.

Components

The following sections discuss the various functional components of Oracle Application Server. Services, which affect the overall operation of AS, are described later in "System Services."

HTTP Server

The Oracle HTTP Server (OHS) that is part of Application Server is the same basic product that we described previously as part of the database. OHS in AS is based on Apache, but provides some additional modules, known as *mods*, including:

mod_oc4j
> Directs requests for Java modules to the Oracle Containers for Java component, described later

mod_jserv
> Used for Java Server Pages

mod_webdav
> Supports versioning through WebDAV (Web-based Distributed Authoring and Versioning)

mod_osso
> Provides built-in single sign-on functionality

You can add other *mods* to OHS, but Oracle Support may ask you to remove unsupported modules if a problem occurs.

The Oracle HTTP Server includes the ability to use server-side includes, which can be used to add code to the headers and footers of all pages served, to implement standardized behaviors and look and feel.

OHS provides virtual host capabilities, which let you use a single instance of OHS to map to multiple host names. OHS can act as a proxy server or a reverse proxy server, and it can also support URL rewriting, which allows administrators to change the location of a page without requiring users to change the way they access the page. OHS includes a proxy plug-in for Internet Information Server and SunONE server, which lets requests to these servers be automatically rerouted to OHS. These plug-ins can provide the load balancing functionality, described in the later section on "Clustering and load balancing," for Oracle Containers for J2EE, described in the following section.

Containers for J2EE (OC4J)

The core Java capabilities of Oracle Application Server are provided by Oracle Application Server Containers for J2EE, also known as OC4J. This component is a Java Virtual Machine, providing support for a wide range of Java 1.3 standards, including session beans, entity beans (with both bean-managed and session-managed persistence), and message-driven Java beans, Java Server Pages 1.2 and Servlets 2.3, and Java Message Service.

You can scale OC4J by having multiple instances of OC4J on a single machine as well as having multiple threads, each running a single application module, in an individual OC4J instance.

OC4J also implements JDBC connections to the Oracle database, which can include connection pooling.

TopLink

TopLink provides object-relational mapping, the ability to associate object attributes with relational tables and columns. Because TopLink performs this mapping, a developer can change the mapping without changing the Java code that accesses the underlying data.

TopLink also provides caching and optimization to reduce database and network traffic.

Development tools

Oracle Application Server 10g includes several development kits:

XML Development Kit
Provides components, tools, and utilities for working with XML in applications

Content Management Kit
Integrates with Oracle content management products in Collaboration Suite, and provides a variety of capabilities, including security, versioning, workflow, and search and retrieval operations

MapViewer
Makes it easier to build maps to represent themes or locations

The increased need for integration of diverse applications has thrust web services to the forefront of application development. Oracle Application Server supports a range of web service standards, including SOAP, WSDL, and UDDI. AS includes the ability to easily publish both stateful and stateless J2EE classes as web services, automatically generating WSDL descriptions and client-side proxy stubs.

Of course, the course of standards bodies, like that of true love, never runs smooth. AS already provides integration between .NET SOAP and Java SOAP, and Oracle has stated its intention to continue this type of integration.

Development servers

Oracle's traditional development tools, including Oracle Forms Developer (known as Developer in the past), Oracle Reports, and JDeveloper, are part of the Oracle Developer Suite of products, as are Oracle Designer and Discoverer. However, AS includes runtime services for Forms and Reports.

Oracle Application Server, Enterprise Edition, comes with a Forms Services component. This component allows a user to run the user interface to a Forms application as a Java applet on the client. The Forms Service creates a server process to handle HTTP requests from the Java client.

AS Enterprise Edition also includes a Reports Server. The Reports Server creates and manages reports processes to handle user requests. Reports can be cached for a specified length of time, so that subsequent requests are satisfied by retrieving the report, rather than by running the queries for the report again. Reports can be scheduled to run and be delivered to multiple recipients.

Portal

Oracle Application Server Portal has gone through some significant changes in its history. When it was first released under the name of WebDB as part of the Oracle database, Portal was seen as a tool to create HTML-based applications, a role now taken by HTML DB, described earlier. WebDB was renamed Oracle Portal, and the focus of the product was changed to concentrate on bringing together separate sources of information into a common desktop.

Entire books have been written on Portal alone, so the description in this section is, of necessity, a very brief overview of the range of Portal capabilities.

Portal uses pages, which can consist of static or dynamic information and which use a theme for overall look and feel. Portal includes wizards for easy creation of pages. Portlets are applications that can get information from a wide variety of sources, from a database to a web source, and can be plugged into the Portal framework. The Portal framework provides a look and feel as well as navigation controls for all the information displayed in it (see Figure 14-2).

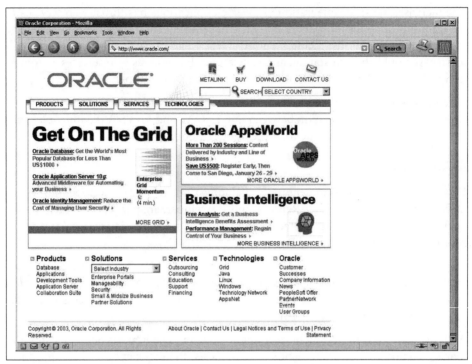

Figure 14-2. A well-known Portal application

Developers can allow users to customize some parts of portlet and page display, and Portal will automatically save these customizations. Portal provides a single sign-on capability to identify users and secure content.

A user can search across all information in a portal with a built-in search mechanism. Developers can also add categorization to pages to aid in searches.

A single Portal deployment can also deploy multiple versions of pages in different languages.

Wireless

OracleAS Wireless is a set of services and applications that form a development platform that can be used to create applications to address a variety of mobile devices and forms, including PDAs, cell phones, and other wireless devices.

OracleAS Wireless supports three modes:

Pull mode
    In this mode, a wireless user requests information.

Push mode
    In this mode, information is sent to a wireless user.

Persistent mode
> In this mode, a wireless user can maintain an application even when she is out of wireless contact.

This component also includes a set of *mobile enablers*, which provide services that wireless applications commonly need. These enablers include:

- Content and data syndication, which translates web and WAP content for mobile devices
- Location services
- Personalization
- Analytics, used to understand user behaviors
- Commerce, used for mobile wallets and payment integration
- Provisioning, used for phone and device settings
- Synchronization, used for phones and devices, as well as data synchronization with Oracle Lite
- Notification, used to provide multichannel conditional and time-based alerts

OracleAS Wireless also includes three mobile applications:

Mobile Office
> Includes basic productivity applications for mobile devices

Multi-Channel Messaging
> Lets you send a message to different mobile devices

Mobile Location
> Helps to add location awareness with driving directions, a business finder, and maps

Security

Security features are used to limit access to data, applications, and computing resources. The Oracle database has a complete security system, as described in Chapter 5. Oracle Application Server can be used to authenticate users, store security credentials, and implement a concept known as *identity management*.

Identity management allows an administrator to establish and maintain a security identity for a user and enforce it across an entire set of computing components, such as databases, application servers, and applications. Oracle Application Server uses the Oracle Internet Directory (OID) to store security information and provide user authentication. OID is an LDAP (Lightweight Directory Access Protocol) compliant store of information. Any application can access OID, including the Oracle database.

Identity management also includes a number of other features, including:

- A user provisioning framework that can be integrated with other applications, such as the HR system, provided by OID

- Directory integration tools, provided with OID
- PKI certificate management, provided with AS Certificate Authority
- Tools for managing security, implemented as part of Enterprise Manager

In addition, AS provides a single sign-on capability. As the name implies, this service allows a user to log on once; the user's information is then used by various computing entities to retrieve the authenticated identity of the user.

Oracle's identity management solution can also be integrated with other third-party identity management products.

Integration

Integration is a broad area that encompasses bringing together information from different sources. The Oracle database has a number of features for integration, including Streams and Heterogeneous Gateways. Application Server includes its own set of features for integration, including:

Integration Modeler
This is an HTML-based tool that can model business processes and map data transformations. The results of this tool are stored in a repository, and they can be changed at any time.

Integration Manager
This tool handles the runtime processes used for integration.

Adapters
Oracle Application Server includes a set of adapters for packaged applications, such as SAP and Peoplesoft, as well as other databases and messaging systems. You can also create your own adapters with an Adapter SDK.

To complement these main features, Oracle AS includes a repository for the storage of integration information, such as transformations, and analysis tools to provide intelligence on how business processes are being integrated. Enterprise Manager is used to manage the integration processes defined with AS Integration.

Business intelligence

Business intelligence can encompass a wide spectrum of options. Oracle provides three modules that are classified as being business intelligence features of Application Server (Portal is also sometimes added to this category):

Reports Services
These services are discussed earlier in the "Development servers" section.

Discoverer
Discoverer is a tool that business analysts use to obtain business intelligence data from an Oracle database. Analysts use Discoverer to query and retrieve data via a browser-based interface and to manipulate it in a variety of ways, including drill-down, pivoting, and changing the layout and presentation of data into various

forms, such as tabular and crosstab forms. Administrators set up an End User Layer to simplify complex access to multiple data sources, complete with appropriate aggregation. Because Discoverer can also present data in a graphical format, Figure 14-3 is worth the remaining thousand words of description.

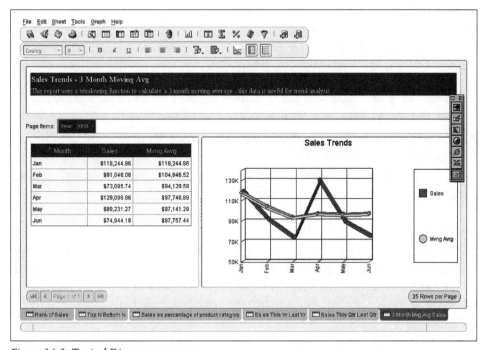

Figure 14-3. Typical Discoverer output

Personalization

Personalization, the final component of the AS business intelligence solution, uses data mining algorithms on data gathered from customer transactions, web site clicks, and demographics. These help build a recommendation engine that can be used to create recommendations for individual customers as they traverse the web site. Personalization can be deeply complex in setup, but the benefits that come from successful personalization of sites like web stores can directly result in higher sales volumes.

We cover business intelligence in the Oracle database in more depth in Chapter 9.

System Services

The remaining areas of Application Server capabilities provide services that affect more than one of the functional areas described earlier:

- Management capabilities address the entire AS stack

- Caching improves performance across many areas of functionality
- Clustering (of several types) and load balancing provide for scalability and reliability

Management

With the Oracle Database 10g release, the scope of Enterprise Manager has been broadened to encompass AS. Enterprise Manager now provides availability and performance tracking for both Application Server and the Oracle database. For instance, Enterprise Manager automatically provides information on the web pages that take the longest to serve, and it does this by mining the log files for Application Server, so there is virtually no impact on performance.

AS now lets you archive the configuration of an individual instance, either to act as a backup before making configuration changes or to apply to any other instance.

For more information on other extended features of Enterprise Manager, see the "Management" section under "Grid Computing" later in this chapter.

Caching

Caching is a standard concept in computing—caching speeds up the retrieval of frequently used information by saving it somewhere where it can be rapidly retrieved. In the database, this means keeping frequently used data in memory, rather than retrieving it from disk. For Reports Server, described earlier, this means saving a report rather than running it again.

Oracle Application Server includes two specific components meant to provide additional caching capabilities: the Web Cache and the Java Object Cache.

Web Cache. The idea behind the Web Cache is fairly simple—maintain copies of frequently requested information in a cache so the information does not have to be retrieved every time it is requested. The Oracle Application Server Web Cache works on HTML pages and parts of pages. It can cache either static or dynamic data and includes validation routines that you can implement to specify when the data should be refreshed. Web Cache is aware of individual user and application dependencies on data, so it automatically caches and delivers situation-specific information.

HTML code uses Edge Side Includes to indicate where partial page content goes, and Web Cache will use those directives to assemble pages with cached data. The Web Cache can also cache images, audio, video, Java, and search results.

Web Cache can also compress web content, which can speed delivery to clients. Both cache validation rules and compression rules can be implemented with regular expressions for flexibility.

Web Cache instances can be on the same node as Application Server instances, or on their own servers, as shown in Figure 14-4. Web Cache instances can be clustered with a load balancer and use a built-in clustering capability. This capability provides a shared distributed cache, where each cache instance is aware of the contents of the other cache instances. Web Cache can be used with Forms and Reports.

The Web Cache includes a technology Oracle refers to as *surge protection*. Surge protection proactively monitors the load on each server and implements actions to prevent the servers from being overwhelmed by a spike in traffic or a denial-of-service attack.

In Oracle Application Server 10g, Web Cache is used to collect the data on page service times used by Enterprise Manager's Application Performance Monitoring feature, which is described later in the "Grid Computing" section.

Java Object Cache. The Java Object Cache is implemented with a set of Java classes. As its name implies, this cache stores frequently used Java objects in memory or on disk. Developers use a set of attributes associated with a Java object to define how an object is loaded into the cache, where an object is stored, and validation rules that specify when an object is moved out of the cache.

Clustering and load balancing

Oracle Application Server instances can be clustered together, for higher performance and availability. You can cluster Web Cache, Java Container, Portal, Forms Service, Report Servers, or OID instances. In addition, you can use Real Application Clusters to provide clustering capabilities for the AS infrastructure or Portal. A multi-tier set of clusters is shown in Figure 14-4.

mod_oc4j, which directs requests to the Oracle Container for Java from the Oracle HTTP Server, provides load balancing across multiple instances of the Java Container, based on several different types of schemes, including varieties of random assignment, round robin, and metric-based.

You can implement load balancing for either stateless requests or requests that carry state. State-based load balancing is implemented with cookies, and can be done either explicitly or with the Java Object Cache. Oracle Java Containers are aware of nodes that share state information, so they can provide high availability for stateful load balancing by redirecting requests to a failed node to another node that shared application state with the failed node.

In Oracle Application Server 10g, you can create policies that can reallocate a node from one cluster to another without having to restart the cluster.

Application Server includes a high-availability framework, which monitors instances for their health, informs the system of problems, and automatically attempts to

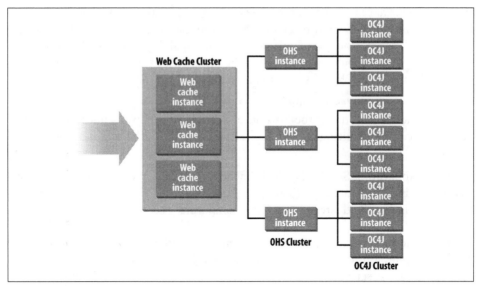

Figure 14-4. Multiple levels of clustering in Application Server

restart failed instances. Each node in a cluster contains its own configuration information, so if the node containing the repository that describes the cluster becomes unavailable, OHS can rebuild the repository on a designated backup node, eliminating this potential single source of failure.

Application Server can be installed to use underlying hardware cluster functionality in what is called a *Cold Failover Cluster*. This configuration uses a shared disk attached to multiple machines. If the primary server should fail, operations fail over to a backup server. The 10*g* release of AS also supports *Active Failover Clusters* (AFCs). (Note that the initial release of AS 10*g* does not support this configuration in a production environment.) AFCs require a load balancer in front of the active nodes, but both nodes can operate at the same time, providing scalability with high availability. Figure 14-5 shows the difference between these two types of failover configurations.

> Of course, many uses of Application Server involve multiple services, such as Java, identity management, and database access. To use clustering for high availability, you must avoid single points of failure for all of these services. This can require careful planning and multiple clustering and failover schemes.

For easier creation of clusters, AS comes with a feature called Distributed Configuration Management (DCM), which simplifies creating clones of existing nodes and redistributes J2EE components to the new node.

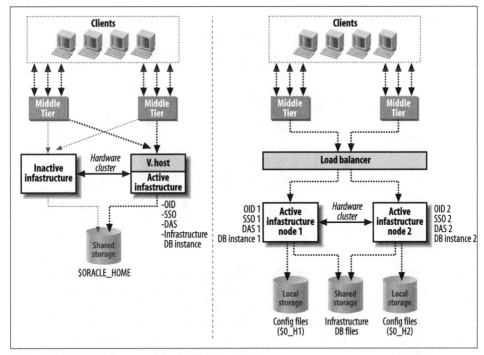

Figure 14-5. Cold Failover and Active Failover Clusters

The Application Server 10g release also includes a feature in the database called *failover notification*. Prior to this release, an Application Server instance had to wait for a TCP/IP timeout to know that a database server node had failed. With this new release, the cluster management software for the database cluster proactively informs the Application Server instance of a failure, reducing failover time.

Grid Computing

As with the Internet (the *i* in Oracle8*i* and Oracle9*i*), Oracle Corporation has signaled its intent to embrace the new paradigm of grid computing (see Figure 14-6) with a letter—the letter attached to the version number of Oracle Database 10g. Grid computing is, circa 2003, a hot buzzword, but the grid computing architecture is the result of the more powerful aspects of the last two paradigm shifts, client/server computing and Internet computing.

Grid computing seeks to capitalize on the most profound economic benefit of the client/server explosion for IT—low-cost commodity servers. Grid computing is based on the premise that using multiple commodity machines is less expensive than using larger SMP machines. Four commodity servers with 4 CPUs are less expensive than a single SMP machine with 16 servers—in most cases, significantly less expensive.

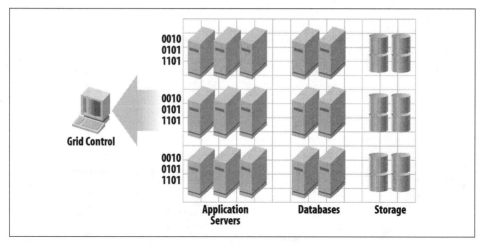

Figure 14-6. Oracle's vision of grid computing

Grid computing is also the extension of the simplicity provided by Internet computing. Internet computing relies on a simple user interface, which requires only a URL to locate a resource. In the grid, a client simply plugs into computing resources, whose location, distribution, and topology are completely transparent. The computing resources that provide the power for the client appear to be seamless and result in a framework for adding infrastructure resources needed by applications when they are needed.

Features for Grid Computing

There are several concepts central to the idea of grid computing. Although none of these concepts are completely new with the grid, each of them has taken on added importance in this latest architecture. Before drilling down into further detail, we note that this book covers grid computing as Oracle has defined it with the initial Oracle Database 10g release.

The definitions presented here may be somewhat different from other visions or definitions of grid computing you've encountered. Keep in mind that Oracle's vision is also based upon off-the-shelf products rather than upon lengthy custom-built software development efforts.

At the time of this writing, an Oracle-based grid implementation would consist of database instances running in a RAC configuration with up to 64 instances running on a common operating system/set of platforms. The other key components in the configuration are the following:

- Oracle Application Server 10g, the subject of much of this chapter
- Oracle Enterprise Manager 10g, discussed here relative to the grid, but more fully described in Chapter 5

- Network-attached storage devices, which will probably use Oracle Database 10*g*'s Automatic Storage Management (ASM) capability

Of course, Oracle's database interchange mechanisms allow the exchange of data with other database grid implementations, enabling extension beyond a single database. The next sections describe key software capabilities that enable the building of such configurations.

Provisioning

Years ago, the computing universe revolved around the sun of the mainframe. In terms of centralized computing power, the cloud of the grid occupies the same position as the once mighty mainframe.

The grid is based on consolidating the computing power provided by multiple servers and clusters. Once consolidated, these resources must be reallocated to the users and applications that need them. This allocation, in turn, must be both flexible and transparent for the grid to deliver on its promised efficiencies.

The mechanism used by the grid for accomplishing this allocation is termed *provisioning*. A grid computing architecture must be able to match requests and resources. Because the grid is meant to handle the whole world of varying requests, provisioning should be easy and able to dynamically respond to changes in the composition of any particular workload.

One of the requirements for flexible provisioning is the concept of *virtualization*, where resources are delivered in a virtual chunk. The underlying support for a virtual resource can be changed, in response to demand or failure, without having to disturb the connection between the resource and its consumer.

If grid computing is to be achievable without an unacceptable management burden, provisioning and virtualization are required.

Resilience

Consolidation is a virtue, but it has a dark side. Does a single computing resource imply a single point of failure? If so, this one potential problem could outweigh all the virtues of grid computing.

The grid must be, of necessity, highly *resilient*. If one part of the grid fails, the failure must not endanger the rest of the grid. In order to truly implement a transparent source of computing power, transparent failover must be an integral part of the grid.

On the database side of Oracle's grid vision, Real Application Clusters provide one part of this type of high availability. If a node in a RAC database fails, the rest of the nodes just keep on running. The other part of this equation is supplied by Data Guard, which protects against disaster scenarios, such as media or site failure.

Oracle Application Server has the ability to cluster its HTTP, Web Cache, and J2EE servers, as well as the Oracle Internet Directory, which provides security services to the grid, and Oracle Application Server Portal, which can deliver a desktop to all users.

Integration

From the outside, the grid looks like one big hunka hunka computing resource. But there are reasons why there may still be separate groups of resources, from different locations participating in the grid to a raft of political and organizational issues. The grid must be able to integrate these loosely coupled resources together transparently.

The Oracle database has a few different technologies aimed at integration. Oracle has supported transparent gateways for quite a while; these allow a user or application to access data in other databases with the same API as Oracle. You can access data that lives outside the Oracle database through the use of external tables.

Oracle Streams is intended to be a complete integration solution for data in different Oracle databases (through replication), as well as between Oracle and other data sources (through Advanced Queueing).

Web services are another way that separate computing sources can combine their efforts. The Oracle database allows you to expose queries (as well as PL/SQL packages) as web services, and can act as a consumer of other web services. Oracle Application Server also includes many ways to create, define, manage, and integrate web services.

Finally, Oracle Application Server includes its set of integration technologies to bring together all types of heterogeneous services without too great a management burden.

Management

You may have noticed that we lightly skipped over a huge potential problem with combining multiple servers—the corresponding multiplication in management effort. In fact, the increasing reduction in the price of hardware makes management overhead one of the largest factors in the overall cost of computing today.

Oracle Database 10g, as described in Chapter 5 and elsewhere, provides a wide range of features for improved management. The easier it is to manage individual servers, the lower the overall management costs for the grid.

Some features described earlier in the book, such as providing identity management across the enterprise environment, ease the management burdens that could result from the consolidation of the grid. Oracle has also expanded the scope and feature set of Enterprise Manager (EM) in order to help implement and maintain a grid computing environment. EM changes in Oracle Database 10g include:

Management of Oracle database and AS
> The first big change is the ability to manage both the Oracle database and Oracle Application Server from within Enterprise Manager. EM gives you a set of monitoring and management capabilities for Application Server that are similar

to those available for the Oracle database—for example, automatically tracking the time taken by the HTML pages that are slowest to serve to the client.

Enterprise Configuration Management

Another new area, Enterprise Configuration Management (ECM), tracks and stores the configuration details of all monitored servers. You can find out which servers have a particular configuration option, compare servers against each other to spot differences, run reports to see which servers have certain options or vary from an established baseline, or clone a new server node with a pre-established configuration.

Performance management

One other new area of functionality in EM revolves around the need to manage user expectations of performance. Performance has always been a slippery topic: although you may calibrate performance based on measurements such as CPU cycles or I/O time, your users have their own, occasionally orthogonal, view of performance as measured by response time. Enterprise Manager 10*g* includes a feature known as Application Performance Management (APM), which focuses on the end-user view of performance. The inherent complexity of a grid computing architecture may be invisible to an end user, but it can still affect the performance he receives.

APM is implemented by establishing agents, known as *beacons*, to run transactions from various user sites. These transactions can be defined as any type of user interaction. They are run at regular intervals, and the results are sent back to the Enterprise Manager repository. EM provides graphical historical tracking of these results, which can help you to quickly see whether a particular performance problem exists across the grid or whether the source of the problem is located on the path to a particular location.

You can also set warning levels for transaction performance, which will cause alerts to be proactively sent if performance degrades to a specified level.

A Final Thought on Grid Computing

Is grid computing just another marketing buzzword, or is it truly a new and inevitable destination for the world of IT? We think the answer is, well, both.

The factors that have created the marketing embrace of grid computing are certainly real—low-cost machines and simplified end-user access. And these factors are not only lasting, but will continue to display considerable appeal to CEOs looking to avoid increases in IT spending, while still providing more IT services.

Will the IT universe end up as one big grid? It's not a bad idea, but there are formidable personal and political barriers to this type of widespread cooperation. Whether the world, or even one organization, ends up using a grid computing architecture is, to some extent, beside the point. Everywhere that IT wants to save money through increased efficiency and consolidation, the features that benefit grid computing will provide value.

What's New in This Book
for Oracle Database10*g*

When we wrote the first edition of *Oracle Essentials* in 1999, our goal was to offer a new kind of book about Oracle, one that would clearly and concisely cover all of the essential features and concepts of the Oracle database. In order to keep our focus on those essentials, we limited the scope of the book. For instance, we decided not to cover SQL, or PL/SQL, in depth; these complex topics would have required a level of detail that would have run counter to the purpose of our book, and they are amply described in other books.

The latest release of the Oracle database, Oracle Database 10*g*, contains an enormous number of new features. Most of these features build on the existing foundation of Oracle database technology. We have tried to add details about these features in the chapters in which their discussion seemed most appropriate, but there are of course some enhancements in the new release that are outside the scope of this book.

The following sections summarize the new features of Oracle Database 10*g* that are covered in this new edition, chapter by chapter. Although many of these features are mentioned in multiple chapters, they are listed here according to where the most relevant discussion occurs.

Chapter 1, Introducing Oracle

This introductory chapter was extensively updated to reflect the packaging changes in Oracle Database 10*g*. It also briefly mentions features described in more detail in other chapters.

Chapter 2, Oracle Architecture

Bigfiles
Bigfiles can hold up to 8 exabytes of data in a single file, depending on the limitations of the underlying operating system. Tablespaces support bigfiles, which eliminate the need for multiple datafiles in a tablespace as a consequence of size limitations.

DROP DATABASE statement
   Can be used to drop an entire database with a single statement.

Automatic archiving
   The ALTER DATABASE ARCHIVELOG statement automatically marks redo logs for archiving as they are filled, eliminating the need for the LOG_ARCHIVE_START=TRUE initialization parameter.

Reduced configuration parameters
   Oracle Database 10g reduces the number of initialization parameters that require manual specification to fewer than 40 parameters.

Chapter 3, Installing and Running Oracle

Faster installation
   You can install Oracle Database 10g in 20 minutes from a single disk.

Database Upgrade Assistant
   This tool is a part of Oracle Database 10g that simplifies the upgrade process from an earlier version of Oracle.

Rolling upgrades
   You can perform a rolling upgrade to new versions by using Real Application Clusters and upgrading only some of the nodes in the cluster at a time.

Automatic Storage Management
   Automatic Storage Management (ASM) provides automatic striping and mirroring for datafiles without requiring any other software. ASM also lets you add or remove disks without stopping the database, and performs automatic disk tuning to avoid the performance problems of "hot spots" on disk.

Automatic Workload Repository
   The Automatic Workload Repository (AWR) stores snapshots of your Oracle environment that can be used to identify potential problems in the environment.

Export directory entries
   You can export configuration information from Oracle Internet Directory (OID, an LDAP-compliant directory) to a local version of the *TNSNAMES.ORA* file, in case the directory is not available.

Simplified host naming
   You can identify a host with either the host name or the TCP/IP address.

LDAP.ORA
   This file is no longer needed if the directory is registered with the Domain Name Server (DNS).

Chapter 4, Data Structures

Globalization Development Kit

The Globalization Development Kit (GDK) makes it easier to develop multilingual applications.

Accent- and case-insensitive queries

Oracle Database 10g supports queries that ignore accent marks and/or case.

Increased CLOB size

A CLOB or NCLOB can now hold up to 128 terabytes of data.

SCN pseudocolumn

A new pseudocolumn, ORA_ROWSCN, holds the System Change Number (SCN) for the last transaction that changed the row.

Expression filter

This filter allows a complex expression to be stored as part of a row. You can use the EVALUATE function to evaluate the expression and to limit rows returned in queries based on the evaluation.

No recompilation of PL/SQL needed for synonym changes

If you change the location referenced by a synonym, you no longer have to recompile PL/SQL procedures that use the synonym.

Sorted hash clusters

These clusters save information in a hash cluster in the order it was added.

Automatic statistics collection

In Oracle Database 10g, statistics collection for the cost-based optimizer can be automated.

Rule-based optimizer de-supported

The rule-based optimizer is no longer supported in Oracle Database 10g.

I/O statistics

The cost-based optimizer now uses CPU and I/O statistics.

SQL Tuning Advisor

This tool collects additional statistics, which are then stored and used by the cost-based optimizer to create a better execution plan.

Chapter 5, Managing Oracle

This chapter has been reorganized to highlight the new manageability features for Oracle Database 10g and the grid.

HTML-based console for Enterprise Manager 10g

Enterprise Manager now has an HTML-based interface, as well as a Java-based interface.

Scheduler
Oracle Database 10g includes a sophisticated scheduling application for database jobs.

Automatic Database Diagnostic Monitor
The Automatic Database Diagnostic Monitor (ADDM) uses information stored in the Automatic Workload Repository to spot potential problems and suggest solutions.

Automatic shared memory tuning
Shared memory is automatically tuned in Oracle Database 10g, eliminating the possibility of an out-of-memory condition for an undersized shared pool.

Automatic Undo Management Tuning
This feature automatically determines optimal undo retention time based on system activity and uses this information to maximize the use of the UNDO tablespace.

Fine-grained auditing
Fine-grained auditing controls (FGAC) have been enhanced in the new release to cover UPDATE, INSERT, and DELETE operations.

Policies in Enterprise Manager
Policies, which define best practices as well as security alerts and other crucial patch issues, are used to automatically check all target servers.

Kerberos support
Oracle Database 10g provides authentication for users with Kerberos credentials and Kerberos-based authentication across database links.

Segment Advisor
This tool simplifies segment management.

Image copy backups
Image copy backups can now be made for the database, a tablespace, or a datafile.

Recovery Manager enhancements
These RMAN enhancements include automatic retry of failed backups and automatic use of older backup files if a corrupt or unusable backup is discovered.

Backup set compression
RMAN now compresses backup sets.

Chapter 6, Oracle Performance

Portable clusterware
Oracle Database 10g includes clusterware and a cluster filesystem that works on the Windows and Linux platforms.

Automatic SGA configuration

You no longer need to define individual memory pools for the System Global Area (SGA); these pools will be adjusted according to the overall size of the system's SGA.

Automatic PGA configuration

Oracle Database 10g provides automatic sizing for different memory pools in the Program Global Area (PGA).

Cluster workload management

This is a feature that provides dynamic allocation of cluster nodes in response to node failure.

Chapter 7, Multiuser Concurrency

Workspaces enhancements

A child workspace can have more than one parent workspace, use SQL*Loader to load bulk data into workspaces, and trigger events based on workspace operations.

Chapter 8, Oracle and Transaction Processing

Connection Manager enhancements

With these enhancements you can modify configuration parameters without shutting down Connection Manager and can use improved access rules for filtering traffic.

Improvements to the Database Resource Manager

Using the new version of Database Resource Manager (DRM), you can define a service group by service name, application, host machine, or the operating system username of a user.

Oracle Streams enhancements

With Oracle Database 10g, it is easier to programmatically interact with queues.

Chapter 9, Oracle and Data Warehousing

Improved optimization

Optimizer predictions for decision support operations are compared with actual results, and there will be subsequent adjustments in future predictions if indicated.

MODEL clause

This clause in the SELECT statement allows relational data in a query to be treated as a multidimensional array, which can also have formulas applied to them.

Cross-platform transportable tablespaces
Transportable tablespaces can be used to move data between different operating system platforms.

Downstream capture of change information
Change information can be captured from log files, rather than from the database.

Data Pump
This is a high-speed data transfer application.

Data mining enhancements
These enhancements include text mining and BLAST similarity searches.

Additional analytics and statistics
The database includes new hypothesis testing and distribution statistics, crosstabs, and descriptive statistics. The OLAP option adds support for custom members and measures.

Chapter 10, Oracle and High Availability

Flashback capabilities
Oracle Database 10g provides greatly expanded flashback capabilities, including the ability to flash back the database, a transaction, a table, or a DROP statement.

Incremental backups for image backups
Recovery Manager can now apply incremental backups to image backups.

Single command for hot backup mode
In Oracle Database 10g, you can use a single ALTER DATABASE statement to put all tablespaces into hot backup mode.

Disk-based backup and recovery
Recovery Manager can now back up all necessary files to an area of disk, and automatically manage backups to maintain a specified retention period.

Asynchronous change data capture
In Oracle Database 10g, Oracle Streams can transfer changed data asynchronously.

Chapter 11, Oracle and Hardware Architecture

Dynamic service provisioning
This feature provides the ability to automatically reassign nodes in a Real Application Cluster when a node fails or comes back online.

Chapter 12, Distributed Databases and Distributed Data

Support for remote functions
> Oracle Database 10g adds support for remote functions through Heterogeneous Gateways.

Oracle Streams enhancements
> These enhancements include notification via email, HTTP, or PL/SQL, as well as a migration tool from Advanced Replication to Streams.

Chapter 13, Extending Oracle Datatypes

Proximity searching
> Oracle Database 10g provides the ability to use proximity searching (NEAR) for text.

Character set and language detection
> Oracle Database 10g can determine the character set and language in a document.

Native indexing for XMLType
> You can add Oracle native indexing for XMLType columns.

Java support
> Oracle Database 10g provides a text application generator for JDeveloper.

GeoRaster
> This feature is used for storing, indexing, querying, analyzing, and delivering raster image data, associated spatial vector geometry data, and metadata.

Topology and network management
> These management features include the ability to manipulate nodes and edges in a topology or network, or faces in a topology.

Chapter 14, Network Deployment Models

This chapter has undergone the most extensive revisions of any chapter in the book; even its name has changed (from *Oracle and The Web*). The Oracle Database 10g release claims to take Oracle beyond the Web into the grid, so in addition to briefly covering features described in previous editions—for example, Oracle Application Server[*]—it also includes a summary of the needs of grid computing and how the Oracle Database 10g release is addressing them.

---

[*] For more information on Oracle Application Server 10g than we can include in this chapter, see the book *Oracle Application Server 10g Essentials*, expected to be released later in 2004.

HTML DB

This is a development tool for creating HTML-based applications, creating and modifying database structures, and importing data into the Oracle database.

Direct calls to Java stored procedures

You no longer have to create a PL/SQL wrapper to call a Java stored procedure.

XML DB

XML DB is a set of improvements for the XML capabilities of the Oracle database.

Failover notification

Oracle Application Server 10g is notified of a failure in a Real Application Cluster node.

Enterprise Configuration Manager

This tool is a part of Enterprise Manager 10g that allows you to discover, compare, and modify the configuration of servers across your enterprise.

Application Performance Management

This new tool allows you to set up beacons, which run user-defined transactions from remote locations and send the results back to the Enterprise Manager repository.

Additional Resources

In this concise volume, we've attempted to give you a firm grounding in all the basic concepts you need to understand Oracle and use it effectively. We hope we've accomplished this goal.

At the same time, we realize that there is more to using a complex product such as Oracle than simply understanding how and why it works the way it does. Although you can't use Oracle without a firm grasp of the foundations of the product, you will still need details if you're actually going to implement a successful system.

This appendix lists two types of additional sources of information for the topics covered in this book—relevant web sites, which act as a constantly changing resource for a variety of information, and a chapter-by-chapter list of relevant books, articles, and Oracle documentation.

For the chapter-by-chapter list, the sources fall into two basic categories: Oracle documentation and third-party sources. Typically, the Oracle documentation provides the type of hands-on information you will need regarding syntax and keywords, and the third-party sources cover the topics in a more general and problem-solving way. We've listed the third-party sources first and ended each listing with the relevant Oracle documentation. Also note that some of the volumes listed here include previous Oracle release names in their titles. You can assume that by the time you are reading this, similar volumes exist (or will soon exist) for whatever version of Oracle you may be using (for example, Oracle Database 10g).

Web Sites

Oracle Corporation—http://www.oracle.com
> The home of the company. Latest information and marketing, as well as some good technical and packaging information.

Oracle Technology Network—http://otn.oracle.com

The focal point of Oracle Corporation's attempt to reach a wider audience of developers. You can find tons of stuff at the Oracle Technology Network (OTN), including low-cost developer versions or free downloads of most Oracle software and lots of information and discussion forums.

International Oracle Users Group (IOUG)—http://www.ioug.org

The International Oracle Users Group web site includes information on meetings, links to Oracle resources, a technical repository, discussion forums, and special interest groups.

OraPub, Inc.—http://www.orapub.com

Craig Shallahamer's site devoted to all things Oracle. Craig was a long-time Oracle employee in the performance analysis group and acted as one of the tech reviewers for this book.

RevealNet—http://www.revealnet.com

The Quest Software site for all things PL/SQL-oriented, as well as information on Oracle database administration, Java database programming, and other topics.

O'Reilly & Associates, Inc.—http://www.oreilly.com

The O'Reilly web site, which contains web pages for each book and a variety of other helpful information. See *http://www.oreilly.com/catalog/oressentials3/* for errata and other information for this book.

EMC/Cisco/Oracle Infrastructure (ECOstructure)—http://www.eECOstructure.com

A site containing blueprints validated in a joint development center by EMC, Cisco, and Oracle. Available blueprints include "Resilient," for highly available and secure single sites; "Recovery," which extends Resilient for failover and fallback to and from a standby site; and "Accelerated," which incorporates storage networking and content caching.

Books and Oracle Documentation

The following books and Oracle documentation provide additional information for each chapter in this book.

Chapter 1, Introducing Oracle

Ellison, Lawrence. *Oracle Overview and Introduction to SQL*. Belmont, CA: Oracle Corporation, 1985.

Kreines, David, and Brian Laskey. *Oracle Database Administration: The Essential Reference*. Sebastopol, CA: O'Reilly & Associates, 1999.

Loney, Kevin, and Bob Bryla. *Oracle Database 10g DBA Handbook*. New York, NY: Oracle Press/Osborne McGraw-Hill, 2004.

Ralston, Anthony, ed. *Encyclopedia of Computer Science and Engineering*. New York, NY: Nostrand Reinhold Company, 1983.

Thome, Bob. *Achieving a 24x7 e-Business Leveraging the Oracle Database*. Belmont, CA: Oracle Corporation, 2000.

Oracle Database 10g Concepts. Redwood Shores, CA: Oracle Corporation, 2004.

Oracle Database 10g New Features. Redwood Shores, CA: Oracle Corporation, 2004.

Oracle9i Database: The Power of Globalization Technology. Belmont, CA: Oracle Corporation, 2001.

Oracle HTML DB (Oracle Feature Overview). Redwood Shores, CA: Oracle Corporation, 2003.

Chapter 2, Oracle Architecture

Kreines, David, and Brian Laskey. *Oracle Database Administration: The Essential Reference*. Sebastopol, CA: O'Reilly & Associates, 1999.

Oracle Database 10g Concepts (Part II). Belmont, CA: Oracle Corporation, 2004.

Chapter 3, Installing and Running Oracle

Kreines, David, and Brian Laskey. *Oracle Database Administration: The Essential Reference*. Sebastopol, CA: O'Reilly & Associates, 1999.

Loney, Kevin, and Bob Bryla. *Oracle Database 10g DBA Handbook*. New York, NY: Oracle Press/Osborne McGraw-Hill, 2004.

Toledo, Hugo, and Jonathan Gennick. *Oracle Net8 Configuration and Troubleshooting*. Sebastopol, CA: O'Reilly & Associates, 2000.

Oracle Database 10g Concepts. Redwood Shores, CA: Oracle Corporation, 2004.

Oracle Database 10g Installation Guide. Redwood Shores, CA: Oracle Corporation, 2004.

Oracle Database 10g Net Services Administrators Guide. Redwood Shores, CA: Oracle Corporation, 2004.

Oracle Enterprise Manager Basic Installation and Configuration. Redwood Shores, CA: Oracle Corporation, 2004.

Chapter 4, Data Structures

Ensor, Dave, and Ian Stevenson. *Oracle Design*. Sebastopol, CA: O'Reilly & Associates, 1997.

Harrington, Jan L. *Relational Database Design Clearly Explained.* San Francisco, CA: AP Professional, 1998.

Oracle Database 10g Concepts (Part II). Belmont, CA: Oracle Corporation, 2004.

Chapter 5, Managing Oracle

Feuerstein, Steven with Bill Pribyl. *Oracle PL/SQL Programming, 3rd Edition.* Sebastopol, CA: O'Reilly & Associates, 2002.

Freeman, Robert G., and Matthew Hart. *Oracle9i RMAN Backup and Recovery.* New York, NY: Oracle Press/Osborne McGraw-Hill, 2002.

Finnigan, Peter. *Oracle Security: Step-by-Step.* Bethesda, MD: SANS Institute, 2003.

Greenwald, Rick, and David Kreines. *Oracle in a Nutshell: A Desktop Quick Reference.* Sebastopol, CA: O'Reilly Associates, 2002.

Himatsingka, Bhaskar, and Juan Loaiza. "How to Stop Defragmenting and Start Living: The Definitive Word on Fragmentation." Paper no. 711. Belmont, CA: Oracle Corporation, 1998.

Kreines, David, and Brian Laskey. *Oracle Database Administration: The Essential Reference.* Sebastopol, CA: O'Reilly & Associates, 1999.

Kuhn, Darl, and Scott Schulze. *Oracle RMAN Pocket Reference.* Sebastopol, CA: O'Reilly & Associates, 2002.

Loney, Kevin, and Bob Bryla. *Oracle Database 10g DBA Handbook.* New York, NY: Oracle Press/Osborne McGraw-Hill, 2004.

Manning, Paul, and Angelo Pruscino. *Simplify Your Job—Automatic Storage Management* (white paper), Oracle Corporation, 2003.

Theriault, Marlene L., and Aaron Newman. *Oracle Security Handbook*, New York, NY: Oracle Press/Osborne McGraw-Hill, 2001.

Velpuri, Rama, Anand Adkoli, and George Williams. *Oracle8i Backup and Recovery.* New York, NY: Oracle Press/Osborne McGraw-Hill, 2000.

Feature Overview: Oracle Enterprise Manager EM2Go. Redwood Shores, CA: Oracle Corporation, 2004.

Legato Storage Manager Administrator's Guide. Belmont, CA: Oracle Corporation, 1999.

Managing the Complete Oracle Environment with Oracle Enterprise Manager (white paper). Redwood Shores, CA: Oracle Corporation, 2004.

Oracle Advanced Security Administrator's Guide. Redwood Shores, CA: Oracle Corporation, 2003.

Oracle Database 10g Administrator's Guide. Redwood Shores, CA: Oracle Corporation, 2004.

Oracle Database 10g Backup and Recovery Basics. Redwood Shores, CA: Oracle Corporation, 2004.

Oracle Database 10g Concepts (Chapters 12, 14–15). Redwood Shores, CA: Oracle Corporation, 2004.

Oracle Enterprise Manager Concepts. Redwood Shores, CA: Oracle Corporation, 2004.

Oracle Label Security Administrator's Guide. Redwood Shores, CA: Oracle Corporation, 2004.

Chapter 6, Oracle Performance

Gurry, Mark. *Oracle SQL Tuning Pocket Reference*. Sebastopol, CA: O'Reilly Associates, 2002.

Kyte, Thomas. *Effective Oracle by Design*. New York, NY: Oracle Press/Osborne McGraw-Hill, 2003.

Kyte, Thomas. *Expert One-on-One Oracle*. Berkeley, CA: APress, 2003 (reprint).

Lewis, Jonathan. *Practical Oracle8i: Building Efficient Databases*. Reading, MA: Addison Wesley, 2001.

Millsap, Cary with Jeff Holt. *Optimizing Oracle Performance*. Sebastopol, CA: O'Reilly & Associates, 2003.

Niemiec, Rich, Bradley Brown, and Joe Trezzo. *Oracle Performance Tuning Tips & Techniques*. Belmont, CA: Oracle Corporation, 1999.

Oracle Database 10g Concepts. Redwood Shores, CA: Oracle Corporation, 2004.

Oracle Database 10g Real Application Clusters Administration. Redwood Shores, CA: Oracle Corporation, 2004.

Oracle Database 10g Performance Tuning Guide. Redwood Shores, CA: Oracle Corporation, 2004.

Chapter 7, Multiuser Concurrency

Oracle Database 10g Concepts (Chapter 13). Redwood Shores, CA: Oracle Corporation, 2004.

Chapter 8, Oracle and Transaction Processing

Gray, Jim, and Andreas Reuter. *Transaction Processing: Concepts and Techniques*. San Francisco, CA: Morgan Kaufmann Publishers, 1992.

Edwards, Jeri, with Deborah DeVoe. *3-Tier Client/Server at Work*. New York, NY: John Wiley & Sons, 1997.

Oracle Database 10g Streams Advanced Queuing Users Guide and Reference. Redwood Shores, CA: Oracle Corporation, 2003.

Oracle Database 10g Application Developer's Guide—Fundamentals. Redwood Shores, CA: Oracle Corporation, 2003.

Oracle8i Call Interface Programmer's Guide. Belmont, CA: Oracle Corporation, 1999.

Oracle Database 10g Concepts Guide. Redwood Shores, CA: Oracle Corporation, 2004.

Oracle Database 10g Java Developer's Guide. Redwood Shores, CA: Oracle Corporation, 2004.

Oracle Database 10g Net Services Reference Guide. Redwood Shores, CA: Oracle Corporation, 2004.

Oracle Database 10g Real Application Clusters Administration. Redwood Shores, CA: Oracle Corporation, 2004.

Chapter 9, Oracle and Data Warehousing

Berry, Michael J.A., and Gordon Linoff. *Data Mining Techniques*. New York, NY: John Wiley & Sons, 1997.

Dodge, Gary, and Tim Gorman. *Oracle8 Data Warehousing*. New York, NY: John Wiley & Sons, 1998.

Hobbs, Lilian and Susan Hillson and Shilpa Lawande. *Oracle9iR2 Data Warehousing*. England: Butterworth-Heinemann, 2003.

Inmon, W.H. *Building the Data Warehouse*. New York, NY: John Wiley & Sons, 1996.

Kelly, Sean. *Data Warehousing, The Route to Mass Customisation*. Chichester, England: John Wiley & Sons, 1996.

Kimball, Ralph. *The Data Warehouse Toolkit*. New York, NY: John Wiley & Sons, 1996.

Peppers, Don, and Martha Rogers. *Enterprise One to One*. New York, NY: Currency Doubleday, 1997.

Peppers, Don, Martha Rogers, and Bob Dorf. *One to One Fieldbook*. New York, NY: Currency Doubleday, 1999.

Stackowiak, Robert. "Why Bad Data Warehouses Happen to Good People." *The Journal of Data Warehousing*, April 1997.

Oracle Data Mining Concepts. Redwood Shores, CA: Oracle Corporation, 2004.

Oracle Database 10g Concepts (Chapter 17). Redwood Shores, CA: Oracle Corporation, 2004.

Oracle Database 10g Data Warehousing Guide. Redwood Shores, CA: Oracle Corporation, 2004.

Oracle Warehouse Builder User's Guide. Redwood Shores, CA: Oracle Corporation, 2004.

Chapter 10, Oracle and High Availability

Chen, Lee, Kate Gibson, and Patterson Gibson. "RAID: High Performance, Reliable Secondary Storage." *ACM Computing Surveys*, June 1994.

Kreines, David, and Brian Laskey. *Oracle Database Administration: The Essential Reference*. Sebastopol, CA: O'Reilly & Associates, 1999.

Peterson, Erik. *"No Data Loss" Standby Database*. Belmont, CA: Oracle Corporation and Paul Manning, EMC Corporation, 1998.

Oracle Database 10g Backup and Recovery Basics. Redwood Shores, CA: Oracle Corporation, 2004.

Oracle Database 10g Concepts (Chapter 16). Redwood Shores, CA: Oracle Corporation, 2004.

Oracle Database 10g Advanced Replication. Redwood Shores, CA: Oracle Corporation, 2004.

Oracle Data Guard Concepts and Administration. Redwood Shores, CA: Oracle Corporation, 2004.

Oracle High Availability Architecture and Best Practices. Redwood Shores, CA: Oracle Corporation, 2004.

Chapter 11, Oracle and Hardware Architecture

Morse, H. Stephen. *Practical Parallel Computing*. Cambridge, MA: AP Professional, 1994.

Pfister, Gregory. *In Search of Clusters*. Upper Saddle River, NJ: Prentice Hall PTR, 1995.

Oracle Grid Computing (business white paper). Redwood Shores, CA: Oracle Corporation, 2004.

Chapter 12, Distributed Databases and Distributed Data

Cerutti, Daniel, and Donna Pierson. *Distributed Computing Environments.* New York, NY: McGraw-Hill, 1993.

Dye, Charles. *Oracle Distributed Systems.* Sebastopol, CA: O'Reilly & Associates, 1999.

Ortalie, Robert, Dan Harkey, and Jeri Edwards. *The Essential Distributed Objects Survival Guide.* New York, NY: John Wiley & Sons, 1996.

Oracle Streams Advanced Queuing User's Guide and Reference. Redwood Shores, CA: Oracle Corporation, 2003.

Oracle Database 10g Concepts. Redwood Shores, CA: Oracle Corporation, 2004.

Oracle Database 10g Advanced Replication. Redwood Shores, CA: Oracle Corporation, 2004.

Oracle Services for Microsoft Transaction Server. Redwood Shores, CA: Oracle Corporation, 2004.

Chapter 13, Extending Oracle Datatypes

Bales, Donald. *Java Programming with Oracle JDBC.* Sebastopol, CA: O'Reilly & Associates, 2001.

Siegal, Jon. *CORBA Fundamentals and Programming.* New York, NY: John Wiley & Sons, 1996.

Taylor, David A. *Object-Oriented Technology: A Manager's Guide.* Alameda, CA: Servio Corporation, 1990.

Oracle Database 10g Concepts (Part IV). Redwood Shores, CA: Oracle Corporation, 2004.

Oracle interMedia User's Guide. Redwood Shores, CA: Oracle Corporation, 2004.

Oracle interMedia Reference. Redwood Shores, CA: Oracle Corporation, 2004.

Oracle Database 10g Java Developer's Guide. Redwood Shores, CA: Oracle Corporation, 2004.

Oracle Database 10g Application Developer's Guide—Object Relational Features. Redwood Shores, CA: Oracle Corporation, 2004.

Oracle Spatial User's Guide and Reference. Redwood Shores, CA: Oracle Corporation, 2004.

OracleSpatial Georaster Guide. Redwood Shores, CA: Oracle Corporation, 2004.

Oracle Database 10g SQLJ Developer's Guide and Reference. Redwood Shores, CA: Oracle Corporation, 2004.

Oracle Text Reference. Redwood Shores, CA: Oracle Corporation, 2004.

Oracle Ultra Search User's Guide. Redwood Shores, CA: Oracle Corporation, 2004.

Chapter 14, Network Deployment Models

Gennick, Jonathan, and Peter Linsley. *Oracle Regular Expressions Pocket Reference.* Sebastopol, CA: O'Reilly & Associates, 2003.

Greenwald, Richard, Robert Stackowiak, and Don Bales. *Oracle Application Server Essentials.* Sebastopol, CA: O'Reilly & Associates, 2004.

Muench, Steve. *Building Oracle XML Applications.* Sebastopol, CA: O'Reilly & Associates, 2000.

Oracle Database 10g Java Developer's Guide and Reference. Redwood Shores, CA: Oracle Corporation, 2004.

Oracle Database 10g SQLJ Developer's Guide and Reference. Redwood Shores, CA: Oracle Corporation, 2004.

Oracle XML DB Users Guide. Redwood Shores, CA: Oracle Corporation, 2004.

Oracle Application Server 10g, (technical white paper). Redwood Shores, CA: Oracle Corporation, 2004.

Oracle Application Server 10g—Grid Computing (Oracle white paper). Redwood Shores, CA: Oracle Corporation, 2004.

Oracle 10g: Infrastructure for Grid Computing (Oracle white paper). Redwood Shores, CA: Oracle Corporation, 2004.

Index

We'd like to hear your suggestions for improving our indexes. Send email to *index@oreilly.com*.

C

C and C++ programming languages, 11
  Oracle Lite, 29
cache, 16
  AS (Oracle Application Server), 15
  memory allocation to, 164
Cache Fusion, 26, 205, 280
caching, 330
cardinality, 219
cascade deletes, 101
case-insensitive queries, 82
Central Console, 120
Change Management Pack, 23
CHAR datatype, 81
character datatypes, 81
check constraints, 101
checkpoints, 243
  completed, records of, 243
  I/O activity, and, 244
  size value, impact on recovery time,
    performance, 244
  structure, 38
chunk size, 154
CKPT (Checkpoint) process, 50
class, 304
clean data, 226
client processes, 68
  dedicated server processes, and, 71
CLOB datatype, 82, 85
clustered systems, 279
  locking model requirements, 279
clusters, 96
  IOTs, and, 91
CMAN (Connection Manager), 14, 201
COBOL, 11
Codd, Dr. Edward F., 2
cold backup, 260
Cold Failover Cluster, 332
collections, 303
  types, 304
columns, 80, 88
COMMIT statements, 176
commits, 75
Common Warehouse Metadata Interchange
  (CWMI), 233
complete database recovery, 261
complete site failure
  data redundancy solutions, 270
  preparation for, 266
  preparedness, options for,
    comparison, 273

component redundancy, 246
composite partitioning, 25
COMPUTE STATISTICS option, ANALYZE
  statement, 107
concatenation operator (||), 86
concentrators, 14
concurrency, 175–176, 176–179
  contention, 178
  features in Oracle, 181
  integrity problems, 178
  locks, 177
  performance, and, 185
  transaction isolation, and, 179
  transactions, 176
concurrent user access, 175
  multiversion read consistency, 179
CONFIG.ORA, 46
configuration files, 63
  hand-coded, problems with, 63
  Oracle Net, 64
CONNECT INTERNAL syntax, 130
Connection Manager (CMAN), 14, 201
connection pooling, 201
  application servers, 197
constraining tables runtime errors, 103
constraints, 99–102
  vs. triggers, 102
Content Management Kit, 324
content-based publishing and
  subscribing, 19
contention, 178
  of write operations, 184
control files, 34–37
  backup, 36
  checkpoint records, 243
  multiple files, 37
  multiplexing, 37
  parameters, 35–37
  performance, impact on, 37
CONTROL_FILES parameter, 36, 67
correlation functions, 222
cost-based optimization
  statistics, use of, 106
    saving, 108
    updating, 108
cost-based optimizers, 105
  star schemas, queries against, 218
CPUs (central processing units)
  non-database workload and Oracle
    performance, 171
  quantity and parallelism value, 160

---

query optimization, 104–115
  cost-based optimizers, 105
  decision support queries, 218–221
  execution path, 104
  ORDER BY conditions, 104
  rule-based optimizers, 105
query optimizers, 5
query processes, parallelizable
    operations, 159

R

RAC (Real Application Clusters), 26, 174,
    204, 219, 253–257, 279, 335
  availability advantages, 205
  availability, and, 254
  Cache Fusion support, 205
  hardware failover, compared to, 253
  high availability support, 206
  node failure management, 255
  physical distancing of clusters, 266
  scalability and, 255
RACGuard, 256
RAD (Rapid Application Development), 28
RAID (Redundant Array of Inexpensive
    Disks), 148–155, 247
  control files, need for backup, 36
  levels, 149, 247
    selection, 249
RAID-S arrays, 151
range partitioning, 224
ranking functions, 221
Rapid Application Development (RAD), 28
RAW datatype, 84
RDBMS (relational database management
    systems), 3
  Oracle products family, 6
READ COMMITTED isolation level, 180
read locks, 177
read operations, example, 185
read-only tablespaces, 262
  backup and recovery, 262
Real Application Clusters (see RAC)
records, 4
recovery, 24, 137–140
  backups, using, 260
  complete database recovery, 261
  fault-tolerant disk arrays, and, 148
  options, 139
  PITR, 263
  planning, 259

  preparations, 137
  RECO (Recover) process, 51
  targeted and rollforward, 261
  testing, 139, 259
  (see also RMAN)
RECYCLE buffer pool, 49
redo log buffer, 49
  size and performance, 166
redo logs, 39–45
  archive logs, isolation from, 148
  archives, 42–45
  checkpoint records, 243
  cold backups, and, 261
  device assignment, 147
  fast commits, and, 76
  filenames, 41
  mirroring to remote site, 269
  multiplexing, 39, 41
  naming conventions, 41
  online, 43
  sequence numbers, 41
  suppression of logging, 40
  threading, 39
REF datatype, 304
relational databases (see databases,
    relational)
Relational Online Analytical Processing
    (ROLAP), 230
Relational Software, Incorporated (RSI), 2
relationships, 98
replication, 18, 206, 295
  advanced, 18
  bandwidth, and, 271
  overhead, 272
Replication Manager, 296
reporting aggregate functions, 221
reporting tools, 229
Reports Server, AS 10g Enterprise
    Edition, 325
request queues, 72
resilience, 335
resumable space allocation, 57
RETENTION AREA parameter, 139
Reuter, Andreas, 191
reverse key indexes, 92
REVOKE statement, 129
RMAN (Recovery Manager), 24, 138, 264
  incremental backups, 264
ROLAP (Relational Online Analytical
    Processing), 230
roles, 128
rollback, 75, 245

About the Authors

Rick Greenwald has been active in the world of computer software for nearly two decades, including stints with Data General, Cognos, and Gupta. He is currently an analyst with Oracle Corporation. He has published six books and countless articles on a variety of technical topics, and has spoken at conferences and training sessions across six continents. In addition to *Oracle Essentials: Oracle Database 10g*, Rick's books include *Oracle in a Nutshell* (principal author with David C. Kreines, O'Reilly & Associates); *Oracle9iAS Portal Bible* (principal author with Jim Milbery, John Wiley & Sons); and *Administering Exchange Server* (principal author with Walter Glenn, Microsoft Press).

Robert Stackowiak is Senior Director of Business Intelligence in Oracle Corporation's Technology Business Unit. He works with Oracle's largest customers in North America, providing insight into the company's products and data warehousing strategy. In addition, he frequently assists Oracle Corporate in developing product strategy and training. Prior to joining Oracle in 1996, Robert was the Decision Support Segment Manager in IBM's RISC System/6000 Division. There, he met with IBM's largest customers throughout North America who were implementing RS/6000s and the IBM RS/6000 SP. He also previously worked as a Senior Field Analyst at Harris Computer Systems and as Chief of Programming at the St. Paul District of the U.S. Army Corps of Engineers. Articles written by Bob have appeared in publications including *The Journal of Data Warehousing*, *Database Trends and Applications*, *Informix Tech Notes*, and *AIXcellence Magazine*.

Jonathan Stern has more than 13 years of IT experience, including senior positions in consulting, systems architecture, and technical sales. He has in-depth experience with the Oracle RDBMS across all major open systems hardware and operating systems, covering tuning, scaling and parallelism, Oracle Parallel Server, high availability, data warehousing, OLTP, object-relational databases, *N*-tier architectures, and emerging trends such as Java and CORBA. He has authored papers and presented at internal and external conferences on topics such as scaling with Oracle's dynamic parallelism and the role of reorganizing segments in an Oracle database. Jonathan is the Technical Director at Ariba, Inc., the leading vendor of value-chain solutions for electronic commerce. Previously, he led a team of highly experienced database specialists at Oracle Corporation, providing technical depth and strategic assistance to Oracle's largest customers in the north central USA.

Colophon

Our look is the result of reader comments, our own experimentation, and feedback from distribution channels. Distinctive covers complement our distinctive approach to technical topics, breathing personality and life into potentially dry subjects.

The animals on the cover of *Oracle Essentials: Oracle Database 10g* are cicadas. There are about 1,500 species of cicada. In general, cicadas are large insects with long thin wings that are perched above an inch-long abdomen. Their heads are also large and contain three eyes and a piercing and sucking mechanism with which to extrude sap from trees. Cicadas are known for their characteristic shrill buzz, which is actually the male's mating song, one of the loudest known insect noises.

Cicadas emerge from the ground in the spring or summer, molt, then shed their skin in the form of a shell. They stay near trees and plants, where they live for 4 to 6 weeks with the sole purpose of mating. The adult insects then die, and their young hatch and burrow into the ground. They attach to tree roots and feed off the sap for 4 to 17 years, after which time they emerge and continue the mating cycle. Cicadas have one of the longest life spans of any insect; the most common species is the periodical cicada, which lives underground for 13 to 17 years.

Reg Aubry was the production editor and proofreader for *Oracle Essentials: Oracle Database 10g*. Genevieve d'Entremont, Marlowe Shaeffer, and Claire Cloutier provided quality control. John Bickelhaupt wrote the index.

Ellie Volckhausen designed the cover of this book, based on a series design by Edie Freedman. The cover image is an original 19th-century engraving from *Cuvier's Animals*. The cover layout was produced by Emma Colby with QuarkXPress 4.1 using the ITC Garamond font.

David Futato designed the interior layout. This book was converted by Julie Hawks to FrameMaker 5.5.6 with a format conversion tool created by Erik Ray, Jason McIntosh, Neil Walls, and Mike Sierra that uses Perl and XML technologies. The text font is Linotype Birka; the heading font is Adobe Myriad Condensed; and the code font is LucasFont's TheSans Mono Condensed. The illustrations that appear in the book were produced by Robert Romano and Jessamyn Read, using Macromedia FreeHand 9 and Adobe Photoshop 6. The tip and warning icons were drawn by Christopher Bing. This colophon was written by Nicole Arigo.

Related Titles Available from O'Reilly

Oracle PL/SQL

Learning Oracle PL/SQL

Oracle PL/SQL Best Practices

Oracle PL/SQL Developer's Workbook

Oracle PL/SQL Language Pocket Reference, *2nd Edition*

Oracle PL/SQL Programming, *3nd Edition*

Oracle Books for DBAs

Oracle DBA Checklists Pocket Reference

Oracle RMAN Pocket Reference

Unix for Oracle DBAs Pocket Reference

Oracle SQL and SQL Plus

Mastering Oracle SQL

Oracle SQL Plus: The Definitive Guide

Oracle SQL Tuning Pocket Reference

Oracle SQL*Plus Pocket Reference, *2nd Edition*

Oracle SQL: The Essential Reference

Oracle

Building Oracle XML Applications

Java Programming with Oracle JDBC

Oracle Regular Expressions Pocket Reference

Oracle in a Nutshell

Perl for Oracle DBAs

TOAD Pocket Reference

Keep in touch with O'Reilly

1. Download examples from our books

To find example files for a book, go to:

www.oreilly.com/catalog

select the book, and follow the "Examples" link.

2. Register your O'Reilly books

Register your book at *register.oreilly.com*

Why register your books?
Once you've registered your O'Reilly books you can:

- Win O'Reilly books, T-shirts or discount coupons in our monthly drawing.
- Get special offers available only to registered O'Reilly customers.
- Get catalogs announcing new books (US and UK only).
- Get email notification of new editions of the O'Reilly books you own.

3. Join our email lists

Sign up to get topic-specific email announcements of new books and conferences, special offers, and O'Reilly Network technology newsletters at:

elists.oreilly.com

It's easy to customize your free elists subscription so you'll get exactly the O'Reilly news you want.

4. Get the latest news, tips, and tools

www.oreilly.com

- "Top 100 Sites on the Web"—PC Magazine
- CIO Magazine's Web Business 50 Awards

Our web site contains a library of comprehensive product information (including book excerpts and tables of contents), downloadable software, background articles, interviews with technology leaders, links to relevant sites, book cover art, and more.

5. Work for O'Reilly

Check out our web site for current employment opportunities:

jobs.oreilly.com

6. Contact us

O'Reilly & Associates, Inc.
1005 Gravenstein Hwy North
Sebastopol, CA 95472 USA

TEL: 707-827-7000 or 800-998-9938
         (6am to 5pm PST)

FAX: 707-829-0104

order@oreilly.com
For answers to problems regarding your order or our products. To place a book order online, visit:

www.oreilly.com/order_new

catalog@oreilly.com
To request a copy of our latest catalog.

booktech@oreilly.com
For book content technical questions or corrections.

corporate@oreilly.com
For educational, library, government, and corporate sales.

proposals@oreilly.com
To submit new book proposals to our editors and product managers.

international@oreilly.com
For information about our international distributors or translation queries. For a list of our distributors outside of North America check out:

international.oreilly.com/distributors.html

adoption@oreilly.com
For information about academic use of O'Reilly books, visit:

academic.oreilly.com

O'REILLY®

Our books are available at most retail and online bookstores.
To order direct: 1-800-998-9938 • *order@oreilly.com* • *www.oreilly.com*
Online editions of most O'Reilly titles are available by subscription at *safari.oreilly.com*